Dedicated to the memory of
Kathryn J. Alston

Phalaenopsis

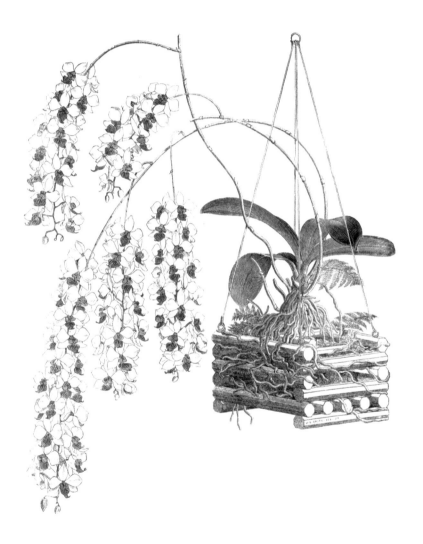

Phalaenopsis×intermedia var. *portei*. (From the *Gardeners' Chronicle*.)

Phalaenopsis

A Monograph

Eric A. Christenson

sponsored by the
International Phalaenopsis Alliance

Timber Press
Portland • London

Frontispiece illustration by W. G. Smith.

Published in 2001 by
Timber Press, Inc.
The Haseltine Building
133 S.W. Second Avenue, Suite 450
Portland, Oregon 97204
www.timberpress.com

2 The Quadrant
135 Salusbury Road
London NW6 6RJ
www.timberpress.co.uk

ISBN: 978-1-60469-171-9

The Library of Congress has cataloged the hardcover edition as follows:

Christenson, Eric A., 1956–
    Phalaenopsis : a monograph / Eric A. Christenson ; sponsored by the
International Phalaenopsis Alliance.
        p. cm.
    Includes bibliographical references (p.).

    1. Phalaenopsis. I. Title.

QK495.O64 C39 2001
584'.4—dc21

00-056830

Contents

Preface

I began growing orchids as a junior in high school in 1972, and one of my first acquisitions was a large plant of *Phalaenopsis* Dos Pueblos, purchased during the final days of the famous Thomas Young Nursery in New Jersey. Shortly thereafter I considered several different universities and selected the University of Connecticut. At least part of that decision was influenced by Gustav Mehlquist, who snapped off a keiki of *P. lueddemanniana* to foster my budding passion for orchids. Little did I know that nearly 30 years later I would write a revision of the genus!

This revision is made possible by one man and one organization. The man is the late Herman Sweet. His meticulous revision of *Phalaenopsis*, including all the "grunt" work of locating and drawing types and critical specimens, laid the basis for this revisiting of the genus. His research admirably achieved its goals of defining the species and stabilizing the names in use.

The organization that made this revision possible is the International Phalaenopsis Alliance (IPA). Their support of my research made this revision a reality. I have learned many things from countless hours of discussing minutiae with its membership and can hardly wait for the arguments—make that "discussions"—that seeing this book in print will engender.

Sweet approached the chaos that was *Phalaenopsis* with the intention of bringing order to that chaos. My approach, in addition to incorporating new species and information that has come to light after Sweet's 1980 monograph, differs in three principal ways. First, I have a much broader circumscription of the genus than did Sweet and include the genera *Doritis* and *Kingidium* within *Phalaenopsis*. Second, with most of

9

the detailed species-level problems resolved by Sweet, I have concentrated on how the infrageneric groups are interrelated. I feel that the classification presented here, including the use of the subgeneric rank, produces groups that are more equivalent to each other than were Sweet's equally ranked sections. Third, my approach includes strong consideration of the utility of this revision to the sizeable trade in the genus that has arisen since Sweet's work. Thus infraspecific variation is formally described and given names for use by phalaenopsis breeders and enthusiasts as well as those involved with conservation efforts. The characterization of these variants separates significant subspecies from more trivial forms. All too frequently botanists opt to ignore these matters, which are generally considered too trivial among academic circles.

My rather multifaceted experience—including a bachelor's degree in horticulture, a master's degree in genetics, a Ph.D. in orchid taxonomy, and more than five years' experience as director of a micropropagation laboratory specializing in the clonal propagation of *Phalaenopsis*—gives me a rather unique view on the biology, taxonomy, conservation, and commercial industry of these plants. I hope that this view has been communicated in the following pages.

Acknowledgments

With an interest in *Phalaenopsis* spanning almost 30 years, I have before me a difficult task: selecting who to thank and why. The first choice that comes to mind are the four men who have most influenced my intellectual development: Gustav A. L. Mehlquist, Howard Wm. Pfeifer, Gunnar Seidenfaden, and Leslie A. Garay. Combined, these mentors have guided this impulsive orchid-centric protagonist through all dimensions of botany and horticulture.

As my undergraduate professor, Mehlquist taught me the most important lesson I learned in horticulture—that all the book learning in the world is of no use in horticulture without a grounded sense of practical application. That sense of the feasible has guided me ever since and in many ways. Pfeifer, when not conveying the deliciously archaic details of herbarium science, had the painful task of teaching me to write. To this day I do not know who had the greater pain (and psychological scars!). I attribute many of my strong communication skills to the Socratic process that brought about that first excruciating article on *Cleisostoma* back in 1982 and all that followed.

Both Garay and Seidenfaden have freely shared their extensive knowledge and archives with me throughout my experience as an orchid researcher. Many of the quirky intellectual insights I have had into problematic taxonomic situations have resulted directly from crucial bits of information provided by these men at equally crucial moments of investigation. Both have taught me the need for and value of critically interpreting early plant descriptions and types. I only hope I have lived up to whatever potential they miraculously saw in my early days as a very green graduate student.

The second group of people to be thanked are all the unsung heroes that slave and have slaved away in herbaria throughout the world. Perhaps nobody outside the discipline can appreciate the phenomenal resource herbaria represent and the tedious labors that create and maintain them.

The third group to be thanked are all the growers, both commercial and hobbyist, who have opened their collections to me. Often overly self-deprecating, little do they know how observing each and every growing situation added to my experience. Perhaps my notoriety allows me to get away with the proverbial murder, but I do appreciate their resolve to remain silent while I shoved flowers toward my nose and seemed to want to feel every flower in the greenhouse. From smelling the distinct fragrance of *P. corningiana* in Minnesota to seeing my first true *P. kunstleri* (the plant of a friend, who just wanted to see if the name was right), each tidbit has lodged somewhere in my cranium and added to the greater whole.

The fourth group that deserves recognition are all those poor suckers who found their lot in life included a vice-presidency and hence program chairperson in a local orchid society. As a lecturer I always do "sing for my supper" rather literally. What is hard to convey at the time is how deeply I appreciate the opportunity to see people's orchid collections and do snippets of herbarium research in neighboring institutions, tangentially funded for the most part by this vast network of local societies.

The fifth group that I wish to thank are all the photographers who have generously shared their documentation with me and contributed so many images to the final version of this book. What would a flower book be without those spectacular pictures?

The sixth group that deserves my heartfelt thanks are my personal friends, who have endured every groaning moment of this odyssey with me. Finally conversations will be free of my automatic opening of "almost finished" and the rejoinder to "finish the #@^@#^% thing!" Loving thanks go to Brian, Dave, David, Jim, John, Marni, Michael, Richard, Roy, and Scott. I promise not to start a new book for a little while, at least.

Finally, but in no way least of all, I thank the IPA. Their support has been nice, but their patience as one deadline after the other fell by the wayside has been epic. The period in which I researched and wrote this revision has had many personal bumps along the way, but through it all the IPA stood stoically by me and waited. I hope they are pleased with the final product and that it fills the void they so astutely sensed in the literature.

CHAPTER 1

History

It is unimaginable that when Swedish botanist Linnaeus described the "showy" *Epidendrum, E. amabile*, he could have foreseen a world in which millions of phalaenopsis plants would be grown annually for the general public. Even less would he have imagined a world in which these wondrous tropical exotics would be grown in test tubes and shipped around the world, adorning the pages of glossy magazines in everyone's home and spawning a specialist organization like the International Phalaenopsis Alliance (IPA). Linnaeus, the father of plant taxonomy, stood at the early threshold of the Age of Discovery and lived to see only the very first torrent of orchid diversity then being collected in the mysterious and dangerous unknowns of the tropics. Could his mind have comprehended the thousands upon thousands of orchids that awaited collection, study, and classification?

Beginning in the early 19th century and coinciding with the orchid craze that swept Europe, new species of *Phalaenopsis* found their way to wealthy patrons in England, France, and Germany in a more or less steady stream over time. Even within the rarified elite of orchid growers at that time, phalaenopsis were a cut above the flock. Lacking pseudobulbs or other storage mechanisms, phalaenopsis were hardly the easiest or least expensive plants to ship around the globe in sailing vessels. Upon their arrival and re-establishment in Europe, phalaenopsis rarely lent themselves to easy or even periodic propagation the way that cattleyas or paphiopedilums would. Some of these phalaenopsis plants generated sideshoots that could be removed and some produced plantlets, or keikis (singular "keiki," the Hawaiian term for "baby"), but most had a limited, albeit highly pampered, life span. Everyone who grows phalaenopsis knows the scourge of bacterial crown rot and other noxious diseases. Just imagine a time without electric fans and with only the most basic of chemical weapons in the arsenal.

Still, the graceful arching sprays of pink or white flowers made the larger-flowered species an essential part of the finer collections of orchids at the time. Phalaenopsis might have remained curiosities except for two pivotal developments in the first half of the 20th century. First, Professor Morel in France and Professor Knudson in the United States developed sterile culture techniques that allowed phalaenopsis and nearly all other tropical epiphytic orchids to be successfully propagated in large numbers at low cost. Suddenly plants of *Phalaenopsis* could be produced at a rate and cost comparable to other genera.

Quick on the heels of sterile culture techniques was the occurrence of some chance tetraploid seedlings in a cross named *P.* Doris. While charming and graceful, phalaenopsis flowers derived from *P. amabilis* and other larger-flowered species had been notoriously short-lived until that time. Their thin-textured flowers had a relatively short life span and were frustratingly susceptible to air pollution and other factors that could decrease longevity even further. The appearance of *P.* Doris changed all that and allowed *Phalaenopsis* hybrids to be used for a greater range of purposes including cut-flowers. Few orchid flowers lend themselves as well to wedding bouquets and personal arrangements as do large, opaque, stark-white phalaenopsis.

Following World War II, inexpensive orchids were produced in quantity with newfound ease, and orchid production shifted first from a rich man's hobby to a commercial industry and then from a commercial pot-plant and cut-flower market to one geared toward the hobbyist and backyard grower. This broader market coincided with the influx of many new or previously obscure species to horticulture. Quickly hybridizers started to mingle large-flowered standard hybrids with smaller-flowered colorful species that had previously been disdained by growers fixated on exhibition plants and cut-flowers.

The Royal Horticultural Society (RHS) in England, charged with the daunting task of registering all orchid hybrids made throughout the world, quickly saw the writing on the wall and requested Dr. Herman Sweet of the Oakes Ames Orchid Herbarium at Harvard University to revise the genus. This Sweet did in a superlative fashion, and his efforts largely stabilized the taxonomy, identifications, and names in use for the next 30 years. There remained bones of contention with Sweet's work—both within the phalaenopsis community and by the RHS itself —but his treatise preëmpted incalculable confusion.

Today new species of *Phalaenopsis* continue to be discovered. Some, like *P. chibae*, are valid new species; others are exciting new finds only until they flower and prove to be acutely expensive purchases of well-known older species. It is an exciting time for phalaenopsis growers, with almost limitless possibilities on the horizon. At this point seedling production is a routine no-brainer, and tissue culture of select clones is widespread and has become both commonplace and inexpensive. The humongous demand for mass market, pot-plant phalaenopsis makes selection of incredible clones from large populations a hybridizer's dream, and laboratory sciences have advanced so that answers can be obtained to almost any question that could be asked. Plants can be manipulated to a grower's whim in ways undreamt of only a few years ago.

Timeline of events affecting Phalaenopsis

1753   Description of *Epidendrum amabile* by Swedish botanist Linnaeus.

1825   Erection of the genus *Phalaenopsis* by Dutch botanist Blume.

1827   Erection of the genus *Polychilos* by Dutch botanist Breda.

1833   Erection of the genus *Doritis* by English botanist Lindley.

1853   Recognition of *Phalaenopsis×intermedia* as a stabilized natural hybrid by Lindley before the theory of evolution was proposed by Darwin and Wallace.

1886   Rolfe investigates the species of *Phalaenopsis* in a series of articles for the *Orchid Review*.

1917   Erection of the genus *Kingiella* by English botanist Rolfe.

1933   *Doritis* reduced to a section of *Phalaenopsis* by J. J. Smith.

1940   *Phalaenopsis* Doris establishes modern tetraploid hybrids leading to renaissance of phalaenopsis breeding.

1968–69   A revision of *Phalaenopsis* by Sweet appears in a series of articles in the *American Orchid Society Bulletin*.

17

1980 A revised edition of *The Genus Phalaenopsis* by Sweet is published as a book by the Orchid Digest Corporation.

1988 Seidenfaden's Vandeae of Thailand clarifies many problematic species of subgenus *Aphyllae* and leads the way for de-emphasizing pollinia number as a generic character.

1996 Rediscovery of *Phalaenopsis lowii.*

2001 A new monograph of *Phalaenopsis* is produced under the auspices of the IPA.

CHAPTER 2

Ecology and Distribution

Despite the popularity of *Phalaenopsis* species in cultivation, very little is known about their ecology and distribution in nature. Botanical gathering of phalaenopsis for herbaria and living research collections has been almost nonexistent in recent decades and hence little hard data about habitat and flowering season has been recorded. Examination of the holdings of the world's major herbaria has turned up only a scattering of collections that postdate Sweet's revision. Although there has been and continues to be active collecting of plants from the wild for the horticultural trade, no reliable information accompanies these living samples, which tend to be largely ephemeral in cultivation. To draw reasonable conclusions about ecology and distribution, more information must be supplied—something better than simply "Borneo" or "exported from Thailand."

Unlike numerous published articles on the native habitats of other popular orchid genera, such as *Paphiopedilum*, scant information has been shared by botanists, hobbyists, or naturalists who have visited habitats that support *Phalaenopsis* in the wild. Ideally, sharing information would be one of the ways that phalaenopsis enthusiasts who live in tropical Asia could contribute to our understanding of the genus. Habitat data not only adds to our primary knowledge but proves invaluable to *ex situ* conservation efforts when translated to applied horticultural practice.

In many cases the lack of available information is quite remarkable in its scope and longevity. A good example of such a gap concerns the elevation of *P. lindenii* in the wild. The literature consistently repeats Quisumbing's statement from 1947 that *P. lindenii* comes from "higher altitudes," but to this day no actual elevation has been reported. Growers take their clue from this scrap of information and have greater success growing *P. lindenii* at cooler temperatures than those typically recommended for phalaenopsis. Commercial collectors continue to harvest plants from the wild without relaying any useable habitat information. More precise data is needed about the specific habitat and ecology of this species, however, since even the most experienced growers will admit that *P. lindenii* remains problematic in long-term cultivation.

Ecology

In nature, *Phalaenopsis* occurs mostly in three distinct habitats: seasonally dry areas, seasonally cool areas, and constantly moist or humid areas. The plants show adaptations to each of these.

Phalaenopsis species that grow in monsoonal areas with a pronounced wet and dry cycle have adapted to the stress of the dry season in several ways. One method of adaptation is to become directly adapted to xerophytic conditions by increased succulence. This may be the approach taken by *P. cornu-cervi* and related species, which have much thicker leaves and roots than other species of similar vegetative size. Unsubstantiated reports claim that in at least part of its range *P. cornu-cervi* is semideciduous, dropping a portion of its leaves toward the end of the dry season as a final response to extreme desiccation. Certainly a precedent for this survival strategy exists in related genera such as *Aerides* and *Vanda*. This may not be a direct adaptation to seasonal dryness, however, because *P. pantherina*, a sister species to *P. cornu-cervi*, is recorded from high in the forest canopy, where it is exposed to bright diffuse light unlike most of the other species in Borneo, which occur toward the base of trees under low-light conditions. This increased succulence may simply be a response to degree of exposure independent of seasonal dryness.

The most extreme form of adaptation seen in *Phalaenopsis* species native to seasonally dry habitats is a deciduous habit. Leaves are the primary route by which water is transpired from a plant; as such, they are a significant liability during drought conditions, and their loss is a common adaptation to a seasonally severe water deficit. This adaptation is seen in several primarily Himalayan groups of *Phalaenopsis*, including subgenera *Aphyllae, Parishianae,* and *Proboscidioides.* Not surprisingly, this extreme adaptation is not seen in those members of the genus with centers of distribution outside of the Himalayan region, where the wet-dry cycle is less pronounced. While the species in these three subgenera may retain some leaves during the dry season, and usually do so under the mild conditions offered by horticulture, in most cases all their leaves are shed over the course of the dry season.

Phalaenopsis species that have adapted to seasonally cool to cold conditions also occur in regions that are seasonally dry. And, in the manner of the chicken and the egg, it is difficult to say which adaptation came first, since many adaptations apply to both extremes equally. The only truly cool- to cold-growing species of *Phalaenopsis* are those of subgenus *Aphyllae.* Chinese species of this subgenus are recorded as high as 2200 m, an elevation typical of cold-growing orchid genera such as *Odontoglossum* and unlike those one usually thinks of as typical for *Phalaenopsis.*

All these cold-growing *Phalaenopsis* species are deciduous or semi-deciduous in nature. Concomitant with this deciduous habit is a strong dormant rest period. This dormancy, with its high carbon to nitrogen ratio and low water content of the leaf tissue, allows some protection from cold damage. It is questionable whether this cold tolerance can be transferred to many hybrids because most other species do not exhibit a pronounced dormancy.

The most common habitat for the majority of species in the genus, those of subgenera *Phalaenopsis* and *Polychilos,* is one that is steadily warm and moist throughout the year. These are the lowland conditions that most growers emulate and that serve well for most species and hybrids. *Phalaenopsis* species most commonly occur in evergreen forests without an appreciable dry season; while seasonality is sufficient to trigger flowering and other physiological changes, the seasons are not pronounced enough to deleteriously stress the plants. Within these forests is a mosaic of habitats, and *Phalaenopsis* species occur in most of them.

Some species, such as *P. gigantea* and *P. pantherina,* occur relatively high in the canopy under rather exposed conditions. As a consequence, plants of these species have extremely leathery leaves to prevent desiccation and will tolerate higher light levels than will many other species.

21

Growers know to hang their plants of *P. gigantea* in areas of bright light to obtain healthy plants and prevent pathogens.

The other extreme is represented by those species that grow under extremely low light levels in nature, much lower light levels than given to standard phalaenopsis in cultivation. This appears to be the case with *P. tetraspis*. The original description of the habitat recorded *P. tetraspis* as coming from extremely dark locations. Growers who have emulated this low light level, by placing their plants under the greenhouse benches below their other phalaenopsis plants, have experienced great success with this species. *Phalaenopsis fuscata* also appears to respond to extremely low light levels, and limited data suggests it also inhabits dark locations in nature.

Many species of *Phalaenopsis* occur in riparian habitats, along streams and rivers that provide a constant high level of humidity regardless of fluctuations in local rainfall. Other species, such as *P. violacea*, are inhabitants of swamps for the same reason.

Some species of *Phalaenopsis* are able to grow either as epiphytes or opportunistically as lithophytes. *Phalaenopsis sumatrana* and *P. lowii* have been recorded as lithophytes. Life on large boulders may provide the plants with a steadier moisture supply or may take advantage of the light gap often associated with rock outcroppings in otherwise continuous forest.

The most unusual ecology in *Phalaenopsis* is the obligate terrestrial or lithophytic habit of the three species of section *Esmeralda* (formerly the genus *Doritis*) and some Australian populations of *P. amabilis* subsp. *rosenstromii*. Both appear to be derived conditions within the genus, and an epiphytic habit is accepted as the ancestral character for the genus as a whole. In the cases of *P. buyssoniana*, *P. pulcherrima*, and *P. regnieriana*, the terrestrial habit appears to be an adaptation, in part, to an extremely pronounced dry season. Direct access to the soil and accumulated leaf litter presumably provide supplemental water during the dry season. Life on the ground for these three species, which are native to more or less deciduous forests, also presumably provides some shade even when the forest canopy is leafless. These species also show perhaps the strongest tendency for the leaves to turn reddish purple under intense solar radiation or water stress, another defense under extreme conditions.

The case of *P. amabilis* subsp. *rosenstromii* appears to be somewhat more complex. At one end of its extensive range, the terrestrial and lithophytic habit of Australian plants of *P. amabilis* subsp. *rosenstromii* may be an adaptation to a combination of seasonally very dry and cool conditions. Throughout the rest of its range, *P. amabilis* inhabits wet habitats without pronounced dry or cool seasons.

Phalaenopsis plants are generally thought to require low to medium light levels. While true for most species and standard hybrids bred from them, this generalization falls apart for many of the less frequently cultivated species. Many species grow under quite bright light levels in nature. Personal experience with *P. taenialis* in northeast India as well as in cultivation suggests that this species as well as other members of subgenus *Aphyllae* grow best when given bright light levels similar to those given cattleyas. This may, in part, be linked to the importance of root photosynthesis in these species.

One largely overlooked aspect of phalaenopsis research is pollination biology. The only species with documented pollination biology is *P. amabilis*, which is visited by large carpenter bees of the genus *Xylocopa*. Pollination events are frequent and successful in *P. amabilis*, judging by the high percentage of fruit set in the wild (up to 50 percent of the flowers are pollinated). It is reasonable to assume that similar large bees pollinate other species of section *Phalaenopsis* with comparable lip and callus structure.

It is unlikely that this pollination syndrome can be extrapolated to cover many other groups of species in the genus. Flower sizes, colors, fragrances, longevity, attitude of presentation, and callus and lip structures differ widely among other sections. The pollinator success rate is also dramatically different. Herbarium records, which represent a largely impartial sampling by botanical collectors without any bias toward orchids, suggest that pollination of most species is a remarkably rare event. In *P. lueddemanniana* and its relatives in the Philippines, for example, usually only one or two capsules appear to be produced by each plant during a season, if any are produced at all (noting that a nonfruiting, non-flowering plant would be ignored by botanical collectors).

Looking at most species of subgenus *Polychilos*, it is reasonable to hypothesize that they are pollinated by a group of bees smaller than the massive *Xylocopa*. These *Phalaenopsis* species, such as *P. bellina* and *P.*

sumatrana, have strongly day-fragrant flowers typical of bee-pollinated flowers. The longevity of the flowers are in part a result of the infrequent pollination events in nature. Jim Comber (pers. comm.), expert on the orchids of Java and Sumatra, relates how one observes the same flowers over time on a plant *in situ* without any evidence of pollinator visitation (i.e., the anther is intact and no post-pollination senescence has taken place).

It is difficult to even speculate what classes of pollinators visit other groups of species. Nothing is known of the function of the variably expressed spur in subgenus *Aphyllae* or the mobile lip of subgenus *Parishianae* and how these structures relate to pollination. Answering these questions, which can only be resolved by long-term field work, is one more contribution that can be made by residents, and especially amateur enthusiasts, in the tropics where *Phalaenopsis* species are native. Unfortunately pollination studies often have a low success rate (especially where pollination events are rare) and are time consuming, frequently unpleasant to perform, and underfunded relative to more glamorous high-tech botanical researches.

Distribution

Species of *Phalaenopsis* are found throughout tropical Asia and the larger islands of the Pacific Ocean. They reach their westernmost limit in Sri Lanka and South India and their easternmost limit in Papua New Guinea and adjacent Australia. In the north they occur in southern China (Yunnan), Taiwan, and the Philippines. Although the genus is comparatively small, this distribution more or less parallels larger Asian genera such as *Dendrobium* and *Eria*.

The subgenera of *Phalaenopsis* have distinct geographic distributions. The subgenera *Aphyllae, Parishianae,* and *Proboscidioides* are Himalayan with centers of diversity in southern China, India to northern Vietnam, and Myanmar to Thailand, respectively. Subgenus *Polychilos* has a few species as far west as northeast India but is primarily centered in southeast Asia, with at least two separate radiations in Indonesia and the Philippines; the Philippine species form a closely interrelated complex (i.e., those species formerly included in the all-encompassing *P. lueddemanniana*). Finally, subgenus *Phalaenopsis* is centered in the Phil-

24

ippines with two extensions to Taiwan (*P. aphrodite* subsp. *formosana* and Taiwanese plants of *P. equestris*) and one wide-ranging species found from Indonesia to Australia but actually rather rare in the Philippines proper (*P. amabilis*).

Data pinpointing the exact distribution of the individual species is wanting for most species. Precise information from museum specimens is available for only a few species whose range coincides with historically active botanical collecting, primarily species from the Philippines and the former British India. Outside of these few species little is known other than the country of origin or general provenance of samples. Thus we have significant horticultural species, such as *P. celebensis*, whose distribution in the wild is wholly unknown except for its origin somewhere in Sulawesi. Early horticultural collectors purposefully obscured the origins of their plants. Sadly their modern counterparts offer little additional information on the origins of contemporary examples.

Just as accurate information on distribution is wanting, so is data on the elevational ranges of most species. While general elevational ranges of most species have been established from historic records, word-of-mouth from the collectors, or observation of plants under cultivation, precise information and ranges are again lacking.

Finally, next to nothing is known about the spatial distribution of individual plants of *Phalaenopsis* within the forest. For some species we have limited data about their vertical stratification in the canopy, from clustered near the base of the host trees to relatively high up in canopy. Almost no information is available regarding horizontal stratification of these plants in nature. Do the plants exist primarily on primary tree trunks, on horizontal branches, or in the axils of branches where leaf litter accumulates? Species with consistently successful pollinations that produce large numbers of fruits and seeds are colonizers in the wild. Thus it is usual to see species like *P. amabilis* or *P. aphrodite* occur in large numbers in rather dense colonies on an individual host tree, on the primary tree trunks or on large branches proximal to the main trunk. Other species appear to occur as more isolated individuals, although the population of a given area may still be fairly dense provided that the habitat is conducive to germination and seedling establishment.

CHAPTER 3

Morphology

With the exception of a few species that show specialized ecological adaptations, *Phalaenopsis* is uniform in the vegetative and floral morphology of its plants. Most may be easily recognized to genus by even neophyte hobbyists and non-orchid people. This chapter presents the morphological variation within *Phalaenopsis* and cites the implications of this variation on classification of the genus.

Plants

Plants of *Phalaenopsis* all have short stems. This is in keeping with Holttum's theory that stem length in monopodial orchids is generally an adaptation to light requirements: genera that require high light levels have long internodes and, hence, long vining stems (*Arachnis, Renanthera*), while genera that require low light levels have short internodes (*Grosourdya, Phalaenopsis*). *Phalaenopsis* is distinguished by stems that might almost be called acaulous (literally "without stems"): the internodes, or the spaces between leaves, are extremely short. Elongate internodes occasionally occur as anomalous growth characters in the genus, usually through etiolation caused by overly wet conditions or as an aberrant growth most likely occurring through a genetically controlled internal hormone imbalance. The latter is most often seen where the apical meristem of the stem is consumed in the production of an inflorescence that initially bears large, basal, subfoliaceous bracts toward the base.

Typically the stems in *Phalaenopsis* are borne at right angles to vertical host stems. And unlike other genera in the Aeridinae, no species of *Phalaenopsis* has been recorded growing primarily on horizontal host branches. This is in keeping with the architecture of the leaves. Leaves in *Phalaenopsis* are typically laxly arching-pendent in nature. Borne on an essentially horizontal stem, this arrangement allows rain water to drain away from the growing point (the crown of the plant) along the midvein of the leaves. In so doing, pathogens—and especially bacterial rots—are avoided in nature.

Exceptions to this scheme are the species of section *Esmeralda* (*Doritis*, in the narrow sense). These terrestrial species bear erect stems with leaves that typically form a catch-basin. The individual leaves are more or less cupped and effectively direct water toward the crown. This is most likely an adaptation to a limited water supply during the dry season.

Roots

Roots in *Phalaenopsis* are of three kinds: aerial, prostrate epiphytic, and substrate. Aerial roots are typically cylindric and unbranched, unless they have suffered physical damage, and bear large, elongate, pigmented root tips. The root tips may be either green or purple and, like leaf pigmentation, appear to be governed by a simple, probably single-allele, inheritance pattern. Epiphytic roots (or those roots that follow a host stem, with one side appressed to the host stem and the other side exposed to the air without any substrate covering) are typically flattened and ribbon-like. In subgenus *Parishianae* and certain species of section *Phalaenopsis* (especially *P. philippinensis*, *P. schilleriana*, and *P. stuartiana*), the exposed surfaces are heavily wrinkled, although no real study has been made for this characteristic throughout the genus. Substrate roots are typically cylindric, larger in diameter than the corresponding aerial roots, and usually lacking pigment in the root tips. Individual roots may show one or more of these stages depending on their environment.

The roots of *Phalaenopsis* are usually unbranched unless they are damaged (branching is a standard wound response in the Aeridinae) or unless they obtain significant length with age.

Root tissue has been used for the micropropagation of *Phalaenopsis* with varying success. Root tissue of orchids in general appears to be physiologically "determined" to be root tissue. The hormonal forcing of root parenchyma (largely undifferentiated cells that are capable of cell division, or mitosis) to initiate mitosis and subsequently form the tissue for generating protocorm-like-bodies (PLBs) has a number of drawbacks, especially a sizeable inducement of macro-mutations. One species, *P. stuartiana*, flies in the face of this pattern. *Phalaenopsis stuartiana* has often been recorded as generating plantlets from root primordia. Typically, a large plant of *P. stuartiana* establishes itself on a bench or plaque in a greenhouse; if the plant is removed, the broken root segments remaining on the bench or wall produce plantlets. I am unaware of any situation wherein *P. stuartiana* produces plantlets from the roots of an undisturbed parent plant. Nor have I seen this phenomenon in the closely related *P. schilleriana*.

Leaves

Although leaf thickness varies from species to species, the overall leaf texture and morphology are similar throughout the genus. All species of *Phalaenopsis* bear succulent, fleshy leaves. This is consistent with the plants lacking any other water storage organs, such as pseudobulbs, with which to endure the dry season. Unlike high light requiring genera of the Aeridinae such as *Aerides* and *Vanda*, most *Phalaenopsis* species do not appear to use their root systems as storage organs during the dry season (i.e., shedding their leaves and transferring water storage and carbohydrate reserves to the roots during the dry season). Their relatively close, humid natural environments shield the plants from excessive drying.

Plants of subgenera *Aphyllae*, *Parishianae*, and *Proboscidioides* are normally deciduous in nature. Native to areas governed by monsoonal climate with a pronounced dry season, these plants shed their leaves to avoid excessive dehydration. This could be considered a shared evolutionary character (a synapomorphy in cladistic terms) but could equally represent independent evolution of the character as a parallel response to the environment (convergent evolution). These plants do not require a severe dry period and in cultivation watering should be sufficient to avoid leaf loss.

The leaves do show some variation in pigmentation, in both the basic ground color and the superposed patterns. In section *Fuscatae* the leaves are a drab olive green, unlike other species in the genus. In subgenus *Parishinae* the upper leaf surface is a dark bluish green and often somewhat prismatic. In some species of subgenus *Phalaenopsis* the leaves are overlain with a silver sheen and richly marked with darker purple spots. Color patterning of the leaves appears to correlate strongly with traditionally recognized species complexes. In those species with unmarked leaves, the presence or absence of purple suffusion on the lower leaf surfaces appears to be variable and again, controlled by a simple, probably one-allele system.

The leaves of many species of subgenus *Polychilos* show mosaic patterning of several more or less pallid green shades that may be a result of nutritional deficiencies in cultivation. Species related to *P. lueddemanniana*, in particular, typically produce foliage mottled with minute sectors of paler green coloration. Although falsely attributed to a "possible" virus, the cause of this mottling is unknown. Specific studies should be undertaken to ascertain the possibility of a calcium or other mineral deficiency in this species cluster.

Inflorescences

The inflorescences, or flower stalks, of *Phalaenopsis* range from short, few-flowered racemes to long-scapose racemes, to variously branched panicles. Some species produce panicles with every blooming (*P. schilleriana, P. stuartiana*) while others produce either racemes or panicles depending on the vigor of the plant and/or the age of the inflorescence. Simple unbranched racemes appear to be recessive in breeding, judging from the multiflora hybrids that have been created using such species as *P. lobbii*.

The peduncle, or the non-flowering portion of the inflorescence, is usually terete and bears several nodes, each concealed by a solitary, tightly fitting tubular bract. Each node produces a quiescent growing point (meristem) that is visible to the naked eye when the bract is removed. This primary meristem is flanked by a pair of much smaller meristems, which may not be visible prior to their activation and growth. If the rachis is damaged, if none of the flowers are pollinated, or if the rachis is removed shortly after the flowers fade, the primary meristems of the uppermost node(s) will typically initiate growth. In most species this growth results in new branches of the inflorescence, which go on to produce a secondary flush of flowers.

Occasionally these nodes produce keikis rather than additional flowering branches. Roots on these plantlets are adventitious from the leaf axils toward the base of the stem. For vegetative propagation in horticulture, at least two roots should be developed on each plantlet before severing from the parent plant. Plantlet formation can be induced artificially using plant hormones applied topically. In addition, if young (short) secondary branches of the inflorescence are broken off, the secondary meristems at the nodes often go on to produce plantlets rather than additional inflorescence.

The rachis, or the flowering portion of the inflorescence, may be terete or variously flattened. A highly flattened rachis and/or floral bracts are characteristic of some species, such as those of the *P. cornu-cervi* complex. The flowers may be arranged in a spiral manner around the rachis (section *Stauroglottis*) or alternate, distichous forming a two-ranked inflorescence (*P. bellina*). The rachis may be few- to many-flowered. Floral bracts in *Phalaenopsis* are small relative to the length of the pedicel and ovary. The bracts may be fleshy and persistent or thin-textured and withering. The rachis is terminated by a quiescent meristem. In *P. equestris* this meristem typically grows into a plantlet following flowering. This feature is seen sporadically in other species. In some species this meristem produces additional rachis and flowers following the first flush of flowers. In most species, however, this meristem never reinitiates growth.

Flowers

Flowers of *Phalaenopsis* are resupinate, that is to say, the pedicel and ovary will twist as needed to orient the flower with the lip in the lowermost position. In an erect inflorescence this is achieved by a 180° twist. In a pendent inflorescence (or at least the rachis pendent) no twisting is needed. The flowers range from very fleshy-succulent to thin and membranous. Regardless of their texture, most flowers in the genus are long-lasting, usually remaining in good condition for at least three weeks. Flowers most frequently are borne more or less simultaneously, although some species, such as those in the *P. cornu-cervi* complex, produce flowers sequentially, one at a time, over long periods. Some species bear strongly fragrant flowers while others do not appear to produce any scent detectable to either the human nose or the gas chromatograph.

The sepals and petals, collectively termed the perianth, are usually more or less similar in size, shape, and coloration. The dorsal sepal is erect and uppermost in the flowers. The lateral sepals are oblique, they may be divergent or subparallel, and they often bear markings and/or more saturated pigments not seen on the other segments. The petals are usually about the same size as the sepals, but they may be either much more narrow than the sepals, and especially the lateral sepals (section *Polychilos*), or much broader than the sepals (section *Phalaenopsis*). The perianth segments may be flat, cupped, or with strongly revolute margins. The most unusual petals are found in *P. celebensis*, which bears incurved petals with revolute margins and a central brown stain. This arrangement mimics a peloric flower wherein the petals approach the lip in configuration and coloration.

The lips of flowers in *Phalaenopsis* are always three-lobed. The lateral lobes may be subparallel (subgenus *Polychilos*) or curved to form a cylindric chamber (sections *Phalaenopsis* and *Stauroglottis*). The morphology of the lateral lobes is useful in the classification of the genus. Subgenus *Phalaenopsis* bears lateral lobes of the lip that are smooth over their inner surfaces and with gently rounded apices; the other four subgenera bear lateral lobes of the lip that each have an oblique tooth on their inner surfaces and that have variously toothed apices.

The midlobe of the lip may be acute, bluntly rounded, notched, or embellished with tendril-like lobules at the apex. The blade may be concave or convex and variously ornamented with keels, teeth, and trichomes (hairs). In subgenus *Parishianae* the midlobe is mobile.

Toward the base of the lip, between the lateral lobes, are between one to three sets of calli. When two sets of calli are present (the callus then said to be biseriate), the posterior callus may be glandular. When three sets of calli are present (the callus then said to be triseriate), the posterior callus is always glandular. The number and morphology of the calli are significant characters for species determinations as well as the infrageneric classification of the genus. Subgenus *Phalaenopsis* has only one callus while all other subgenera have at least two sets of calli. Most species of subgenus *Parishianae* have a transverse anterior callus unique in the genus.

The column and the broad stigmatic cavity are the only totally consistent characters for the genus. Columns in *Phalaenopsis* are more or less straight, subcylindric, and dilated toward the apex. The base of the column may be unadorned or have a pair of swollen "knees." These knees presumably play a role in pollination and are absent or much reduced in subgenus *Phalaenopsis*. The clinandrium (anther bed) may be unadorned or extended in a concave hood. The hooded clinandrium defines section *Zebrinae*. The rostellum of nearly all *Phalaenopsis* species is elongate and held over and parallel to the apex of the stigmatic cavity. The exception is *P. lowii*, which has a highly elongate rostellum (and corresponding stipe of the pollinarium). The elongate rostellum of *P. lowii* is the primary reason for placing it in the monotypic subgenus *Proboscidioides*.

The anther in *Phalaenopsis* may be more or less rounded or angularly lobed with a central channel. The morphology of the pollinarium, comprised of a viscidium, stipe, and pollinia, is uniform throughout the genus. The only exceptions are the elongate stipes found in subgenus *Proboscidioides* and section *Esmeralda*. Pollinia number has traditionally been a heavily weighted character in the classification of orchid genera. That is less true today as we continue to find multiple exceptions within otherwise tightly defined genera, such as *Aerides* and *Gastrochilus*. *Phalaenopsis* has either four pollinia borne in two appressed pairs or two pollinia with a cleft or suture on one side. The evolutionary progression from four to two pollinia appears to have occurred twice within the genus, in the subgenera *Phalaenopsis* and *Polychilos*.

Fruits

With the traditional emphasis in orchid taxonomy on floral, and especially lip morphology, characters of the fruit have been largely overlooked in study of the family. In the case of *Phalaenopsis*, no particularly significant differences have been noted among the species with the exception of chlorophylly in subgenera *Aphyllae* and *Polychilos*. In most species of the genus, the perianth withers following pollination. The perianth is persistent and remains attached to the apex of the ovary as small, shrivelled structures for the duration of the fruit. Although the full extent of chlorophylly in *Phalaenopsis* is not known because the fruits of some species have not been recorded to date, species of sub-genera *Aphyllae* and *Polychilos* appear to consistently display chloro-phylly. In these subgenera the perianth turns green (i.e., loses all the other pigments, revealing the underlying chlorophyll) following effec-tive pollination and the segments remain fleshy and leafy for the com-plete duration of the fruit.

The ovary of *Phalaenopsis*, which eventually develops into a fruit, is termed inferior. This means that the ovary is located wholly below the floral segments, which are fused to the apex of the ovary. In most plants, and a few orchid genera, there is a clear distinction between the ovary and the stalk that bears the individual flower. The stalk for each flower (i.e., the string-like "stem" you pull off an apple or cherry) is called the pedicel. In *Phalaenopsis* the ovary, defined by the region which has ovules and/or seeds present, internally tapers at the base to a sterile segment, the pedicel. These regions are usually visually undif-ferentiated prior to pollination, although the pedicel becomes obvious once the ovary has swollen.

The fruits of *Phalaenopsis* are commonly called seed "pods." This is a slang horticultural term: the fruits of *Phalaenopsis* (and almost all orchids) are correctly called capsules. A capsule is a many-seeded fruit that is dry at maturity and opens to release its seeds. The capsule in *Phalaenopsis* is composed of six parallel segments akin to the stays of a barrel. Prior to opening, these convex-rounded segments translate as six grooves (i.e., the fruit is said to be six-sulcate). Fruits of *Phalaenopsis* may be green or variously pigmented. In particular, the fruits of sub-genus *Aphyllae* are purple suffused and heavily mottled with dark purple-brown, similar to species of *Ascocentrum* and *Luisia*.

Chromosomes

All species of *Phalaenopsis*, with the exception of the naturally occur-ring tetraploid *P. buyssoniana*, have 38 chromosomes (2n = 38). *Phalae-nopsis buyssoniana* has 76 chromosomes (2n = 4x = 76). This is consistent with the subtribe Aeridinae (= Sarcanthinae), which displays a remark-ably uniform diploid number of 38, with only occasional tetraploid and hexaploid species and/or races. Differences in chromosome num-bers are not a factor leading to sterility or other incompatability when breeding interspecific hybrids based on normal (chemically untreated) species.

Chromosomes in the genus do differ in size and morphology. Most research to date has focused on species of subgenera *Phalaenopsis* and *Polychilos*, however, and nothing like a complete picture of variation has been produced. Species of sections *Phalaenopsis* and *Stauroglottis* appear to have the shortest chromosomes in the genus. Depending on the particular combination of parents, chromosome morphology can be useful in determining the validity of reported hybrid combinations (see the discussion under section *Esmeralda* in Chapter 9).

Non-traditional characters

Despite the popularity of *Phalaenopsis* and the relative ease with which research material can be obtained, little modern work has been attempted using newer technologies, although almost every avenue taken has shown promise. Analysis of floral fragrances has been shown to have utility in separating closely related species pairs (Christenson and Whitten 1995). Electrophoretic banding patterns show taxonomic utility for separating species as well as analyzing hybrids. Although flavonoids have not revealed any useful chemo-taxonomic patterns, flavonoid co-pigments have shown great promise (Griesbach 1990 and unpubl.). Finally, limited DNA work using the matK gene (Jarrell unpubl.) has independently supported the generic restructuring presented here.

Clearly more molecular work is needed, preferably using this monograph as a working hypothesis. In particular, a better understanding of the genera related to *Phalaenopsis* is needed, despite the extreme rarity of many genera purported to be close relatives based on floral morphology (*Lesliea, Nothodoritis*). With the realization that *Doritis* is not a closely related genus (an "outgroup" in cladistic terminology) but rather a central part of *Phalaenopsis* and that *Sarcochilus*, traditionally considered a sister group to *Phalaenopsis*, is not particularly closely related (Jarrell unpubl.) despite the presence of intergeneric hybrids, knowledge of the closest relatives to *Phalaenopsis* and the rather highly derived *Nothodoritis* remains obscure.

CHAPTER 4

Generic and Infrageneric Classification and Taxonomy

Phalaenopsis Bl.

Bijdr. 7:294. 1825. Type: *Epidendrum amabile* L. (= *Phalaenopsis amabilis* (L.) Bl.).

Synadena Raf., Fl. Tellur. 4:9. 1838. Type: *Synadena amabilis* (L.) Raf. (= *Phalaenopsis amabilis* (L.) Bl.).

Polychilos Breda in Kuhl and van Hasselt, Gen. and Sp. Orch. 1. 1827. Type: *Polychilos cornu-cervi* Breda (= *Phalaenopsis cornu-cervi* (Breda) Bl. & Rchb.f.).

Doritis Lindl., Gen. and Sp. Orch. Pl. 178. 1833; *Phalaenopsis* section *Doritis* (Lindl.) J. J. Sm., Repert. Spec. Nov. Regni Veg. 32:366. 1933, nom. inval. Type: *Doritis pulcherrima* Lindl. (= *Phalaenopsis pulcherrima* (Lindl.) J. J. Sm.).

Polystylus Hassk., Natuurk. Tijdschr. Nederl. Indië 10:3. 1856. Type: *Polystylus cornu-cervi* Hassk. (= *Phalaenopsis cornu-cervi* (Breda) Bl. & Rchb.f.).

Stauroglottis Schauer, Nov. Act. Acad. Nat. Cur. 19, suppl. 1:432. 1843. Type: *Stauroglottis equestris* Schauer (= *Phalaenopsis equestris* (Schauer) Rchb.f.).

Kingiella Rolfe, Orchid Rev. 25:197. 1917; *Kingidium* P. F. Hunt, Kew Bull. 24:97. 1970. Lectotype (in Hunt 1971a): *Kingidium taeniale* (Lindl.) P. F. Hunt (= *Phalaenopsis taenialis* (Lindl.) E. A. Christ. & U. C. Pradhan).

Grafia Hawkes, Phytologia 13:306. 1966. Type: *Grafia parishii* (Rchb.f.) Hawkes (= *Phalaenopsis parishii* Rchb.f.).

Monopodial terrestrials, lithophytes, and epiphytes. **Stems** short, leafy, concealed by imbricating persistent leaf sheaths, rooting at the base. **Leaves** alternate, distichous, succulent, persistent or sometimes deciduous, oblong to broadly elliptic, sometimes marbled or suffused with purple or silver. **Inflorescences** axillary pedunculate racemes or panicles, erect to laxly pendent, the peduncle terete, the rachis terete or bilaterally compressed, rarely swollen relative to the peduncle, the floral bracts inconspicuous, persistent, succulent or papery. **Flowers** few to many, resupinate, inconspicuous to showy, membranous to thickly fleshy, produced simultaneously or in succession over time, often extremely long-lasting, often fragrant, immaculate or variously marked with spots, marbling, or bars. **Sepals** and **petals** free, spreading, subsimilar to dimorphic, the lateral sepals usually oblique and larger than the dorsal sepal. **Lip** three-lobed, clawed, continuous with the foot, sometimes saccate or subsaccate, the lateral lobes erect and subparallel, often callose, the midlobe oblong-elliptic to obtrullate, rarely transverse, sometimes pubescent to villose, the **callus** uni-, bi- or triseriate, longitudinal, rarely transverse. **Column** stout, often subtended by a pair of fleshy knee-like protrusions, without wings, with a foot, usually dilated lateral to the stigma. **Pollinia** two or four, on a common spatulate stipe and viscidium. **Pedicel** and **ovary** terete, slender, shallowly six-sulcate. **Capsule** pedicellate.

Until quite recently pollinia number was considered an absolute taxonomic character in defining orchid genera. When Sweet revised *Phalaenopsis* this was the overwhelming consensus within the botanical community. Subsequently this consensus changed, and while pollinia number is still a useful character, it is no longer a character given absolute weighting in an analysis.

This is particularly significant for an approach to a classification of *Phalaenopsis*. Under the philosophy in place during Sweet's research, plants segregated as *Doritis* and *Kingidium* could not by definition be considered part of *Phalaenopsis*. *Phalaenopsis*, as typified by *P. amabilis*, has two pollinia while *Doritis* and *Kingidium* have four pollinia. It should also be remembered that Sweet was coping first and foremost with species-level problems and not a generic revision of the Aeridinae. Details of the pollinarium and pollinia numbers play an insignificant role in species-level determinations in *Phalaenopsis*.

The first crack in Sweet's classification has been the pollinia numbers of species he placed in his section *Aphyllae*. The availability of new material from this group (treated here as subgenus *Aphyllae*) has established that these species have four pollinia. It has similarly been established that the *P. parishii* group (subgenus *Parishianae*) and *P. lowii* (subgenus *Proboscidioides*) also have four pollinia.

The species included by Sweet in *Phalaenopsis* form a natural group: never has there been any question that they all belong to a single genus. The position taken here is that several additional groups, traditionally treated as separate genera, should be added to Sweet's concept to make a truly inclusive genus. The end result of these findings is a classification which recognizes that having two pollinia is a derived condition in the genus, one that has arisen independently in two lineages: once in subgenus *Polychilos* and once in sections *Phalaenopsis* and *Stauroglottis* of subgenus *Phalaenopsis*.

The genus *Kingidium* has been a minor bone of contention among students of *Phalaenopsis*. First is the question of what to include in a separate *Kingidium* and then the question of whether to include all or only some of its components in a more broadly defined *Phalaenopsis*. I am of the camp that splits the traditional genus *Kingidium* into different parts of *Phalaenopsis*, some as part of subgenus *Aphyllae* and some as section *Deliciosae* of subgenus *Phalaenopsis*. Once the absolute character of pollinia number is dismissed, the only character that holds *Kingidium* together is the presence of a small saccate spur. Within the species placed here in subgenus *Aphyllae* are every possible degree of spur development, from a conspicuous spur in *P. braceana* and *P. taenialis* to no spur whatsoever in *P. wilsonii*.

The other half of a traditional *Kingidium*, exemplified by *P. deliciosa*, is unrelated to subgenus *Aphyllae* and is part of the same clade that includes both *Doritis* and the remainder of subgenus *Phalaenopsis*. This pattern of relationship is strongly supported by molecular taxonomy based on matK (Jarrell unpubl.).

This brings us to *Doritis*, a second genus traditionally separated from *Phalaenopsis* because of pollinia number. As discussed in Chapter 9 under section *Esmeralda*, the supposed distinctiveness of *Doritis* was enhanced by misinterpretation of the lip structures and an overemphasis of the adaptations of these three species to a terrestrial habit. The placement of *Doritis* within subgenus *Phalaenopsis* as a section next to section *Deliciosae* is also strongly supported by molecular taxonomy (Jarrell unpubl.).

In addition to these changes at the generic level, I have inserted five groups at the rank of subgenus into the classification of *Phalaenopsis*. Sweet and other earlier authors did not use this rank in their classifications of the genus. With one exception I agree with Sweet's nine sections but feel that his sections do not warrant the equal weighting he gave them. In particular I include far more species and several of Sweet's sections in one clade defined as subgenus *Polychilos*. Having both subgenera and sections, in my opinion, more accurately represents the phylogenetic history of the genus.

Taxonomy and species treatments are presented in the next five chapters, each devoted to one of the five subgenera; my proposed revision of Sweet's ranking, to the sectional level, is as follows:

Genus *Phalaenopsis* Bl.
    Subgenus *Proboscidioides* (Rolfe) E. A. Christ., stat. nov.
    Subgenus *Aphyllae* (Sweet) E. A. Christ., stat. nov.
    Subgenus *Parishianae* (Sweet) E. A. Christ., stat. nov.
    Subgenus *Polychilos* (Breda) E. A. Christ., stat. nov.
        Section *Polychilos* (Breda) Rchb.f.
        Section *Fuscatae* Sweet
        Section *Amboinenses* Sweet
        Section *Zebrinae* Pfitz.
    Subgenus *Phalaenopsis*
        Section *Phalaenopsis*
        Section *Deliciosae* E. A. Christ.
        Section *Esmeralda* Rchb.f.
        Section *Stauroglottis* (Schauer) Benth.

CHAPTER 5

Subgenus *Proboscidioides*

Subgenus *Proboscidioides* (Rolfe) E. A. Christ., stat. nov.

Basionym: *Phalaenopsis* section *Proboscidioides* Rolfe, Gard. Chron., n.s., 26:276. 1886. Type: *Phalaenopsis lowii* Rchb.f.

This monotypic subgenus is problematic in several ways. It is unique in a broadly defined *Phalaenopsis* in having an extremely long, beak-like rostellum; Sweet (1980) likened it to an elephant's head and trunk. Unlike other species of *Phalaenopsis* noted for their longer than typical rostellums (such as those of section *Esmeralda*), the rostellum of *P. lowii* far surpasses the stigma and is about as long as the entire column. This long rostellum, at a more or less right angle to the column, positions the viscidium very differently from other species. *Phalaenopsis lowii* also differs from all other species in the genus by having the lateral lobes of the lip in the form of recurved hooks.

Restricted to a rather small area of Myanmar and Thailand, *P. lowii* has a deciduous habit and bears four separate pollinia, characters it shares with subgenera *Aphyllae* and *Parishianae*.

I have speculated elsewhere on the possible relationship of *P. lowii* to the monotypic *Nothodoritis* Tsi of China, and I still believe that *Nothodoritis* is the most closely related genus to *Phalaenopsis* as circumscribed here. They share the characters of a deciduous habit, an elongate rostellum (and concomitant elongate stipe of the pollinarium), and four separate pollinia. The lip of *P. lowii*, however, is unlike the highly unusual lip found in *Nothodoritis* and similar to other species of *Phalaenopsis* in the callus morphology, in the presence of slightly raised teeth on the lateral lobes of the lip, and in overall gestalt, especially evident in recent color photographs. Also, there is no trace of the peculiar column appendage found in *Nothodoritis* in *P. lowii*. Emphasizing the similarity in lip morphology, I retain *P. lowii* in a broadly defined *Phalaenopsis*, noting the isolated position it occupies.

A different and equally valid approach would be to separate *P. lowii* as a new genus on the basis of its rostellum morphology. Such a "solution" would have the advantage of removing a somewhat discordant morphology from *Phalaenopsis*, albeit altering a stable nomenclature in the process. I do not take this approach: the general consensus among taxonomists working on paleotropical orchids is to try to avoid making new monotypic genera just to provide a "quick fix" to a monograph in hand. This is especially true in the Aeridinae, already rife with monotypic genera, where generic limits have been confused until relatively recently. Fine tuning of generic limits is not to be done casually because of the ramifications of altering names and should preferably proceed only after molecular data or data from other modern techniques has been considered. Having said that, I should also state that if *P. lowii* had been described historically as a separate genus, I would not rush to merge such a genus with *Phalaenopsis* until new data became available. Most likely, subgenus *Proboscidioides* is a basal group to the rest of the genus, and its removal would not change the scientific integrity of *Phalaenopsis* (i.e., removing *P. lowii* from *Phalaenopsis* in the broad sense would not create any paraphyletic groups).

Phalaenopsis lowii Rchb.f.

> Bot. Zeit. 20:214. 1862; *Polychilos lowii* (Rchb.f.) Shim, Malayan Nat. Journ. 36:24. 1982. Type: Myanmar. Moulmein, *Parish 125* (holotype: W; isotype: K). Photograph of the isotype published in Sweet (1980:43).

> *Phalaenopsis proboscidioides* Parish ex Rchb.f., Xenia Orch. 2:139. 1868, nom. nud.

Miniature lithophytes (on limestone) and epiphytes. **Roots** numerous, flattened, appressed to the substrate, exposed to the air without any associated accumulated organic matter, very long (Fitch records them as "several feet" in length). **Leaves** one to five, ovate-lanceolate to oblong-

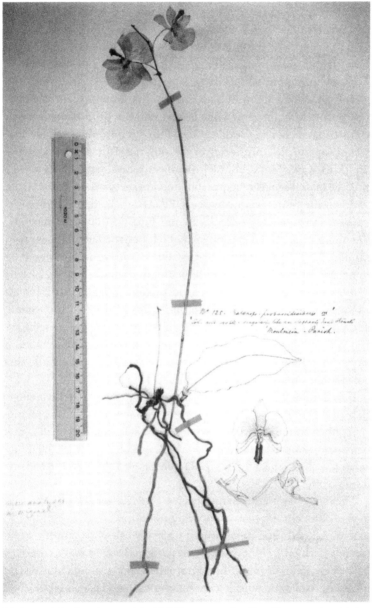

Phalaenopsis lowii, an isotype (*Parish 125*) conserved at Kew. Photographer: E. A. Christenson. Reproduced with the kind permission of the Trustees of the Royal Botanic Gardens, Kew.

lanceolate, acute, to 9 × 3 cm, articulated and deciduous in nature, dark green above, speckled with purple underneath. **Inflorescences** arching to pendent, few-flowered racemes to massive panicles, usually to 30 cm long, the floral bracts triangular, acute, 3–4 mm long. **Flowers** showy, membranous, white with variable degrees of pink suffusion, the lateral lobes of the lip white with bright yellow-orange teeth, the midlobe purple with a narrow white border and five diffuse longitudinal white stripes including the dorsal keel, the column and rostellum white except for purple suffusion over the pollinia. **Dorsal sepal** oblong-elliptic to ovate-elliptic, obtuse (broadly subacuminate), 15–20 × 9–12 mm, the **lateral sepals** subequal, obliquely ovate to ovate-elliptic, acute or subobtuse, with revolute margins. **Petals** flabellate-reniform, cuneate, broadly rounded, 17–22 × 18–24 mm. **Lip** three-lobed, 15 mm long, 10 mm wide across the expanded lateral lobes, the lateral lobes erect, parallel, in the form of acute retrorse hooks, with a tooth terminating along the leading edge, the midlobe fleshy, obovate, convex, bluntly acute, with an irregular-subdenticulate margin, the upper surface with a longitudinal keel for its length, the **callus** biseriate, with a small, fleshy bilobed callus at the base, a larger bilobed callus between the lateral lobes. **Column** arching, subtriangular in cross-section, ca. 8 mm long, with a long narrowly bifid rostellum at right angle to and subequal to the column. **Pedicel** and **ovary** to 4 cm long.

   Distribution: Myanmar and adjacent western Thailand. **Etymology**: Named for Hugh Low, whose nursery first flowered this species in England. **Illustrations**: Bot. Mag. 88: t. 5351. 1862; Fitch 1996:808, 809; Gruss and Röllke 1992b:153, 154, 155; Gruss and Wolff 1995:69; Lindenia 6: t. 272. 1890; Orchids 65(7):803; Sweet 1969:239, 1980:43, 44; Xenia Orch. 2:151. 1868.

   The range of variation in this species is little known. Plants cultivated in the 19th century, such as those figured in *Lindenia*, bore white to pale pink sepals and petals with a darker blush pink center. An extremely dark pink clone was figured in *Xenia Orchidacea*, but this may have been an error in printing where the white ground color was replaced with medium pink. Recent collections from Thailand have white sepals and petals with minimal pink blush. Whether this is an artifact of geography or a bias of small sample size is unknown at this time.

   Similarly, the floral and vegetative potential of *P. lowii* is unknown.

Historic illustrations (as well as the type specimens and recent collections) show plants with unbranched racemes that bear only two to four flowers. Orchid collector E. S. Berkeley, however, reported seeing plants in Moulmein with inflorescences three feet long bearing many side branches and "at least a hundred flowers out at a time." There is no reason to doubt Berkeley's observation; no other orchid in Myanmar could be confused with *P. lowii*. The extreme seasonal drought of its native habitat, which leads to the shedding of the plants' leaves, may account for the species' limited ability to produce large numbers of flowers in nature (as well as on recently imported plants). In cultivation, where supplemental watering is provided, the plants are not stressed and may be able to produce larger branched inflorescences. This is certainly the case with such other Aeridinae as *Aerides crassifolia* Burb.; populations of this species, dwarfed by seasonally arid conditions, produce only few-flowered short racemes in nature but rebound in cultivation, producing massive, branched panicles bearing many flowers on larger, non-stunted plants.

Plants of *P. lowii* collected in Thailand as lithophytes (Fitch 1996) bore a solitary leaf, as did the type collection. Plants growing nearby as epiphytes were not subjected to the same degree of drying and retained more leaves. Like other deciduous species, *P. lowii* should not be dried out in cultivation to the point of causing leaf drop. Under optimal cultivation the plants should retain three to five leaves year-round.

Fitch also reported finding this species at an elevation of ca. 800 m. This suggests that plants of *P. lowii* should be grown at intermediate temperatures and not the warmer conditions that are optimal for most other species and hybrids in the genus.

No hybrids are known to have been made with *P. lowii* in the 19th and early 20th century during the species' first round of cultivation (1862 until at least 1904) and nothing is known of its genetic affinities. The flowers of *P. lowii* superficially resemble those of *P. amabilis* and its allies on the basis of the white ground color and very broad petals. On the basis of the species biogeography, four separate pollinia, and deciduous habit, however, *P. lowii* is only distantly related to the *P. amabilis* group and is probably most closely related to species of subgenus *Parishianae*.

Because of the similarities of *P. lowii* to the rare Chinese genus

43

Nothodoritis, and the relatively obscure publication of the latter, a description based on the original article is included here.

Nothodoritis Tsi

Acta Phytotax. Sinica 27(1):58. 1989. Type: *Nothodoritis zhejiangensis* Tsi.

Miniature epiphytes with very short stems. **Leaves** few, distichous at the articulate base, sheathing. **Inflorescences** elongate, unbranched, densely multiflowered, the peduncle furnished with a few sheaths, the bracts distichous, narrow and rather small. **Flowers** patent, rather small, texture almost membranous. **Dorsal sepal** ovate-elliptic, concave, covering over the column, the **lateral sepals** obliquely ovate, larger than the dorsal sepal. **Petals** obovate, narrowed at the base in a short claw. **Lip** three-lobed, the lateral lobes narrow, in the form of a sulcus except for the separate upper parts, the middle lobe narrowly boat-shaped, the base saccate, equipped with an appendage at the mouth of the sac, the sac short, nearly hemi-globose. **Column** short, subcylindric, in front with an awl-shaped appendage near the base, the foot very short, the stigma near the base of the column, the rostellum spreading, decidedly elongate and narrowed; the anther operculate, somewhat hemispheric, in front triangular-extended. **Pollinia** four, subglobose, the stipe linear, elongate, the viscidium disc subcircular.

Tsi contrasted his new genus with *Doritis* Lindl. (section *Esmeralda* in this work) by the structure of the pollinarium, the non-clawed labellum, the appendaged column, the very short column foot lacking a mentum, and the decidedly elongate and narrowed rostellum.

Nothodoritis zhejiangensis Tsi

Acta Phytotax. Sinica 27(1):59. 1989. Type: China. Zhejiang: Linan, Xitianmu Shan, 350 m, on trunks and branches of trees, 14 June 1986, *Z. H. Tsi 86-006* (holotype, PE; isotype: K).

Downward-hanging epiphytes. **Stems** decidedly abbreviated, ca. 3 mm long. **Roots** originating at the base of the stem, 1.2–1.5 mm in diameter, numerous, lightly flexuous, unbranched, more or less compressed, glabrous, fleshy, green when alive. **Leaves** one to three, distichous, somewhat coriaceous, deciduous in winter, the blades obovate or obovate-oblong, 2–6.8 cm long, 1.5–2.1 cm wide, apex obtuse and sometimes a little oblique, narrowed and articulated at the base, articulate beneath the sheath, green on both sides, upper surface and margins for the most part purple-spotted, with numerous fine nerves. **Inflorescences** solitary scapose, produced laterally at the base of the stem, hanging down, slender, unbranched, 8–13 cm long, 1 mm thick, greenish, provided above the base with one or two sheaths and below the rachis with two or three sterile bracts, the raceme 5–8 cm long, 8- to 19-flowered, the floral bracts narrowly lanceolate, 2–3 mm long, apices acuminate, yellowish green. **Flowers** white, not fragrant, the sepals and petals three-nerved, equipped on the upper side with transverse purple bars. **Dorsal sepal** ovate-elliptic, concave, completely covering the column, 6 mm long, at the middle 3 mm wide, apex obtuse, near the base a little narrowed, the **lateral sepals** obliquely ovate, 6 mm long, above the middle 6 mm wide, apex obliquely truncate, contracted at the base in a short claw. **Petals** obovate, 5 mm long, at the middle 2.5 mm wide, apex obtuse, clawed at the base. **Lip** three-lobed, the lateral lobes erect, 1.5 mm long, apex purple, in the form of a sulcus except for the separate upper parts, the sulcus ca. 7 mm long, white, the midlobe horizontally spreading, narrow, boat-shaped, white outside, dark purple inside, 8 mm long, ca. 1.2 mm wide, the apex somewhat bilobed and acute-recurved, provided with a suboblong, somewhat concave, white basal appendage, 2.5 mm long, 1.2 mm wide, the sac white, nearly hemispheric, ca. 2 mm long. **Column** for the most part cylindric, 5 mm long, ca. 2 mm wide, yellow in front, near the base provided with an awl-shaped, downward curving, yellow-green appendage, ca. 1.2 mm long, the stigma near the base of the column, the rostellum spreading, ca. 5.5 mm long, apex bilobed and hooked, pale above, purplish below; the anther operculate, yellowish green, in front triangular-extended. **Pollinia** four, subglobose, the stipe 5.5 mm long, 0.5 mm wide; the viscidium subcircular, ca. 0.7 mm wide. **Pedicel** and **ovary** slender, ca. 1 cm long, brownish. **Capsule** ellipsoid, 8 mm long, ca. 4 mm wide.

Distribution: *Nothodoritis zhejiangensis* is known only from the type locality and Ningbo (*L. C. Jin 1844*, PE?) in eastern Zhejiang, where it grows on branches about 5 cm in diameter at 300–900 m in elevation. **Illustrations:** Chen et al. 1998:298.

CHAPTER 6

Subgenus *Aphyllae*

Subgenus *Aphyllae* (Sweet) E. A. Christ., stat. nov.

Basionym: *Phalaenopsis* section *Aphyllae* Sweet, Amer. Orchid Soc. Bull. 37:872. 1968; *Kingidium* section *Aphyllae* (Sweet) Gruss & Röllke, Die Orchidee 44(4):189. 1993. Type: *Phalaenopsis stobartiana* Rchb.f.

Kingiella Rolfe, Orchid Rev. 25:197. 1917; *Kingidium* P. F. Hunt, Kew Bull. 24:97. 1970. Lectotype (in Hunt 1971a): *Kingidium taeniale* (Lindl.) P. F. Hunt (= *Phalaenopsis taenialis* (Lindl.) E. A. Christ. & U. C. Pradhan).

Kingidium section *Conspicuum* Gruss & Röllke, Die Orchidee 48(6):267. 1997. Type: *Kingidium minus* Seidenf. (= *Phalaenopsis minus* (Seidenf.) E. A. Christ.).

This subgenus is characterized by having small deciduous plants, strongly flattened roots, short, unbranched or branched, few-flowered inflorescences, small scarious floral bracts, subequal, subsimilar floral segments, lateral labellum lobes with flap-like flanges, biseriate callus, four pollinia on a spatulate stipe, obscure to prominent spur, pink or green flowers, and the corolla chlorophyllous and persistent in post-pollination. Flower color may be variable within a species consisting of a green or pink state.

Subgenus *Aphyllae* is restricted to the Himalayan region from Nepal to Thailand with a center of diversity in southern China (Yunnan). DNA studies (Jarrell unpubl.) shows this subgenus to be basal to both subgenus *Phalaenopsis* and subgenus *Polychilos*.

Species-level taxonomy in the group is highly problematic because of the very limited material available for study. Except for *P. taenialis* and *P. wilsonii*, herbarium specimens are practically nonexistent. German horticulturists Olaf Gruss and Lutz Röllke published a long series of short papers on this group between 1993 and 1997, treating the plants as species of *Kingidium*. Even though they made several new taxonomic combinations and published a number of historic drawings and type photographs, their failure to recognize salient features of the inflorescences, lip structures, and significance of color variation within some species largely confused the situation.

In addition, Gruss and Röllke erred in assigning types to this and other elements of a broadly defined *Kingidium*. They cited *Kingidium taeniale* as the type species of *Phalaenopsis* section *Aphyllae*, the basionym for their *Kingidium* section *Aphyllae* and this subgenus. Sweet explicitly stated the type species as *P. stobartiana*. Similarly, Gruss and Röllke cited the type species of the genus *Kingidium* as *P. deliciosa*, although Hunt (1971a) explicitly cited *K. taeniale* as the type. The latter led to their formal publication of a superfluous *Kingidium* section *Kingidium* (Gruss and Röllke 1993c:189).

Although most species have been introduced recently to cultivation, few permanent specimens for study have been preserved. Most species have not persisted in cultivation in any sort of quantity. In the United States this has been due primarily to the quite distinct horticultural requirements of these seven species from the majority of other species and hybrids of *Phalaenopsis* (see Chapter 10).

Key to the species of subgenus *Aphyllae*

1. Spur prominent, a continuation of the angle formed by the junction of the labellum midlobe and sidelobes.
  2. Dorsal sepal 8–9 mm long; flowers pink; column stout, broadly dilated at the stigma; labellum midlobe flat. . . . . *P. taenialis*
  2. Dorsal sepal 12–15 mm long; flowers green or green suffused with bronze; column cylindric, not dilated at the stigma; labellum midlobe convex. . . . . *P. braceana*
1. Spur not prominent, apparently absent or forming a small nipple-shaped structure beneath the posterior callus.

47

3. Labellum midlobe acute. . . . . *P. minus*
3. Labellum midlobe obtuse.
   4. Labellum midlobe obcordate with a central apical fleshy knob.
      . . . . *P. wilsonii*
   4. Labellum midlobe not obcordate, without a terminal notch.
      5. Flowers deep green; labellum midlobe oblanceolate without
         any conspicuous constriction. . . . . *P. stobartiana*
      5. Flowers rose-pink; labellum midlobe with conspicuous con-
         striction.
         6. Labellum midlobe flared below the apex producing a three-
            lobulate midlobe; flowers pink. . . . . *P. hainanensis*
         6. Labellum midlobe widest below the apex, the apical mar-
            gins reflexed along the midvein, forming a subtubular apex
            that may appear emarginate in natural position; flowers
            pink to pale green. . . . . *P. honghenensis*

Phalaenopsis braceana (J. D. Hook.) E. A. Christ.

Selbyana 9:169. 1986; *Doritis braceana* J. D. Hook., Fl. Brit. Ind. 6:
196. 1890; *Kingidium braceanum* (J. D. Hook.) Seidenf., Opera Bot.
95:187. 1988. Type: Bhutan, leg. Gamble, drawing by *Brace* (CAL).

Kingidium naviculare Tsi ex Hashimoto, New Orchids 3:40. 1984;
Biermannia naviculare Tang & Wang ex Gruss & Röllke, Die Orchidee 48(2):56. 1997. Type: China. Yunnan, Hort. *Hashimoto
s.n.*; lectotype, here designated: color photographs published in
Hashimoto, loc. cit.

Miniature epiphytes with large numbers of roots which form large, flattened mats against the substrate. **Leaves** one or two, deciduous, rarely
present, oblong-elliptic, subacute, to 2.4 × 0.8 cm. **Inflorescences**
suberect to erect racemes, the peduncle subequal to the rachis, with
one or two distant tubular bracts, the floral bracts lanceolate, acuminate, concave, spreading, 0.3–0.5 cm long. **Flowers** four to six, spreading, variable in color, the sepals and petals yellow, green, or greenish
bronze variously suffused with pink, the labellum dark rose. Sepals and
petals subsimilar, subequal, elliptic, obtuse, the **dorsal sepal** to 1.5 ×
0.5 cm, the **lateral sepals** to 1.5 × 0.6 cm, the **petals** subspatulate, to 1.3

× 0.6 cm. **Lip** three-lobed, spurred, to 0.7 cm long from the apex of the lip to the spur apex, the lateral lobes oblong, obtuse, to 0.4 cm long, the midlobe oblong-oblanceolate, obtuse, convex, +/– constricted at the apex, the spur cylindric, straight, formed as a continuation of the midlobe base, to 0.3 cm long from the juncture of the lateral lobes and midlobe, the **callus** biseriate, the basal callus fleshy, bifid with the tips recurved and horn-like, on the backwall of the spur, the apical callus slender, bifid, on the front wall of the spur becoming free at the base of the midlobe. **Column** stout, cylindric, straight, to 0.4 cm long, the foot to 0.2 cm long. **Pedicel** and **ovary** to 1.5 cm long.

Distribution: Bhutan and China. Chen et al. (1998) record *P. braceana* (as *Kingidium braceanum*) growing at elevations of 1100–1700 m, and one specimen (*Yü 16329*, AMES) was collected at 2100 m in elevation. **Illustrations**: Chen et al. 1998:272; Gruss and Röllke 1997b:54, 1997c:56 (both as *Biermannia naviculare*); Hooker, Ann. Roy. Bot. Gard. Calcutta 1895: pl. 60; Seidenfaden 1988b:186, fig. 115.

For most of its history this species was known only from a drawing by Brace. This drawing was interpreted as a somewhat stylized version of *P. taenialis*, and the name *D. braceana* was maintained in the former's synonymy until critical study of the group by Seidenfaden. Examination of recent collections shows *P. braceana* to be a distinct species differing especially in the form of the labellum apex, which is shaped like an inverted boat, forming a hollow cavity beneath, and in the length of its spur.

Phalaenopsis braceana is one of two species in the subgenus that forms a conspicuous spur as a continuation of the base of the midlobe. Only *P. braceana* and *P. taenialis* have spurs that are unambiguously noticeable to the naked eye. As distinguished in the key, the flowers of *P. braceana* are larger and always have a green to greenish bronze color; in contrast, the flowers of *P. taenialis* are always pale pink.

Flower color in *P. braceana* appears to be somewhat variable. The type was described as having had yellow flowers with a reddish brown midvein ("flavis costa rufescente"). Horticultural material in Japan known as *Kingidium naviculare* Tsi ex Hashimoto bears brownish bronze flowers. One collection from Yunnan (*Yü 16329*, AMES) recorded the flowers with "outer perianth brownish green, inner pinkish red" (the inner perianth in this case probably referred to the lip). Chen et al. (1998)

49

show a bronze flower with a rose-purple lip. A flower from a cultivated plant grown by Carri Raven-Riemann in Connecticut represented a rather clear green-flowered phase.

Gruss and Röllke (1997b:53) reduced *P. braceana* to the synonymy of *P. taenialis*, despite the arguments presented by Christenson (1996) and Seidenfaden (1988b). This is all the more surprising since they illustrated their change, in part, with a watercolor of *P. stobartiana* (misidentified as *Kingidium braceanum*), which clearly shows elongate racemes of dark green flowers with broadly obovate-subspatulate petals completely unlike their abundantly illustrated treatment of *P. taenialis* (Gruss and Röllke 1997a:49–53). Similarly, they reduce *Kingidium naviculare* to the synonymy of *P. taenialis* (Gruss and Röllke 1997c:56).

Phalaenopsis hainanensis Tang & Wang

Acta Phytotax. Sinica 12:47. 1974. Type: China. Hainan: Pai Sha Dist., *Lau 27549* (holotype: PE; isotype: AMES).

Phalaenopsis chuxiongensis F. Y. Liu, Acta Bot. Yunnan. 18(4):411. 1996, syn. nov. Type: China. Yunnan: Chuxiong, 1990 m, *F. Y. Liu 92001* (holotype: KUN).

Phalaenopsis hainanensis, the single flower of the isotype conserved at the Orchid Herbarium of Oakes Ames. Photographer: L. A. Garay.

Miniature epiphytes with large numbers of roots which form large, flattened mats against the substrate. **Stems** short, to 1.5 cm long. **Leaves** deciduous, obliquely oblong, retuse, to 4 × 1 cm. **Inflorescences** racemes or few-branched panicles to 42–55 cm long, with the rachis to 27–30 cm long, the peduncle with sparse broadly ovate bracts 0.3–0.5 cm long, the floral bracts ovate, 0.3–0.4 cm long. **Flowers** eight to ten, pale pink, the lip darker rose-pink. **Sepals** oblong, obtuse, the dorsal sepal to 1.3 × 0.3 cm, the lateral sepals broader, to 1.3 × 0.6 cm. **Petals** oblanceolate-spatulate, obtuse, to 1.2 × 0.6 cm. **Lip** three-lobed, to 1.1 cm long, to 0.8 cm across the expanded lateral lobes, the lateral lobes erect, oblong-rectangular in outline, to 0.4 × 0.2 cm, the anterior corner tooth-like, the blade with a thin, bilobed flange, the midlobe obovate, obtuse-rounded, dorsally keeled, with a pair of small subapical reflexed flaps, to 0.7 × 0.5 cm, the **callus** biseriate, the base of the lip with a low bifid callus, the base of the midlobe with a larger, suberect pair of teeth. **Column** straight, to 0.7 cm long. **Pedicel** and **ovary** slender, 2.2 cm long.

Distribution: China (Hainan, Yunnan). **Illustrations**: Chen and Tsi 1985. Icon. Cormophy. Sinicorum 5:752 (as *P. wilsonii*); Gruss and Röllke 1996:152–153 (as *Kingidium wilsonii*).

Sweet (1980) included this species in the synonymy of *P. stobartiana* Rchb.f. I disagree with his position. In addition to having pink rather than green to greenish bronze flowers, *P. hainanensis* differs by having a lip broadened just below the apex. Prior to the discovery of plants described as *P. chuxiongensis*, *P. hainanensis* was known from a single dried flower of the type plant. In the case of *P. hainanensis*, the broadening of the labellum does not appear to be an aberration of pressing (i.e., the sometimes revolute midlobe margin found in some species of this subgenus was not flattened to falsely yield the broadened apex) as evidenced by drawings of the type (Seidenfaden unpubl.), a recent second collection (see Chen and Tsi 1985), and an earlier drawing published in the *Flora Hainanensis* (see the reproduction in Gruss and Röllke 1996:153).

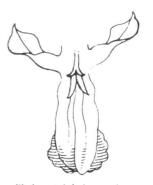

Phalaenopsis hainanensis, lip drawing from the original publication of its synonym, *P. chuxiongensis*.

I include the recently described *P. chuxiongensis* Liu in synonymy here with some trepidation; others may wish to keep them separate. With the exception of fewer, somewhat larger flowers and longer ovaries, I find no significant characters that distinguish the two. Liu gives the sepals and petals of *P. chuxiongensis* as 1.8 cm long compared to the 1.3 cm given here (based on the type description of *P. hainanen-*

Phalaenopsis hainanensis, line drawing from the original publication of its synonym, *P. chuxiongensis.*

sis) and an ovary length of 4 cm. Some of the difference in measurements may be based on measuring fresh versus reconstituted flowers, but it is doubtful that that fully explains the recorded differences. Our limited knowledge of these populations, based on a scant handful of specimens, does not allow a final assessment at this time.

Phalaenopsis honghenensis F. Y. Liu

Acta Bot. Yunnan. 13(4):373. 1991. Type: China. Yunnan: Honghe, 2000 m, 1 Apr. 1988, *F. Y. Liu 88002* (holotype: KUN).

Miniature epiphytes with minutely warty roots forming flattened mats against the substrate. **Stems** short, to 1 cm long. **Leaves** one or two, obliquely elliptic, acute, 5–7 × 1.5–2.5 cm, the sheathing bases persistent, spotted purple-red, ca. 0.5 cm long. **Inflorescences** short pedunculate racemes to 7.7 cm long including the 3.5–4.5 cm long rachis, the peduncular bracts broadly ovate, the floral bracts ovate, to 0.6 cm long. **Flowers** three to six, to 2.9 cm across, the sepals and petals ranging from rose-pink to pale green, the lip purple. **Dorsal sepal** oblong-elliptic, obtuse, to 1.3 × 0.6 cm, the **lateral sepals** obliquely elliptic-ovate, obtuse, to 1.3 × 0.6 cm. **Petals** spatulate, obtuse, to 1.1 × 0.6 cm. **Lip** three-lobed, minutely spurred, the lateral lobes oblong, obliquely truncate, to 0.7 × 0.2 cm, the midlobe oblong, obtuse, tapered at both ends, to 0.8 × 0.2 cm, the spur short, nipple-like, to 1.5 mm long, the **callus** biseriate, the posterior callus fleshy, bifid, terminating at the base of the midlobe, the anterior callus plate-like, bifid, extending beyond the base of the midlobe. **Column** stout, conspicuously dilated to either side of the stigma, to 0.9 cm long.
Pedicel and **ovary** 1.6–2.2 cm long.

Distribution: China (Yunnan) at 2000 m in elevation. **Illustrations**: Gruss and Röllke 1995e:234 (as *Kingidium* ×*stobartianum*), 1995f:237, 1996:155 (as *Kingidium* ×*stobartianum*).

Phalaenopsis honghenensis, lip drawing from the original publication.

Liu contrasted *P. honghenensis* with his earlier *P. minor* (see *P. wilsonii*) thus: "Species nova proxima *P. minore* F. Y. Liu sed floribus minoribus purpureo-rubris, sepalis et petalis 10–13 mm longis[,] labelli lobo medio ligula[t]o, polliniis orbiculatis distincta" [translation: New species near *P. minor* F. Y. Liu but distinguished by the smaller, purple-red flowers, the sepals and petals 10–13 mm long, the labellum midlobe ligulate, and the pollinia orbiculate].

Despite Liu's straightforward original description and type illustration, *P. honghenensis* has caused considerable confusion, in part because the original publication was obscure, largely unknown and unavailable to the horticultural community.

Phalaenopsis honghenensis is distinguished by having short, few-flowered inflorescences, a short, nipple-like spur, and an oblong lip midlobe that is slightly tapered at both ends. Liu described the lip apex as emarginate but this is an illusion caused by the subapical lateral margins being strongly deflexed-revolute. The resulting apical tube results in an apex that casually appears to be emarginate but is actually obtuse when flattened. Liu also described the inflorescences as simple or branched, but I have yet to document a branched inflorescence among several hundred flowering plants seen in cultivation.

Flower color is somewhat variable in *P. honghenensis*. Most clones are a pale rose-pink with a darker lip. Not infrequently one sees this same color infused with varying amounts of pale green. The pastel green seen in this species is unlike the dark greens seen in *P. braceana* and *P. stobartiana* and is unlikely to be a source of confusion.

Phalaenopsis honghenensis has been exported from China in rather astonishing quantities. Nearly all these exportations have been mislabeled *P. wilsonii*, which has added to the confusion surrounding these species in cultivation. Many provisional AOS awards for *P. wilsonii* have been rejected as mislabeled plants of *P. honghenensis*. Clones of *P. honghenensis* have also been mislabeled as other species in this subgenus, including plants awarded as *P. hainanensis* 'Memoria Herman Sweet', CBR/AOS (see *Awards Quarterly* 24(1):74. 1993) and *P. stobartiana* 'Limrick', CBR/AOS (see *Awards Quarterly* 25(4):199. 1994).

Phalaenopsis minus (Seidenf.) E. A. Christ., comb. nov.

Basionym: *Kingidium minus* Seidenf., Opera Bot. 95:188. 1988.
Type: Thailand. Loei, *Hort. Suphachadiwong S. 736* (holotype: C).

Description after Seidenfaden: Epiphytes with short stems. **Leaves** elliptic, to 9 cm wide. **Inflorescences** laxly arching-pendent racemes (?). **Flowers** congested, the sepals and petals reflexed, white with pale brown longitudinal barring, the inner halves of the lateral sepals purple-spotted, the lip white with purple blotches at the center, the column white with pale brown barring. **Dorsal sepal** oblong, acute, concave, to 0.8 cm long, the **lateral sepals** obliquely oblong-ovate, obtuse, to 0.8 × 0.4 cm. **Petals** oblanceolate-subspatulate, obtuse, to 0.7 × 0.2 cm. **Lip** three-lobed, to 1 × 1.1 cm when expanded, the lateral lobes erect, suborbicular, broadly rounded in front, the posterior corner extended as a slender falcate-triangular tooth, the midlobe narrowly lanceolate, acute-acuminate, shallowly incurved, the **callus** biseriate, the posterior callus short, bifid, ca. 0.1 cm long, the apex held over a shallow depression, the anterior callus ligulate, bifid at the apex, ca. 0.2 cm long. **Column** erect, hooded, to 0.5 cm long, with a pair of broadly rounded vertical wings lateral to the stigma. **Pedicel** and **ovary** ca. 1.3 cm long.

 Distribution: Endemic to Thailand. **Illustrations**: Gruss and Röllke 1997d:259–260; Seidenfaden, Opera Bot. 95:188.

 Seidenfaden compared this species to *P. stobartiana* thus: "Kingidio stobartiano (Rchb.f.) Seidenf. praecipue affine, floribus minoribus, dente falcate triangulo e margine posteriore cujusque lobi lateralis labelli surgente, binis alis, verticalibus e columna prominentibus ut aliis notis ab eo diversum" [translation: Chiefly allied to *Kingidium stobartianum* (Rchb.f.) Seidenf. but differing by its smaller flowers, the falcate-triangular tooth rising up from the posterior margin of the lateral lobes of the lip, and a prominent pair of vertical column wings].

 Phalaenopsis minus is an oddball of sorts and does not appear to be closely related to the other species in the subgenus. Its inclusion here is mainly based on Seidenfaden's placement of the species in *Kingidium* and the presence of a shallow depression underneath the posterior callus. Originally known only from a single flower and a color photograph of an inflorescence tip from a plant in cultivation, no final decision can be made about the placement of this species until more material becomes available. A second photograph (reproduced in the color plate section of this book) shows the base of a plant with leaves dissimilar to those found in other species of the subgenus but offers little other information.

Gruss and Röllke used *P. minus* to establish a monotypic section they called *Kingidium* section *Conspicuum*. They characterized the section thus: "Folia et forma lobi medio labelli simili sectione Aphyllae. Lobi laterale con dente falcate triangulo e margine posteriore" [translation: Leaves and form of the lip midlobe similar to those of section *Aphyllae*. The lateral lobes with a falcate-triangular tooth on their posterior margin].

I choose not to maintain this division since the tooth on the lateral lip lobes, although more pronounced in *P. minus*, is homologous to the structure found in the other species of the subgenus.

Phalaenopsis minus is easily distinguished by the combination of strongly reflexed sepals and petals and broad, suborbicular lateral lobes of the lip with a conspicuous falcate-triangular posterior tooth.

Phalaenopsis stobartiana Rchb.f.

Gard. Chron., n.s., 8:392. 1877; *Phalaenopsis wightii* var. *stobartiana* (Rchb.f.) Burb., The Garden 22:19. 1882; *Kingidium stobartianum* (Rchb.f.) Seidenf., Opera Bot. 95:188. 1988. Type: Origin unknown, *Hort. Stobart s.n.* (holotype: W).

Miniature epiphytes with massive root systems. **Leaves** deciduous in nature, oblong-lanceolate, acute, to 10 × 5 cm. **Inflorescences** arching-pendent racemes, never with branches, to 20 cm long, the floral bracts ovate, concave, subacuminate, to 0.5 cm long. **Flowers** seven to nine, with sepals and petals saturated apple green to dark olive green, the lip and column brilliant rose. **Dorsal sepal** oblong-elliptic to obovate, obtuse-rounded, to 1.5 × 0.7 cm, the **lateral sepals** obliquely ovate to elliptic-ovate, obtuse-rounded, to 1.6 × 0.7 cm. **Petals** obovate to subspatulate, obtuse-rounded, to 1.4 × 0.8 cm. **Lip** three-lobed, to 1.1 cm long, to 1.2 cm across the expanded lateral lobes, the lateral lobes erect, oblong, gently rounded at the apex, the posterior corner a short tooth, the anterior corner semicircular, the midlobe narrowly elliptic-obovate, obtuse-rounded, convex with a low median keel, with a shallow dimple-like depression at the base, the **callus** biseriate, subequal, bidentate. **Column** somewhat arching, to 0.6 cm long. **Pedicel** and **ovary** to 1.5 cm long.

Distribution: China (Yunnan) at 800–900 m in elevation. **Illustrations**: Gruss and Röllke 1995e:235 (as *Kingidium×stobartianum*), 1997b: 54 (watercolor as *Kingidium braceanum*), 1997c:56 (as *Kingidium ×stobartianum*); Yang et al. 1995:145 (as *Kingidium* sp.).

Phalaenopsis stobartiana is known only from four clones: the type, a color photograph published in Yang et al. (1995), one cultivated plant that perished in the United States, and one cultivated plant (that may yet be alive!) in Japan. This species is easily recognized by the combination of a multi-flowered raceme of seven to nine olive-green flowers, broadly subspatulate petals, a narrowly elliptic-obovate midlobe, and a minute dimple-like depression at the base of the lip. The midlobe of the lip of *P. stobartiana* is most similar to *P. honghenensis*; the two were combined by Gruss and Röllke (1995e:233), but the latter species differs by its usually rose-colored flowers on short, few-flowered racemes. Reichenbach's watercolor of the type specimen clearly shows eight flowers on one inflorescence, a high flower count also seen in the clone 'Tahitian Dancer'. In its dark green color *P. stobartiana* is most similar to *P. braceana*, but that species differs by having proportionately narrower petals and a conspicuous spur.

The origin of this species was not recorded and subsequent reports for Myanmar (based on *Haase s.n.*, AMES) and Hainan (based on *Lau 27549*; see *P. hainanensis*) are now disregarded. The distribution in Yunnan is based on the color photograph in Yang et al. (1995), where the elevational range is given as 800–900 m.

Plants of *P. braceana* (as *Kingidium naviculare*) were hybridized in Japan in the early 1980s with plants thought to be *P. hainanensis*. The resulting hybrids were given a tentative informal name of *Phalaenidium ×tsiae* and were speculated to be the same as the long-lost *P. stobartiana*. The possibility that *P. stobartiana* could result from such a hybrid is unlikely given the lower flower count and proportionately narrower petals of both putative parents. The

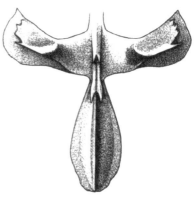

Phalaenopsis stobartiana drawn from the type. Illustrator: H. R. Sweet.

57

subsequent appearance of additional clones of *P. stobartiana* from the wild also argues against a hybrid origin. Even so, Gruss and Röllke (1995e:233) followed this logic in proposing a hybrid origin for *P. ×stobartiana*, pro. spec. They also reduced *P. honghenensis* to the synonymy of *P. stobartiana* despite its characteristically low flower count and usually pink flowers.

A few promising hybrids have been made with *P. stobartiana* in Japan. Crossing this species with a standard tetraploid red-lipped hybrid resulted in a large, full-shaped flower with pastel olive-green sepals and petals. When crossed with the diploid *P. bellina*, the result was *P.* China Wonder, which produces a range of flowers with vibrant green sepals and petals. The possibility of breeding truly green-flowered hybrids with *P. stobartiana* is quite real.

Phalaenopsis taenialis (Lindl.) E. A. Christ. & U. C. Pradhan

Selbyana 9:168. 1986; *Aerides taeniale* Lindl., Gen. and Sp. Orch. Pl. 239. 1833; *Doritis taenialis* (Lindl.) J. D. Hook., Fl. Brit. Ind. 6:31. 1890; *Kingiella taenialis* (Lindl.) Rolfe, Orchid Rev. 25:197. 1917; *Biermannia taenialis* (Lindl.) Tang & Wang, Acta Phytotax. Sinica 1(1):95. 1951; *Kingidium taeniale* (Lindl.) P. F. Hunt, Kew Bull. 24:98. 1970; *Polychilos taenialis* (Lindl.) Shim, Malayan Nat. Journ. 36:28. 1982. Type: Nepal. Without precise locality, *Wallich s.n.* (holotype: K).

Aerides carnosa Griff., Not. 3:365. 1851. Type: Bhutan. Panukka, *Griffith s.n.* (holotype: K).

Miniature epiphytes with numerous flattened roots. **Stems** very short, concealed by small scarious bracts and leaf sheaths. **Leaves** one or two, obliquely lanceolate, acute, dark green, to 10 × 2 cm, usually about half that size. **Inflorescences** pedunculate racemes to 10 cm long, the floral bracts lanceolate, to 0.3 cm long. **Flowers** six to eight, to 2 cm across, the sepals and petals pale pink, the lip and anther rose-purple. **Dorsal sepal** oblong, obtuse, to 0.8 × 0.3 cm, the **lateral sepals** obliquely elliptic-ovate, obtuse, to 0.8 × 0.4 cm. **Petals** elliptic-obovate, obtuse, to 0.8 × 0.3 cm. **Lip** three-lobed, spurred, to 0.8 cm long from the base of the spur to the midlobe apex, the lateral lobes erect, oblong, obtuse, to

6 × 1.5 mm, the midlobe oblong-elliptic, obtuse, arching, to 6 mm long, the **callus** biseriate, the posterior callus fleshy, bidentate, on the backwall of the spur, the anterior callus ligulate, deeply bifid, attached to the frontwall at the base of the midlobe. **Column** stout, strongly dilated at the middle to either side of the stigma, to 0.4 cm long. **Pedicel** and **ovary** to 1.6 cm long.

Distribution: Nepal, northeast India, Bhutan, Myanmar, and Thailand at 1000–2500 m in elevation. Flowering in nature is reported in April and May. **Illustrations**: Amer. Orchid Soc. Bull. 54:324. 1985; Christenson 1995:21; Die Orchidee 38(3):58. 1987; Gruss and Röllke 1997a:49–52; U. C. Pradhan in Indian Orch. 2:550. 1979.

Phalaenopsis taenialis has always been the best known of the species in this subgenus. It is abundant in nature, and numerous herbarium specimens have been available for study and critical comparison. Until recent restrictions on the export of wild-collected plants by India and their importation into the United States by the enactment of CITES legislation, *P. taenialis* was frequently exported from northeast India for horticulture. It is easily recognized by its pale pink flowers with a conspicuous spur. Only *P. braceana* has a similar spur and that species has significantly larger green to greenish bronze flowers.

Garay (pers. comm.) suggests that *Aerides carnosa* may represent a separate species as the spur appears to be shorter and more broadly rounded than in *P. taenialis*. The paucity of material from Bhutan makes the significance of this difference hard to judge. Further study of this question is left to the botanists preparing the Orchidaceae for the *Flora of Bhutan* at the Royal Botanic Garden, Edinburgh. Spur length in *P. taenialis* may represent a cline, or perhaps the recognition of a distinct subspecies is warranted.

Phalaenopsis wilsonii Rolfe

Kew Bull. 1909:65. 1909. Type: China. Western China, without precise locality, *Wilson 4576* (holotype: K; isotype: BM).

Phalaenopsis minor F. Y. Liu, Acta Bot. Yunnan. 10(1):119. 1988. Type: China. Yunnan, Malipo, 1500 m, 4 Apr. 1981, *S. Q. Bao 81001* (holotype: KUN).

Miniature epiphytes and lithophytes with massive root systems. **Leaves** deciduous in nature, oblong-elliptic, acute to 2.5 × 0.9 cm. **Inflorescences** elongate arching racemes, never branched, to 20 cm long, the floral bracts spreading, ovate, concave, acute, to 0.8 cm long. **Flowers** 10 to 15, opening simultaneously, the sepals and petals pastel pink grading to medium rose at their bases, the lip dark rose-purple, the column white. **Dorsal sepal** oblong-elliptic, cuneate, acute, to 2.2 × 0.8 cm, the **lateral sepals** obliquely elliptic, acute, subequal to dorsal sepal. **Petals** oblanceolate-subspatulate, obtuse-rounded, to 2.1 × 0.9 cm. **Lip** three-lobed, to 2 cm long, to 1.4 cm across the expanded lateral lobes, the lateral lobes erect, oblong, falcate, obtuse, the midlobe obovate, notched at the apex, convex, with a raised elliptic pad below the apex, with a raised median at the base, the **callus** biseriate, subsimilar and subequal, sulcate, bilobed. **Column** straight, stout, to 1 cm long. **Pedicel** and **ovary** to 4 cm long.

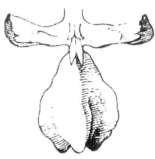

Phalaenopsis wilsonii, lip drawing from the original publication of the type of its synonym, *P. minor.*

Distribution: China (Szechuan, Yunnan) and eastern Tibet at 800–2200 m in elevation; to be expected in northern Vietnam. **Illustrations**: Baker and Baker 1989:133 (as *P. minor*); Chen et al. 1998:353; Die Orchidee 42(1):84. 1991; Die Orchidee 43(6):47. 1991; Gruss and Röllke 1996:150, 151; Gruss and Röllke 1997f:264; Yang et al. 1995: 152, 153.

Phalaenopsis wilsonii is easily recognized by the combination of elongate, multi-flowered racemes of 10 to 15 flowers and the obcordate lip midlobe. Despite its distinctive and well-illustrated lip structure, *P. wilsonii* has been a source of recent confusion because the name has been widely misapplied

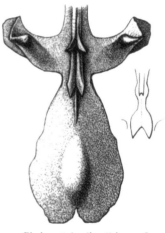

Phalaenopsis wilsonii drawn from the type. Illustrator: H. R. Sweet.

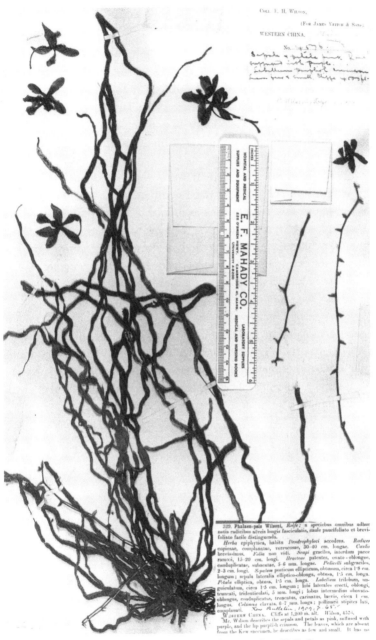

The holotype of *Phalaenopsis wilsonii*. Photographer: H. R. Sweet

to plants of *P. honghenensis* exported from China. The latter has short inflorescences of four to six flowers and oblong lip midlobes. Chen et al. (1998) report that *P. wilsonii* flowers from April to July, but this account may include some data from *P. honghenensis*.

Gruss and Röllke (1996:152) reduced *P. hainanensis* to synonymy under *P. wilsonii*. While both species are similar in having pink flowers with lip midlobes that are obovate in outline, *P. hainanensis* has an obtuse-rounded lip midlobe that is at once distinct from the apically notched midlobe of *P. wilsonii*.

Phalaenopsis minor is accepted as a synonym of *P. wilsonii*, and the type illustration clearly shows the obcordate midlobe of the lip, which is unique in this subgenus. Note should be made that the apparent small stature of *P. minor*, shown in the type illustration, is a reflection of the particular plant illustrated and/or the artist's rendition. The text clearly states that the inflorescences are 16.5–30 cm long, in keeping with the holotype of *P. wilsonii*. *Phalaenopsis wilsonii* and *P. stobartiana* have the longest inflorescences in the subgenus.

The type of *P. minor* was collected in Malipo, just over the border of northern Vietnam. *Paphiopedilum malipoense*, also described from Malipo, occurs in great abundance in northern Vietnam, and most plants in cultivation originated in Vietnam and not China, relates Averyanov (pers. comm.). *Phalaenopsis wilsonii* may also be found in northern Vietnam.

CHAPTER 7

Subgenus *Parishianae*

Subgenus *Parishianae* (Sweet) E. A. Christ., stat. nov.

Basionym: *Phalaenopsis* section *Parishianae* Sweet, Amer. Orchid
Soc. Bull. 37:872. 1968. Type: *Phalaenopsis parishii* Rchb.f.

Grafia Hawkes, Phytologia 13:305. 1966. Type: *Phalaenopsis
parishii* Rchb.f.

The four species in this complex form a highly cohesive group of species characterized by their deciduous leaves, four pollinia, mobile lip
midlobe, and prominent swellings ("column wings") at the base of the
column. In addition, all four appear to have the lateral lobes of the
lip erect, subparallel, and diverging at the middle to form a U-shaped
compound structure. The distinctive nature of this group was recognized by Hawkes, who proposed the segregate genus *Grafia* for these
species. Following the broad circumscription of *Phalaenopsis* followed
here, this group is treated as one of five subgenera.

The leaves are normally deciduous in their native habitat, which is
subjected to a pronounced monsoonal climate of alternating wet and
dry seasons. In cultivation the leaves are normally evergreen. Growers
with less than optimal growing conditions may grow these species on
the cool and dry side during the winter months.

The relative isolation of this group within the genus is supported by
anecdotal information from orchid breeders. Although species of this
subgenus, particularly *P. lobbii*, have been crossed with those of other
subgenera, such hybrids are very difficult to make and usually show
high levels of sterility. An aberration appears to be the hybrid of *P. lob-*

bii with *P. pulcherrima,* which shows surprising fertility (Griesbach pers. comm.) as supported by the microspore studies of Aoyama et al. (1994, as *P. parishii*).

Sweet included *P. mysorensis* Saldanha in this group, a species poorly known to him, with reservations. Additional material of that species indicates it is not related to the *P. parishii* complex as indicated by Saldanha but is rather a third member of section *Deliciosae* (see Chapter 9). With the removal of *P. mysorensis,* subgenus *Parishianae* ranges from the Himalayas to Indochina.

Key to the species of subgenus *Parishianae*

1. Sepals and petals white spotted with violet, the midlobe white with violet margins and streaks; the midlobe of the lip with multiple, longitudinal, toothed keels. . . . . *P. appendiculata*
1. Sepals and petals white without any other pigmentation, the midlobe marked with yellow, brown, or wine-color, but never with violet margins or streaks; the midlobe of the lip without multiple keels.
    2. Midlobe of lip shallowly three-lobulate, with a definite sinus between the apex and lateral points, white with a pair of large transverse yellow spots. . . . . *P. gibbosa*
    2. Midlobe of lip broadly rounded without any lobing, pigmentation different.
        3. Midlobe of lip wine-colored; below the long filiform callus with a transverse ridge bearing long, whisker-like appendages. *P. parishii*
        3. Midlobe of lip with two longitudinal brown stripes on either a white or a yellow base color; below the long filiform callus with a transverse ridge at most obscurely denticulate. . . . . *P. lobbii*

Phalaenopsis appendiculata C. E. Carr

Gard. Bull. Straits Settlem. 5:16. 1929; *Polychilos appendiculata* (C. E. Carr) Shim, Malayan Nat. Journ. 36:24. 1982. Type: Malyasia. Pahang State, Tembeling, *Carr 299* (holotype: K). Photograph of the holotype reproduced in Sweet (1969:324, 1980:50).

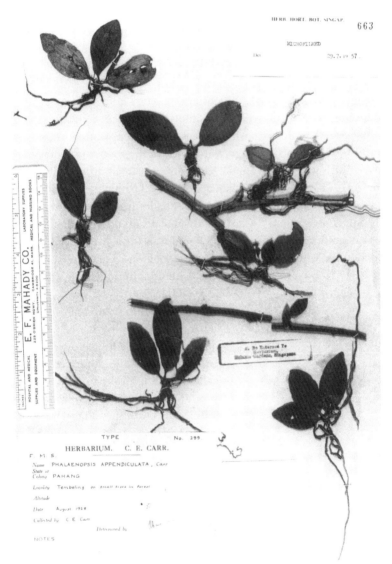

The holotype of *Phalaenopsis appendiculata* conserved at the Singapore Botanical Garden. Photographer: H. R. Sweet.

Miniature epiphytes growing on small-diameter host branches (twigs) in nature. **Stems** very short, completely concealed by imbricating leaf bases. **Leaves** two to four, elliptic to oblong-elliptic, acute or obtuse, to 7 × 3.5 cm, the petiolate base ca. 5 mm long. **Inflorescences** short, few-flowered, suberect racemes, much shorter than the leaves. **Flowers** produced in succession, the segments white, the sepals and petals spotted with violet, the lip with white lateral lobes tipped in pale violet, the anterior teeth pale yellow with violet spots, the midlobe white with violet margins and streaks, the posterior callus white with violet spots, the anterior callus pale violet, the filiform extensions white, the lateral rows of teeth violet with white apices, the column white with purple suffusion lateral to the stigma, the apex of the foot pale yellow bordered with pale violet. **Dorsal sepal** obovate to suborbicular, deeply concave, with erose-denticulate margins, 4 × 3.5 mm, the **lateral sepals** obliquely broadly ovate to subrotund, shallowly concave, obtuse, 5 × 4.5 mm. **Petals** suborbicular, broadly cuneate, obtuse-rounded with an erose-denticulate margin, 4 × 3.5 mm. **Lip** three-lobed, the lateral lobes fused with the column foot, erect, oblong-linear, erose-denticulate, with an anterior tooth, the midlobe mobile, transverse, 5.5 × 7 mm, triangular-subdeltoid with shallow sinuses separating the points, the margin minutely and obscurely erose-denticulate, the base with two superposed bifid **calli** extending to the middle and beyond the middle respectively, the posterior callus with secondary divisions, with four lateral keels composed of irregularly serrulate teeth. **Column** short, broad, fleshy. **Pedicel** and **ovary** 5 mm long.

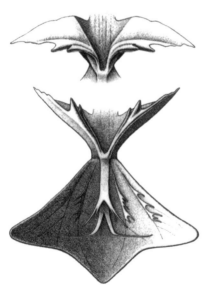

Phalaenopsis appendiculata, lip drawn from the type. Illustrator: H. R. Sweet.

Distribution: Endemic to Malaysia (Malaya Peninsula). **Etymology**: From the Latin, *appendiculatus* ("with small appendages"; -*ul* is a Latin diminutive), presumably an allusion to the longitudinal rows of teeth lateral to the two central calli on the lip. **Illustrations**: Carr 1929: t. 8, loc. cit.; Gruss and Wolff 1995:75, 76; Sweet 1969:324, 1980:50.

Phalaenopsis appendiculata is still known only from two independent collections at the type locality. It has never been in cultivation, although the color notes provided with the type specimen indicate that the patterned flowers and dwarf habit might find a place in modern novelty breeding.

Phalaenopsis gibbosa Sweet

Amer. Orchid Soc. Bull. 39:1095. 1970; *Polychilos gibbosa* (Sweet) Shim, Malayan Nat. Journ. 36:25. 1982. Type: Vietnam. Prov. Hoa Binh, Muong Thon, *Petelot 5425* (holotype: AMES).

Epiphytes with stems completely concealed by imbricating leaf bases. **Leaves** elliptic to elliptic-obovate, cuneate, acute, grading in size to 12 × 4.5 cm. **Inflorescences** slender, arching racemes or panicles, to 15 cm long, the peduncle terete, equal to the rachis, the rachis slightly flattened, fractiflex (zigzag), usually eight- to ten-flowered, the floral bracts alternate, distichous, ovate, acute, concave, to 4 mm long. **Flowers** white with greenish suffusion toward the apices of the sepals and petals, the base of the column and the swellings at the base of the column bright yellow, the lateral lobes of the lip white with the leading edge brown barred on yellow, the midlobe of the lip with a pair of large, clear, bright yellow spots. **Dorsal sepal** ovate-elliptic, obtuse-rounded, concave, to 7 × 3.5 mm, the **lateral sepals** obliquely ovate, subacute, adnate to the column foot, to 6 × 4.5 mm. **Petals** narrowly ovate-elliptic, obtuse-rounded, to 5 × 3 mm. **Lip** three-lobed, the lateral lobes erect, linear, retrorse-falcate, acuminate, to 2 mm long, the two lobes nearly touching at the middle with the combined structure U-shaped, the midlobe triangular-reniform, to 7 × 6 mm, obscurely three-lobulate, the lateral lobules rounded, the central lobules subacute, the **callus** biseriate, the basal callus four thread-like appendages superposed over a transverse, crescent-shaped denticulate callus. **Column** short, to 4 mm long, fleshy, laterally swollen at the base. **Pedicel** and **ovary** slender, arching, to 4 mm long.

Distribution: Vietnam and Laos. **Etymology**: From the Latin, *gibbosus* ("with a pouch-like swelling"), a reference to the excavated area of the lip beneath the anterior callus. **Illustrations**: Gruss and Wolff 1995:76; Seidenfaden 1992c:425; Sweet 1980:49.

Although this species has only recently been introduced to cultivation, it does not appear to be particularly rare in nature. Recent introductions have entered horticulture through the Hanoi flower market, the plants collected to the northwest of the city within a few hours' ride by bicycle (Averyanov pers. comm.). Small-flowered orchids, such as *P. gibbosa*, are of little value in the internal Vietnamese market and are routinely discarded by vendors when they realize their "mistake."

The very clear flower colors, which lack any purple-toned pigmentation, appearing almost like an alba form of *P. parishii*, suggest this species might be useful in breeding concolor miniature hybrids. In addition, this is the only species in this subgenus reported to have branched inflorescences.

The measurements given here are based on Sweet's original description, which was based on a rehydrated flower from an herbarium specimen; Seidenfaden (1992c:424) reported slightly larger measurements based on a fresh flower. Seidenfaden also emended the original description, noting that *P. gibbosa* has four pollinia in two pairs. Examination of fresh flowers also shows that the apices of the sepals and petals are not acute as noted by Sweet from the type specimen. The sepals and petals are rounded-obtuse, in the same manner as other species in this subgenus. Finally, Sweet's drawing of the type specimen exaggerates, to an extent, the degree to which the column foot forms a free segment between the point of attachment of the sepals and the lateral lobes of the lip.

Phalaenopsis lobbii (Rchb.f.) Sweet

Genus *Phalaenopsis* 53. 1980; *Phalaenopsis parishii* var. *lobbii* Rchb.f., Refug. Bot. 2: sub t. 85. 1870; *Polychilos lobbii* (Rchb.f.) Shim, Malayan Nat. Journ. 36:25. 1982. Type: "Eastern Himalaya." Without precise locality, leg. Lobb, *Hort. Veitch s.n.* (holotype: W).

Phalaenopsis listeri Berkeley, Gard. Chron., ser. 3, 1:280. 1887, nom. nud.

Miniature epiphytes forming clusters of stems by basal branching, with copious flattened roots. **Leaves** broadly elliptic, obliquely two-lobed at the apex, to 13 × 5 cm. **Inflorescences** erect, few- to six-flowered racemes, the floral bracts minute, elliptic, obtuse. **Flowers** white, the swollen base of the column with a few irregularly distributed brown spots, with a regular pair of darker brown spots below the apices of the swellings, the leading edges of the lateral lobes of the lip brown spot-

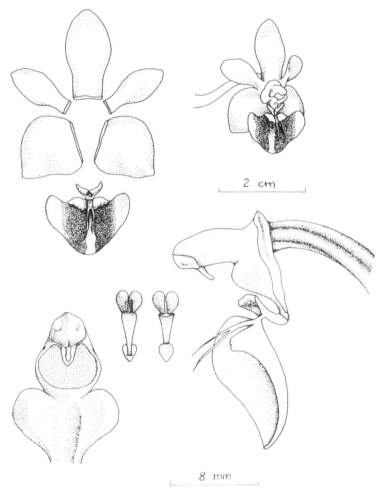

Phalaenopsis lobbii. Illustrator: F. Pupulin.

69

stripes. **Dorsal sepal** oblong-elliptic, obtuse, concave, to 10 × 5 mm,
the **lateral sepals** obliquely ovate to suborbicular, obtuse-rounded,
lightly reflexed, to 8 × 7 mm. **Petals** obovate-subspatulate, obtuse-
rounded, to 8 × 4 mm. **Lip** three-lobed, the lateral lobes erect, falcate,
acute, parallel to the middle and then diverging forming a U-shaped
structure, to 3 × 1 mm, the midlobe kidney-shaped, rounded-obtuse,
concave with the lateral margins shallowly incurved, to 6 × 10 mm, the
basal **callus** of four thread-like appendages superposed over a semicircular (+/− kidney-shaped) callus with minutely irregular-subdenticulate margins. **Column** short, somewhat arching, to 5 mm long. **Pedicel**
and **ovary** to 15 mm long.

ted, the midlobe white with two broad, longitudinal chestnut-brown stripes. **Dorsal sepal** oblong-elliptic, obtuse, concave, to 10 × 5 mm, the **lateral sepals** obliquely ovate to suborbicular, obtuse-rounded, lightly reflexed, to 8 × 7 mm. **Petals** obovate-subspatulate, obtuse-rounded, to 8 × 4 mm. **Lip** three-lobed, the lateral lobes erect, falcate, acute, parallel to the middle and then diverging forming a U-shaped structure, to 3 × 1 mm, the midlobe kidney-shaped, rounded-obtuse, concave with the lateral margins shallowly incurved, to 6 × 10 mm, the basal **callus** of four thread-like appendages superposed over a semicircular (+/− kidney-shaped) callus with minutely irregular-subdenticulate margins. **Column** short, somewhat arching, to 5 mm long. **Pedicel** and **ovary** to 15 mm long.

Distribution: India, Bhutan, Myanmar, and Vietnam. In my experience, most species that show a Myanmar-Bhutan/Vietnam disjunct distribution will eventually be found in Yunnan, China (for example, *Aerides rosea* Lindl. & Paxt.). **Etymology**: Named in honor of prodigious Victorian plant collector Thomas Lobb. **Illustrations**: Amer. Orchid Soc. Bull. 57:116, 122. 1988; Amer. Orchid Soc. Bull. 60:125. 1991; Amer. Orchid Soc. Bull. 61:672. 1992; Ann. Roy. Bot. Gard. Calcutta 6: t. 263. 1898; Awards Quart. 18(4):213. 1987; Awards Quart. 21(2):90, 96. 1990; Christenson 1995:21; Die Orchidee 42(4):31. 1991; Die Orchidee 43(6):46. 1991; Die Orchidee 46(4):55. 1995; Grubb, Select Orch. Pl. 2:54. 1962; Gruss 1992a:133; Gruss and Röllke 1990a:159, 1994a:6; Gruss and Wolff 1995:70, 71; Karnehl 1991:138, 140; Pradhan 1981:33, 34; Pradhan 1982:235; Sweet 1980:48, 53.

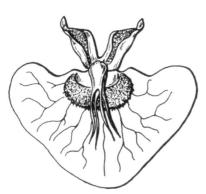

Phalaenopsis lobbii drawn from the type. Illustrator: H. R. Sweet.

Phalaenopsis lobbii has long been confused with *P. parishii*. In the absence of true *P. parishii* in cultivation (and the rare specimens in herbaria), it was plausible to consider *P. lobbii* a color variant of *P. parishii* with some differences in the callus. This treatment was reinforced over the past 30 years by the thousands of *P. lobbii* that have entered horticulture from northeast India (Kalimpong and environs)

70

and the void of *P. parishii* in cultivation until very recently. Examination of numerous clones of *P. parishii* confirm that Sweet was correct: *P. lobbii* is a fully distinct species with no particularly close affinity to *P. parishii* relative to other species in this subgenus. *Phalaenopsis lobbii* also appears to differ from *P. parishii* by having very dark, almost sea-green leaves that are more or less prismatic.

The several color morphs of *P. lobbii* are based on lip coloration. The midlobe of the lip may have brown stripes on a white background (agreeing with the holotype of the species as explicitly stated by Reichenbach); brown stripes on a yellow background; brown stripes with a white stripe in the center and yellow stripes to the outside; or a solid yellow color without any brown stripes. A "blue-lipped" phase of this species has even been rumored; this appears to stem from a printing error (Karnehl 1991:138) in which a standard *P. lobbii* was printed with false blue colors (even the root tips are blue!). It is unlikely given the yellow and brown pigments found in *P. lobbii* that a blue form would arise. And although it is possible for a blue form to arise from the wine-colored lip of *P. parishii*, no such color morph has surfaced to date.

Only one of the four legitimate color morphs has been described. I take the opportunity to describe a second morph because of its horticultural significance and desirability in breeding programs.

Phalaenopsis lobbii f. *flava*
(Gruss & Röllke) E. A. Christ., comb. nov.

> Basionym: *Phalaenopsis parishii* var. *lobbii* f. *flava* Gruss & Röllke, Die Orchidee 43(1):42. 1992, nom. inval. Lectotype, here designated: photographs on p. 43, loc. cit.

Etymology: From the Latin, *flavus* ("yellow"), a reference to the yellow ground color of the lip midlobe.

Gruss and Röllke described this color morph, which bears flowers with the midlobe of the lip having reddish brown stripes overlain on a solid yellow ground color rather than over a white ground color. Unfortunately, they failed to designate a type specimen, and thus their name is technically invalid under the International Code of Botanical Nomenclature. Designating a lectotype here rectifies that oversight, although for purposes of priority the name dates from this publication and not from 1992.

Phalaenopsis lobbii f. *flavilabia* E. A. Christ., f. nov.

Differt a specie typica labello flavo et non bruneo.

Type: Without precise locality, *Hort. Trudel 585* (holotype: photograph reproduced in color plate section of this book).

Etymology: From the Latin, *flavus* ("yellow") and *labium* ("lip"), a reference to the pure yellow lip of this form.

This morph has a pure yellow lip that lacks any brown pigment on the midlobe. A clone of it has been awarded as *P. parishii* var. *lobbii* 'Yellow Lip', CHM/AOS.

Phalaenopsis parishii Rchb.f.

Bot. Zeit. 23:146. 1865; *Grafia parishii* (Rchb.f.) Hawkes, Phytologia 13:306. 1966; *Polychilos parishii* (Rchb.f.) Shim, Malayan Nat. Journ. 36:26. 1982. Type: Myanmar. Moulmein, *Parish 110* (holotype: W; isotype: K).

Aerides decumbens Griff., Notul. Pl. Asiat. 3:365. 1851, nomen confusum. Type: Myanmar. Magoung, *Griffith s.n.* (holotype: K).

Miniature epiphytes with numerous roots. **Leaves** obovate-elliptic, cuneate, acute or obtuse, grading in size to 12 × 5 cm. **Inflorescences** initially erect, then arching, five- or six-flowered, lightly fractiflex racemes to 14 cm long, the floral bracts ovate, concave, acute, to 3 mm long. **Flowers** white, the base of the column spotted with dark brown, the lateral lobes of the lip light brown spotted over a yellow ground, the midlobe of the lip wine-colored with white apex and white base to the leading edge of the transverse callus. **Dorsal sepal** broadly elliptic, obtuse-rounded, concave, 6–8 × 3–5 mm, the **lateral sepals** obliquely obovate to suborbicular, obtuse-rounded, slightly reflexed, 7–10 × 5–7 mm. **Petals** oblanceolate-subspatulate, obtuse-rounded, concave, 6–8 × 3–4 mm. **Lip** three-lobed, the lateral lobes erect, retrorsely falcate, parallel and nearly touching at the middle, forming a U-shaped struc-

Phalaenopsis parishii from Saunders' *Refugium Botanicum* 2: t. 85. 1870.

ture, the midlobe triangular-reniform, obtuse, minutely notched at the apex, 4–7 × 5–10 mm, the **callus** biseriate, the basal callus of four thread-like filaments projected above a depression and superposed over a transverse, semicircular callus terminating in a fringe of long teeth-like fimbriations. **Column** short, with large swellings laterally on the base. **Pedicel** and **ovary** to 15 mm long.

Distribution: "Eastern Himalayas," India, Myanmar, and Thailand. **Etymology**: Named in honor of Samuel Bonsall Parish (1838–1928), whose collections from Myanmar (Burma) remain unparalleled. **Illustrations**: Awards Quart. 26(4):228. 1995; Die Orchidee 43(6):46. 1991; Die Orchidee 44(1):99. 1993; Gruss 1992a:133; Gruss and Röllke 1990a: 158, 159, 160; Gruss and Röllke 1992a:42, 43; Gruss and Wolff 1995:72, 73, 74; Karnehl 1991:138, 141; Seidenfaden 1988c:239; Sweet 1969: 322, 1980:48, 52.

Phalaenopsis parishii has long been confused with *P. lobbii*. In addition to differences in the callus (the transverse semicircular plate minutely irregular-denticulate in *P. lobbii* versus long-fimbriate in *P. parishii*), the lip of *P. parishii* is consistently a solid wine-color.

The name *Aerides decumbens* was published earlier than *P. parishii* and would normally take precedence. That name, however, has been consistently misapplied to *P. deliciosa* Rchb.f. (see Chapter 9). The reason for this appears to have been the now discontinued practice of mounting more than one collection per herbarium sheet to conserve money and space. The herbarium sheet at Kew that bears the holotype of *A. decumbens* also bears subsequent collections of *P. deliciosa* as well as drawings of *P. deliciosa*. This misled several generations of taxonomists into thinking that Griffith's plant was actually *P. deliciosa*. Careful examination of Griffith's plant reveals that his plant is a member of subgenus *Parishianae*. Because of the consistent misapplication of the name and the confusion that would ensue if the specific epithet *decumbens* were applied to what we call *P. parishii*, the name *Aerides decumbens* (and its derivatives) is rejected as a *nomen confusum*, literally a confused name, despite the priority of *A. decumbens*.

A Thailand collection of *P. parishii* (*Kerr 466*, K) was collected at 500 m in elevation. Other than that, no information is known on its native habitat and ecology.

Most hybrids registered to date that supposedly used *P. parishii* as a parent were actually made with *P. lobbii*: for example, *P.* Formosa Dream (*amabilis* × *lobbii*, not *amabilis* × *parishii*) and *P.* Micro Nova (*lobbii* × *maculata*, not *parishii* × *maculata*). A number of these hybrids were illustrated in Gruss and Wolff (1995) using the name *P. parishii* as one of the parents. The recognition of *P. lobbii* as separate from *P. parishii* affects the horticultural community, as hybrids with true *P. parishii* are now maturing and will need to be distinguished from earlier misnamed hybrids. It also affects the scientific community where plants of *P. lobbii* have also been lumped under *P. parishii* (Aoyama et al. 1994).

CHAPTER 8

Subgenus *Polychilos*

Subgenus *Polychilos* (Breda) E. A. Christ., stat. nov.

Basionym: *Polychilos* Breda in Kuhl and van Hasselt, Gen. and Sp. Orch. 1. 1827. Type: *Polychilos cornu-cervi* Breda (= *Phalaenopsis cornu-cervi* (Breda) Bl.).

Polystylus Hassk., Natuurk. Tijdschr. Nederl. Indië 10:3. 1856. Type: *Polystylus cornu-cervi* Hassk. (= *Phalaenopsis cornu-cervi* (Breda) Bl.).

This subgenus bears fleshy, long-lasting flowers with two pairs of calli on the lip (biseriate), the lateral lobes of the lip producing a raised tooth along the leading edge, and two pollinia. The base of the posterior callus may be irregular (and presumably glandular) or a separate field of glandular tissue may occur at the base of the lip, technically yielding a triseriate callus. This triseriate condition is most pronounced in section *Polychilos*. With a few exceptions (*P. floresensis*, for one), the flowers of this subgenus are richly pigmented, usually bear spots or bars on the sepals and petals, and are often fragrant.

Shim (1982) separated *Polychilos* as a genus separate from a narrowly defined *Phalaenopsis*. Although his classification is not followed here, his broad circumscription of *Polychilos*, one that includes several sections recognized by Sweet (essentially all the "colorful" species), is followed here at the subgeneric level. According to a modern phylogenetic (cladistic) approach, the recognition of a *Polychilos* as a genus distinct from *Phalaenopsis* requires further division of *Phalaenopsis* (i.e., the removal of *Polychilos* produces a paraphyletic *Phalaenopsis* in the strict sense). Such an action, which would split *Phalaenopsis* into at least five genera (the subgenera put forward in this book), is an alternative approach not taken here. Shim's classification has never gained acceptance, and it is unlikely that any classification which radically divides the genus as circumscribed today will find disciples.

Species of subgenus *Polychilos* readily produce interspecific hybrids within the subgenus and produce hybrids with other subgenera with some difficulty. Arends (1970) found a high level of meiotic chromosome homology in hybrids between species of subgenus *Polychilos* (mean total of 19.00 in the hybrid *lueddemanniana* × *mannii*; 18.92 in the hybrid *amboinensis* × *mannii*) and lower levels of meiotic chromosome homology in hybrids between species of subgenus *Polychilos* and subgenus *Phalaenopsis* (mean total of 5.00 in the hybrid *equestris* × *mannii*; 12.13 in the hybrid *amboinensis* × *sanderiana*). These inferred relationships have been robustly supported by anecdotal information from phalaenopsis breeders.

The richly colored, often fragrant flowers are probably bee pollinated, but no observations have been made under natural conditions. From the limited number of field-pressed herbarium specimens and personal observations (Comber pers. comm.), it appears that pollination is a relatively rare event in nature. This perhaps helps to explain the remarkable longevity of the flowers. Several species, especially those related to *P. lueddemanniana*, exhibit post-pollination chlorophylly of the perianth. After initiating a fruit, the flowers turn green (i.e., they lose their other pigments), and the sepals and petals persist throughout the life of the fruit. It is assumed that these persistent perianths augment the photosynthate coming from the parent plant.

Section *Polychilos* (Breda) Rchb.f.

Bot. Zeit. 22:298. 1864. Type: *Polychilos cornu-cervi* Breda (= *Phalaenopsis cornu-cervi* (Breda) Bl.).

This section is characterized by having a fleshy flattened rachis (terete in *P. mannii*), non-fragrant flowers produced singly in succession over long periods of time, petals conspicuously narrower than the sepals, a triseriate callus, a slightly saccate lip base created by folding, the mid-

lobe of the lip transversely anchoriform or lunate, the lip base continuous with the column foot, and a pair of fleshy knee-like projections at
the base of the column. The flowers of this section do not exhibit post-
pollination chlorophylly of the perianth.

At the base of the lip is a glandular callus, usually surrounding a
small depression, that is highly variable in morphology (see the discussion under *P. cornu-cervi*) and therefore, as with glandular tissue in
other orchids (for example, the *Aerides odorata* complex), not a useful
taxonomic character. In its most extreme it terminates as an elongate,
erect tongue that bends 180° backward along the back of the lip base.
In the center of the lip is a flat, sheet-like callus that terminates in two
narrow, elongate teeth, like the forked tongue of a snake. This callus
plate may have lateral teeth as well, but these too are variable, and individual flowers may often have one lateral tooth on one side and no tooth
or two lateral teeth on the other side. Finally, an erect, terminal, bilaterally flattened, tooth-like callus stands between the elongate teeth of
the central plate. Some taxonomic weighting has been given the relative width of this structure, but in my experience the width of this callus is variable and appears to have little taxonomic utility.

Of all the groups of species in *Phalaenopsis*, section *Polychilos*—with
the exception of *P. mannii*—has proven the most difficult to resolve at
the species level to my complete satisfaction. On casual inspection of
the flowers, without some foreknowledge of what to look for, *P. cornu-
cervi*, *P. borneënsis*, and *P. pantherina* appear identical, and under a micro-
scope, their floral characters present a mosaic pattern of variability. In
particular, the width of the apical tooth, its length relative to the elongate teeth of the central plate-like callus, and the degree to which the
lateral margins of the midlobe are entire versus irregularly denticulate—all display a wide range of variability. The only clear difference
among the three is found in the width of the lip midlobe. *Phalaenopsis
cornu-cervi* has a midlobe to 0.9 cm wide, while *P. borneënsis* and *P. pantherina* have a midlobe to 1.2 cm wide. On the basis of several hundred
clones examined for this revision these measurements appear to represent well-defined groups without any intermediates.

Unfortunately very little material, either in herbaria or in cultivation,
bears any verifiable or detailed locality data, and thus no comments
can be made about clinal variation, elevational isolation, or other dis-

tribution patterns that might explain the complex morphological variation seen in the flowers. Several unpublished horticultural names have been attached to populations of newly imported plants; but while these may each present distinctive facies, upon analysis of the flowers, no characters on which to base new species or subspecies are displayed.

Key to the species of section *Polychilos*

1. Rachis of inflorescence terete, the floral bracts free; numerous flowers produced simultaneously. .... *P. mannii*
1. Rachis of inflorescence flattened, the floral bracts strongly two-ranked along the rachis edges; flowers produced sequentially with only one or two flowers open at a time.
 2. Midlobe of lip to 0.9 cm wide. .... *P. cornu-cervi*
 2. Midlobe of lip to 1.2 cm wide.
  3. Midlobe of lip sessile, flat, glabrous. .... *P. borneënsis*
  3. Midlobe of lip clawed, with a fleshy center raised only on the upper surface into a slight pad, the pad with a few sparse trichomes. .... *P. pantherina*

Phalaenopsis borneënsis Garay

Lindleyana 10:182. 1995. Type: Borneo. Without precise locality, *Hort. J. Levy 1450* (holotype: AMES).

An augmented free translation of the type description (in Latin): Epiphytes, with elongate, glabrous roots 3–4 mm thick. **Stems** erect with distichous leaves, 3 cm long. **Leaves** coriaceous, linear-oblanceolate, acute, with unequal apices, conduplicate at the base, to 30 cm long, 3–4 cm wide. **Inflorescences** axillary, elongate, arching, to 45 cm long, the peduncle subterete, somewhat compressed, at the middle with rather short, ovate-cucullate, acute bracts, the rachis simple or branched, flattened, +/- fractiflex, to 15 cm long, the floral bracts in two rows, flattened, ovate-cucullate, 5 mm long. **Flowers** produced sequentially, with spreading segments, yellow-green, with transverse brown spots. **Dorsal sepal** elliptic, with recurved margins, obtuse, dorsally mucronulate, 2.2 × 0.8 cm, the **lateral sepals** similar but wider, 2.2 × 1.1 cm. **Petals** obovate-oblanceolate, acute, 1.6 × 0.6 cm. **Lip** three-lobed, 1.3 cm long, 1.1 cm wide when expanded, the lateral lobes broadly subquadrate, bearing a parallel **callus** between, the midlobe sessile with a cuneate base, transversely lunate, without an isthmus, without a callus, erosulate on both margins, below the apex shortly mucronate, the disc excavated with a central erect linear-triangular, highly acuminate structure above a lamina with deeply bifurcated, filiform processes. **Column** arching, 1 cm tall, with a pair of prominent basal knees. **Ovary** rather long-pedicellate.

Distribution: Endemic to Borneo. **Etymology**: With the Latin suffix -*ensis*, indicating its place of origin in Borneo. **Illustrations**: Garay, Hamer, and Siegerist 1995:180; Gruss and Wolff 1995:79 (as *P. cornu-cervi*).

Phalaenopsis borneënsis is known only from horticultural sources said to be from Borneo but with no other locality data. It has been in cultivation for a number of years masquerading either as a large-flowered form of *P. cornu-cervi* or more commonly as the rare *P. pantherina*. *Phalaenopsis borneënsis* is similar to *P. pantherina* in having a broad lip midlobe up to 1.2 cm wide, well above the maximum size seen in *P. cornu-cervi*. It is instantly separable from *P. pantherina* by its flat midlobe, which lacks a raised pad of tissue on the upper surface and is without any trichomes.

When describing *P. borneënsis*, Garay made strong reference to its lip being sessile from a cuneate base in contrast to the clawed lip of *P. pantherina*. Although I have included this character in the key to section *Polychilos*, I find this feature somewhat variable based on the limited sample of these two rare species available to me.

Phalaenopsis cornu-cervi (Breda) Bl. & Rchb.f.

Hamb. Gartenz. 16:116. 1860; *Polychilos cornu-cervi* Breda in Kuhl and van Hasselt, Gen. and Sp. Orchid., t. 1. 1827. Type: Indonesia. Java, Bantam Prov., *van Hasselt s.n.* (holotype: L).

Polystylus cornu-cervi Hassk., Natuurk. Tijdschr. Nederl. Indië 10:3. 1856. Type: Indonesia. Java, without precise locality, *Lobb s.n.* (holotype: K).

Phalaenopsis cornu-cervi var. *picta* (Hassk.) Sweet, Amer. Orchid Soc. Bull. 38:514. 1969; *Polystylus cornu-cervi* var. *picta* Hassk., Natuurk. Tijdschr. Nederl. Indië 10:4. 1856. Neotype, designated by Sweet (loc. cit.): Bot. Mag. 92: t. 5570. 1866.

Phalaenopsis devriesiana Rchb.f., Hamb. Gartenz. 16:116. 1860. Type: Indonesia. Java, without precise locality, *DeVries s.n.* (holotype: W).

Phalaenopsis lamelligera Sweet, Amer. Orchid Soc. Bull. 38:516. 1969, syn. nov.; *Polychilos lamelligera* (Sweet) Shim, Malayan Nat. Journ. 36:25. 1982. Type: Borneo. Without precise locality, *Bull 83* (holotype: K).

Phalaenopsis cornu-cervi var. *assamica* Mayr, Die Orchidee 37(4):178. 1986, nom. nud., ex icon.

Epiphytes with extremely thick white roots. **Stems** elongate for the genus, 5–10 cm long. **Leaves** oblanceolate, obtuse, coriaceous, pale green, to 22 × 4 cm. **Inflorescences** pedunculate racemes or panicles, variable in length and branching, 9–42 cm long, the peduncle terete, several times longer than the rachis, the rachis strongly flattened, the floral bracts succulent, continuous with the rachis, long-persistent. **Flowers** strongly two-ranked in plane with the flattened rachis, produced singly in succession over long periods of time, translucent yellow with reddish brown spots and transverse bars, the lip midlobe clear whitish yellow to pale yellow. **Dorsal sepal** oblong-elliptic, acute, often carinate, shallowly concave, to 2.3 × 0.8 cm, the **lateral sepals** obliquely elliptic-ovate, acute, to 2.3 × 0.9 cm. **Petals** oblong, obtuse, to 1.8 × 0.6 cm. **Lip** three-lobed, to 0.8 × 1 cm, the lateral lobes erect, obscurely bilobulate, the posterior lobule oblong, truncate, the anterior lobule subsimilar to the posterior lobule but half its length, the midlobe highly variable, transverse, +/− crescent-shaped, obtuse, the **callus** triseriate, the posterior callus glandular, variable, the central callus a bifid plate with long primary filiform divisions, often with a pair of smaller divisions to either side, the anterior callus a suberect bilaterally flattened tooth that separates the divisions of the central callus. **Column** somewhat arching, dilated toward the apex lateral to the stigma, to 0.8 cm long, with prominent basal knees. **Pedicel** and **ovary** terete, 1.5–3 cm long.

Distribution: Northeast India and the Nicobar Islands to Java and Borneo from sea level to 800 m in elevation. Comber (1990:304) notes that *P. cornu-cervi* is a colonizing species and when left undisturbed "seeding is prolific, several hundred plants may then be found on the one tree." **Etymology**: From the Latin, *cornu cervi* ("horn of a deer"), a reference to the antler-like flattened rachis of the inflorescence. **Illustrations**: Amer. Orchid Soc. Bull. 49:865. 1980; Awards Quart. 18(3):157. 1987; Batchelor 1983:10; Chan et al. 1994:236, pl. 15b; Die Orchidee 33(2): back cover. 1982; Die Orchidee 37(2): back cover. 1986; Gruss 1990:117; Mayr 1986:178; Pradhan 1981:32, 1982:235; Seidenfaden 1988c:240–241, pl. 26a-b.

Of all the species of *Phalaenopsis*, *P. cornu-cervi* has caused me the most difficulty. In the past botanists frequently called such species "highly variable." In most cases subsequent research and new specimen collection rendered these "variable" species as complexes of superficially similar valid species with clearly defined morphological differences. The neotropical *Encyclia oncidioides* and *Epidendrum difforme* "complexes" exemplify such broad catch-all groups. Based on all available evidence, however, *P. cornu-cervi* must be relegated to the rank of a "highly variable" species. Despite concerted research efforts, no discernible pattern of variation has emerged to explain the remarkable variation seen in this species, broadly defined here.

An argument could be made concerning the variability of the back-wall, basal callus in this species—a variability that gave rise to the description of *P. lamelligera*. It is the wide variation in lip midlobe shape, both in two-dimensional outline and in three dimensions, that yields significant confusion. The two-dimensional outline of *P. cornu-cervi* as treated here comes in several shapes. The majority of clones examined have midlobes that are transverse and anchoriform or crescent-shaped. A minority of clones have midlobes that are lunate and similar to but smaller than those of *P. borneënsis* and *P. pantherina* or are obscurely three-lobulate. The latter is clearly illustrated in Chan et al. (1994:236).

The three-dimensional shape of the midlobe also is variable and appears to follow no particular geographic pattern. Some clones examined have midlobes that are thickened in the center both above and below the blade, with the lower portion jutting out like a chin. I liken this type to a sphinx's head, with the cloth flaps of the headpiece equivalent to the thin lamina of the blade. This three-dimensional structure is true of the clone illustrated by Sweet (1980:55), the type of *P. lamelligera* (Sweet 1980:58), and most of the plants I have seen imported from Thailand (Seidenfaden 1988c:240–241).

In contrast, a second group of clones examined have midlobes that are not thickened in the center. Instead, these plants have a shallowly channeled lip midlobe. This is the lip shape shown for some plants from Borneo (Chan et al. 1994:236, pl. 15b) and Sumatra (Comber 1990:304).

A smaller number of clones examined have more or less flat midlobes without any central thickening or shallow channel. The lip midlobes of these plants are most similar to but smaller than those of *P. borneënsis*. In addition, these clones exhibit the most variable two-dimensional shapes as well, including clones with lunate midlobes and midlobes with finely crenulate-erosulate posterior margins.

A study of the infraspecific variation in *P. cornu-cervi* would make an excellent research topic, perhaps using modern molecular tools. The difficulty resides in obtaining plants of known provenance. Although widespread in horticulture from plants recently collected in the wild, most have no locality data or such sketchy information as "said to be from Borneo"—hardly sufficient information to attempt detailed genetic and geographic analyses.

After examining more than 100 clones of plants that I would assign to the broadly defined concept of *P. cornu-cervi* presented here, I choose to reduce *P. lamelligera* to synonymy. I have never encountered a clone exhibiting three organized basal callus plates as illustrated by Sweet but have seen enough variability in this glandular basal callus to consider it within the possible range of variation for the species. In all other ways, and especially in the three-dimensional structure of the lip midlobe, the type of *P. lamelligera* is inseparable from *P. cornu-cervi*.

In his key to the species, Sweet (1980:54) included *P. lamelligera* under those species that produce a terete flowering portion of the inflorescence (rachis). This decision is baseless. *Phalaenopsis lamelligera*, as known to and interpreted by Sweet, consisted of a single flower without any inflorescence. *Phalaenopsis mannii* is the only species in this section with a terete rachis.

Phalaenopsis cornu-cervi is extremely variable in color. Throughout its range the species appears to exhibit a range of markings from sparse spot-like short brown bars to quite heavily marked flowers with larger bars arranged in transverse rows. Sweet recognized the latter as var. *picta*. Sweet neotypified the name, which was based on a plant presumably from Indonesia and originally described by Hasskarl, with a published illustration presumably based on plants from Moulmein. I do not recognize this variety, in part because I consider this within the normal range of variation within all populations of the species, and in part because it is unknown where Breda's type of *Polychilos cornu-cervi* fell in this range of markings. Thus it cannot be established whether the type variety was lightly or heavily marked. Mayr's var. *assamica* is identical to and presumably of the same provenance as the neotype of var. *picta* and has the same unmarked, pure yellow inner halves of the lateral sepals (to either side of the lip). It should be noted in passing that the photograph used to illustrate var. *picta* in Sweet's book (Sweet 1980:48) is probably *P. borneënsis*, given the very broad subsaccate fold in the claw of the lip.

Three color morphs deserve formal designation because of their significance in horticulture.

Phalaenopsis cornu-cervi f. *flava*

(Braem) E. A. Christ., stat. nov.

> Basionym: *Phalaenopsis cornu-cervi* var. *flava* Braem, Schlechteriana 1(3):113. 1990. Type: Indonesia. Sumatra, *Braem 89/23c* (holotype: SCHLE).

Distribution: To date only recorded from Sumatra but expected spontaneously from throughout the range of the species. **Etymology**: From the Latin, *flavus* ("yellow"), a reference to the concolor flowers. **Illustrations**: Amer. Orchid Soc. Bull. 49:865. 1980; Awards Quart. 19(2): 104. 1988; Die Orchidee 31(1):16. 1980; Die Orchidee 32(2):6. 1981; Die Orchidee 33(2): back cover. 1982; Die Orchidee 37(2): back cover. 1986; Pradhan 1982:235.

This anthocyanin-free form of *P. cornu-cervi* bears pure yellow flowers without any spots or bars on the sepals and petals.

Phalaenopsis cornu-cervi f. *sanguinea*

E. A. Christ., f. nov.

A forma typica floribus sanguineis differt.

Holotype: Photograph on the right in van Holle-de Raeve (1990c:111).

Phalaenopsis cornu-cervi var. *rubescens* Braem, Die Orchidee 37(2): back cover. 1986, nom. nud.

Etymology: From the Latin, *sanguineus* ("blood-red"), a reference to the saturated flower color. **Illustrations**: Mayr 1986:179.

This phase of the species represents a nearly red flower brought about by the coalescing of red spots and bars. The pattern is still visible and a yellow picotee (narrow border) is still evident. The vibrant color is reminiscent of the red flush seen in most clones of *P. corningiana*. This form differs from the *thalebanii* form by having the visible ground color.

I know this form only through the photograph cited. The midlobe of the lip appears to be more lunate (moon-shaped) than most clones of *P. cornu-cervi*, but this may be an artifact of the photograph and the angle from which the flower was captured on film.

Phalaenopsis cornu-cervi f. *thalebanii*

(Seidenfaden) E. A. Christ., comb. et stat. nov.

Basionym: *Phalaenopsis thalebanii* Seidenfaden, Opera Bot. 95:241. 1988, syn. nov. Type: Thailand. Surat just north of the border to Perlis, Thaleban Sanctuary, Yaroi Falls, *Seidenfaden & Smitinand 9354* (holotype: C).

With some trepidation, I reduce *P. thalebanii* to the synonymy of *P. cornu-cervi*. Ignoring for the moment the possibility that Thai and Indochinese plants of *P. cornu-cervi* are distinct from the Javan type population, I do not think that the type of *P. thalebanii* is distinct at the species-level from other Thai plants of *P. cornu-cervi*. The history of *P. thalebanii* and the circumstances of its description are rather complex so I will endeavor to relate the history as I understand it.

The holotype (original specimen) of *P. thalebanii* was collected in the Thaleban Sanctuary in northern Thailand. Seidenfaden remarked on two outstanding characters of the flowers: the larger than usual flower size (dorsal sepal to 20 mm long) and the uniform cinnamon-brown flowers. The flowers may be on the large size for *P. cornu-cervi*, but they are certainly within the range of floral measurements for *P. cornu-cervi* throughout its geographic range: Sweet (1980), for example, gives a dorsal sepal length of 18–23 mm. The flower color, however, is exceptional—a rich, deep, cinnamon brown without any noticeable markings.

First, from orchid growers familiar with the orchid industry in Thailand, it appears that *P. thalebanii* is known in cultivation from only one or two clones. Clonal divisions, although rare, are just now finding their way to connoisseur collections (Grove pers. comm.; Michel pers. comm.). It is not known if the clones in cultivation are the same as the type collection or from the isolated, limited population at Thaleban. Second, Seidenfaden's drawings in this complex are problematic. Specifically, Seidenfaden's drawing of *P. cornu-cervi* (Seidenfaden 1988c: 240, fig. 150) is inaccurate in that the central laminate callus is drawn as two separate lamina (the callus appearing four-seriate rather than three-seriate). To my knowledge no known plant of *P. cornu-cervi* has such a four-seriate callus. When this error, probably the result of a misunderstanding during the inking of the drawing for publication, is resolved by merging the "two" laminate calli, Seidenfaden's drawings of *P. cornu-cervi* and *P. thalebanii* become identical. Third, the color photograph of *P. thalebanii* published with the type description (Seidenfaden 1988c: pl. 26b) is not that concept ("found in a single specimen") but is instead a faded, and hence red-infused, flower of typical *P. cornu-cervi*. The photograph is based on *Seidenfaden & Smitinand 9342*, and not the type number of *Seidenfaden & Smitinand 9354*.

With that history presented, and in the absence of any morphological differences or evidence of a sizeable population in nature, I choose to treat *P. thalebanii* as nothing more than a remarkably deeply pigmented form of *P. cornu-cervi*. This situation is perhaps analogous to the rare but dramatic vinicolor forms of *Paphiopedilum callosum* (Rchb.f.) Stein.

Although this form is quite similar to the *sanguinea* form, the extreme desirability of the *thalebanii* form in horticulture and the lack of any yellow ground color whatsoever warrants formal designation here.

Phalaenopsis mannii Rchb.f.

Gard. Chron. 902. 1871; *Polychilos mannii* (Rchb.f.) Shim, Malayan Nat. Journ. 36:25. 1982. Type: India. Sikkim, Upper Assam, *Mann 10* (holotype: W).

Phalaenopsis boxallii Rchb.f., Gard. Chron., n.s., 19:274. 1883. Type: Myanmar. Without precise locality, *Boxall s.n.* (holotype: W).

Phalaenopsis mannii var. *maculata* Trudel, Die Orchidee 37(4): back cover. 1986, nom. nud., syn. nov., ex icon.

Epiphytes eventually forming clumps by basal stem branches. **Leaves** oblong-oblanceolate to narrowly elliptic, acute, medium green to pale silvery green, often with fine brown submarginal spotting especially toward the base of the leaves, to 37 × 7 cm. **Inflorescences** arching-subpendent racemes or panicles, loosely many-flowered, the peduncle and rachis terete, the floral bracts oblong-lanceolate, concave, acute, to 1 cm long. **Flowers** numerous, waxy, glossy, long-lasting, the sepals and petals yellow with dark brown spotting and barring, the midlobe of the lip white, the column yellow. **Dorsal sepal** oblong-oblanceolate, acute, margins revolute, to 2.4 × 0.8 cm, the **lateral sepals** obliquely elliptic-oblanceolate, subfalcate ("bowlegged") at the apex, acute, margins revolute, to 2.5 × 1.1 cm. **Petals** lanceolate, acute, often incurved, to 2.0 × 0.6 cm. **Lip** three-lobed, to 1.1 cm long, to 1.1 cm across the expanded lateral lobes, the lateral lobes erect, appressed, oblong-subquadrate, obliquely truncate, the midlobe transverse, anchor-shaped, the margins fimbriate-erose, the apex a swollen knob with sparse trichomes, the **callus** triseriate, the posterior callus a small glandular patch, the middle callus a bifid plate with long, filiform divisions, the anterior callus an erect, bilaterally compressed tooth. **Column** arching, club-shaped, to 0.8 cm long, with prominent basal knees. **Pedicel** and **ovary** to 3 cm long.

Distribution: Northeast India, Nepal, and China to Vietnam at 500–1400 m in elevation. **Etymology**: Named for Gustav Mann, the original collector of the species in Sikkim. **Illustrations**: Awards Quart. 17(1):24. 1986; Awards Quart. 18(1):34. 1987; Awards Quart. 23(2):129. 1992; Baker and Baker 1989:71; Chen et al. 1998:352; Christenson 1999a: 367; Pradhan 1981:30, 31, 32; Pradhan 1982:234; Williams 1984:238.

Note: *Phalaenopsis mannii* 'Black MAJ' (Awards Quart. 24(4):312. 1993) is questionably identified given the very narrow midlobe of the lip and might possibly be a plant of *P. bastianii.*

Phalaenopsis mannii, exported in quantity over time from northeast India, was a frequently grown species in horticulture until quite recently. It is an easily recognized species and the only member of this

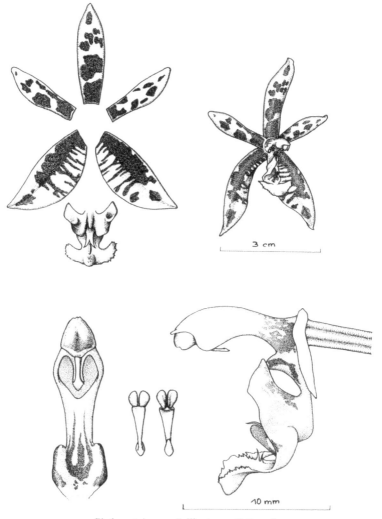

Phalaenopsis mannii. Illustrator: F. Pupulin.

section that produces both a terete inflorescence peduncle and rachis. Once an active component of novelty and yellow hybrid breeding programs, the species lost favor because of several undesirable floral qualities, including narrow revolute floral segments and a tendency for the yellow pigments to fade. This disfavor, combined with difficulties in obtaining inexpensive wild-collected plants because of CITES regulations and India's own conservation measures, has made *P. mannii* surprisingly scarce in modern collections.

The species is variable in its leaf color and to a lesser extent in flower color and form. The leaves of typical plants are a medium green. Toward the leaf bases and somewhat concentrated along the basal margins one finds small purple spots. These spots are enhanced by growing under bright light levels, cool temperatures, or dry conditions —the same conditions that promote darker anthocyanin pigments in purple or pink flowers. Select clones of *P. mannii* produce quite silvery green leaves.

Flower color and shape are also somewhat variable. Typical clones produce pale yellow flowers indifferently marked with brown spots and transverse bars. Trudel described var. *maculata* from a clone that produced particularly large dark spots on the sepals and petals. While this

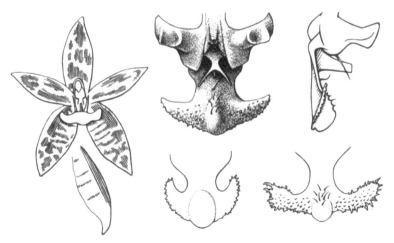

Phalaenopsis mannii drawn from the type (upper center) and associated specimens (lower center and lower right) in the Reichenbach Herbarium. Illustrator: H. R. Sweet.

is one extreme variant, it is within the normal range seen in the species. Such variation is best treated at the clonal level rather than formally designated. The most striking variant is the immaculate form described here, which produces clouds of pure yellow flowers or yellow flowers with green tips.

Phalaenopsis mannii f. *flava* E. A. Christ., f. nov.

A forma typica floribus flavis differt.

Type: Photograph reproduced in the color plate section of this book.

Phalaenopsis mannii var. *concolor* Trudel, Die Orchidee 37(4): back cover. 1986, nom. nud., ex icon.

Etymology: From the Latin, *flavus* ("yellow"), a reference to the pure yellow flowers of this form. **Illustrations**: Awards Quart. 18(2):65. 1987; Awards Quart. 22(3):164. 1991; Awards Quart. 26(1):26. 1995; Awards Quart. 26(4):229. 1995; Gruss and Wolff 1995:82; Pradhan 1981:31, 1982:234.

This is the anthocyanin-free form of the species. Although informally designated in horticulture under a variety of names (such as varieties *alba* and *concolor*), a valid botanical name for it has never been published.

Phalaenopsis pantherina Rchb.f.

Bot. Zeit. 22:298. 1864; *Polychilos pantherina* (Rchb.f.) Shim, Malayan Nat. Journ. 36:25. 1982. Type: Borneo. Without precise locality, *Low s.n.* (holotype: W).

Epiphytes with extremely thick white roots. **Stems** leafy throughout, to 15 cm long. **Leaves** oblong to narrowly oblong-elliptic, obliquely obtuse and sublobulate, pale green, to 20 × 4 cm. **Inflorescences** pedunculate racemes or few-branched panicles, to 25 cm long, the peduncle terete, to 20 cm long, the rachis fleshy, strongly flattened, the floral bracts fleshy, distichous. **Flowers** produced singly in succession over long periods of time, the sepals and petals yellow with reddish brown spots and +/– transverse bars, the column base dark red, the column apex yellow, the lip white. **Dorsal sepal** elliptic-lanceolate, acute, with revolute lateral margins, to 3.3 × 0.9 cm, the **lateral sepals** obliquely ovate, acute, with revolute basal margins, to 3 × 1.1 cm. **Petals** oblong-elliptic, acute, to 1.9 × 0.7 cm. **Lip** three-lobed, to 1.5 cm long, to 1 cm wide across the lateral lobes, the lateral lobes erect, oblong, obliquely truncate, to 0.6 × 0.3 cm, the midlobe lunate, clawed, to 1.2 cm wide, with a fleshy central pad bearing sparse trichomes, the **callus** triseriate, the basal callus glandular, variable in structure, the central callus plate-like, deeply bifid, usually with a smaller tooth to each side, the apical callus an erect bilaterally compressed tooth held between the bifid arms of the central callus. **Column** somewhat arching, dilated lateral to the stigma, to 0.8 cm long, with a pair of basal knees. **Pedicel** and **ovary** to 1.5 cm long.

Distribution: Endemic to Borneo from sea level to 800 m in elevation. **Etymology**: Named for the leopard-like markings on the sepals and petals. **Illustrations**: Chan et al. 1994:248, pl. 16b; Sweet 1980:48 (as *P. cornu-cervi* var. *picta*). **Note**: The photograph in Gruss and Wolff (1995:84) is not *P. pantherina* and appears to be an exception clone of *P. cornu-cervi* (tetraploid?) with very flat, broad segments.

Phalaenopsis pantherina has been rarely collected either for botany or horticulture. It is readily distinguished from related species by the large white lip midlobe, which bears on its upper surface a central raised

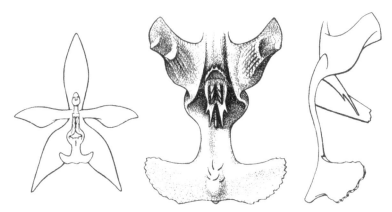

Phalaenopsis pantherina drawn from the type. Illustrator: H. R. Sweet.

keel with sparse trichomes. In horticulture *P. borneënsis* was confused with *P. pantherina* because of the similar large lip midlobe, both species attaining lip midlobes to 1.2 cm wide. The lip midlobe of *P. borneënsis* is usually ivory-white to pale yellow, not the stark white of *P. pantherina*.

Phalaenopsis pantherina is easy to recognize once you have seen a flower of the true species. Because of its rarity, however, most identifications of plants in horticulture as *P. pantherina* have been reidentified as *P. borneënsis* or *P. cornu-cervi*. A particularly thorough and well-illustrated treatment of *P. pantherina* can be found in Chan et al. (1994).

Sweet's decision to include *P. luteola* Burb. in the synonymy of *P. pantherina* was based on a specimen, later identified as *P. pantherina*, that Burbidge had sent to Reichenbach in Vienna. Subsequent to Sweet's publication, Leslie Garay located Burbidge's unpublished original watercolor of *P. luteola*, including floral dissections, at the Natural History Museum (BM). Examination of the drawing (reproduced in the color plate section of this book) shows that *P. luteola* is not synonymous to *P. pantherina* or other species of section *Polychilos* and is not linked to the herbarium specimen of *P. pantherina* in Vienna.

Section Fuscatae Sweet

Amer. Orchid Soc. Bull. 37:873. 1968. Type: *Phalaenopsis fuscata* Rchb.f.

These four species represent a very natural group characterized by having concave striped lips with a longitudinal keel, pale yellow flowers variously marked with brown, and, with the exception of *P. cochlearis*, strongly revolute sepals and petals. The lip shape and coloration is distinct and strongly dominant in breeding. The previously problematic species-level taxonomy of this group was thoroughly elucidated by Sweet.

Members of section *Fuscatae* are not common in cultivation. Most growers have difficulty keeping plants of these species for long periods of time, and they are in disfavor among phalaenopsis breeders because of their strongly revolute floral segments. Field research to establish the unique habitat requirements of these species is urgently required.

Key to the species of section *Fuscatae*

1. Sepals completely unmarked; petals with a narrow brown band at the base. . . . . *P. cochlearis*
1. Sepals variously marked with transverse brown bars and blotches; petals marked with brown to at least beyond the middle.
   2. Flowering portion of inflorescence (rachis) fleshy-thickened; lip with violet stripes. . . . . *P. viridis*
   2. Flowering portion of inflorescence not thickened relative to the base (peduncle); lip with cinnamon-colored stripes.
      3. Column slender, cylindric; basal callus originating between the lateral lip lobes (i.e., the central groove between the calli stops at the claw). . . . . *P. fuscata*
      3. Column squat, bulbous; basal callus originating at the base of the claw (i.e., the central groove between the calli extends to the base of the claw). . . . . *P. kunstleri*

Phalaenopsis cochlearis Holtt.

Orchid Rev. 72:408. 1964; *Polychilos cochlearis* (Holtt.) Shim, Malayan Nat. Journ. 36:24. 1982. Type: Sarawak. Without precise locality, leg. Kho, *Hort. Kew s.n.* (holotype: K).

Lithophytes and epiphytes. **Leaves** oblong-elliptic to elliptic-obovate, subacute, to 22 × 8 cm. **Inflorescences** panicles to 50 cm long, many-flowered, the peduncle erect, the branches arching-subpendent, to 6 cm long, the floral bracts ovate, concave, to 0.5 cm long. **Flowers** with shallowly convex segments, glossy, clear pale yellow, the base of the petals with a solitary trans-verse brown bar, the lip brighter yellow with radiating reddish brown stripes, the column white at the base becoming pale yellow toward the apex. **Dorsal sepal** oblong-elliptic, obtuse, to 2 × 0.9

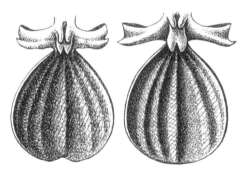

Phalaenopsis cochlearis. Illustrator: H. R. Sweet.

cm, the **lateral sepals** obliquely oblong to elliptic, acute, to 2.2×0.7 cm. **Petals** oblong, acute, to 1.8×0.5 cm. **Lip** three-lobed, to 1.2 cm long, to 1 cm wide across the expanded lateral lobes, the lateral lobes oblong-oblanceolate, subtruncate with the corners extended as teeth, the midlobe obovate-suborbicular, broadly obtuse-rounded, concave, with five raised ridges, the **callus** biseriate, subequal, the posterior callus sulcate, notched-bilobed, the anterior callus subsimilar, not sulcate. **Column** straight, dilated at the apex, to 0.7 cm long. **Pedicel** and **ovary** to 2 cm long.

Distribution: Malaysia (Malay Peninsula) and Indonesia (Sarawak). It occurs at 500–700 m in elevation. **Etymology**: From the Latin, *cochlearis* ("concave like a spoon"), an allusion to the lip shape. **Illustrations**: Die Orchidee 30(6):11. 1979; Die Orchidee 33(2): back cover. 1982; Die Orchidee 42(1): Orchideenkartei Seite 631. 1991; Gruss and Wolff 1995:86; Orchid Digest 52:73. 1988; Sweet 1980:71.

Phalaenopsis cochlearis is unusual in the section by having flat sepals and petals, unmarked sepals, and almost unmarked petals. It is distinctive for its unmarked pale yellow segments and could hardly be confused with any other species in the genus.

Shortly after its original description *P. cochlearis* was brought into cultivation. The wild-collected plants were grown, selfings and sibcrosses were distributed, and experimental hybrids were made. Very quickly thereafter both the adult plants and seedlings died off, and the species became rare in cultivation, which situation remains largely unchanged. The species is exceedingly rare in modern collections. Even many of the top phalaenopsis breeders do not own a plant of *P. cochlearis*. Clearly some critical cultural details are missing.

Phalaenopsis fuscata Rchb.f.

Gard. Chron., n.s., 2:6. 1874; *Polychilos fuscata* (Rchb.f.) Shim, Malayan Nat. Journ. 36:25. 1982. Type: Malaysia. Malay Peninsula, without precise locality, *Hort. Bull s.n.* (holotype: W).

Phalaenopsis denisiana Cogn., Gard. Chron., ser. 5, 26:82. 1899. Type: The Philippines. Without precise locality, *Hort. Denis s.n.* (holotype: BR).

Epiphytes. **Leaves** oblong-obovate to oblong-elliptic, acute, fleshy, shiny, to 30 × 10 cm. **Inflorescences** many-flowered panicles, to 40 cm long, with the peduncle erect and the rachis arching-pendent, the floral bracts ovate-triangular, acute, concave, to 0.5 cm long. **Flowers** glossy, rigid, the sepals and petals yellow with a coalesced field of brown spots at the base, with strongly revolute margins ("soda straws"), the lip

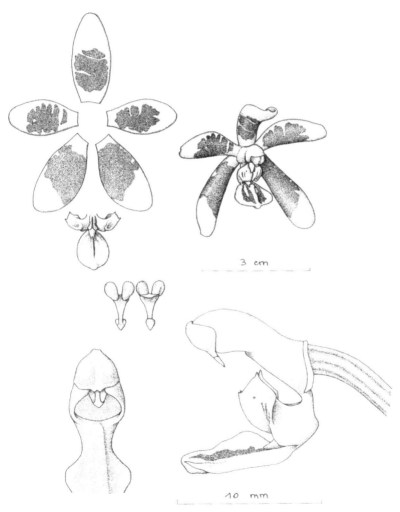

Phalaenopsis fuscata. Illustrator: F. Pupulin.

yellow with longitudinal brown stripes, the column yellow. **Dorsal sepal** elliptic-ovate, obtuse, to 1.7 × 1 cm, the **lateral sepals** obliquely elliptic, obtuse, to 1.7 × 1 cm. **Petals** oblong-elliptic to elliptic-obovate, obtuse, to 1.5 × 0.8 cm. **Lip** three-lobed, to 1.4 cm long, to 1.4 cm across the expanded lateral lobes, the lateral lobes subfalcate oblong-elliptic, subtruncate with a rounded apex, the corners extended as small teeth, the midlobe obovate-suborbicular, obtuse-rounded, concave with a low median keel, the **callus** biseriate, the posterior callus sulcate, bilobed, the lobes divergent, the anterior callus smaller, shallowly bifid. **Column** erect, straight, to 9 mm long. **Pedicel** and **ovary** 2–3 cm long.

Distribution: Malaysia (Malay Peninsula), Borneo (West Koetai), and the Philippines. **Etymology**: From the Latin, *fuscatus* ("darkened"), a reference to the dark brown blotches on the lower halves of the sepals and petals. **Illustrations**: Die Orchidee 46(5): Orchideenkartei Seite 811. 1995; Freed 1981a:937; Gruss and Wolff 1995:88, 89; Orchid Digest 49:164. 1985; Schmidt 1985:216; Sweet 1980:68, 69.

Phalaenopsis fuscata and *P. kunstleri* are the only two *Phalaenopsis* species that have bicolored sepals and petals with the basal halves brown and the apical halves yellow. They both also have sepals and petals with strongly revolute margins (see under *P. kunstleri* for a discussion of the technical differences).

Sweet described the inflorescences of *P. fuscata* as few-flowered, which is true of wild-collected specimens and the newly established cultivated plants then available to him. In my experience this is anything but true, and mature plants of *P. fuscata* regularly produce panicles in cultivation. Although each branch is relatively few-flowered, plants of *P. fuscata* are quite floriferous in their entirety.

The only record of the species for the Philippines is the cultivated type plant of *P. denisiana* from 1897. It has never been recollected in the Philippines, and it is quite possible this record was mislabeled.

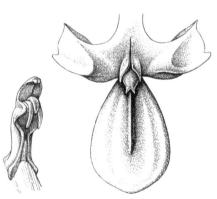

Phalaenopsis fuscata drawn from the type of *P. denisiana.* Illustrator: H. R. Sweet.

Phalaenopsis amabilis. The holotype of *P. grandiflora*, a synonym of *P. amabilis*, in the Lindley Herbarium. Photographer: E. A. Christenson. Reproduced with the kind permission of the Trustees of the Royal Botanic Gardens, Kew.

Phalaenopsis amabilis. Grower and photographer: J. A. Kopias.

Phalaenopsis amabilis var. *aurea* from Sabah, East Malaysia. Grower: The Marie Selby Botanical Gardens. Photographer: R. Wands.

Phalaenopsis amabilis 'Susan'. Grower and photographer: J. Hutchinson.

Phalaenopsis amabilis. Grower and photographer: J. A. Kopias.

Phalaenopsis amabilis. Grower: F. & M. Kaufmann. Photographer: G. Atkins.

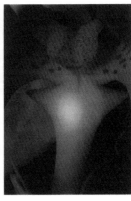

Phalaenopsis amabilis subsp. *rosenstromii* (left) compared with *Phalaenopsis amabilis* subsp. *amabilis* from Java. Grower and photographer: M. A. Clements.

Phalaenopsis amabilis, a close-up of the lip showing the characteristic shield-shaped callus. Grower and photographer: J. A. Kopias.

Phalaenopsis amabilis subsp. *rosenstromii*. Grower and photographer: M. A. Clements.

Phalaenopsis amabilis subsp. *rosenstromii*. Photograph courtesy Christenson Archives.

Phalaenopsis amboinensis var. *flavida* 'Wallbrunn'. Grower and photographer: J. Hutchinson.

Phalaenopsis amboinensis var. *flavida* 'Dragon Fire', HCC/AOS. Grower: Mistral's Orchids. Photographer: M. Steen.

Phalaenopsis amboinensis var. *flavida* 'Gold Digger', HCC/AOS. Grower: Mistral's Orchids. Photographer: M. Steen.

Phalaenopsis amboinensis var. *flavida* 'Boulder Valley', HCC/AOS. Grower: Mistral's Orchids. Photographer: M. Steen.

Phalaenopsis amboinensis. Grower and photographer: R. Griesbach.

Phalaenopsis amboinensis. Grower and photographer: R. Griesbach.

Phalaenopsis amboinensis. Grower: F. & M. Kaufmann. Photographer: G. Atkins.

Phalaenopsis amboinensis, showing the floriferous nature and few-flowered individual inflorescences of a mature plant. Grower: F. & M. Kaufmann. Photographer: G. Atkins.

Phalaenopsis aphrodite photographed in nature on Butan, the Philippines. Photographer: J. A. Fowlie.

Phalaenopsis aphrodite from the Philippines. Grower: F. Fuchs. Photographer: E. A. Christenson.

Phalaenopsis aphrodite subsp. *formosana*, the seed strain most commonly seen in cultivation, which bears smaller, rounder flowers than the Philippine subspecies. Grower: The Orchid House. Photographer: E. A. Christenson.

Phalaenopsis bastianii. Grower and photographer: P. Tuskes.

Phalaenopsis bastianii in sideview, showing the flat nature of the flowers. Grower and photographer: P. Tuskes.

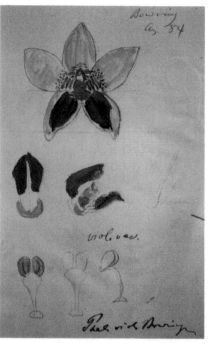

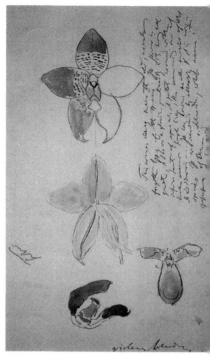

Phalaenopsis bellina f. *bowringiana*, showing the spots and transverse bars of pigment at the bases of the dorsal sepal and petals. Reichenbach's original watercolor of *P. violacea* var. *bowringiana*, conserved at the Reichenbach Herbarium, Vienna. Photographer: L. A. Garay.

Phalaenopsis ×*singuliflora*, the natural hybrid between *P. bellina* and *P. sumatrana*. Reichenbach's original watercolor of *P. violacea* var. *schroederiana*, conserved at the Reichenbach Herbarium, Vienna. Photographer: L. A. Garay.

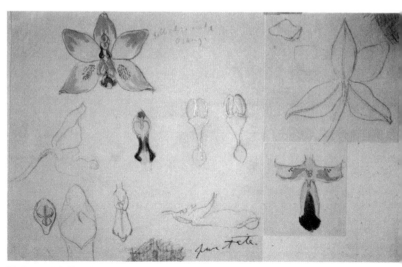

Phalaenopsis bellina f. *punctata*, showing the purple bands of pigment on the lateral sepals broken up into a series of small spots. Reichenbach's original watercolor of *P. violacea* var. *punctata*, conserved at the Reichenbach Herbarium, Vienna. Photographer: L. A. Garay.

Phalaenopsis bellina 'Chestnut Hill'. Grower:
& L Orchids. Photographer: L. B. Kuhn.

Phalaenopsis bellina. Grower and photographer:
P. Tuskes.

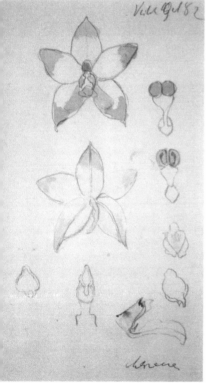

Phalaenopsis bellina. Reichenbach's original
watercolor of *P. violacea* var. *chloracea*, conserved at the Reichenbach Herbarium, Vienna.
Photographer: L. A. Garay.

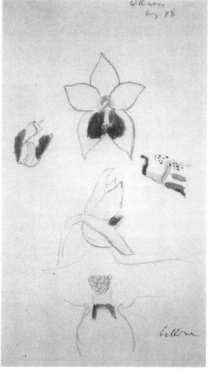

Phalaenopsis bellina. Reichenbach's original
watercolor of the type, conserved at the Reichenbach Herbarium, Vienna. Photographer:
L. A. Garay.

Phalaenopsis bellina, awarded a CCM/AOS and AM/AOS in July 1965, notable for the green sepals and petals. Grower: J & L Orchids. Photograph courtesy American Orchid Society.

Phalaenopsis bellina 'Ponkan', an outstanding example of a modern selection derived from line-breeding plants in cultivation. Photograph courtesy Christenson Archives.

halaenopsis borneënsis, the type plant. Grower and hotographer: J. Levy.

Phalaenopsis borneënsis. Grower: F. & M. Kaufmann. Photographer: G. Atkins.

halaenopsis braceana. Grower: Mistral's Orchids. Photographer: M. Steen.

Phalaenopsis buyssoniana from a select seed strain with darker flowers than typically seen in wild-collected plants. Grower: The Orchid Man. Photographer: E. A. Christenson.

Phalaenopsis celebensis, a clone with a yellowish white ground color. Grower and photographer: J. A. Kopias.

Phalaenopsis celebensis, showing the semipendent habit and richly patterned leaves. Grower: The Orchid Man. Photographer: E. A. Christenson.

Phalaenopsis cochlearis. Grower: The Marie Selby Botanical Gardens. Photographer: J. L. Henderson.

Phalaenopsis cochlearis, wild-collected in Sarawak. Grower: Truford Orchids. Photographer: T. Marsh.

Phalaenopsis chibae. Grower and photographer: J. Dixler.

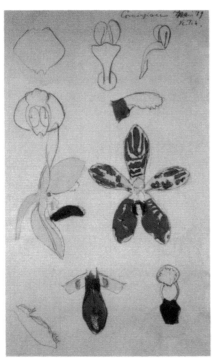

Phalaenopsis corningiana. Reichenbach's original watercolor of the type, conserved at the Reichenbach Herbarium, Vienna. Photographer: L. A. Garay.

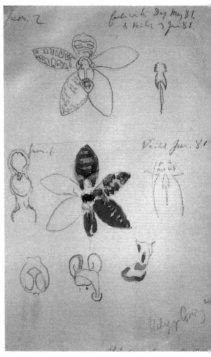

Phalaenopsis corningiana. Reichenbach's original watercolor of the type of *P. sumatrana* var. *sanguinea*, a synonym of *P. corningiana*, conserved at the Reichenbach Herbarium, Vienna. Photographer: L. A. Garay.

Phalaenopsis corningiana 'Crestwood', AM/AOS, showing the solid red phase of the species. Grower: Crestwood Orchids. Photographer: E. S. Boyett Jr.

Phalaenopsis corningiana 'Garnet Flame', a select seed strain with nearly solid garnet-red flowers. Grower: Orchids Unlimited. Photographer: J. L. Fischer.

Phalaenopsis corningiana 'Janet'. Grower: J & L Orchids. Photographer: L. B. Kuhn.

Phalaenopsis cornu-cervi, exhibiting large, dark spots on the sepals and petals. Grower and photographer: P. Tuskes.

Phalaenopsis cornu-cervi, exhibiting fine markings on the sepals and petals. Grower and photographer: P. Tuskes.

Phalaenopsis cornu-cervi 'Wallbrunn'. Grower and photographer: J. Hutchinson.

Phalaenopsis cornu-cervi 'OrchidPhile', a very darkly marked flower. Grower: C. Raven-Riemann. Photograph © Charles Marden Fitch.

Phalaenopsis deliciosa, showing the undulate leaf margins characteristic of the species. Grower and photographer: P. Tuskes.

Phalaenopsis deliciosa. Grower and photographer: P. Tuskes.

Phalaenopsis deliciosa. Grower and photographer: R. Griesbach.

Phalaenopsis deliciosa. Grower: Truford Orchids. Photographer: T. Marsh.

Phalaenopsis deliciosa subsp. *hookeriana* in sideview. Grower and photographer: E. A. Christenson.

Phalaenopsis deliciosa subsp. *hookeriana.* Grower and photographer: E. A. Christenson.

Phalaenopsis doweryënsis. Grower and photographer: D. M. Lowder.

Phalaenopsis equestris 'Fleur de Lys', a famous early peloric form from Fred Thornton. Grower: E. A. Christenson. Photographer: M. Kindlmann.

Phalaenopsis equestris with white flowers that retain yellow markings on the lip. Grower: Mistral's Orchids. Photographer: M. Steen.

Phalaenopsis equestris var. *rosea* from a wild-collected plant. Grower and photographer: E. A. Christenson.

Phalaenopsis equestris 'Helen's Choice', AM/AOS, a choice clone derived from the famous clone *P. equestris* 'Riverbend', AM/AOS. Grower: H. Jones. Photograph courtesy American Orchid Society.

Phalaenopsis equestris. Grower and photographer: P. Tuskes.

Phalaenopsis equestris 'Sabetto 1 of 3', AM/AOS. Grower and photographer: J. Hutchinson.

Phalaenopsis equestris 'Elizabeth', AM/AOS. Grower and photographer: J. Hutchinson.

Phalaenopsis equestris, a nearly pure white flower with only a pigmented callus. Grower: F. & M. Kaufmann. Photographer: G. Atkins.

Phalaenopsis equestris, showing its floriferous nature on small plants. Grower: F. & M. Kaufmann. Photographer: G. Atkins.

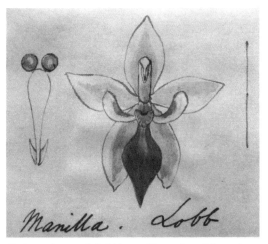

Phalaenopsis equestris. Lobb's type illustration of *P. rosea* in the Lindley Herbarium. Photographer: E. A. Christenson. Reproduced with the kind permission of the Trustees of the Royal Botanic Gardens, Kew.

Phalaenopsis equestris f. *alba* 'Orchid-Phile', HCC/AOS. Grower: C. Raven-Riemann. Photograph © Charles Marden Fitch.

Phalaenopsis equestris f. *alba* 'Tinkerbelle', HCC/AOS. Grower: C. Raven-Riemann. Photograph © Charles Marden Fitch.

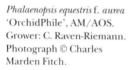
Phalaenopsis equestris f. *aurea* 'OrchidPhile', AM/AOS. Grower: C. Raven-Riemann. Photograph © Charles Marden Fitch.

Phalaenopsis fasciata 'Maria', AM/AOS. Photograph courtesy Christenson Archives.

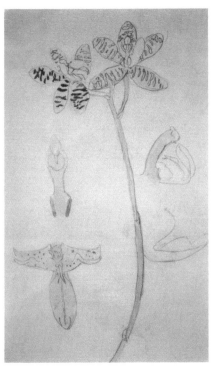

Phalaenopsis fasciata. Reichenbach's original watercolor of the type, conserved at the Reichenbach Herbarium, Vienna. Photographer: L. A. Garay.

The widely used breeding clone 'John E', which is in fact a hybrid between *Phalaenopsis fasciata* and *P. lueddemanniana*. Grower and photographer: P. Tuskes.

Phalaenopsis fasciata. Grower and photographer: J. Barrick.

Phalaenopsis natural hybrid awarded as *P. lueddemanniana* var. *ochracea* 'J & L', AM/AOS. This supposedly select form of the species now known as *P. fasciata* is actually a natural hybrid between *P. fasciata* and *P. hieroglyphica.* Grower: J & L Orchids. Photographer: E. Waxman.

Phalaenopsis fimbriata 'J & L', CBM/AOS. Grower: J & L Orchids. Photographer: L. B. Kuhn.

Phalaenopsis floresensis with a fully open and expanded flower. Grower and photographer: P. Tuskes.

Phalaenopsis floresensis, showing the dense trichomes on the lip midlobe. Grower and photographer: P. Tuskes.

Phalaenopsis fimbriata. Grower and photographer: P. Tuskes.

Phalaenopsis fuscata 'J & L', CBM/AOS, with one of the lateral lip lobes removed to reveal the callus. Grower: J & L Orchids. Photographer: L. B. Kuhn.

Phalaenopsis fuscata. Grower: J & L Orchids. Photographer: G. Kennedy.

Phalaenopsis fuscata from Malaya, southwest of Kampar. Grower: Truford Orchids. Photographer: T. Marsh.

Phalaenopsis fuscata in sideview. Grower and photographer: P. Tuskes.

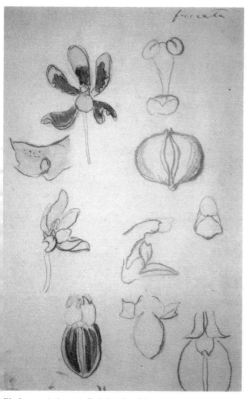

A variant of *Phalaenopsis fuscata* that may represent a new species. The clone was collected in Borneo, east of Ranau, at 600 m in elevation in 1983. Grower: Truford Orchids. Photographer: T. Marsh.

Phalaenopsis fuscata. Reichenbach's original watercolor of the type, conserved at the Reichenbach Herbarium, Vienna. Photographer: L. A. Garay.

The expanded lip of the same variant of *Phalaenopsis fuscata.* Grower: Truford Orchids. Photographer: T. Marsh.

Phalaenopsis fuscata. Grower and photographer: P. Tuskes.

Phalaenopsis gibbosa with a still expanding flower. Grower and photographer: P. Tuskes.

Phalaenopsis gibbosa with the flowers fully open and the segments lightly reflexed. Grower and photographer: P. Tuskes.

Phalaenopsis gibbosa flowering on atypically short inflorescences on a newly established plant. Grower and photographer: P. Tuskes.

Phalaenopsis gigantea 'Dale', HCC/AOS.
Grower: Marshall Orchids. Photograph courtesy American Orchid Society.

Phalaenopsis gigantea 'Orchidglade', CCM/AOS,
AM/AOS, a famous early clone, showing the
large leaf produced in the wild and a smaller
leaf produced in cultivation. Grower: Jones &
Scully Orchids. Photograph courtesy American
Orchid Society.

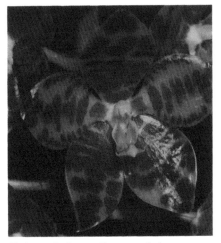

Phalaenopsis gigantea. Grower and photographer: J. A. Kopias.

Phalaenopsis hainanensis imported into Kalimpong, India, from an unknown locality in Myanmar. Grower: G. M. Pradhan. Photographer: E. A. Christenson.

Phalaenopsis hainanensis. Grower: Mistral's Orchids. Photographer: M. Steen.

Phalaenopsis hieroglyphica. Grower and photographer: R. Griesbach.

Phalaenopsis hieroglyphica, a particularly large-flowered example derived from select line-breeding in cultivation. Grower: The Orchid Man. Photographer: E. A. Christenson.

Phalaenopsis hieroglyphica. Grower and photographer: J. A. Kopias.

Phalaenopsis honghenensis in sideview. Grower: World of Orchids. Photographer: K. Richards.

Phalaenopsis honghenensis, a particularly dark pink clone. Grower and photographer: J. Levy.

Phalaenopsis honghenensis, a clone that blends green and pink coloration. Grower: World of Orchids. Photographer: K. Richards.

Phalaenopsis honghenensis 'Memoria Herman Sweet', CBR/AOS, a greenish flower with almost no pink coloration in the sepals and petals. Grower and photographer: J. Levy.

Phalaenopsis honghenensis. Grower and photographer: P. Tuskes.

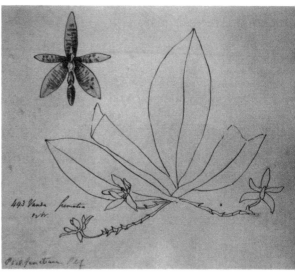

Phalaenopsis inscriptiosinensis. This watercolor in the Lindley Herbarium, which served as the basis for *P. sumatrana*, has been reinterpreted as *P. inscriptiosinensis.* Photographer: E. A. Christenson. Reproduced with the kind permission of the Trustees of the Royal Botanic Gardens, Kew.

Phalaenopsis inscriptiosinensis, showing the characteristically short inflorescences, which usually bear single flowers in succession. Grower: Simanis Orchids. Photographer: J. B. Comber.

Phalaenopsis inscriptiosinensis with a pronounced yellowish ground color. Grower: F. & M. Kaufmann. Photographer: G. Atkins.

Phalaenopsis inscriptiosinensis, exhibiting the characteristically short inflorescences that typically bear single flowers in succession. Grower: F. & M. Kaufmann. Photographer: G. Atkins.

Phalaenopsis inscriptiosinensis. Grower and photographer: J. Barrick.

Phalaenopsis ×intermedia var. *portei* 'J & ❚ which represents the darkest lip color the species. Grower: J & L Orchids. Ph◌ tographer: L. B. Kuhn.

The peloric forms of *Phalaenopsis ×intermedia* from the island of Leyte, to which the informal vari◌ etal name *diezii* has been applied. Grower and photographer: P. Tuskes.

Phalaenopsis javanica. Grower and photographer: P. Tuskes.

Phalaenopsis kunstleri. Grower: R. Finley. Photographer: E. A. Christenson.

Phalaenopsis javanica. Grower and photographer: P. Tuskes.

Phalaenopsis ×*leucorrhoda* (*aphrodite* × *schilleriana*), a manmade remake of the natural hybrid. Grower and photographer: R. Griesbach.

Phalaenopsis lindenii in sideview.
Grower and photographer: P. Tuskes.

Phalaenopsis lindenii. Grower and photographer: P. Tuske

Phalaenopsis lindenii. Grower and photographer: P. Tuskes.

Phalaenopsis lindenii. Grower and photographer: R. Griesbach.

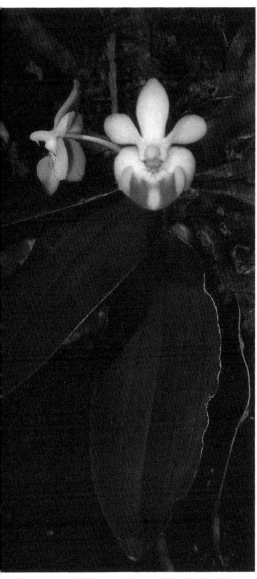

Phalaenopsis lobbii. Grower and photographer: E. A. Christenson.

Phalaenopsis lobbii f. *flava.* Grower and photographer: N. Trudel.

Phalaenopsis lobbii f. *flava.* Grower: Mistral's Orchids. Photographer: M. Steen.

Phalaenopsis lobbii f. *flava.* Grower and photographer: P. Tuskes.

Phalaenopsis lobbii f. *flava.* Grower and photographer: N. Trudel.

The type of *Phalaenopsis lobbii* f. *flavilabia* based on *Trudel* 585. Grower and photographer: N. Trudel.

Phalaenopsis lobbii f. *flava*. Grower and photographer: N. Trudel.

Phalaenopsis lobbii. Grower and photographer: P. Tuskes.

Phalaenopsis lowii flowering as a lithophyte in nature. Photographer: Teerapong.

Phalaenopsis lowii as an epiphyte in nature. Photograph © Charles Marden Fitch.

Phalaenopsis lowii flowering in the wild. Photographer: Teerapong.

Phalaenopsis lueddemanniana var. *ochracea* 'Crestwood', exhibiting the lack of any purple anthocyanin pigments. Grower and photographer: J. Hutchinson.

Phalaenopsis lueddemanniana. Grower and photographer: R. Griesbach.

Phalaenopsis lueddemanniana var. *delicata* 'OrchidPhile'. Grower: C. Raven-Riemann. Photograph © Charles Marden Fitch.

Phalaenopsis lueddemanniana 'Jo San', HCC/AOS, one of many clones that represent preferential selection of natural hybrids over pure species in cultivation. The influence of *P. hieroglyphica* is seen in the broad, flat sepals and petals and the more intricate markings. Grower: Mistral's Orchids. Photographer: M. Steen.

Burbidge's original watercolor of *Phalaenopsis luteola*, conserved at the Natural History Museum (BM). Photographer: L. A. Garay. Reproduced with the kind permission of the Trustees of the Natural History Museum.

Phalaenopsis luteola. Grower and photographer L. Röllke.

Phalaenopsis maculata. Reichenbach's original watercolor of the type, conserved at the Reichenbach Herbarium, Vienna. Photographer: L. A. Garay.

Phalaenopsis maculata. Grower and photographer: P. Tuskes.

Phalaenopsis maculata f. *flava* 'Magnifico', CHM/AOS, the type of this color form. Grower and photographer: J. Levy.

Phalaenopsis maculata. Grower: J & L Orchids. Photographer: L. B. Kuhn.

Phalaenopsis maculata, a clone with particularly intense red markings and lip. Grower and photographer: J. Barrick.

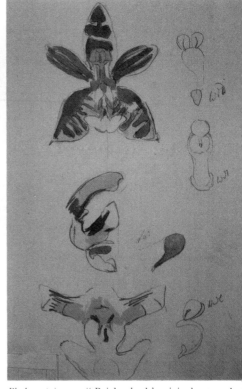

Phalaenopsis mannii lip in sideview, showing two of the three sets of calli that characterize the species of section *Polychilos.* Grower: J & L Orchids. Photographer: G. Kennedy.

Phalaenopsis mannii. Reichenbach's original watercolor of *P. boxallii,* considered a synonym of *P. mannii,* conserved at the Reichenbach Herbarium, Vienna. Photographer: L. A. Garay.

Phalaenopsis mannii. Grower and photographer: P. Tuskes.

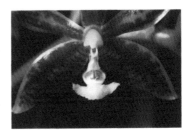

Phalaenopsis mannii, a close-up of the lip. Grower and photographer: P. Tuskes.

Phalaenopsis mannii f. *flava*. Grower: MAJ Orchids. Photographer: E. A. Christenson.

Phalaenopsis mannii f. *flava*. Grower and photographer: P. Tuskes.

Phalaenopsis mannii. Grower and photographer: A. Black.

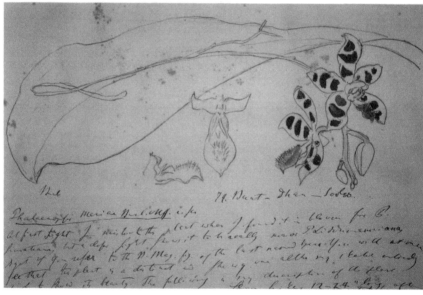

Phalaenopsis mariae. Reichenbach's watercolor of Burbidge's original drawing, conserved at the Reichenbach Herbarium, Vienna. Photographer: L. A. Garay.

Phalaenopsis mariae. Grower and photographer: P. Tuskes.

Phalaenopsis mariae in sideview, showing the large tuft of trichomes on the lip. Grower and photographer: P. Tuskes.

Phalaenopsis mariae. Grower: Marie Selby Botanical Gardens. Photographer: L. B. Kuhn.

Phalaenopsis micholitzii. Grower and photographer: P. Tuskes.

Phalaenopsis minus. Grower: Suphachadiwong.
Photographer: R. Griesbach.

Phalaenopsis modesta. Grower and photographer: P. Tuskes.

Phalaenopsis pallens. Grower and photographer:
P. Tuskes.

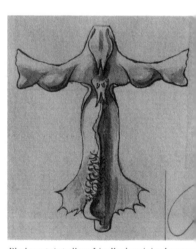

Phalaenopsis pallens. Lindley's original water
color of the type of *Trichoglottis pallens,* the
basionym of *P. pallens,* in the Lindley
Herbarium. Photographer: E. A. Christenson. Reproduced with the kind permission
of the Trustees of the Royal Botanic Gardens, Kew.

Phalaenopsis pantherina. Grower: Tenom Research Center. Photographer: E. A. Christenson.

Phalaenopsis parishii. Photograph courtesy Christenson Archives.

Phalaenopsis parishii, a newly opened flower that has yet to have its sepals and petals reflex. Grower and photographer: P. Tuskes.

Phalaenopsis parishii. Grower and photographer: P. Tuskes.

Phalaenopsis philippinensis, showing the species' tendency for mass, simultaneous flowering. Grower: Mistral's Orchids. Photographer: M. Steen.

Phalaenopsis pulcherrima. Grower: J & L Orchids. Photographer: L. B. Kuhn.

Phalaenopsis pulcherrima, a slightly bluish phase. Grower: F. & M. Kaufmann. Photographer: G. Atkins.

Phalaenopsis pulchra. Grower and photographer: P. Tuskes.

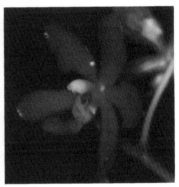

Phalaenopsis pulchra 'Orchidglade', SM/SFOS, which clone has been consistently confused in horticulture with *P. speciosa.* Grower and photographer: E. A. Christenson.

Phalaenopsis pulchra 'Oscar', AM/AOS, perhaps the finest, flattest clone in cultivation. Grower and photographer: J. Hutchinson.

Phalaenopsis pulcherrima, exhibiting the characteristic erect inflorescences. Grower: F. & M. Kaufmann. Photographer: G. Atkins.

Phalaenopsis reichenbachiana 'OrchidPhile', CBR/AOS. Grower: C. Raven-Riemann. Photograph © Charles Marden Fitch.

Phalaenopsis reichenbachiana, exhibiting the dense trichomes on the lip and flat sepals and petals that distinguish it from the closely related *P. fasciata*. Grower and photographer: R. Griesbach.

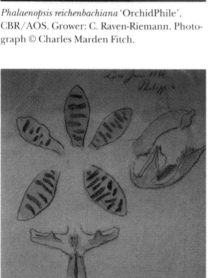

Phalaenopsis reichenbachiana. Reichenbach's original watercolor of the type, conserved at the Reichenbach Herbarium, Vienna. Photographer: L. A. Garay.

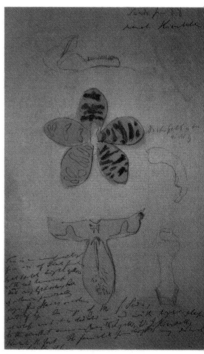

Phalaenopsis reichenbachiana. Reichenbach's original watercolor of *P. sumatrana* var. *kimballiana*, conserved at the Reichenbach Herbarium, Vienna. Photographer: L. A. Garay.

Phalaenopsis sanderiana, an extremely dark pink clone achieved by selective line-breeding in cultivation. Grower: Arthur Freed Orchids. Photographer: E. A. Christenson.

Phalaenopsis sanderiana f. *alba* 'J & L', CBM/AOS. Grower: J & L Orchids. Photographer: L. B. Kuhn.

Phalaenopsis sanderiana f. *alba.* Grower and photographer: P. Tuskes.

Phalaenopsis sanderiana 'South Olive', FCC/AOS, one of the finest clones ever in cultivation. Grower: L. & V. Vaughn. Photographer: L. B. Kuhn.

Phalaenopsis sanderiana, showing the pale pink blush typical of the species. Grower: J & L Orchids. Photographer: L. B. Kuhn.

Phalaenopsis sanderiana, showing the light pink flowers typical of select strains in cultivation. Grower and photographer: P. Tuskes.

Phalaenopsis sanderiana 'Varina', FCC/AOS, another of the finest clones in cultivation. Grower: L. & V. Vaughn. Photographer: L. B. Kuhn.

Phalaenopsis sanderiana. Grower: F. & M. Kaufmann. Photographer: G. Atkins.

Phalaenopsis schilleriana, a wild-collected diploid selection of the species. Grower: J & L Orchids. Photographer: L. B. Kuhn.

Phalaenopsis schilleriana 'Varina', an exceptional early tetraploid selection of the species. Grower: L. & V. Vaughn. Photographer: L. B. Kuhn.

Phalaenopsis speciosa. Reichenbach's original watercolor of the type, conserved at the Reichenbach Herbarium, Vienna. Photographer: L. A. Garay.

Phalaenopsis stobartiana. Reichenbach's original watercolor of the type, conserved at the Reichenbach Herbarium, Vienna. Note the many-flowered inflorescence and the minute, nipple-like spur. Photographer: L. A. Garay.

Phalaenopsis stobartiana 'Tahitian Dancer', showing the many-flowered inflorescence that distinguishes this rare species from other green-flowered members of the subgenus. Photograph courtesy Christenson Archives.

Phalaenopsis stobartiana from a plant in cultivation in Japan. Photograph courtesy Paphanatics, unLtd.

Phalaenopsis stuartiana, showing the typical distribution of pigments in the flower. Grower and photographer: P. Tuskes.

Phalaenopsis stuartiana. Grower: Mistral's Orchids. Photographer: M. Steen.

Phalaenopsis stuartiana f. *punctatissima* 'Larkin Valley', AM/AOS, showing the richly spotted sepals and petals of what is commonly called the Larkin Valley strain or type. Grower and photographer: P. Tuskes.

Phalaenopsis stuartiana 'Apopka', a select clone with particularly broad, rounded petals. Grower and photographer: J. Hutchinson.

Phalaenopsis stuartiana, the richly mottled leaves. Grower: The Orchid Man. Photographer: E. A. Christenson.

Phalaenopsis sumatrana. Grower: Simanis Orchids. Photographer: J. B. Comber.

Phalaenopsis sumatrana from the southern Philippines. Photograph courtesy Christenson Archives.

halaenopsis sumatrana 'J & L', CBM/AOS, representing e green phase that appears to be restricted to the and of Borneo. Grower: J & L Orchids. Photograph urtesy American Orchid Society.

Phalaenopsis sumatrana. Grower and photographer: P. Tuskes.

halaenopsis sumatrana, a heavily pigmented form that ay represent introgression with *P. corningiana*. ower: F. & M. Kaufmann. Photographer: G. Atkins.

Phalaenopsis taenialis. Grower and photographer: E. A. Christenson.

Phalaenopsis taenialis. Grower and photographer: E. A. Christenson.

Phalaenopsis tetraspis in sideview, showing the conspicuous boss of trichomes on the lip. Grower and photographer: P. Tuskes.

Phalaenopsis tetraspis. Grower and photographer: P. Tuskes.

Phalaenopsis ×*veitchi-ana* (*equestris* × *schil-leriana*), a manmade remake of the natural hybrid, with silvery leaves showing the influence of *P. schilleri-ana* as parent. Grower and photographer: R. Griesbach.

Phalaenopsis ×*veitchiana* 'Stones River', AM/AOS, a superior clone resulting from the artificial crossing of select parents. Grower: Stones River Orchids. Photographer: E. S. Boyett Jr.

Phalaenopsis venosa 'Brown Summit', HCC/ AOS. Grower: Mistral's Orchids. Photographer: M. Steen.

Phalaenopsis venosa. Grower and photographer: P. Tuskes.

Phalaenopsis venosa 'Ontario', HCC/AOS. Grower: Mistral's Orchids. Photographer: M. Steen.

Phalaenopsis violacea f. *alba.* Grower: J. Watkins. Photographer: E. A. Christenson.

Phalaenopsis violacea f. *coerulea*. Grower: The Orchid Man. Photographer: E. A. Christenson.

Phalaenopsis violacea, a particularly dark clone. Grower: F. & M. Kaufmann. Photographer: G. Atkins.

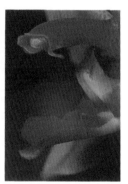

Phalaenopsis violacea, a close-up of the lip. Grower and photographer: J. A. Kopias.

Phalaenopsis violacea. Grower and photographer: P. Tuskes.

Phalaenopsis viridis. Grower: Mistral's Orchids. Photographer: M. Steen.

Phalaenopsis viridis. Grower and photographer: P. Tuskes.

Phalaenopsis wilsonii with average coloration, blooming on an atypically short inflorescence from a newly established import. Grower and photographer: P. Tuskes.

Phalaenopsis wilsonii 'Carri's Envy', one of the darkest clones obtained from the ecologically dwarfed population described as *P. minor.* Grower: Mistral's Orchids. Photographer: M. Steen.

Phalaenopsis kunstleri J. D. Hook.

Fl. Brit. India 6:30. 1890; *Polychilos kunstleri* (J. D. Hook.) Shim, Malayan Nat. Journ. 36:25. 1982. Type: Malaysia. Perak, *Kunstler s.n.* (lectotype, here designated: K; isolectotype: CAL).

Phalaenopsis fuscata var. *kunstleri* Hort., Orchid Rev. 75: index p. 10. 1967, nom. nud.

Epiphytes. **Leaves** two to four, oblanceolate-obovate, acute, to 24 × 8 cm. **Inflorescences** arching to suberect long-pedunculate racemes or panicles, to 40 cm long, the floral bracts ovate, acute, to 0.5 cm long. **Flowers** opening simultaneously, glossy, rigid, the sepals and petals pale yellow with a coalesced field of brown spots at the base, with strongly revolute margins ("soda straws"), the lip pale yellow with longitudinal brown stripes, the column very pale yellow. **Sepals** elliptic, obtuse, to 2 × 1.1 cm. **Petals** subsimilar to the sepals, to 1.5 × 0.8 cm. **Lip** three-lobed, to 1.2 cm long, to 1 cm wide across the expanded lateral lobes, the lateral lobes oblong, retrorsely curved, with tooth-like corners and a thickened callus-like center, the midlobe elliptic-suborbicular, concave with a central longitudinal keel, the **callus** biseriate, the posterior callus a pair of parallel low ridges from the base of the claw to near the base of the midlobe, the anterior callus a pair of small teeth directly in front of the posterior callus and just extending to the base of the midlobe. **Column** stout, squat, somewhat bulbous, to 0.9 cm long. **Pedicel** and **ovary** to 2 cm long.

Distribution: Myanmar and the Malay Peninsula. **Etymology**: Named for the original collector of the species, Hermann H. Kunstler, a professional plant collector for Sir George King. **Illustrations**: Amer. Orchid Soc. Bull. 35:752. 1966 (as *P. fuscata*); Awards Quart. 20(3):123. 1989; Gruss and Wolff 1995:90; Orchid Digest 40: 88. 1976; Sweet 1980:69, 73.

Phalaenopsis kunstleri is remarkable because of its astonishing simi-

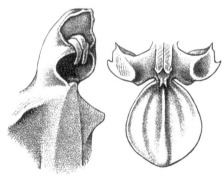

Phalaenopsis kunstleri drawn from the type. Illustrator: H. R. Sweet.

larity to *P. fuscata*. Without examination of the callus under magnifica-
tion the two species are nearly identical, sharing identical coloration,
similar flower size, and strongly revolute floral segments. *Phalaenopsis*
kunstleri has always been rather rare in cultivation, and many growers
have questioned whether *P. kunstleri* is really just a variant of *P. fuscata*.
They are amply distinct because of the consistent differences in the
column and the basal callus.

The column of *P. kunstleri* is squat and bulbous compared to the
slender, cylindric column of *P. fuscata*. In *P. kunstleri* the fleshy central
ridge below the stigma abuts the stigma. In *P. fuscata* the ridge is indistinct for some distance below the stigma. The basal callus of *P. kunstleri*
arises from the base of the lip claw and the groove separating the two
halves of the callus is clearly visible on the claw. In *P. fuscata* the callus
originates from above the claw at the bases of the lateral lip lobes.

Phalaenopsis viridis J. J. Sm.

Bull. Dept. Agric. Ind. Néerl. 5:21. 1907; *Polychilos viridis* (J. J.
Sm.) Shim, Malayan Nat. Journ. 36:26. 1982. Type: Indonesia.
Sumatra, east coast, Deli, *Held s.n.* (holotype: BO).

Phalaenopsis forbesii Ridl., J. Bot. 63, suppl.:118. 1925. Type: Indonesia. Sumatra, hills near Paoe, Palembang, *Forbes 2521* (holotype: BM).

Epiphytes. **Leaves** ovate to elliptic-ovate, tapered to the base, acute or
subobtuse, leathery, shiny, to 30 × 8 cm. **Inflorescences** erect racemes
or few-branched panicles, to 40 cm long, long-pedunculate, the rachis
fleshy-thickened, the floral bracts ovate, acute, concave, to 0.3 cm long.
Flowers opening simultaneously, the sepals and petals with a greenish
yellow ground color almost completely obscured by a dark brown overlay, the lip and column white, all segments with strongly revolute margins. **Dorsal sepal** oblong-elliptic to oblong-obovate, obtuse, to 2 × 0.9
cm, the **lateral sepals** subsimilar to the dorsal sepal, oblique, acute, to
1.7 × 0.9 cm. **Petals** elliptic to elliptic-ovate, acute, to 1.6 × 0.8 cm. **Lip**
three-lobed, to 1 cm long, to 1 cm across the expanded lateral lobes,
the lateral lobes elliptic, truncate at the apex with both corners extended as narrow teeth, the midlobe elliptic-obovate, obtuse-rounded,

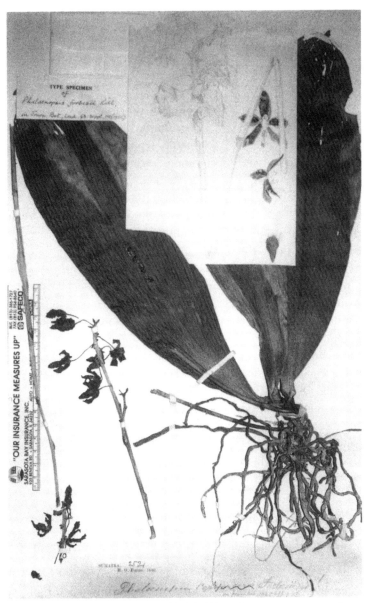

Phalaenopsis viridis. The holotype of *P. forbesii* from Sumatra, a synonym of
P. viridis, conserved at the Natural History Museum (BM). Photographer:
E. A. Christenson. Reproduced with the kind permission of the Trustees of
the Natural History Museum.

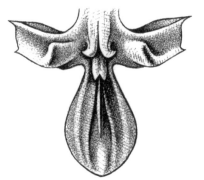

Phalaenopsis viridis drawn from the type. Illustrator: H. R. Sweet.

shallowly concave with a low median keel, the **callus** biseriate, the posterior callus sulcate, bilobed, the anterior callus oblong, notched at the apex. **Column** stout, almost straight, to 0.8 cm long. **Pedicel** and **ovary** to 2 cm long.

Distribution: Endemic to Indonesia (Sumatra). It is recorded from 1000 m in elevation. **Etymology**: From the Latin, *viridis* ("green"), an allusion to the flower color. **Illustrations**: Awards Quart. 21(3): 142. 1990; Die Orchidee 42(2): Orchideenkartei Seite 643. 1991; Gruss and Wolff 1995:91; Orchid Digest 49: 89. 1985; Sweet 1980:67.

Phalaenopsis viridis is a little-known species with rather small nondescript flowers. Although it is in cultivation, one rarely sees it exhibited. Having little to contribute to offspring, the species is not often used in hybridization. It should be noted, however, that mature plants have a high flower count. The flowers open simultaneously, but the inflorescences continue to elongate and periodically reflower, each flush comprising five or six flowers. The preserved inflorescences of *Forbes 2210* (BM) had about 35 flowers on the primary rachis.

Sweet knew this species only from three herbarium specimens and a few color photographs. One additional record has been subsequently located at the Natural History Museum (BM) in the form of a drawing by C. J. Brooks made in October 1916 of a plant seen in Sumatra at Benkoelen, Lebong Tandai.

Section Amboinenses Sweet

Amer. Orchid Soc. Bull. 37:874. 1968. Type: *Phalaenopsis amboinensis* J. J. Sm.

Phalaenopsis subsection *Glabrae* Sweet, Amer. Orchid Soc. Bull. 37:874. 1968, syn. nov. Type: *Phalaenopsis modesta* J. J. Sm.

Phalaenopsis subsection *Hirsutae* Sweet, Amer. Orchid Soc. Bull. 37:874. 1968, syn. nov. Type: *Phalaenopsis pallens* (Lindl.) Rchb.f.

Phalaenopsis subsection *Lueddemannianae* Sweet, Genus *Phalaenopsis* 15. 1980, syn. nov. Type: *Phalaenopsis lueddemanniana* Rchb.f.

Sweet accepted a section *Amboinenses* separate from a section *Zebrinae* on the basis of relative petal width.[*] Section *Amboinenses* was defined by having rotuliform (wheel-shaped) flowers (petals broadly elliptic, twice or less long as wide) as compared to section *Zebrinae*, in which the flowers are stellate (petals narrowly obovate or oblanceolate, more than twice as long as wide). While there are practical conveniences to erecting sections based on easy-to-observe characters, I do not think that use of this particular character results in a valid subdivision of the genus.

Instead, I choose to emphasize the hooded anther bed of *P. sumatrana* and its allies and maintain a narrowly defined section *Zebrinae*, one which corresponds to Sweet's subsection *Zebrinae*. The remaining three subsections of Sweet's section *Zebrinae* are transferred to and placed in the synonymy of section *Amboinenses*, characterized by having an unadorned anther bed.

Dividing the species into subsections as done by Sweet does not appear to produce natural groupings of species, and I reject them. Subsection *Glabrae* was based primarily on the two species having a glabrous lip (devoid of trichomes). That feature is not valid even for the type species, *P. modesta*, as acknowledged by Sweet and later authors. Subsection *Lueddemannianae* was distinguished from subsection *Hirsutae* by its having the posterior callus "variously tuberculate." The presence of and degree to which irregularly shaped glandular tissue develops ("tuberculate") I have not found to be a significant taxonomic character, even at the species level. The other characters mentioned, such as the degree of trichomes on the midlobe of the lip in subsection *Hirsutae*, form a mosaic pattern. They are variable and occur in Sweet's other groups; for example, *P. pulchra*, placed in subsection *Lueddemannianae* by Sweet, has trichomes on the midlobe of the lip similar to *P. pallens*, placed in subsection *Hirsutae* by Sweet. In the absence of nonmorphological data, I think it best to treat all these species as part of a single, broadly defined section *Amboinenses*.

---

[*] The other characters cited by Sweet (1980) for section *Amboinenses*—"the midlobe of lip fleshy, always convex with a single thin median keel"—are found throughout both section *Amboinenses* and section *Zebrinae*.

Key to the species of section *Amboinenses*

1. Dorsal sepal of one color (+/– green at the apex), without spots or bars of darker pigment.
  2. Sepals and petals pink to purple.
    3. Flowers glossy, purple, the lateral sepals usually with revolute margins, the apex of the midlobe of the lip fan-shaped with an irregular margin.
    . . . . *P. pulchra*
    3. Flowers not glossy, pink, the lateral sepals usually flat, the apex of the midlobe of the lip gently rounded with a smooth margin. . . . . *P. violacea*
  2. Sepals and petals white, greenish or yellowish.
    4. Lateral sepals with a large purple stain along their inner halves, the lip without any trichomes. . . . . *P. bellina*
    4. Lateral sepals unmarked or with small spots or bars, the midlobe of the lip with trichomes.
      5. Lateral sepals without any markings. . . . . *P. micholitzii*
      5. Lateral sepals with small markings toward the base.
        6. Midlobe of the lip purple with the lateral margins lobulate and incurved (erect), the lateral sepals with transverse pink barring.
        . . . . *P. fimbriata*
        6. Midlobe of the lip white with the lateral margins not lobulate and not incurved, the lateral sepals with very pale brown spotting.
        . . . . *P. floresensis*
1. Dorsal sepal of more than one color, with prominent spots and bars of darker pigment.
      7. Midlobe of the lip +/– glabrous.
        8. Lateral lobes of the lip about one-fourth the length of the midlobe. . . . . *P. robinsonii*
        8. Lateral lobes of the lip more than half the length of the midlobe.
          9. Inflorescences pendent, the sepals and petals broad, forming a round flower with overlapping segments. . . . . *P. gigantea*
          9. Inflorescences erect to arching, the sepals and petals not broad, resulting in a star-shaped flower without overlapping segments.
            10. Sepals and petals with a yellow or greenish yellow ground color.

11. Callus biseriate, the posterior callus a boss of retrorse
fleshy tubercles. . . . . *P. fasciata*
11. Callus biseriate, the posterior callus bidentate.
  12. Sepals and petals broadly obtuse-rounded; the midlobe
  of the lip with a terminal fleshy pad. . . . . . *P. doweryënsis*
  12. Sepals and petals acute; the midlobe of the lip convex,
  without a distinct fleshy pad. . . . . *P. luteola*
10. Sepals and petals never with a yellow ground color, at most
off-white.
    13. Flowers white with pink-purple transverse barring, the
    lip purple. . . . . *P. modesta*
    13. Flowers off-white with reddish brown spots or very
    broad barring, the lip scarlet. . . . . *P. maculata*
7. Midlobe of the lip always with trichomes present, usually in a dense
boss.
    14. Inflorescences pendent.
      15. Flowers strongly cupped, the sepals and petals
      patterned with stripes composed of squarish bars.
      . . . . *P. javanica*
      15. Flowers not strongly cupped, the sepals and petals
      patterned with large red or violet transverse bars
      not arranged in longitudinal stripes. . . . *P. mariae*
    14. Inflorescences erect to arching.
      16. Midlobe of the lip with a sulcate, double-edged
      keel with serrulate margins. . . . . . *P. amboinensis*
      16. Midlobe of the lip with a single keel with entire
      margins.
        17. Midlobe of the lip with entire margins.
          18. Flowers with white or off-white ground
          color, heavily marked with purple barring,
          the bases of the sepals and petals not
          marked differently, the lip mostly purple-
          pink. . . . . *P. lueddemanniana*
          18. Flowers with yellow ground color all but ob-
          scured by dense overlay of brown barring,
          the bases of the sepals and petal white, the
          lip mostly white. . . . . *P. venosa*

17. Midlobe of the lip with small teeth along the margins lateral to the apex.
    19. Ground color of the sepals and petals uniformly pale yellow.
        20. Apex of the lip acute, the lateral lobes of the lip notched. . . ***P. reichenbachiana***
        20. Apex of the lip obtuse, bluntly rounded, the lateral lobes of the lip flat. . . . . ***P. pallens***
    19. Ground color of the sepals and petals white, +/− pale pink suffusion or yellow suffusion toward the apices.
        21. Sepals and petals marked with several large transverse solid brownish red bars, lip purple with only the very apex white. . . . . ***P. bastianii***
        21. Sepals and petals marked with numerous intricate transverse pinkish brown bars often forming open ellipses, lip white with pinkish base and center. . . . . ***P. hieroglyphica***

Phalaenopsis amboinensis J. J. Sm.

Bull. Dept. Agric. Ind. Néerl. 45:23. 1911 (Mar.); *Polychilos amboinensis* (J. J. Sm.) Shim, Malayan Nat. Journ. 36:24. 1982. Type: Indonesia. Molucca Archipelago, Ambon, leg. Lach de Bère, *Hort. Bogor s.n.* (holotype: BO; isotype: AMES). Original watercolor of the holotype reproduced in Sweet (1969:326).

Phalaenopsis psilantha Schltr., Repert. Spec. Nov. Regni Veg. 10:193. 1911. Type: Indonesia. Sulawesi, District Toli-Toli, Djangdjang, *Schlechter 20667* (holotype: B, destroyed; lectotype, here designated: drawing of the holotype by Schlechter, AMES). Copy of the lectotype drawing published in Sweet (1980:80).

Phalaenopsis hombronii Finet, Not. Syst. 2:253. 1912. Type: Indonesia. Molucca Archipelago, Ambon, *Hombron 1841* (holotype: P).

Epiphytes. **Leaves** usually three or four, elliptic to obovate, tapered at the base, obtuse-rounded, to 24 × 10 cm. **Inflorescences** arching racemes or panicles longer than the leaves, to 45 cm long, with each branch few-flowered, with the rachis fractiflex, the bracts ovate, concave, acute, keeled, to 7 mm long. **Flowers** fleshy, creamy white or yellow with transverse brown bars which frequently form +/− concentric circles, the lip mottled with brown, the column white. **Dorsal sepal** elliptic-ovate, acute-carinate, to 30 × 15 mm, the **lateral sepals** obliquely

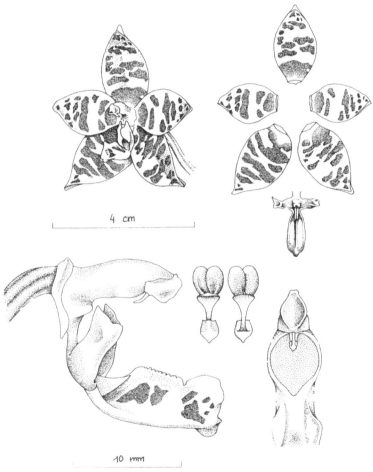

Phalaenopsis amboinensis. Illustrator: F. Pupulin.

broadly ovate, acute-carinate, to 30 × 15 mm. **Petals** elliptic, broadly cuneate, obtuse to subacute, subequal to but slightly shorter than the dorsal sepal. **Lip** three-lobed, to 22 mm long, to 18 mm across the expanded lateral lobes, the lateral lobes erect, triangular-oblong, truncate, the anterior corner a short tooth, the posterior corner an elongate lanceolate tooth, the midlobe oblong-elliptic, cuneate, obtuse, convex, the apex below extended in a fleshy chin, above with a high, bilaterally compressed, fleshy tooth, the blade with a central, raised, sulcate (two-edged) keel having minutely serrulate margins, the **callus** biseriate, the posterior callus bilobed, the lobes bluntly obtuse, the anterior callus sulcate, bifid, the divisions filiform. **Column** arching, to 8 mm long. **Pedicel** and **ovary** to 3 cm long.

Distribution: Indonesia (Molucca Archipelago and Sulawesi). **Etymology**: With the Latin suffix *-ensis*, indicating its place of origin on the island of Amboin. **Illustrations**: Amer. Orchid Soc. Bull. 49:260, 261 (the latter as *P. psilantha*). 1980; Awards Quart. 23(3):153, 191. 1992; Awards Quart. 24(2):121. 1993; Awards Quart. 24(4):291. 1993; Batchelor 1983:8; Fowlie 1993:35; Freed 1980a:469; Griesbach 1983a:204; Gruss and Wolff 1995:93 (line drawing and photograph on the left); Martin 1985:413; Orchid Digest 52:102. 1987; Shim and Fowlie 1983: 126, 128; Sweet 1969:329, 1980:72, 73; Williams 1984:239. **Note:** *Phalaenopsis amboinensis* 'Queen' (Gruss and Wolff 1995:93) is a complex hybrid probably bred from *P.* Princess Kaiulani or similar hybrid.

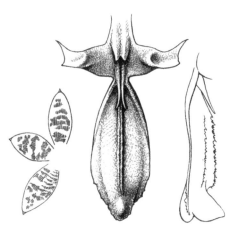

The original plant of *P. amboinensis* described by Smith produces flowers with a white ground color. This is the same color form that came into cultivation in the 1960s, exemplified by the 'Orchidglade' clone and its progeny. A more recent strain with a greenish yellow to yellow ground color has come into cultivation and all but supplanted the original color morph. This duality of a white and yellow phase parallels the color morphs seen in *P.*

Phalaenopsis amboinensis drawn from the type. Illustrator: H. R. Sweet.

gigantea. Ironically, this yellow phase has never been formally described. The extent and exact distribution of the yellow phase in nature is unknown, and thus it is described as a variety, pending further information from field research.

The name *P. psilantha* was applied in error to plants of *P. venosa* that entered into cultivation in 1979. An original drawing of *P. psilantha* was subsequently located and showed that the name *P. psilantha* was a synonym of *P. amboinensis* and that *P. venosa* was at that time an undescribed species. At least one Indonesian exporter informally reduced *P. psilantha*

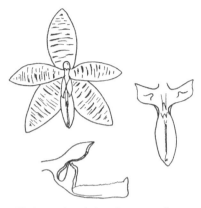

Phalaenopsis amboinensis, a copy of Schlechter's original pencil sketch of its synonym *P. psilantha*. Illustrator: H. R. Sweet.

to a variety of *P. amboinensis* (see *American Orchid Society Bulletin* 51:1125. 1982), even though the color morph of *P. amboinensis* that this name has been applied to (see *American Orchid Society Bulletin* 49:261. 1980), having few brown bars on the floral segments, is at odds with the type drawing of *P. psilantha.* The name *P. psilantha* has also been applied to a cultivated plant in Australia (Smythe 1994); that plant, known only from one clone that had been cultivated in Australia for more than 20 years, is said to be from Sulawesi but may represent an old hybrid. Nothing definitive can be said until further collecting takes place in Sulawesi near the type locality of Djangdjang; only then can we establish exactly what Schlechter had in mind when he described *P. psilantha.*

Phalaenopsis amboinensis var. *flavida*

E. A. Christ., var. nov.

A varietatibus typica floribus flavidis differt.

Type: Indonesia. Sulawesi, lower right photograph in Sweet (1980:73) labeled *P. amboinensis* 'Golden Treasure' (reproduced in Shim and Fowlie 1983:126).

Etymology: From the Latin, *flavidus* ("yellowish"). **Illustrations**: Amer. Orchid Soc. Bull. 49:261. 1980; Awards Quart. 16(1):18. 1985; Awards

Quart. 16(2):88. 1985; Awards Quart. 19(1):38. 1988; Awards Quart. 20(1):10. 1989; Awards Quart. 22(4):260. 1991; Awards Quart. 23(1):32. 1992; Awards Quart. 24(3):230. 1993; Awards Quart. 26(1):28. 1995; Die Orchidee 33(4):15. 1982; Die Orchidee 33(6): back cover. 1982; Die Orchidee 39(1):30. 1988; Die Orchidee 42(4):27. 1991; Gordon 1988b: 17, 1989a:232; Gruss 1990:116; Harper 1985:951, 1993:138; Koopowitz and Hasegawa 1985b:197; Orchid Digest 51:102. 1987. **Notes**: *P. amboinensis* 'Yellow Strain' (Gruss and Wolff 1995:94) is a complex hybrid bred from *P.* Barbara Moler or similar hybrid. Many modern clones show signs of mistaken hybridization in cultivation.

Originally introduced with greenish yellow to pale yellow ground colors, this variety has been line-bred and selected in cultivation for more intensely golden yellow flowers that are favored by plant breeders. Shim and Fowlie (1983) recorded their plant from Sulawesi as did Fitch (Amer. Orchid Soc. Bull. 49:261. 1980), but it is unknown if this color morph also occurs on Ambon or if the white ground color variety (var. *amboinensis*) also occurs in Sulawesi.

Phalaenopsis bastianii Gruss & Röllke

Die Orchidee 42(2):76. 1991. Type: The Philippines. Without precise locality, *Hort. Röllke s.n.* (holotype: herbarium of the Deutsche Orchideen-Gesellschaft).

Phalaenopsis deltonii Hort. ex Gruss & Röllke, Die Orchidee 42(2):76. 1991, pro syn.

Phalaenopsis bastianii f. *flava* Gruss & Röllke, Die Orchidee 42(2):79. 1991. Type: The Philippines. Without precise locality, *Hort. Röllke s.n.* (holotype: not designated; lectotype, here designated: photograph on p. 79, loc. cit.).

Epiphytes. **Leaves** two to ten, obovate-elliptic, cuneate, rounded and notched at the apex, 15–23 × 5–7 cm. **Inflorescences** erect racemes or panicles, 15–50 cm long, the branches with two to seven flowers. **Flowers** flat, glossy, 3.5–4 cm wide, greenish white to yellow overlaid with large, transverse, reddish brown bars, the lip rose-purple with pinkish white to rose-purple lateral lobes, the lateral lobes with yellow (if over a whitish ground color) or orange (if over a purple ground color) ridges, the column white or purple. **Dorsal sepal** elliptic to obovate, acute, shallowly convex by lightly revolute margins, 16–18 × 6.5–7.5 mm, the **lateral sepals** subsimilar, oblique, acuminate-subcarinate, divergent or subparallel, 15–17 × 7–8 mm. **Petals** oblanceolate, obtuse, 15–17 × 5–6 mm. **Lip** three-lobed, 9 mm long, 9 mm wide across the expanded lateral lobes, the lateral lobes erect, subparallel, falcate at the apices, 3.5 mm long, the midlobe elliptic-obovate, obtuse, 8 × 4 mm, with a central keel terminating in a raised subapical mound, concave below, the lateral margins irregularly denticulate, the sparse trichomes below the apex, the **callus** biseriate, the posterior callus sulcate, notched, the anterior callus bifid. **Column** nearly straight, 6–7 mm long. **Pedicel** and **ovary** to 2 cm long.

Distribution: Endemic to the Philippines. Reported by Wallbrunn (1989) as coming from the Sulu Archipelago. **Etymology**: Named to honor Bastian Röllke, son of the co-author of this species, Lutz Röllke. **Illustrations**: Awards Quart. 24(3):254. 1993 (cf.); Christenson 1998: 491; Gruss and Röllke 1991a:77, 79; Gruss and Wolff 1995:107; Wallbrunn 1989:93.

This entity has been and continues to be both problematic and confusing. This is attributable in part both to the nature of the plant and to some errors in previous publications. While I accept this entity as a valid species, it is morphologically extremely similar to *P. mariae*, its sister species; if horticultural sources are to be believed, they are from the same region of the Philippines in the Sulu Archipelago. Although other botanists may not accept such a finely split species concept, horticulturists certainly require a name for this distinctive plant. The primary differences between the two species are the erect inflorescences and very flat floral segments of *P. bastianii* compared to the pendent inflorescences and floral segments, generally with strongly revolute margins, in *P. mariae* (evident in Burbidge's drawings of the type of *P. mariae*). *Phalaenopsis mariae* also tends to have a denser mass of trichomes on the midlobe of the lip and to bear greater number of flowers, both on an entire inflorescence and on each side branch—but these are not traditional morphological differences used to delineate species in *Phalaenopsis*.

When this plant came into cultivation, it was thought to represent a natural hybrid of *P. mariae* with *P. lueddemanniana* (an artificially produced hybrid previously registered as *P.* Tigerette). This notion was tested and disproved by Wallbrunn (1989), who raised a population of *P. bastianii* from sib-crossed seed and noted none of the variation to be expected from a hybrid origin. Also, *P. bastianii* never produces the densely flowered inflorescence seen in *P.* Tigerette (see the photograph in *Die Orchidee* 31(1):14. 1980).

When Gruss and Röllke described *P. bastianii*, they compared their new species with *P. cornu-cervi* and *P. maculata*. They did not critically compare *P. bastianii* with *P. mariae* except to say that it had been falsely identified as *P. mariae*. Unfortunately, the type illustration's several inaccuracies have further clouded the issue. The line drawing shows a glabrous lip midlobe with an entire margin, short lateral lobes of the lip, and bluntly obtuse sepals and petals. This disagrees with the photograph of the lip of the type plant (presumably the lip photograph figured with the type description) and all subsequent collections of the species, which have scattered trichomes on the midlobe, irregularly denticulate lateral margins toward the apex of the lip midlobe, lateral lobes of the lip about half again as long as the line drawings, and acute-acuminate sepals and petals.

Gruss and Wolff assigned *P. bastianii* to Sweet's subsection *Zebrinae*, typified by *P. sumatrana*. This is an error since *P. bastianii* lacks the crucial character of a hooded column found in *P. sumatrana* and its allies. Under Sweet's system, *P. bastianii* must be placed next to *P. mariae* in his subsection *Hirsutae*.

Gruss and Röllke described a *flava* form, where the ground color of the sepals and petals are dark yellow. I find little use in trying to maintain this as a distinct form because most flowers of *P. bastianii*, including the type specimen (presumably one of the two clones figured with the type description), have some yellow in the ground color. The clone described as the *flava* form is merely one extreme, as Wallbrunn's plants, with their pale greenish white ground color, are the opposite.

Phalaenopsis bellina (Rchb.f.) E. A. Christ.

Brittonia 47:58. 1995; *Phalaenopsis violacea* var. *bellina* Rchb.f., Gard. Chron., n.s., 22:262. 1884. Type: Origin unknown, *Hort.*

B. S. Williams s.n. (holotype: W). Original watercolor of the holotype reproduced in Sweet (1968:1100, 1980:109).

Phalaenopsis violacea var. *chloracea* Rchb.f., Gard. Chron., n.s., 22:262. 1884. Type: Origin unknown, *Hort. Veitch s.n.* (holotype: W). Original watercolor of the holotype reproduced in Sweet (1968:1100, 1980:105).

Epiphytes. **Leaves** three to several, elliptic-obovate, rounded, acute, waxy, shiny, pale green, 20–25 × 7–12 cm. **Inflorescences** rigid, arching racemes, shorter than the leaves and often resting upon them, the floral bracts ovate, acute, concave, fleshy, bilaterally compressed, to 7 mm long. **Flowers** very fragrant, sequentially produced with one or two flowers open at a time, greenish white to greenish yellow, the basal inner edges of the lateral sepals intensely ssturated purple, the base of the sepals and petals +/– with purple suffusions and fine spotting, the lip purple with yellow lateral lobes. **Dorsal sepal** elliptic-lanceolate, acuminate-carinate, concave below the apex, keeled along the back, to 3.6 × 1.5 cm, the **lateral sepals** subfalcate, obliquely elliptic-ovate, acuminate-carinate, keeled along the back, to 3.5 × 1.7 cm. **Petals** obliquely ovate, acute to subacute, to 3 × 1.7 cm. **Lip** three-lobed, to 2.8 cm long, to 2.3 cm across the expanded lateral lobes, the lateral lobes oblong-ovate, truncate with an irregular margin, the posterior corner of the apex with a recurved lanceolate tip, the midlobe elliptic-obovate, obtuse, with an acute, carinate-triangular keel extending beyond the apex from below, with a dorsal keel extending to a raised, glabrous subapical mound, the **callus** biseriate, the posterior callus a glandular field terminating in a blunt, notched apex, the anterior callus elongate, sulcate, terminally deeply bifid with narrowly linear divisions. **Column** nearly straight, to 1.5 cm long. **Pedicel** and **ovary** 2.6 cm long.

Distribution: Malaysia (Malay Peninsula) and East Malaysia (Sarawak). The photograph of the clone 'Wati' published by Fitch (1983: 709) appears to be the first hard documentation of *P. bellina* on the Malay Peninsula. Chan et al. (1994) report this species below 200 m in elevation. **Etymology**: From the Latin, *bellus* ("beautiful"). **Illustrations**: Amer. Orchid Soc. Bull. 59:17. 1990; Amer. Orchid Soc. Bull. 59:701. 1990; Amer. Orchid Soc. Bull. 64:1339. 1995; Amer. Orchid Soc. Bull. 68:465. 1999; Awards Quart. 15(3):130. 1984; Awards Quart. 16(2):60.

1985; Awards Quart. 17(1):30. 1986; Awards Quart. 17(2):100. 1986; Awards Quart. 18(2):98. 1987; Awards Quart. 19(2):94. 1988; Awards Quart. 20(3):161. 1989; Awards Quart. 20(4):186, 187, 192. 1989; Awards Quart. 21(4):196. 1990; Awards Quart. 22(4):217. 1991; Batchelor 1983:4; Baker and Baker 1990:133; Chan et al. 1994:256, 359; Die Orchidee 32(1): front cover. 1981; Die Orchidee 35(1):34. 1984; Die Orchidee 42(4):32. 1991; Die Orchidee 42(5):33, 274. 1991; Fitch 1983: 709 ('Wati'); Gessner 1979:122; Gordon 1988b:369; Gruss 1990:115, 116; Gruss and Wolff 1995:130; Harper 1985:947; Martin 1985:414; Martin et al. 1993:255; Orchid Digest 50:161. 1986; Orchid Digest 52:73. 1988; Sweet 1980:105, 108, 109.

Phalaenopsis bellina has long been included in the synonymy of a broadly defined *P. violacea*, and indeed they are closely related sister species with very similar lip morphology. Following an examination of floral fragrances and a review of other morphological differences, *P. bellina* was separated from *P. violacea* (Christenson and Whitten 1995). *Phalaenopsis bellina* has been known as the "Borneo" type of *P. violacea*—those plants bearing greenish white flowers with purple suffusion restricted to the lateral sepals, the bases of the dorsal sepal and petals, and the lip and column. These are unlike the true *P. violacea* from Sumatra and the Malay Peninsula, which bear flowers completely suffused with purple (often with greenish tips to the sepals and petals).

The morphological differences were discussed by Christenson and Whitten (1995:58):

> Differences in the calli have been used to define species of *Phalaenopsis* almost to the exclusion of other equally useful floral and vegetative characters. There are no significant differences in the calli between *P. bellina* and *P. violacea*, as one might expect in closely related sister species. There are, however, morphological differences in addition to differences in floral color. In *P. bellina* the petals are ovate and noticeably dilated, whereas in *P. violacea* the petals are elliptic. The petals of *P. bellina* are generally more than 1.3 cm broad, while the petals of *P. violacea* are generally less than 0.7 cm broad. The lateral sepals in *P. bellina* are subfalcate ("bow-legged") and the apices of the three sepals form an isosceles triangle. In *P. violacea* the lateral sepals are not subfalcate and the apices of the three sepals form an

equilateral triangle. Leaf shape is variable (q.v. Dourado, 1978) but in *P. bellina* appears to be consistently broader (generally more than 10 cm wide) than in *P. violacea* (generally less than 8 cm broad).

In addition to these differences, the two species have different floral fragrances, which suggests that they have separate pollinators. Again quoting Christenson and Whitten:

> The lemony fragrance of *P. bellina* is composed almost completely of geraniol (64%) and linalool (32%). These two monoterpenes are widespread in the Aeridinae (Christenson and Whitten, unpubl.) and are products of the mevalonic acid pathway. The spicy fragrance of *P. violacea* also contains these compounds but is dominated by elemicin (3,4,5-trimethoxy-phenylprop-1-ene; 55%) and cinnamyl alcohol (27%). These latter compounds are produced by the shikimic acid pathway.

Phalaenopsis bellina is probably the most fragrant of all species in the genus. If I were to coin a common name for this species it would be the "Fruit Loop orchid," after the popular breakfast cereal whose fragrance it shares. *Phalaenopsis bellina* remains a very popular plant with the general public, in large part because of this strong, pleasant fragrance.

The following four forms may be recognized in horticulture.

Phalaenopsis bellina f. *alba* E. A. Christ., f. nov.

A forma typica floribus albis differt.

Type: East Malaysia. Sarawak, Lundu District, leg. Au Yong Nang Yip, photograph plate 17A in Chan et al., *Orchids of Borneo*, vol. 1.

Etymology: From the Latin, *albus* ("white"), a reference to the pure white flowers. **Illustrations**: Amer. Orchid Soc. Bull. 49:866. 1980; Awards Quart. 23(3):190. 1992; Rotor 1980:855. **Note**: It is difficult in many photographs of alba clones to discern the differences between *P. bellina* and *P. violacea*. The illustrations cited here (and under *P. violacea* f. *alba*) are intended as a guide based on the available information.

White-flowered plants lacking all anthocyanin pigments of *P. vio-*

lacea have been described from Sumatra. Similarly white-flowered plants of *P. bellina* also occur and are widely cultivated but have never been formally described. A readily available color photograph is selected as the type.

Phalaenopsis bellina f. *bowringiana*
(Rchb.f.) E. A. Christ.

> Brittonia 47:59. 1995; *Phalaenopsis violacea* var. *bowringiana* Rchb.f., Gard. Chron., n.s., 22:262. 1884. Type: Origin unknown, *Hort. B. S. Williams s.n.* (holotype: W). Original watercolor of the holotype reproduced in Gruss and Röllke (1993f: 231) and in Sweet (1968:1100, 1980:108).

Etymology: Named to honor plantsman Sir John Charles Bowring (1821–1893).

This form differs from the typical form in having distinct spots and transverse bars of purple at the bases of the dorsal sepal and petals.

Phalaenopsis bellina f. *murtoniana*
(Rchb.f.) E. A. Christ.

> Brittonia 47:59. 1995; *Phalaenopsis violacea* var. *murtoniana* Rchb.f., Gard. Chron., n.s., 10:234. 1878. Type: Origin unknown, *Hort. B. S. Williams s.n.* (holotype: W).

Etymology: Named to honor plantsman Henry James Murton (1853–1881). **Illustrations**: Die Orchidee 39(5):24. 1988 ('Strub', SM/DOG); Orchid Alb. 4: t. 182 (reproduced in Sweet 1980:105).

This name has caused several problems, mostly by its misapplication to the clone 'Country Acres'. When originally described, this form was said to have a ground color of light lemon-yellow sepals and petals, and this is supported by the plate published in the *Orchid Album*, which was based on the type plant. The 'Country Acres' clone has greenish white sepals and petals; one cannot describe them as yellow. The clone 'Country Acres' most closely matches the holotype of *P. bellina*.

It is possible that this form was falsely based on older flowers of typical *P. bellina*, the flowers of which normally turn yellow as they senesce.

I reject this possibility because of the quality of the *Orchid Album* plate
as well as the great expertise of B. S. Williams as a plantsman. One
clone has appeared in Germany ('Strub', SM/DOG); if the color of
the transparency is accurate, it appears to have the lemon-yellow color
of this form.

Recently several orange-flowered plants have been referred to this
form, but study has shown these to be of complex hybrid origin (for example, 'Dorothy Martin', AM/AOS; see *Awards Quarterly* 21(4):229.
1990).

Phalaenopsis bellina f. *punctata* (Rchb.f.) E. A. Christ.

Brittonia 47:59. 1995; *Phalaenopsis violacea* var. *punctata* Rchb.f.,
Gard. Chron., n.s., 22:262. 1884. Type: Origin unknown, *Hort.
ignot. s.n.* (holotype: W). Original watercolor of the holotype
reproduced in Gruss and Röllke (1993f:232) and in Sweet
(1968:1100, 1980:108).

Etymology: From the Latin, *punctatus* ("marked with spots or dots").

This form differs from other forms by having the distinctive purple
bands of pigment along the inner margins of the lateral sepals broken
up into a series of small spots.

Phalaenopsis doweryënsis Garay & E. A. Christ., sp. nov.

Planta epiphytica; radicibus copiosis; caulibus brevibus, laterali-
ter compressis, vulgo bifoliatis (an semper?), 3–4 cm altis; foliis
magnitudine variantibus, carnosis, obovato-ellipticis vel late el-
lipticis, obtusis, apice oblique bilobulatis, usque ad 23 cm longis,
10 cm latis, vulgo minoribus; inflorescentiis erectis, foliis brevi-
oribus, usque ad 20 cm longis; pedunculo paulo compresso,
bivaginato, rhachidi incrassata, subclavata, ca. 3 cm longa, 8 mm
in diametro; bracteis triangulari, acutis, 3 mm longis; floribus
viridi-luteis, sparse brunneo maculatis, labello albo, antice gilvo,
segmentis carnosis, patentibus; sepalis simillimis, e cuneata basi
obovatis, obtusis vel subrotundatis, dorsali 18–23 mm longo,
9–13 mm lato, lateralibus 15–22 mm longis, 9–13 mm latis;

petalis e cuneata basi obovato-ellipticis, obtusis vel subrotundatis, 14–22 mm longis, 7–11 mm latis; labello 3-lobo, lobis lateralibus erectis, oblique triangularibus, margine anteriore versus
callosis, lobo intermedio e rotundata basi oblyrato, in ambitu
subquadrato, antice subtruncato, margine ad dentes lyrae
utrinque lacerato-denticulato; disco inter lobos laterales bicari-
nato et ad conjunctionem lobi intermedii callo libero, anguste
triangulari, bidentato ornato, et lobi intermedii ipse in medio
carinato et sub apice pulvinato incrassato, 10 mm longo, 8 mm
lato; toto labello 13–15 mm longo, inter lobos lateral explanato
14–15 mm lato; columna cylindrica, basin versus leviter dilatata,
re vere apoda, 10 mm alta; ovario pedicellato gracili, cylindrico,
ca. 20 mm longo.

Type: East Malaysia. Sabah, without precise locality; flowered in
cultivation at The Dowery Orchid Nursery, Allisonia, Virginia,
Dwayne Lowder s.n. (holotype: AMES).

Epiphytes with copious, almost fasciculate roots. **Stems** short, compressed, 3–4 cm long. **Leaves** usually two, variable in size, fleshy, ovate-
elliptic to broadly elliptic, obtuse, obliquely bilobulate at the apex, to
23 × 10 cm, usually smaller. **Inflorescences** erect racemes shorter than
the leaves, to 20 cm long, the peduncle somewhat compressed with
two remote sheaths, terminated by a thickened, subclavate rachis, the
rachis to 3 cm long, the floral bracts triangular-lanceolate, acute, 0.3 cm
long. **Flowers** fleshy, the sepals and petals greenish yellow with brown
spots and short transverse bars, the column and lip white, the lip highlighted with bright yellow, the midlobe of the lip with reddish brown parallel stripes.
Sepals similar, obovate, cuneate at the base, obtuse-rounded, the **dorsal sepal** 1.8–2.3 ×
0.9–1.3 cm, the **lateral sepals** 1.5–2.2 × 0.9–1.3 cm. **Petals** elliptic-obovate, cuneate at the
base, obtuse-rounded, 1.4–2.2 × 0.7–1.1 cm. **Lip** three-lobed,

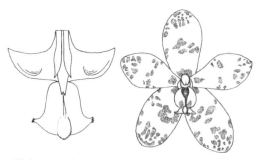

Phalaenopsis doweryënsis drawn from the type. Illustrator: L. A. Garay.

1.3–1.5 cm long, 1.4–1.5 cm wide across the expanded lateral lobes, the lateral lobes erect, obliquely triangular with a cushion-like callus toward the anterior margin, the midlobe porrect, oblyrate from a rounded base, subquadrate in outline, obtuse-rounded at the apex, the lateral hooks of the lyre minutely lacerate-denticulate. **Callus** biseriate, the posterior callus a pair of parallel ridges from the base of the lip to below the base of the midlobe, acute, the anterior callus bifid, the midlobe of the lip with a low keel which terminates in a rather large, elliptic, fleshy, glabrous pad. **Column** cylindric, somewhat widened near the base but not forming a distinct foot, 1 cm long. **Pedicel** and **ovary** slender, ca. 2 cm long.

Etymology: Named for its place of origin, The Dowery Orchid Nursery.

Recently imported from the wild and flowered in cultivation, the plants of *P. doweryensis* are reminiscent of those of *P. javanica*. The flowers, however, closely resemble those of *P. gigantea* by virtue of their flat, round form and shape of the lip. *Phalaenopsis doweryensis* differs from *P. gigantea* by having much smaller, narrower leaves, a footless column, and elliptic-obovate petals which yield an open-shaped flower. The broadly elliptic petals of *P. gigantea* usually overlap or nearly overlap the edges of the sepals.

The flowers of *P. doweryensis* also superficially resemble those of the artificially made primary hybrid *P.* Tridacna (*cochlearis* × *gigantea*). Flowers of *P.* Tridacna (see Gruss and Wolff 1995:87, mislabeled as "*cochlearis* × *mannii*") are slightly cupped, have acute or subacute sepals, and have shallowly concave lips that show the overwhelmingly dominant influence of members of section *Fuscatae*. The stripes on the lip of *P. doweryensis* are straight, parallel, and similar to those of its sister species *P. gigantea*. The stripes on the lip of *P.* Tridacna, in contrast, are curved and radiate from the base.

Phalaenopsis fasciata Rchb.f.

Gard. Chron., n.s., 18:134. 1882; *Polychilos fasciata* (Rchb.f.) Shim, Malayan Nat. Journ. 36:25. 1982. Type: The Philippines. Without precise locality, *Hort. Low s.n.* (holotype: W). Watercolor of the holotype reproduced in Sweet (1968:1096, 1980:101).

Epiphytes. **Leaves** elliptic to obovate, obtuse-rounded, channeled above, keeled below, to 20 × 7.5 cm. **Inflorescences** suberect to arching racemes and panicles, somewhat longer than the leaves, the branches few-flowered, the rachis fractiflex, the floral bracts triangular, acute, concave, to 4 mm long. **Flowers** fleshy, waxy, fragrant, the sepals and petals yellow with transverse brown barring, the lip white with pale pink suffusion, the lateral lobes of the lip bright yellow-orange. **Dorsal**

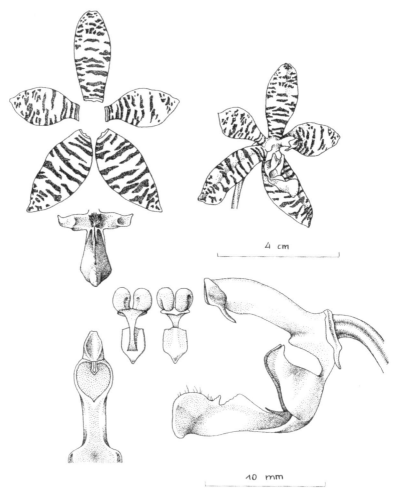

Phalaenopsis fasciata. Illustrator: F. Pupulin.

sepal elliptic, broadly cuneate, obtuse to shallowly notched, to 28 × 13 mm, the **lateral sepals** obliquely ovate-elliptic, channeled toward apex, acute-carinate, to 31 × 15 mm. **Petals** obliquely elliptic-obovate, obtuse, to 26 × 13 mm. **Lip** three-lobed, to 27 mm long, to 18 mm wide across the expanded lateral lobes, the lateral lobes erect, oblong-ovate, obliquely truncate, the posterior corner extended in an acute tooth, the midlobe oblong-obovate, rounded, with a central keel and an apical raised pad of tissue, glabrous or with a few scattered trichomes, the **callus** biseriate, the posterior callus a boss of retrorse fleshy tubercles, the anterior callus bifid. **Column** arching, club-shaped, to 16 mm long. **Pedicel** and **ovary** to 3 cm long.

Distribution: Endemic to the Philippines (Luzon, Bohol, Mindanao). **Etymology**: From the Latin, *fasciatus* ("with transverse marks"), a reference to the broad parallel stripes of color. **Illustrations**: Gruss and Wolff 1995:119, 125 (the latter as *P. lueddemanniana* var. *boxallii*); Sweet 1968:1104, 1969:33, 1970c:302, 1980:93. **Note**: The color photograph in Sweet (1980:101, upper left) is misidentified; the dense boss of trichomes on the lip is clearly visible.

Phalaenopsis fasciata is one of several Philippine species that were incorrectly "lumped" into an overly broadly defined *P. lueddemanniana*. Sweet's revision effectively clarified the species in this complex. The historic confusion surrounding *P. fasciata* stems from the existence of a yellowish phase of the true *P. lueddemanniana*, known as *P. lueddemanniana* var. *ochracea*. The latter is a color morph of *P. lueddemanniana* that lacks most or all of its anthocyanin pigments, resulting in a pale flower with greenish yellow to pale brown barring against an off-white ground color. This is completely different from the intense yellow ground color seen in *P. fasciata*. Unfortunately, early hybrids using *P. fasciata* as a parent were registered as crosses of *P. lueddemanniana* (*P.* Golden Sands, for example).

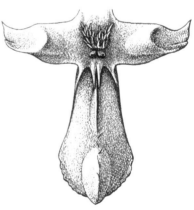

Phalaenopsis fasciata is most easily confused with *P. reichenbachiana*. In *P.*

Phalaenopsis fasciata drawn from the type. Illustrator: H. R. Sweet.

fasciata the sepals and petals usually have more or less revolute margins ("soda straws"), the lip is usually glabrous, and the flowers smell of green apples. In *P. reichenbachiana*, on the other hand, the sepals and petals are lightly concave without revolute margins, the midlobe of the lip consistently has scattered trichomes, and the flowers have a musty odor (Griesbach pers. comm.). The Orchid Registrar has incorrectly considered *P. reichenbachiana* to be a synonym of *P. fasciata*.

As a parent in hybrids, *P. fasciata* lends strong yellow color, a red lip, and fine pale brown spotting over most of the flower. The yellow color does fade with time although not as extensively as hybrids made with such species as *P. mannii*. Most modern yellow *Phalaenopsis* hybrids have some *P. fasciata* in the background.

Phalaenopsis fimbriata J. J. Sm.

Bull. Jard. Bot. Buitenz., ser. 3, 3:300. 1921; *Polychilos fimbriata* (J. J. Sm.) Shim, Malayan Nat. Journ. 36:25. 1982. Type: Indonesia. Java, Blitar, *Tollens s. n.* (holotype: L).

Epiphytes. **Leaves** oblong-elliptic to elliptic-obovate, acute, tapered to the base, channeled above, to 23 × 7 cm. **Inflorescences** racemes or panicles to 27 cm long, simultaneously many-flowered, the rachis obtusely four-angled, the floral bracts ovate, acute, to 4 mm long. **Flowers**

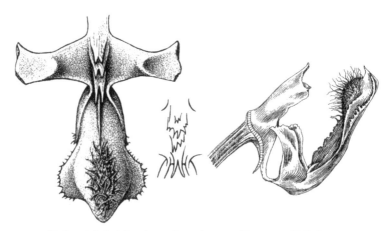

Phalaenopsis fimbriata drawn from the type. Illustrator: H. R. Sweet.

with variously twisted segments, the sepals often undulate and/or with recurved apices, the sepals and petals white to pale green, the sepals with purple barring at the base, the lip purple with a white apex. **Dorsal sepal** oblong-elliptic, obtuse to subacute, to 20 × 9 mm, the **lateral sepals** obliquely ovate-elliptic, acute, channeled toward the apex, to 20 × 12 mm. **Petals** oblong-elliptic, cuneate, subacute, often "bowed" (convex and incurved along the midvein with subrevolute margins), to 18 × 6 mm. **Lip** three-lobed, to 16 mm long, to 14 mm wide across the expanded lateral lobes, the lateral lobes erect, basally triangular, apically obtriangulate, truncate with an undulate margin, the midlobe obovate and trilobulate when flattened, obtuse, with a central keel, the subapical margins fimbriate, involute (upturned), with a subapical raised knob densely covered with long trichomes, the **callus** triseriate, all calli bifid, the anterior callus with narrower divisions. **Column** straight, to 8 mm long. **Pedicel** and **ovary** to 3 cm long.

Distribution: Indonesia (Java, Sarawak, and Sumatra). **Etymology**: From the Latin, *fimbriatus* ("with fringes"), a reference to the long fimbriate trichomes on the midlobe of the lip. **Illustrations**: Die Orchidee 33(3):13. 1982; Die Orchidee 46(3): Orchideenkartei Seite 803. 1995; Gordon 1989a:227; Gruss and Wolff 1995:121; Orchid Digest 49:89. 1985; Sweet 1969:37, 1971b:46, 1980:94, 97.

Phalaenopsis fimbriata has been confused in the past with *P. tetraspis* but is immediately distinguished by having no hood over the anther bed. It is similar both vegetatively and in the flower colors to *P. modesta* but differs by having a subapical pad of soft, downy trichomes unlike the essentially glabrous lip of *P. modesta*.

Phalaenopsis fimbriata subsp. *sumatrana*

(J. J. Sm.) E. A. Christ., stat. nov.

Basionym: *Phalaenopsis fimbriata* var. *sumatrana* J. J. Sm., Bull. Jard. Bot. Buitenz., ser. 3, 12:145. 1932. Type: Indonesia. Sumatra, Bengkoeloe, Rimbo Pengadang, *Ajoeb 195* (BO).

Phalaenopsis fimbriata var. *tortilis* Gruss & Röllke, Die Orchidee 43(2):89. 1992. Type: *Hort. Röllke s.n.* (holotype: not designated; lectotype, here designated: photographs on p. 88, loc. cit.).

Etymology: Named for its place of origin on the island of Sumatra. **Illustrations**: Die Orchidee 46(3): Orchideenkartei Seite 803. 1995; Orchid Digest 49:89. 1985; Sweet 1980:97.

Sumatran plants of *P. fimbriata* represent an isolated, well-marked subspecies that differs from the Javan type by occurring at higher elevations and having longer floral segments (dorsal sepal to 2.7 cm long compared to those of Javan plants to 2 cm long) and twisted sepals, frequently with some purple barring toward the bases of the petals. Plants of subsp. *fimbriata* range from sea level to 450 m in elevation while those of subsp. *sumatrana* have a higher elevational range to 1300 m. Both subspecies have flowers varying from pure white to white with variable degrees of green suffusion. The plant described as the *tortilis* variety represents one extreme of subsp. *sumatrana.*

Phalaenopsis fimbriata f. *alba* Gruss & Röllke

Die Orchidee 43(2):89. 1992. Type: [Indonesia. Java], *Hort. Röllke s.n.* (holotype: not designated; lectotype, here designated: photograph on p. 89, loc. cit.).

Etymology: From the Latin, *albus* ("white"), a reference to the pure white flowers. **Illustrations**: Gruss and Röllke 1992:89.

This anthocyanin-free form of the species was described from a plant having characteristics of the lowland Javan plants of subsp. *fimbriata.*

Phalaenopsis floresensis Fowlie

Orchid Digest 57:35. 1993. Type: Indonesia. Flores, near Wolowaru, east of Ende, 300–500 m, leg. Marthias, *Hort. Los Angeles State and County Arboretum LKW88F2* (holotype: LA; photograph: NY).

Epiphytes. **Leaves** five to seven, narrowly ovate to elliptic, obtuse, to 25 × 9 cm. **Inflorescences** shorter than the leaves, 10–20 cm long, two- or three-flowered, the floral bracts 4 mm long. **Flowers** creamy white, to 4 cm wide, variable suffused with yellowish green suffusion especially toward the apices of the sepals, the bases of the lateral sepals with fine, limited, pale brown transverse markings, the midlobe of the lip with a dull rose keel, laterally with one or more pale rose longitudinal stripes. **Dorsal sepal** elliptic, acuminate-carinate, shallowly concave, 2 × 0.8 cm, the **lateral sepals** broadly elliptic-ovate, acuminate-carinate, 2 × 1.2 cm. **Petals** ovate, acuminate, to 1.8 × 1.2 cm. **Lip** three-lobed, 1.5 cm long, the lateral lobes erect, parallel, narrowly ovate, truncate, the apices minutely crenulate-denticulate, 1.2 cm across when expanded, the midlobe oblong-elliptic, obtuse, with a raised central keel running the length of the midlobe, the apical half covered with a dense mat of fleshy trichomes to 1 mm tall, the **callus** biseriate, the posterior callus sulcate, bluntly bilobed, the anterior callus deeply bifid, the divisions linear-acute. **Column** lightly arching, 6–8 mm long.

Distribution: Endemic to the island of Flores. Fowlie reported this species at 500–1000 ft. (150–300 m) in elevation in the type description but at 1000–1660 ft. (300–500 m) with the type specimen data. **Etymology**: With the Latin suffix *-ensis*, indicating its place of origin on the island of Flores. **Illustrations**: Fessell and Lückel 1994:101, 102; Fowlie 1993:35; Gruss and Wolff 1995:96.

This recently described species caused minor confusion when first published. First, the gestalt of the type photograph suggested a close affinity with *P. javanica*, although Fowlie compared his new species with *P. amboinensis* and, to a lesser extent, with *P. javanica*. Second, the type flower was still expanding when photographed and thus the flower was lightly cupped, again similar to *P. javanica*. Without any published analytical drawings, it appeared at first that *P. floresensis* was merely a pallid form of *P. javanica*.

The second appearance of this species in print (Fessel and Lückel 1994) clarified the characters that separate *P. floresensis* from *P. javanica*, but again the authors used a photograph of a barely open, even more strongly cupped flower similar to *P. javanica*. That their specimen was still maturing its flower is shown by the small floral measurements (they recorded a dorsal sepal 13 mm long compared with the type specimen and subsequent material, which have dorsal sepals +/− 20 mm long). Now that additional plants have flowered in cultivation, it is clear that the flowers of *P. floresensis* expand to a very flat flower similar to better clones of *P. amboinensis* or *P. bellina*.

In *P. floresensis* the flowers are creamy white without any markings on the petals (with only faint pale brown markings toward the base of the lateral sepals), the lateral lobes of the lip are irregularly truncate (flat

like the end of a milled board) and the midlobe in densely covered
with fleshy trichomes for its apical half. In contrast, the flowers of *P. javanica* are marked with longitudinal stripes composed of squarish
transverse bars, the lateral lobes of the lip end in two teeth with the posterior pair of teeth long-acuminate, and the midlobe has a smaller boss
of trichomes restricted to beneath the apex.

Phalaenopsis floresensis is readily separated from *P. amboinensis* by its
different flower color, the lack of an erect tooth at the apex of the midlobe of the lip, and the differently shaped lateral lobes of the lip.

There is a natural disjunction between the plants found on Sumatra
and Java, on the one hand, and on Timor and Flores, on the other.
Widespread species in southeast Asia and Java are frequently "replaced" by a sister species on Timor or Flores. For example, the widespread *Aerides odorata* Lour. is replaced on Timor by the endemic *A.
timorana* Miq. Botanical collecting on Timor and Flores has been almost nonexistent in modern times, and many new species are to be
expected from those islands.

Phalaenopsis ×*gersenii* (Teijsm. & Binn.) Rolfe

Orchid Rev. 25:227. 1917; *Phalaenopsis zebrina* var. *gersenii* Teijsm.
& Binn., Natuurk. Tijdschr. Nederl. Indië 24:320. 1862; *Phalaenopsis sumatrana* var. *gersenii* (Teijsm. & Binn.) Rchb.f., Gard.
Chron. 1865:506. 1865; *Polychilos* ×*gersenii* (Teijsm. & Binn.)
Shim, Malayan Nat. Journ. 36:26. 1982. Type: Indonesia. Sumatra, without precise locality, leg. Gersen, drawing by *Binnendijk*
(lectotype: K). Watercolor of the holotype reproduced in Griesbach (1981b:220) and in Sweet (1968:1097, 1980:116).

Phalaenopsis zebrina var. *lilacina* Teijsm. & Binn., Natuurk.
Tijdschr. Nederl. Indië 24:320. 1862, ex char.; *Phalaenopsis sumatrana* var. *lilacina* (Teijsm. & Binn.) Rchb.f., Gard. Chron. 1865:
506. 1865. Type: Indonesia. Sumatra, without precise locality,
Lobb s.n. (? not preserved).

Distribution: Indonesia (Sumatra). **Etymology**: Named for collector
C. J. Gersen (1826–1877). **Illustrations**: Griesbach 1981b:220, 221; Sweet
1980:116 (as *P. zebrina* var. *gersenii*). **Note**: The illustrations in Awards

Quart. (19(3):137. 1988; 26(4):222. 1995) are doubtfully *P. ×gersenii.*
This concept represents a natural hybrid between *P. violacea* and *P. sumatrana.* Known only from the original collection, it has not been collected again to my knowledge. Despite speculation that this is a "missing species," the original watercolor seems a good match for such a hybrid. Gersen, who also collected the original material of *P. sumatrana,* was in a position to select an aberrant, hybrid individual from a population of *P. sumatrana* in the field. To resolve such an issue, artificially made hybrids need to be raised from known parents (see Griesbach 1981b).

The photograph of a fresh flower labeled *P. gersenii* in Sweet's book (Sweet 1980:117) is not *P. ×gersenii* but rather a complex hybrid of unknown origin. From the white column, strongly divergent lateral sepals, and very flat flower this hybrid appears to have either *P. amboinensis* or *P. floresensis* in its parentage.

Phalaenopsis gigantea J. J. Sm.

Bull. Dept. Agric. Ind. Néerl. 22:45. 1909; *Polychilos gigantea* (J. J. Sm.) Shim, Malayan Nat. Journ. 36:25. 1982. Type: "Borneo" [presumably East Malaysia. Sabah], *Mantri Jaheri s.n.* (holotype: BO). Original watercolor of the holotype reproduced in Sweet (1969:326).

Massive epiphytes. **Leaves** five to six per stem, pendent, leathery, elliptic, broadly rounded, pale drab olive green, shiny on both surfaces, to 68.5 × 25.5 cm. **Inflorescences** pendent racemes or sparsely branched panicles, to 40 cm long, +/– obscured by the leaves, pale chalky green, the floral bracts triangular, acute, concave, to 6 mm long. **Flowers** showy, to 5 cm wide, sweetly fragrant, very shallowly cupped, usually with overlapping segments, the sepals and petals white or yellow densely covered with transverse brown bars that align to form +/– irregular concentric rings, the lip white with six purple longitudinal stripes on

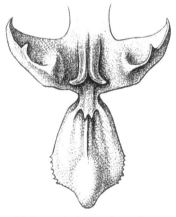

Phalaenopsis gigantea drawn from the type. Illustrator: H. R. Sweet.

the midlobe and with yellow-orange teeth on the lateral lobes, the column white. Sepals subsimilar, ovate-elliptic, obtuse, the **dorsal sepal** to 3.5 × 2.5 cm, the **lateral sepals** to 3.9 × 2.6 cm. **Petals** elliptic, cuneate, obtuse, to 3 × 2.2 cm. **Lip** three-lobed, to 16 mm long, to 1.5 cm wide across the expanded lateral lobes, the lateral lobes erect, triangular-falcate, to 8 × 4 mm, the midlobe obovate, rounded-obtuse with a pointed tip formed by the subapical raised pad of tissue, with small irregular marginal teeth to either side of the apex, to 11 × 7 mm, the **callus** biseriate, the posterior callus larger, bifid, the anterior callus smaller, shallowly notched. **Column** straight, fleshy-thickened at the column foot, to 11 mm long. **Pedicel** and **ovary** 4 cm long.

Distribution: Endemic to Sabah in East Malaysia and adjacent Kalimantan Timur. Chan et al. (1994) record *P. gigantea* from sea level to 400 m in elevation. **Etymology**: From the Latin, *giganteus* ("gigantic"), a reference to the enormous leaves. Hence the common name in Borneo, "elephant ears." **Illustrations**: Awards Quart. 15(1):28. 1984; Awards Quart. 16(2):65. 1985; Awards Quart. 17(3):123. 1986; Awards Quart. 19(3):158. 1988; Awards Quart. 20(4):206. 1989; Awards Quart. 22(3): 148. 1991; Awards Quart. 23(4):221. 1992; Awards Quart. 24(2):144. 1993; Awards Quart. 24(3):239. 1993; Awards Quart. 24(4):285. 1993; Chan et al. 1994:242, 357; Christenson 1999a:364; Die Orchidee 32(5): 30. 1981; Die Orchidee 33(2): back cover. 1982; Die Orchidee 39(1):26. 1988; Die Orchidee 43(6):45. 1992; Gruss and Wolff 1995:97, 98; Mayr 1986:178; Orchid Digest 46:29. 1982; Orchid Digest 51:157. 1987; Sweet 1969:326, 329; Sweet 1980:78; van Holle-de Raeve 1991:3, 5, 6.

Phalaenopsis gigantea produces the largest plants in the genus. Although not difficult to grow, seedlings take significantly longer to reach maturity than other species. As a result, the demand for wild-collected mature plants for the horticultural trade has been and continues to be a problem. *Phalaenopsis gigantea* is probably the only species of *Phalaenopsis* likely to require continued, long-term regulation of its international trade. Unlike other species, which can probably replenish the populations of plants removed from the wild for horticulture, the slow replacement time and large plant size of *P. gigantea* (which makes it easier to truly "collect out" the species) make this species a candidate for conservation efforts above and beyond habitat preservation.

Many growers report some difficulty flowering plants of *P. gigantea*.

The cause is usually insufficient light levels. *Phalaenopsis gigantea* will tolerate and flower well under very bright, cattleya-like, light levels, provided that the leaf temperatures can be controlled. Growers in Florida typically hang plants of *P. gigantea* in bright light directly in front of their cooling pads, getting the high light levels needed to flower while preventing the leaves from overheating and burning.

At first, *P. gigantea* would seem an unlikely candidate for hybridization because of the negative qualities of its huge plant size and pendent inflorescences. Fortunately, both these features are recessive when the species is bred with complex tetraploid hybrids.

The original *P. gigantea* bore flowers that were darkly brown spotted against a white ground color, at least at the center of the flower. Three color morphs occur: brown-red patterns against a white ground color, brown-red patterns against a yellow ground color, and paler brown patterns without red pigments against a yellow background. The latter two color morphs are formally recognized because of their significance to horticulture.

Phalaenopsis gigantea var. *aurea* E. A. Christ., var. nov.

A varietatibus typica floribus aureis differt.

Type: Photograph reproduced in Orchid Digest 51:157. 1987.

Etymology: From the Latin, *aureus* ("golden yellow"). **Illustrations**: Orchid Digest 51:157. 1987.

The original *P. gigantea* has sepals and petals with a white ground color suffused to a varying degree with pale greenish yellow toward their apices. Variety *aurea* has a brighter yellow ground color throughout the sepals and petals (including the area surrounding the column). The white ground color of the typical variety is inherited without any significant influence from the greenish yellow suffusion toward the apices of the sepals and petals. The yellow ground color of var. *aurea* is inherited and produces very different looking progeny. *Phalaenopsis* Marion Fowler (Zada × *gigantea*) made with the typical variety of *P. gigantea* produces rather dull-colored mauve flowers. When remade using *P. gigantea* var. *aurea*, the hybrid produces vibrant raspberry flowers from the overlay of purple on yellow.

Phalaenopsis gigantea f. *decolorata*
(Braem) E. A. Christ., stat. nov.

Basionym: *Phalaenopsis gigantea* var. *decolorata* Braem, Schlechteriana 2(1):7. 1991. Type: East Malaysia. Sabah, Meruatai, *Braem 97/114* (holotype: SCHLE).

Etymology: From the Latin, *decoloratus* ("without color"). **Illustrations**: van Holle-de Raeve 1991:6.

Both the invalidly published *flava* variety (Sweet 1980:76) and the form transferred here appear to be anthocyanin-free forms against a yellow background, although it is unclear from both the photograph in *Schlechteriana* and Braem's minimal type description what the actual ground color of the flower is.

Phalaenopsis hieroglyphica (Rchb.f.) Sweet

Amer. Orchid Soc. Bull. 38:36. 1969; *Phalaenopsis lueddemanniana* var. *hieroglyphica* Rchb.f., Gard. Chron., ser. 3, 2:586. 1887; *Phalaenopsis lueddemanniana* subvar. *hieroglyphica* (Rchb.f.) Veitch, Man. Orchid. Pl., pt. 7:31. 1891; *Polychilos hieroglyphica* (Rchb.f.) Shim, Malayan Nat. Journ. 36:25. 1982. Type: The Philippines. Without precise locality, leg. Boxall, *Hort. Low s.n.* (holotype: W).

Phalaenopsis lueddemanniana var. *palawanensis* Quisumb., Philippine Orchid Rev. 5:2. 1953. Type: The Philippines. Palawan, *Edaño s.n.* (holotype: AMES).

Phalaenopsis lueddemanniana var. *surigadensis* Hort., Amer. Orchid Soc. Bull. 34:542. 1965, nom. nud.

Pendent epiphytes. **Leaves** many, leathery, oblong-ligulate, tapered to the base, acute to obtuse, to 30 × 9 cm. **Inflorescences** arching-subpendent racemes or panicles, to 32 cm long, the branches short, many-flowered, the floral bracts ovate, acute, to 5 mm long. **Flowers** showy, glossy, abundant, long-lasting, creamy white to pastel pink, the sepals and petals with transverse rows of intricate rose to cinnamon-brown bars, the lip white with a rose-pink center, the lateral lobes of the lip yellow. **Dorsal sepal** elliptic, acute-carinate, to 38 × 15 mm, the **lateral sepals** obliquely oblong-elliptic, acute-acuminate, carinate, channeled along the midvein, to 41 × 17 mm. **Petals** ovate-elliptic, cuneate, acute, to 33 × 16 mm. **Lip** three-lobed, to 25 mm long, to 18 mm wide across the expanded lateral lobes, the lateral lobes erect, oblong, bifid, the midlobe oblong-oblanceolate, obtuse-rounded with minutely irregular subapical margins, with a central raised keel grading into a raised knob, the knob covered with trichomes, the **callus** biseriate, the posterior cal-

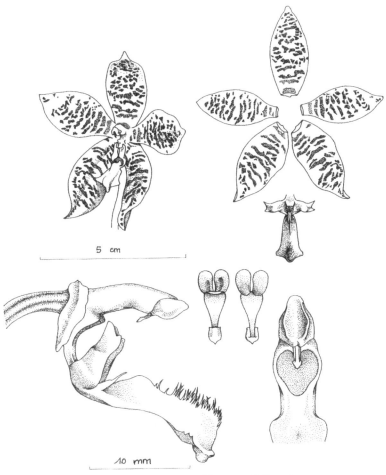

Phalaenopsis hieroglyphica. Illustrator: F. Pupulin.

129

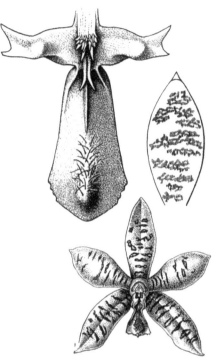

lus a boss of fleshy tubercles, the anterior callus sulcate, bifid. **Column** lightly arching, to 12 mm long. **Pedicel** and **ovary** to 2 cm long.

Distribution: Endemic to the Philippines. **Etymology**: Named for the intricate markings on the sepals and petals, which fancifully resemble Egyptian hieroglyphics. **Illustrations**: Amer. Orchid Soc. Bull. 49:871. 1980; Awards Quart. 15(1):24. 1984; Awards Quart. 25(2):100. 1994; Die Orchidee 45(1): 41. 1994; Freed 1981b:1078; Gruss and Wolff 1995:123, 124; Sweet 1969:37, 1971b:46, 1980:96, 104. **Note**: The clone in Harper (1985:953) appears to represent an intergrade with *P. lueddemanniana*.

Previously included in an overly broad *P. lueddemanniana*, *P. hieroglyphica* is distinguished by having no constriction at the apex of the midlobe, acute-acuminate sepal apices,

Phalaenopsis hieroglyphica drawn from the type. Illustrator: H. R. Sweet.

and differences in the shape of the bars on the sepals and petals. The flowers of *P. hieroglyphica* are larger than other species in the *P. lueddemanniana* complex. In addition, *P. hieroglyphica* has the habit of simultaneously opening all the flowers on a plant. Plants of *P. hieroglyphica* readily make specimen plants that are all but obscured by the profusion of flowers.

Phalaenopsis javanica J. J. Sm.

Bull. Jard. Bot. Buitenz., ser. 2, 26:77. 1918; *Polychilos javanica* (J. J. Sm.) Shim, Malayan Nat. Journ. 36:25. 1982. Lectotype, designated by Sweet (1969:329): Indonesia. Java, Priangan, on south coast between Garoet and Wijnkoops-Bai, *Hort. J. Schuller tot Peursum s.n.* (lectotype: L).

Phalaenopsis latisepala Rolfe, Kew Bull. 1920:130. 1920. Type: [presumably Indonesia. Java], *Hort. Liouville s.n.* (holotype: K). Original watercolor of the holotype reproduced in Sweet (1969:327).

Epiphytes. **Leaves** numerous, glossy, elliptic-obovate, tapered to the base, acute or obtuse, to 22 × 10 cm. **Inflorescences** suberect racemes or occasionally panicles, to 25 cm long, the rachis fractiflex, the floral bracts triangular, acute-acuminate, concave, to 5 mm long. **Flowers** fleshy, strongly cupped, to 3 cm wide, the sepals and petals translucent creamy white with longitudinal brown stripes, the stripes broken and composed of +/− rectangular blocks, the midlobe of the lip rich purple, the lateral lobes of the lip and the column white. **Dorsal sepal** broadly elliptic, obtuse, mucronulate, deeply concave, to 17 × 10 mm, the **lateral sepals** obliquely subrotund, obtuse, mucronulate, deeply concave, channeled along the midvein, to 17 × 22 mm. **Petals** broadly elliptic, rounded with an abruptly acute apex, convex, to 14 × 10 mm. **Lip** three-lobed, to 18 mm long, to 14 mm wide across the expanded lateral lobes, the lateral lobes erect, falcate-lanceolate, bifid, the midlobe oblong, acute, with a low central keel toward the base, with a terminal knob bearing trichomes at the very apex, the **callus** biseriate, the posterior callus oblanceolate, entire, obtuse, the anterior callus sulcate, bifid. **Column** somewhat arching, to 6 mm long. **Pedicel** and **ovary** to 2 cm long.

Distribution: Endemic to Indonesia (Java).
Etymology: Named for its place of origin on the island of Java. **Illustrations**: Die Orchidee 41(5): Orchideenkartei Seite 619, 620. 1990; Gruss and Wolff 1995:100, 102; Sweet 1969: 330, 1980:74, 76.

Phalaenopsis javanica has an unusual color pattern that at first glance makes this species seem desirable for breeding hybrids. And while the color pattern is inherited at the diploid level, the undesirable qualities have outweighed the benefits to date. The combination of concave sepals and convex petals,

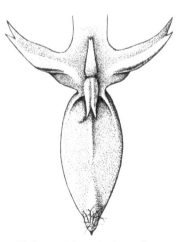

Phalaenopsis javanica drawn from the type. Illustrator: H. R. Sweet.

when the flower size is increased through hybridization, typically results in rather unattractive, poorly shaped flowers.

One color morph needs validation.

Phalaenopsis javanica f. *alba*
Gruss & Röllke ex E. A. Christ., f. nov.

A forma typica floribus albis differt.

Type: [Indonesia. Java]. Photograph in Die Orchidee 41(5): Orchideenkartei Seite 619. 1990.

This is the anthocyanin-free, sporadically occurring form of the species.

Phalaenopsis lueddemanniana Rchb.f.

Bot. Zeit. 23:146. 1865; *Polychilos lueddemanniana* (Rchb.f.) Shim, Malayan Nat. Journ. 36:25. 1982. Type: The Philippines. Without precise locality, *Hort. Lueddemann s.n.* (holotype: W).

Erect epiphytes. **Leaves** several, arching to drooping, oblong-elliptic to elliptic-obovate, tapering to the conduplicate base, rounded, acute to obtuse, to 30 × 9 cm. **Inflorescences** suberect, spreading racemes or panicles, each portion few-flowered, frequently producing apical plantlets (keikis), subequal to or longer than the leaves, the rachis two-ranked, the floral bracts ovate, acute, concave, to 5 mm long. **Flowers** very fleshy, waxy, fragrant, very long-lasting, variable in size and color, to 6 cm wide. **Dorsal sepal** elliptic, obtuse, dorsally keeled, to 30 × 14 mm, the **lateral sepals** obliquely elliptic-ovate, subacute, keeled behind, channeled along the midvein, to 30 × 14 mm. **Petals** broadly elliptic-ovate, cuneate to clawed, obtuse, subequal but smaller than the sepals. **Lip** three-lobed, to 22 mm long, to

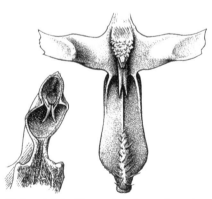

Phalaenopsis lueddemanniana drawn from the type. Illustrator: H. R. Sweet.

18 mm across the expanded lateral lobes, the lateral lobes erect, oblong, obliquely truncate, the apices irregular, the midlobe variable in shape, generally oblong to narrowly obovate, obtuse, abruptly constricted at the apex, convex, with a central raised longitudinal keel, with an apical linear raised pad densely covered with trichomes, the **callus** biseriate, the posterior callus an ovate pad of fleshy, densely packed papillae (nipple-like raised bumps), the anterior callus sulcate, bifid. **Column** lightly arching, to 12 mm long. **Pedicel** and **ovary** to 3.5 cm long.

Distribution: Endemic to the Philippines. **Etymology**: Named to honor Parisian horticulturist Lueddemann, who is credited with the first flowering of this species in Europe. **Illustrations**: Awards Quart. 19(3):138. 1988; Awards Quart. 21(3):160. 1990; Awards Quart. 24(2): 107. 1993; Freed 1981b:1077; Griesbach 1983a:204; Hetherington 1981:97; Martin 1985:416; Martin et al. 1993:256; Sweet 1969:41, 1980: 97, 104. **Note**: The illustrations in Gruss and Wolff (1995:125) are incorrect: the plant labeled *P. lueddemanniana* var. *boxallii* is *P. fasciata* (lip glabrous!), and the plant labeled simply *P. lueddemanniana* (upper right) is a hybrid involving *P. sumatrana*.

Historically, *P. lueddemanniana* was considered to be a "highly variable" species. Some of this variation was and is real, but most of the "variability" was generated by the inclusion of several separate species in the synonymy of an overly broadly defined *P. lueddemanniana*. The species formerly assigned to such a broad concept include *P. fasciata*, *P. hieroglyphica*, *P. pallens*, *P. pulchra*, and *P. reichenbachiana*. Although this taxonomic quagmire was fully resolved by Sweet, his classification of this species complex (followed here) has not been adopted by the Orchid Registrar. Sweet (1980:96) stated bluntly, "This simplistic approach raises havoc with the scientific nomenclature as well as producing a situation in which highly heterogenous and different hybrids must be called by names which do not reflect their true parentage and genealogy." It is hoped that this situation will change as the species of this complex are increasingly used to produce new directions in hybridization.

Even when those species are removed and *P. lueddemanniana* is treated in a narrow sense, a great deal of variation in flower form and color still occurs. With the removal of those species, however, there is no longer any record of a bright or deep yellow phase of *P. lueddeman-*

133

niana. Hence, no yellow hybrids derive that color from *P. lueddemanniana*, those parent plants being misidentified plants of *P. fasciata* or *P. reichenbachiana*. The common color phase of *P. lueddemanniana* is creamy white with more or less concentric rings of transverse amethyst bars and a darker purple lip.

In *P. lueddemanniana* the petals may be gradually tapered (cuneate) at the base or they may be abruptly tapered, resulting in a clearly defined claw; they range in shape from oblong to ovate. Both flower color and the degree and size of the markings are highly variable. Such variability is to be expected in a species with a wide range in an archipelago. In the absence of any data concerning the distribution of this variation in nature, only two historic varieties are recognized here. If a grower or breeder feels that recognition of a plant in cultivation requires naming, descriptive clonal names should be used rather than formal botanical names. Individual plants sometimes show variation consistent with possible introgression with other species in the complex, especially *P. hieroglyphica*.

When *P. lueddemanniana* was first used in hybridization in the 1960s, it was crossed primarily with large, tetraploid whites. The resulting pink-spotted hybrids were mostly sterile triploids and usually had rather pale spotting. *Phalaenopsis lueddemanniana* then fell out of favor only to be used again more recently as part of very complex modern hybrids, where in combination it lends large, bold, intensely pigmented spots to its offspring in addition to great substance to the flowers.

Two horticultural varieties have been named.

Phalaenopsis lueddemanniana var. *delicata* Rchb.f.

Gard. Chron. 1865:434. 1865; *Phalaenopsis lueddemanniana* subvar. *delicata* (Rchb.f.) Veitch, Man. Orchid. Pl., pt. 7:30. 1891. Type: The Philippines. Without precise locality, *Hort. Lueddemann s.n.* (holotype: W).

Etymology: From the Latin, *delicatus* ("dainty"). **Illustrations**: Bot. Mag. 91: t. 5523. 1865.

This color morph differs from the typical variety by having brownish (cinnamon to ocher) bars toward the apices of the sepals and petals that become amethyst-purple toward the center of the flower. The barring is less dense than the typical variety, and the colors are generally less saturated. Carri Raven-Riemann recently flowered a clone that perfectly matches the original concept as illustrated in the *Botanical Magazine*. Plants identified to this variety by Sweet (1970b:236, 1980:104) and others do not match Reichenbach's color notes that precisely.

Phalaenopsis lueddemanniana var. *ochracea* Rchb.f.

Gard. Chron. 1865:434. 1865; *Phalaenopsis lueddemanniana* subvar. *ochracea* (Rchb.f.) Veitch, Man. Orch. Pl., pt. 7:31. 1891; *Phalaenopsis ochracea* (Rchb.f.) Carrière ex Stein, Orchideenbuch 509. 1892. Type: The Philippines. Without precise locality, *Hort. Lueddemann s.n.* (holotype: W).

Etymology: From the Latin, *ochraceous* ("yellowish brown"), a reference to the color of the barring on the sepals and petals. **Illustrations**: Batchelor 1983:7; Sweet 1970c:302; Williams 1984:239.

This variety differs from the typical variety by having almost no anthocyanin pigments in the flowers. Instead of having amethyst-purple barring on the sepals and petals, the barring is pale greenish ocher. Instead of having rich purple lips, the lips of this variety are pallid whitish pink. This name has been widely misapplied to yellow-flowered related species, especially *P. fasciata*, to the consternation of hybridists. The ground color of *P. lueddemanniana* var. *ochracea* is an off-white and is never any color that could be described as yellow.

Phalaenopsis luteola

Burb. ex Garay, E. A. Christ. & Gruss, sp. nov.

Planta lithophytica, muscicola; radicibus carnosis, crassis; caulibus abbreviatus, 3-foliatis; foliis anguste ellipticus, acutis, sessilibus, usque ad 20 cm longis, 5 cm latis; inflorescentiis arcuatis, gracilibus, apice laxe 2-, 3-floris, foliis subaequilongis, floribus conspicuis, pallide aureis, sepia maculatis; sepalis anguste elliptico-lanceolatis, acutis vel subacuminatis, 18–20 mm longis, 6–7 mm latis; sepalis lateralibus arcuatim obliquis, subparallelis;

petalis oblanceolatis, obtusis, 1.6–1.8 cm longis, 0.7–0.9 cm latis; labello carnoso, 3-lobo, explanato T-formi, lobis lateralibus erectis, subquadratis, in medio aculeato callosis, lobo intermedio elliptico, acuto, disco in medio inter lobos laterales callo bidentato ornato, etiamque ad conjunctionem lobi intermedii; toto labello ca. 1.5 cm longo, 1 cm lato; columna cylindrico, 1 cm longa, basi in pedem distinctum producta; ovario pedicellato gracili, ca. 2 cm longo.

Phalaenopsis luteola Burb., The Gardens of the Sun 258. 1880, nom. nud.

Type: Northwest Borneo. Koung, wet mossy rocks, *F. W. Burbidge s.n.* (holotype: Burbidge's original watercolor, conserved in the library of the Natural History Museum, BM, reproduced in the color plate section of this book).

Lithophytes with fleshy roots on wet mossy rocks. **Stem** very short, three-leaved. **Leaves** narrowly elliptic, acute, sessile, to 20 × 5 cm. **Inflorescences** slender arching racemes subequal to the leaves. **Flowers** two or three, the sepals and petals pale yellow with irregular brown bars and blotches (the color on the original painting oxidized darker), the lateral lobes of the lip yellow, the midlobe scarlet. **Sepals** similar, narrowly elliptic-lanceolate, acute to subacuminate, 1.8–2 × 0.6–0.7 cm, the lateral sepals oblique, in natural position falcate-subparallel. **Petals** oblanceolate, obtuse, 1.6–1.8 × 0.7–0.9 cm. **Lip** three-lobed, fleshy, 1.5 cm long, 1 cm wide across the expanded lateral lobes, the lateral lobes erect, subquadrate with an aculeate callus in the middle, the midlobe elliptic, acute, the **callus** biseriate, the posterior callus bidentate between the lateral lobes of the lip, the anterior callus bifid at the base of the midlobe. **Column** cylindric, with a distinct foot, 1 cm long. **Pedicel** and **ovary** ca. 2 cm long.

Etymology: From the Latin, *luteolus* ("yellowish"). **Illustrations:** Die Orchidee 43(2): Orchideenkartei Seite 685. 1992 (as *P. maculata*).

Phalaenopsis luteola is distinguished from *P. maculata* primarily in the larger flowers with a yellow ground color in which the lateral sepals form a semicircle, such that they are falcate-subparallel with each other. In *P. maculata* the flowers have an off-white ground color tinged to varying degrees with pale green and the lateral sepals are divergent. This is also true of *P. maculata* f. *flava*.

Clearly Burbidge's book, *The Gardens of the Sun: A Naturalist's Journal*, was never intended to be the place of formal publication for new species. It is a travelogue that includes specific mention of desirable plants acquired through the author's travels in Borneo and the Sulu Archipelago. Hence, Burbidge's mention of *P. luteola* is brief: "A curious stronggrowing vanilla draped trees in most places, and on some wet mossy rocks beside a rushing torrent, a glossy-leaved phalaenopsis (*P. luteola*) displayed its golden blossoms, each sepal and petal mottled with cinnabar."

Sweet's placement of *P. luteola* in his revision relied on Rolfe's interpretative note on a herbarium sheet at Kew. Subsequent to Sweet's study, Garay was able to locate Burbidge's original paintings in the library of the Natural History Museum in London (formerly the British Museum of Natural History). Critical to identifying the type of *P. luteola* is the phrase written in Burbidge's hand on the watercolor itself, "wet mossy rock," a statement copied verbatim in his book.

Without new material this species would have remained unrecognized. Fortunately, this species was reintroduced to cultivation in Germany, where Gruss and Röllke published excellent color photographs showing salient features.

Phalaenopsis luteola appears to be rare both in cultivation and in nature. Although Reichenbach himself had seen it in the late 1800s, he did not recognize the significance of the distinct angle formed by the lateral sepals, albeit after making an excellent drawing of the specimen from an unknown source. Further collecting is needed in Borneo to locate populations of *P. luteola*, to establish the precise distribution of the species, and to assess the need for possible conservation efforts.

Phalaenopsis maculata Rchb.f.

Gard. Chron., n.s., 16:134. 1881; *Polychilos maculata* (Rchb.f.) Shim, Malayan Nat. Journ. 36:25. 1982. Type: "Borneo." Without precise locality, *Curtis s.n.* (holotype: W). Watercolor of the holotype reproduced in Gruss and Röllke (1993f:231).

Phalaenopsis muscicola Ridl., Trans. Linn. Soc. 3:373. 1893. Type: Malaysia. Malay Peninsula, Pahang State, Tahan River, *Ridley s.n.* (holotype: BM).

Phalaenopsis cruciata Schltr., Repert. Spec. Nov. Regni Veg. 8:457. 1910. Type: "Borneo." Koetai, near Long Sele, *Schlechter 13480* (holotype: B, destroyed).

Miniature epiphytes and lithophytes. **Leaves** oblong-ligulate to oblong-elliptic, acute, upper surface waxy, to 21 × 4 cm. **Inflorescences** arching racemes +/− subequal to the leaves to panicles several times longer

Phalaenopsis maculata. The holotype of *P. muscicola,* a synonym of *P. maculata,* conserved at the Natural History Museum (BM). Photographer: E. A. Christenson. Reproduced with the kind permission of the Trustees of the Natural History Museum.

than the leaves. **Flowers** small, slightly cupped, usually with the dorsal sepal arching over the column, the sepals and petals white to creamy white with transverse reddish brown bars, the lip scarlet, the column white. **Dorsal sepal** oblong-elliptic, acute-carinate, to 18 × 6 mm, the **lateral sepals** obliquely ovate-elliptic, acute-carinate, to 15 × 6 mm. **Petals** narrowly oblong-oblanceolate, obtuse, to 12 × 4 mm. **Lip** three-

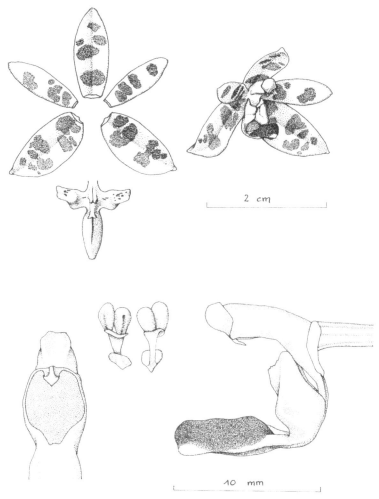

Phalaenopsis maculata. Illustrator: F. Pupulin.

139

lobed, 10 mm long, 8 mm wide across the expanded lateral lobes, the lateral lobes erect, subquadrate, the midlobe oblong-elliptic, obtuse, convex, with indistinct grooves, the **callus** biseriate, the posterior callus larger, sulcate, minutely bifid, the anterior callus smaller, a shallowly notched structure. **Column** slightly arched, 7 mm long. **Pedicel** and **ovary** 1.3 cm long.

Distribution: Malaysia (Pahang), East Malaysia (Sabah, Sarawak), and Indonesia (Kalimantan Timur). Chan et al. (1994) record *P. maculata* from sea level to 1000 m in elevation. The species is recorded from serpentine areas. **Etymology**: From the Latin, *maculatus* ("spotted"). **Illustrations**: Chan et al. 1994:244, 357; Gruss 1992b:209; Gruss and Wolff 1995:137, 138; Orchid Digest 46:29. 1982; Orchid Digest 49:126. 1985; Sweet 1969:232, 1980:115.

Phalaenopsis maculata has a reputation for being difficult to grow. Much of this reputation probably arose from the high mortality rate and general lack of vigor exhibited by earlier wild-collected plants that entered horticulture. Current populations, artifically raised from seed, do not appear to be particularly difficult to grow. *Phalaenopsis maculata* grows at higher elevations than many other species in the genus and displays a preference for moist, heavily shaded habitats; plants of *P. maculata* should be grown under intermediate, rather than warm, temperatures and should be given lower light levels than most other species and hybrids.

Both Sweet (1980) and Chan et al. (1994) record the inflorescences of *P. maculata* as racemes and only rarely panicles. This does not hold up as plants in cultivation typically produce panicles.

The small flower size and the narrow floral segments are drawbacks to hybridizing with *P. maculata*; however, the desirable qualities of the intense scarlet lip and small plant size are dominant in breeding.

One color morph requires formal publication.

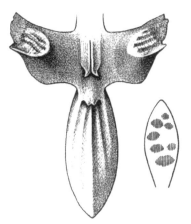

Phalaenopsis maculata drawn from the type. Illustrator: H. R. Sweet.

140

Phalaenopsis maculata f. *flava* E. A. Christ., f. nov.

A forma typica maculis flavis differt.

Holotype: Without precise locality, *Hort. J. Levy 6254*, photograph reproduced in the color plate section of this book.

Etymology: From the Latin, *flavus* ("yellow"). **Illustrations**: Awards Quart. 25(3):188. 1994.

This anthocyanin-free form of the species bears flowers with deep yellow spots and lip.

Phalaenopsis mariae Burb. ex Warn. & B. S. Wms.

Orchid Album 2: t. 80, sub t. 87. 1883; *Polychilos mariae* (Burb. ex Warn. & B. S. Wms.) Shim, Malayan Nat. Journ. 36:25. 1982. Type: The Philippines. Sulu (Jolo) Island, Bunt-Doohan, 600 m, *Burbidge s.n.* (holotype: W).

Epiphytes. **Leaves** few, arching-pendent, oblong to oblong-obovate, acute, to 43 × 10 cm. **Inflorescences** pendent racemes or panicles, subequal to or longer than the leaves, to 61 cm long, the branches pendent, many-flowered, the floral bracts two-ranked, ovate, acute, to 4 mm long. **Flowers** showy, lightly fragrant, sepals and petals creamy white overlain with large, bold, wide, transverse bars of rose, amethyst or reddish brown, the lip rose to dark purple, the column white. **Dorsal sepal** oblong-elliptic to elliptic-obovate, obtuse, with a short carinate-mucronulate extension, with the lateral margins +/– revolute, to 22 × 11 mm, the **lateral sepals** obliquely oblong-elliptic, obtuse, with a short carinate-mucronulate extension, with the lateral margins +/– revolute, to 22 × 12 mm. **Petals** obliquely oblong-oblanceolate, obtuse, to 17 × 9 mm. **Lip** three-lobed, to 15 mm long, to 12

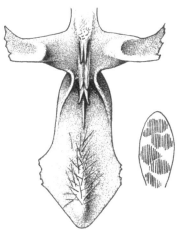

Phalaenopsis mariae. Illustrator: H. R. Sweet.

141

mm wide across the expanded lateral lobes of the lip, the lateral lobes erect, triangular-oblong, obliquely truncate, denticulate-serrulate at the apex, the midlobe oblong, dilated below the apex, obtuse, the lateral margins at the widest point irregularly denticulate, with a short raised central keel to below the middle, with a subterminal linear raised pad covered with trichomes, the **callus** biseriate, the posterior callus continuous with and arising from a minutely tuberculate fleshy base, bifid, the anterior callus subequal, bifid. **Column** lightly arching, to 7 mm long. **Pedicel** and **ovary** to 2.5 cm long.

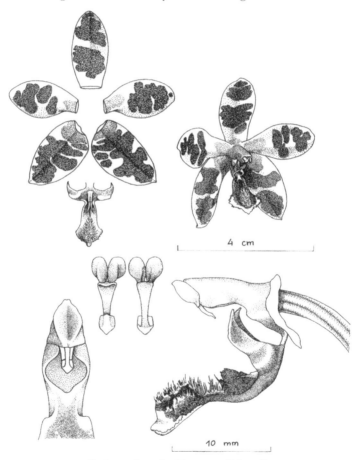

4 cm

10 mm

Phalaenopsis mariae. Illustrator: F. Pupulin.

Distribution: Endemic to the Philippines and Indonesia (Kalimantan, Borneo). **Etymology**: Named to honor the wife of collector Frederick William Thomas Burbidge (1847–1905), superintendent of Trinity College Botanic Garden in Dublin, Ireland. **Illustrations**: Awards Quart. 20(3):116. 1981; Batchelor 1983:11; Christenson 1998:492; Griesbach 1983a:204; Sweet 1969:227, 229, 230; Sweet 1980:112, 113.

Phalaenopsis mariae is a closely related sister species to *P. bastianii*, and some authors, emphasizing the similarities of the lips, may wish to combine the two concepts. The differences are discussed under *P. bastianii*. In the absence of any hard data to support such a merger, however, there are practical reasons for keeping them separate. They are easy to distinguish in cultivation by their flowers (the segments flat in *P. bastianii*, with strongly recurved margins, generally, in *P. mariae*) and the nature of the inflorescences, which are erect in *P. bastianii*, remarkably pendent in *P. mariae* (for an excellent view of the latter, see the photographs in Batchelor 1983). I expect the two will produce markedly different hybrids when crosses are flowered using *P. bastianii* as a parent. For the registration of hybrids and accurate record keeping, we are best served by maintaining these two entities as separate species.

Phalaenopsis mariae has remained surprisingly rare in cultivation, although, other than greater susceptibility to bacterial crown rot, it does not appear to present any particular horticultural challenges. Even with its beautifully marked flowers, aptly likened to stained-glass windows, *P. mariae* has proven to be a disappointing parent when crossed to significantly larger flowers, as the revolute margins of the sepals are all too frequently inherited by the progeny yielding poorly shaped flowers. When crossed with plants bearing similarly sized flowers within this section, however, *P. mariae* has lent a minor influence in breeding red flowers.

Phalaenopsis micholitzii Rolfe

Gard. Chron., ser. 3, 8:197. 1890, nom. nud.; Kew Bull. 1920: 130. 1920; *Polychilos micholitzii* (Rolfe) Shim, Malayan Nat. Journ. 36:25. 1982. Type: The Philippines. Mindanao, *Micholitz s.n.* (holotype: AMES)

Epiphytes with very short stems. **Leaves** pendent, convex, elongate obovate, acute to obtuse, tapered to the base, glossy, to 16 × 6 cm. **Inflorescences** usually numerous, very short, lateral to suberect, much shorter than the leaves, to 5 cm long, the floral bracts ovate, acute-acuminate, concave, to 5 mm long. **Flowers** fleshy-succulent, without any markings on the sepals and petals, stark white to yellowish green, the lip white with yellow to yellow-orange lateral lobes. **Dorsal sepal** elliptic-obovate, acute-carinate, appearing clawed by the revolute margins on the lower half, to 33 × 16 mm, the **lateral sepals** obliquely elliptic-ovate, acute-carinate, channeled below the apex, with revolute margins, to 33 × 17 mm. **Petals** oblique, the upper half elliptic-subrotund, the lower half obovate, obtuse, appearing clawed by the revolute margins on the lower half, to 22 × 17 mm. **Lip** three-lobed, to 22 mm long, to 16 mm wide across the expanded lateral lobes, the lateral lobes erect, oblong-lanceolate with strongly falcate apices, the midlobe broadly elliptic-obovate, rounded, obtuse, with a raised central keel to the middle, with a raised pad from the middle to the apex densely covered with long trichomes, the **callus** biseriate, the posterior callus narrow, minutely bilobed, superposed on the anterior callus, the anterior callus bifid with divergent apices. **Column** lightly arching, somewhat dilated toward the base, to 12 mm long. **Pedicel** and **ovary** to 3 cm long.

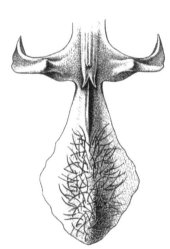

Phalaenopsis micholitzii drawn from the type. Illustrator: H. R. Sweet.

Distribution: The Philippines (Mindanao). Reported from Malaya in error by Rolfe. **Etymology**: Named after a plant collector for the Sander's Nursery, Wilhelm Micholitz (1854–1932), who first discovered this species. **Illustrations**: Awards Quart. 24(1):15. 1993; Die Orchidee 41(6): Orchideenkartei Seite 623–624. 1990; Gordon 1989a: 228; Gruss and Wolff 1995:101, 102; Sweet 1969:330, 1971b:46, 1980:75, 77.

Phalaenopsis micholitzii is easily recognized by its unmarked flowers and very short inflorescences, much shorter than the leaves and the shortest in this

144

subgenus. In addition, *P. micholitzii* usually produces many inflorescences at a time, a feature that has not been exploited in hybridization programs. This species has been rare in cultivation until recent reintroductions and subsequent seed and tissue culture propagation.

Phalaenopsis modesta J. J. Sm.

Icones Bogor. 3:47, t. 218. 1906; *Polychilos modesta* (J. J. Sm.) Shim, Malayan Nat. Journ. 36:25. 1982. Type: "Borneo." Without precise locality, leg. Nieuwenhuis, *Hort. Bogor s.n.* (holotype: BO).

Phalaenopsis modesta subsp. *sabahensis* Fowlie, Orchid Digest 44:189. 1980, nom. nud., ex icon.

Epiphytes usually found toward the base of host trees. **Leaves** one to four per stem, elliptic-obovate, tapering to a subpetiolate base, rounded, acute, glossy, to 23 × 6 cm. **Inflorescences** pendent, usually racemes but sometimes with sparse branches, arching, usually shorter than the leaves, usually few-flowered, the rachis fractiflex, the floral bracts two-ranked, ovate-lanceolate, concave, to 3 mm long. **Flowers** fragrant in the early morning, the sepals and petals white with variable purple transverse barring, the sepals greenish toward their apices, the lip purple, matching the sepal and petal colors in intensity, the teeth on the lateral lobes of the lip yellowish orange, the column white. **Dorsal sepal** oblong-elliptic to obovate, obtuse, convex, to 16 × 7 mm, the **lateral sepals** obliquely elliptic-ovate, acute, apiculate-carinate, to 16 × 9 mm. **Petals** obliquely elliptic, acute, usually with strongly revolute margins, to 15 × 5 mm. **Lip** three-lobed, to 14 mm long, 14 mm wide across the expanded lateral lobes, the lateral lobes erect, oblong, subtruncate, the posterior corner a retrorse, falcate hook, the midlobe oblong-elliptic, rounded, with

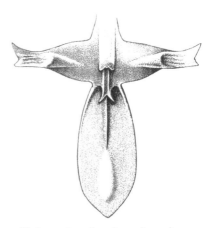

Phalaenopsis modesta drawn from the type. Illustrator: H. R. Sweet.

145

a central longitudinal keel ending in a subapical raised cushion. **Callus** biseriate, the posterior callus sulcate, bifid, the anterior callus narrower, bifid. **Column** nearly straight, to 9 mm long. **Pedicel** and **ovary** to 2 cm long.

Distribution: Endemic to the island of Borneo in East Malaysia (Sabah) and Indonesia (Kalimantan). Chan et al. (1994) report *P. modesta* at 50–900 m in elevation, where it has two flowering peaks, from May to June and again from September to November. **Etymol-

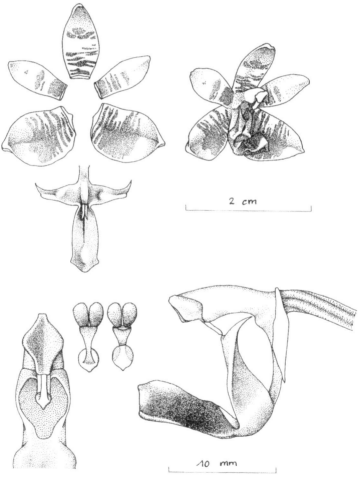

Phalaenopsis modesta. Illustrator: F. Pupulin.

146

ogy: From the Latin, *modestus* ("unassuming"), a reference to the flowers, which are typically partially obscured by the leaves. **Illustrations**: Chan et al. 1994:246, 357, 359; Die Orchidee 46(4): Orchideenkartei Seite 807. 1995; Gruss and Wolff 1995:139; Orchid Digest 46:29. 1982; Orchid Digest 51:102. 1987; Sweet 1969:232, 1980:114.

Phalaenopsis modesta was placed by Sweet in his subsection *Glabrae*, a subsection that I do not recognize here. Chan et al. (1994) confirm Sweet's observations that the midlobe of the lip in *P. modesta* sometimes bears trichomes, an observation that further weakens the case for subsection *Glabrae*. No specimens have been found matching Smith's apparently spurious description, that the midlobe of the lip is velvety hirsute, a characteristic at odds with the available type material.

Phalaenopsis modesta is variable in color, ranging from quite darkly purple-barred clones to pastel lavender-barred clones, to nearly alba clones (a true alba clone will no doubt be found someday). The sepals and especially the lateral sepals may be infused with green in a manner similar to *P. fimbriata*.

This species, with its paucity of small, rather insignificant flowers relative to the plant size, appears to have little to offer growers. While the marking patterns found in the darker clones might prove desirable in breeding, the narrow petals with typically revolute margins will require judicious use by breeders. Most plants of this species have truly modest inflorescences that are more or less hidden by the leaves. A few plants in cultivation exhibit inflorescences almost four times the length of the leaves. Whether these individuals represent a distinct genetic population or are just responding to being fully mature in cultivation is not known.

One problematic variant has been described.

Phalaenopsis modesta var. *bella* Gruss & Röllke

Die Orchidee 43(5):205. 1992. Type: "Borneo." Without precise locality, *Hort. Röllke s.n.* (holotype: not designated but presumably the herbarium of the Deutsche Orchideen-Gesellschaft).

Described from one clone of unknown provenance, this clone is at odds with all other examples of the species. The variety was described as having leaves 30–40 cm long, much larger than usual for the species. It is the cupped flowers and wide floral segments (the dorsal sepal elliptic-ovate, the laterals sepals oblong-obovate, the petals elliptic-oblanceolate), however, that make me suspect this is a hybrid between *P. javanica* and *P. modesta*, labeled as coming from Borneo in error. Variety *bella* certainly does not fit easily into even a broadly defined *P. modesta*, but I hesitate to describe it as a new species until I have seen material of an artificially produced cross of *P. javanica* and *P. modesta*.

Phalaenopsis pallens (Lindl.) Rchb.f.

Ann. Bot. Syst. 6:932. 1864; *Trichoglottis pallens* Lindl., Journ. Hort. Soc. 5:34. 1850; *Stauropsis pallens* (Lindl.) Rchb.f., Hamburg. Gartenz. 16:117. 1860; *Phalaenopsis lueddemanniana* var. *pallens* (Lindl.) Burb., The Garden 22:119. 1882; *Polychilos pallens* (Lindl.) Shim, Malayan Nat. Journ. 36:25. 1982. Type: The Philippines. Without precise locality, *Hort. Duke of Devonshire s.n.* (holotype: K). Original watercolor of the holotype reproduced in Sweet (1969:229).

Phalaenopsis foerstermanii Rchb.f., Gard. Chron., ser. 3, 1:244. 1887. Type: Origin unknown, leg. Foersterman, *Hort. Sander s.n.* (holotype: K).

Phalaenopsis pallens var. *denticulata* (Rchb.f.) Sweet, Amer. Orchid Soc. Bull. 38:227. 1969; *Phalaenopsis denticulata* Rchb.f., Gard. Chron., ser. 3, 3:296. 1888. Type: [The Philippines]. *Hort. Low s.n.* (holotype: W). Original watercolor of the holotype reproduced in Sweet (1969:229, 1980:109).

Epiphytes. **Leaves** arching, elliptic to obovate, tapered to the base, rounded-obtuse, often obliquely bilobed at the tip, to 18 × 6 cm. **Inflorescences** racemes, one- to few-flowered, subequal to the leaves, the rachis fractiflex, the floral bracts ovate, acute, concave, to 4 mm long. **Flowers** rigid, waxy, glossy, evenly pale yellow, the sepals and petals with sparse, light brown transverse bars, the lip white with variable pale pink suffusion on the midlobe in longitudinal stripes, the lateral lobes yellow to yellow-orange, the column white. **Dorsal sepal** elliptic, acute, very shallowly convex, the tip recurved, to 23 × 10 mm, the **lateral sepals** obliquely elliptic-ovate, acute, channeled below the apex, the tip recurved, to 22 × 10 mm. **Petals** obliquely elliptic, acute, lightly constricted below the apex, to 20 × 9 mm. **Lip** three-lobed, to 17 mm long, to 14 mm wide across the expanded lateral lobes, the lateral lobes erect, oblong, truncate, the posterior corner falcate, the midlobe narrowly obovate-oblong, obtuse-rounded, dilated below the apex with irregularly fimbriate lateral margins, with a low central keel to the middle,

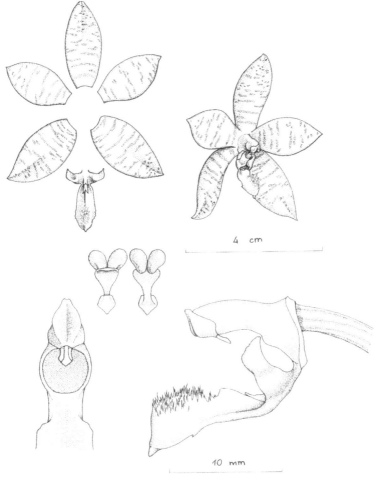

Phalaenopsis pallens. Illustrator: F. Pupulin.

149

then rising to a high keel just below the apex, with a patch of long trichomes above the middle, the **callus** biseriate, subequal, bifid. **Column** lightly arching, dilated toward the base, to 8 mm long. **Pedicel** and **ovary** to 2 cm long.

Distribution: Endemic to the Philippines. **Etymology**: From the Latin, *pallens* ("pale"), a reference to the muted tones of the flowers. **Illustrations**: Gruss and Wolff 1995:135; Sweet 1969:226, 1970c:302, 1980:106.

I am not recognizing *P. pallens* var. *denticulata* as a distinct variety. The supposed distinctions are the markings as broad brown bars or spots and the midlobe of the lip with pale purple longitudinal stripes. First, the spotting pattern of this variety is consistent with the variation found in the species. Second, after examining numerous plants of *P. pallens* over more than 20 years, I have never found a plant that did not have purple stripes on the midlobe of the lip. These stripes vary from very pale, indistinct lines at the very base of the midlobe to clearly delineated stripes from the base to near the apex. Lindley's drawing of the type flower of *P. pallens* shows no trace of purple on the lip, but he may have had one of the more pallid clones before him. Although the lines are very faint in the clone illustrated in Sweet (1980:109, lower right), they are clearly present. I have no evidence to suggest that these are anything but different endpoints of a continuous spectrum of variation.

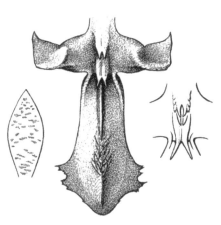

The type illustration of *P. denticulata* is somewhat similar to the recently described *P. bastianii*, especially in the shape of the midlobe and the degree of denticulation lateral to the apex of the midlobe. While the general distribution of pigment on the sepals and petals is similar, in *P. pallens* the pigmentation is less saturated in color and the column and lateral lobes of the lip are white, unlike the deep purple column and lip of *P. bastianii*.

Phalaenopsis pallens drawn from the type. Illustrator: H. R. Sweet.

As might be inferred from the species name, *P. pallens* has never been widely used in hybridization programs, it being neither fish nor fowl. Among its close relatives in the *P. lueddemanniana* complex, it lacks the rich purple pigments of *P. lueddemanniana* and *P. pulchra* as well as the deeper yellows found in *P. fasciata* and *P. reichenbachiana*. Unlike the last two species, however, *P. pallens* produces a very flat flower that lacks strongly revolute sepals. Given its longevity in cultivation even with considerable neglect, *P. pallens* should be investigated for possible disease resistance.

Two variants have been recognized.

Phalaenopsis pallens var. *trullifera* Sweet

Amer. Orchid Soc. Bull. 38:227. 1969. Type: The Philippines. Luzon, Prov. Bataan, Mt. Mariveles, Lanao River, *Whitford 1097* (holotype: AMES).

Sweet provided the following measurements for this variety: **Leaves** to 17 × 4 cm. **Dorsal sepal** 25 × 10 mm, the **lateral sepals** 27 × 10 mm. **Petals** 22 × 8 mm. **Lip** 16 mm long, 12 mm wide across the expanded lateral lobes. **Pedicel** and **ovary** to 3.5 cm.

Etymology: From the Latin, *trullatus* ("like a bricklayer's trowel") and the comparative -*fer* ("bearing"), an allusion to the shape of the midlobe of the lip. **Illustrations**: Gruss and Wolff 1995:136; Sweet 1969:227, 1980:106.

This variety has flowers that are substantially larger than most individuals of *P. pallens* and bear lips with a narrow, tapered base of the midlobe and an acute triangular apex. Known only from the type collection, I suspect that this variety may be an introgression or chance natural hybrid formed by hybridization with *P. reichenbachiana*, which is also known from Mt. Mariveles. Certainly that would

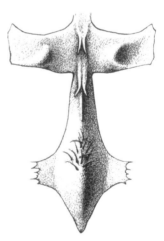

Phalaenopsis pallens var. *trullifera* drawn from the type, a variety that may represent the natural hybrid between *P. reichenbachiana* and *P. pallens*. Illustrator: H. R. Sweet.

explain the shape of the lip apex and the larger floral measurements (especially the wide petals in var. *trullifera*). Field work is needed on Mt. Mariveles to test this hypothesis and establish the variability of both purported parents in that region.

Phalaenopsis pallens f. *alba*
(Ames & Quisumb.) E. A. Christ., stat. nov.

> Basionym: *Phalaenopsis mariae* var. *alba* Ames & Quisumb., Philippine Journ. Sci. 56:461. 1935.

> *Phalaenopsis pallens* var. *alba* (Ames & Quisumb.) Sweet, Amer. Orchid Soc. Bull. 38:226. 1969. Type: The Philippines. Mindanao, Bukidnon, *Phillips s.n.* (holotype: PNH).

Etymology: From the Latin, *albus* ("white"). **Illustrations**: Philippine Journ. Sci. 56: pl. 2, figs. 3, 4; pl. 4, figs. 9–17. 1935.

This form lacks any spotting on the sepals and petals. It has been found only once and is not in cultivation at this time.

Phalaenopsis pulchra (Rchb.f.) Sweet

> Amer. Orchid Soc. Bull. 37:1102. 1968; *Phalaenopsis lueddemanniana* var. *pulchra* Rchb.f., Gard. Chron., n.s., 4:36. 1875; *Phalaenopsis lueddemanniana* subvar. *pulchra* (Rchb.f.) Veitch, Man. Orchid. Pl., pt. 7:31. 1891; *Polychilos pulchra* (Rchb.f.) Shim, Malayan Nat. Journ. 36:26. 1982. Type: The Philippines. Without precise locality, *Hort. Low 187* (holotype: W).

> *Phalaenopsis lueddemanniana* var. *purpurea* Ames & Quisumb., Philippine Journ. Sci. 49:494. 1932. Type: The Philippines. Luzon, Prov. Nueva Ecija, Balete Pass, *Constinoble s.n.* (holotype: PNG; photograph: AMES).

Epiphytes making large loosely organized clumps by frequent plantlet formation at the apices of long flexuous inflorescences. **Leaves** arching, oblong-elliptic to narrowly obovate, acute to subobtuse, to 15 × 6 cm. **Inflorescences** elongate and generally sterile or short, few-flowered, generally shorter than the leaves, the floral bracts triangular,

acute. **Flowers** fleshy, glossy-lacquered, deep purple, the lateral lobes
of the lip bright yellow, the column white. **Dorsal sepal** elliptic to elliptic-oblanceolate, acute, lightly channeled toward the apex, keeled on
the reverse, to 25 × 13 mm, the **lateral sepals** obliquely ovate, acute,
lightly channeled toward the apices, keeled on the reverse, divergent,
to 28 × 15 mm. **Petals** obliquely elliptic, tapered to almost clawed at the
base, subacute, to 23 × 11 mm. **Lip** three-lobed, to 23 mm long, to 20
mm wide across the expanded lateral lobes, the lateral lobes erect, rectangular, truncate, the corners extended in short teeth, the midlobe
cuneate-obovate, the apex a fleshy, blunt knob, the leading edge irregularly toothed, with a raised central keel to the middle, with a few scattered trichomes between the apex and the keel, the **callus** triseriate,
the posterior callus a transverse band of fleshy tubercles, the middle
callus short, bifid, the anterior callus sulcate, bifid, the subulate apices
divergent. **Column** lightly arching, dilated toward the apex, to 13 mm
long. **Pedicel** and **ovary** to 2.5 cm long.

Distribution: Endemic to the Philippines (Luzon, Leyte) at 100–650
m in elevation. Flowering recorded from August to November. **Etymology**: From the Latin, *pulcher* ("beautiful"). **Illustrations**: Gruss and Wolff
1995:127; Sweet 1968:1103, 1980:91, 101.

Historically *P. pulchra* and *P. speciosa* have been confused in horticulture. Unfortunately this confusion continues to the present day, largely
because of a widely distributed clone of *P.
pulchra* erroneously labeled *P. speciosa* 'Orchidglade', SM/SFOS. Other than similar
saturated color, the two species are clearly
separable. *Phalaenopsis speciosa* has a prom-
inently hooded anther bed, a spray of five or
more simultaneously open flowers, and an
inflorescence more or less the length of the
leaves. In *P. pulchra*, on the other hand, the
anther bed is not hooded, the inflorescences
typically bear just one to three flowers, and
the inflorescences are either much shorter
than the leaves or very much longer than the
leaves.

Sweet (1980) described the inflorescences

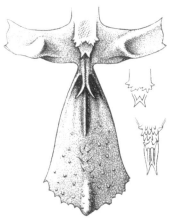

Phalaenopsis pulchra drawn from
the type. Illustrator: H. R. Sweet.

of *P. pulchra* as being "commonly shorter than the leaves." This is, in essence, a half-truth that was no doubt based on his receiving many study plants from cultivation. *Phalaenopsis pulchra* produces two kinds of inflorescences: very long inflorescences to more than a meter in length and very short inflorescences much shorter than the leaves. The long inflorescences sometimes flower, but more frequently they do not hold flowers but instead produce apical plantlets. These apical plantlets, either left attached to the parent plant or separated and placed in a separate growing container, typically flower with short inflorescences. The only other species of *Phalaenopsis* that consistently produces apical plantlets is *P. equestris*. In most other species of *Phalaenopsis* the production of keikis from the inflorescence nodes is an incidental event.

Superior clones of *P. pulchra* are solid deep purple. Less desirable clones show some irregularity in the color with large dark purple transverse patches alternating with paler patches. Most clones show some fading and concomitant irregularity in color as the flowers age.

Phalaenopsis reichenbachiana Rchb.f. & Sander

Gard. Chron., n.s., 18:586. 1882; *Polychilos reichenbachiana* (Rchb.f. & Sander) Shim, Malayan Nat. Journ. 36:26. 1982. Type: The Philippines. Mindanao, *Micholitz s.n.* (holotype: W). Original watercolor of the type reproduced in Sweet (1968: 1096).

Phalaenopsis sumatrana var. *kimballiana* Rchb.f., Gard. Chron., ser. 3, 4:6. 1888. Type: *Hort. Sander s.n.* (not preserved). Original watercolor of the type reproduced in Sweet (1968:1096).

Phalaenopsis kimballiana Gower, The Garden 34:13. 1888. Type: The Philippines. Without precise locality, *Hort. Weathers s.n.* (holotype: BM).

Epiphytes. **Leaves** elliptic-obovate, gradually tapered to base, rounded, to 35 × 7 cm. **Inflorescences** suberect or arching racemes or panicles, equal to or longer than the leaves, to 45 cm long, the floral bracts triangular, acute, concave, to 5 mm long. **Flowers** lightly cupped, fragrant, the sepals and petals greenish yellow with transverse reddish brown bars, often forming +/− concentric circles, the midlobe of the lip evenly pink, the lateral lobes pinkish white with yellow teeth, the column white. **Dorsal sepal** elliptic-obovate, acute-carinate, concave, to 25 × 11 mm, the **lateral sepals** obliquely elliptic-obovate, acute-carinate, concave, to 30 × 12 mm. **Petals** obliquely obovate, acute, concave, to 24 × 12 mm. **Lip** three-lobed, to 20 mm long, to 16 wide across the expanded lateral lobes, the lateral lobes oblong-triangular, two-lobed, the lobes with minute teeth, the midlobe oblong-obtrullate, cuneate, acute, with the lateral margins irregularly serrulate, with a central raised keel, beyond the middle with long trichomes, the **callus** triseriate, the posterior callus consisting of fleshy tubercles, the middle callus bifid, the anterior callus sulcate, bifid, with longer, narrower divisions. **Column** arching, club-shaped, to 12 mm long. **Pedicel** and **ovary** to 2.5 cm long.

   Distribution: Endemic to the Philippines. **Etymology**: Named to honor H. G. Reichenbach, the dominant force in orchid systematics during the latter half of the 19th century. **Illustrations**: Die Orchidee 45(1):44. 1994; Freed 1980c:1099 (as *P. boxallii*); Gruss and Wolff 1995: 132; Sweet 1969:37, 1980:92, 101; Williams 1984:239. **Note**: The photograph labeled *P. fasciata* in Sweet (1980:101, upper left) has obvious trichomes on the midlobe of the lip and is not that species. Most likely it is a flower of *P. reichenbachiana*.

   Only recently brought back into cultivation, *P. reichenbachiana* has been confused with the similar *P. fasciata* and has been considered a synonym of the latter for purposes of hybrid registration. The primary differences between the two species are these: *P. fasciata* is characterized by the glabrous (smooth) midlobe of the lip, poor form (usually) due to revolute margins of the sepals and petals ("soda straws"), and a green apple fragrance, in contrast to the trichome-covered lip midlobe, the shallowly concave sepals and petals (yielding a slightly cupped flower), and the musty odor of *P. reichenbachiana* (Griesbach pers. comm.).

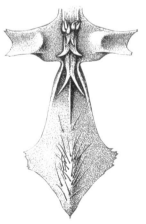

Phalaenopsis reichenbachiana drawn from the type. Illustrator: H. R. Sweet.

155

Sweet carried Reichenbach's *P. sumatrana* var. *kimballiana* as a lost variant of *P. sumatrana*, noting the possible nomenclatural link to *P. kimballiana* and thus *P. reichenbachiana*. In contrast, I am inclined to place this variety in the synonymy of *P. reichenbachiana* on the basis of floral morphology, ignoring for the time, Sweet's hypothesis of a hybrid origin. Even though no type material has been located, the type drawing, based on a Sander plant sent to Reichenbach by Sander's assistant Godseff, lacks the hooded anther bed characteristic of *P. sumatrana* and its allies. In addition, it is suspicious that both *P. kimballiana* and *P. sumatrana* var. *kimballiana* apparently flowered in cultivation for the first time in 1888, the same year that both names were published. Most likely, flowers were sent to Reichenbach in Vienna, and the plant was subsequently seen in England by Gower, who was told the plant would be named by Reichenbach after Mr. Kimball, as requested by Godseff. Gower then innocently reported this new find in *The Garden*, not intending to "scoop" Reichenbach. New introductions were reported quickly in *The Garden*; I am aware of a similar situation, where Burbidge published *Aerides crassifolia* based on an unpublished Parish name before the formal taxonomic paper by Parish and Reichenbach (see Summerhayes 1966).

Sweet's drawing of the midlobe of the lip of the holotype shows a fully expanded midlobe after rehydration of the herbarium material. In fresh flowers the toothed lateral margins of the midlobe are more recurved, and the general shape is closer to that seen in *P. lueddemanniana*.

Phalaenopsis robinsonii J. J. Sm.

Phil. Journ. Sci. 12:259. 1917; *Polychilos robinsonii* (J. J. Sm.) Shim, Malayan Nat. Journ. 36:26. 1982. Type: Indonesia. Molucca Archipelago, Ambon, Hitoe Messen, *Robinson 1627* (holotype: L). Photograph of the holotype reproduced in Sweet (1969:332, 1980:81).

Pendulous epiphytes. **Leaves** four or five, elongate oblong-oblanceolate, cuneate, acute to subobtuse, to 31 × 5.7 cm. **Inflorescences** arching, few-flowered racemes with occasional branches, to 20 cm long, the rachis fractiflex, five- or six-flowered, the floral bracts ovate, acute,

Phalaenopsis robinsonii, the holotype and only known specimen of the species, conserved at the National Herbarium of the Netherlands, in Leiden. Photographer: H. R. Sweet.

concave, distichous, wide-spreading, to 5 mm long. **Flowers** fleshy, white with lilac spots. **Dorsal sepal** narrowly oblong-ovate to elliptic, acute-carinate, 15 × 6 mm, the **lateral sepals** obliquely lanceolate to narrowly elliptic, acute-carinate, bilaterally compressed and subfalcate at the apex, 17 × 5 mm. **Petals** obliquely elliptic, acute, 14 × 6 mm. **Lip** three-lobed, fleshy, 12 mm long, 6 mm wide across the expanded lateral lobes, the lateral lobes triangular, acute, subfalcate, the midlobe elliptic, cuneate, obtuse-rounded, with a swollen subapical knob, the **callus** biseriate, the posterior callus bilobed, the anterior callus sulcate, bifid, the midlobe without any median keel. **Column** 1 cm long. **Pedicel** and **ovary** 1 cm long.

Distribution: Endemic to Indonesia (Ambon). **Etymology**: Named for botanist C. B. Robinson (1871–1913), who collected the type specimen. **Illustrations**: Bull. Jard. Bot. Buitenz., ser. 3, suppl. 3: t. 120; Gruss and Wolff 1995:105; Sweet 1969:332, 1980:81.

Little can be added to the account of this species by Sweet, as this species is still known only from the type collection. The species is remarkable for the very small lateral lobes of the lip, the smallest proportional to the midlobe of any species in the genus. Described from an unopened flower bud, it is unlikely that these small lobes are an artifact of the bud's degree of development. Sweet follows Smith in comparing *P. robinsonii* to *P. amboinensis*; however, the flower color, the delicate few-flowered inflorescences, and the glabrous (smooth) midlobe of the lip would seem to place it closest to *P. modesta. Phalaenopsis robinsonii* differs from the latter only by the shorter lateral lobes of the lip and the broader petals.

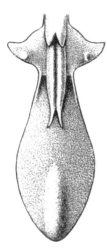

Phalaenopsis robinsonii drawn from the type. Illustrator: H. R. Sweet.

According to Sweet (1980), the flowers of *P. robinsonii* are "produced in succession," although I find no evidence of this from the type specimen. The rachis is five- or six-flowered and likely the flowers are produced more or less simultaneously.

Phalaenopsis ×*singuliflora* J. J. Sm.

Repert. Spec. Nov. Regni Veg. 31:80. 1932. Type: West Borneo. Tajan, east of Pontianak, *Hort. Bogor s.n.* (holotype: BO; isotype: L).

Phalaenopsis violacea var. *schroederiana* Rchb.f., Gard. Chron., n.s., 18:680. 1882; *Phalaenopsis violacea* var. *schroederi* Hort., Journ. Hort. and Cottage Gard., ser. 3, 5:155. 1882. Type: Origin unknown, *Hort. Schroeder s.n.* (holotype: W). Watercolor of the holotype reproduced in Griesbach (1981b:221), Sweet (1968: 1100, 1980:116), and in the color plate section of this book, with *P. bellina*.

Distribution: Western Borneo. **Etymology**: Named for the characteristic of sequentially bearing solitary flowers. **Illustrations**: Sweet 1980:116 (as *P. violacea* var. *schroederiana*).

This is the natural hybrid between *P. bellina* and *P. sumatrana*. It had been placed in synonymy under *P.* ×*gersenii* by Sweet, an entity which represents the natural hybrid between *P. sumatrana* and *P. violacea* (in the narrow sense). The flowering habit, broader petals, and more falcate lateral sepals of *P.* ×*singuliflora* show the strong influence of *P. bellina*.

Phalaenopsis venosa Shim & Fowlie

Orchid Digest 47:125. 1983; *Polychilos venosa* Shim ex Fowlie, Orchid Digest 47:126. 1983, pro syn. Type: Indonesia. Central Sulawesi, pass west of Palopo, 500–600 m, leg. Liem Kie Wie 79-S-1, *Hort. Birk s.n.* (holotype: LA; photograph: NY).

Phalaenopsis venosa var. *ochracea* Fowlie, Orchid Digest 47:124. 1983, nom. nud., ex icon.

Epiphytes. **Leaves** three to five, oblong-elliptic, acute, shallowly undulate, glossy, 10–22 × 5–7.5 cm. **Inflorescences** erect, racemes or panicles with short, densely flowered branches, to 18 cm long, each branch with two to five flowers, the floral bracts triangular, obtuse, concave, to 8 mm long. **Flowers** shallowly cupped, 4–5 cm wide, unpleasantly fragrant, the sepals and petals pale greenish yellow almost completely covered by broad transverse brown barring, the bases of the sepals and petals stark white forming a ring around the column base, the lip white with brown suffusion associated with the callus and median keel on the midlobe and with fine brown spotting on the lateral lobes. **Dorsal sepal** elliptic-ovate, subacute, bluntly apiculate, 17–22 × 12–14 mm, the **lateral sepals** obliquely elliptic, acute-carinate, 18–22 × 10–14 mm. **Petals** obliquely oblong-elliptic to ovate, abruptly subacute, 15 × 11

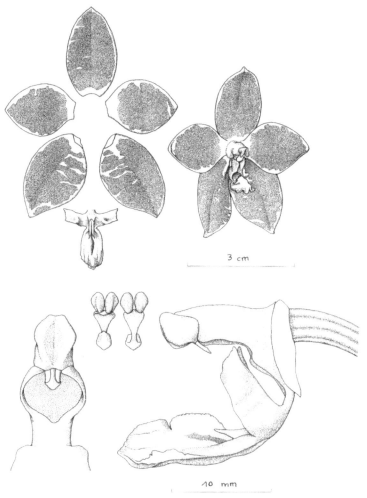

Phalaenopsis venosa. Illustrator: F. Pupulin.

160

mm. **Lip** three-lobed, 18–20 mm long, 13–15 mm wide across the expanded lateral lobes, the lateral lobes oblong-linear, obliquely truncate, the posterior corner extended as a small, falcate tooth, the midlobe elliptic-obovate, acute with a fleshy apicule, the margins irregular toward the apex, with a high central keel, 10 × 6 mm, the **callus** biseriate, the posterior callus a small notched tooth, the anterior callus sulcate, bifid, the divisions divergent. **Column** almost straight, to 9 mm long. **Pedicel** and **ovary** 2.8–3.2 cm long.

Distribution: Endemic to Indonesia (Sulawesi). **Etymology**: From the Latin, *venosus* ("conspicuously veined"). **Illustrations**: Awards Quart. 15(3):133. 1984 (as *P. psilantha*); Awards Quart. 16(2):62, 74. 1985; Awards Quart. 22(2):79. 1991; Awards Quart. 23(4):232, 248. 1992; Awards Quart. 24(3):191. 1993; Awards Quart. 25(4):210. 1994; Awards Quart. 26(2):90. 1995; Die Orchidee 41(4):29. 1990; Die Orchidee 44(3): Orchideenkartei Seite 729. 1993; Frier 1991:215; Gordon 1989a: 237; Gruss and Wolff 1995:103, 104; Norton et al. 1995:476; Orchid Digest 51:102. 1987; Rose et al. 1993:377; Shim and Fowlie 1983:124, 127.

When this species was first introduced to cultivation in 1979 it was confused with the long-lost *P. psilantha*. After this initial misidentification, an original drawing of *P. psilantha* by Schlechter was located (Sweet 1980:80), and it is generally agreed that *P. psilantha* is actually a synonym of *P. amboinensis*. *Phalaenopsis venosa* was also confused with and considered a select form of *P. amboinensis* (see *American Orchid Society Bulletin* 49:260. 1980). When the characteristics of *P. psilantha* were realized, Shim and Fowlie published the plants in cultivation as a new species, *P. venosa*.

Shim and Fowlie frustratingly did not publish a photograph of a flower from the type plant. Instead they elected to illustrate their species with a very dark brown clone collected at a higher elevation (900 m) and a more greenish brown clone they called the *ochracea* variety. That variety was never formally published and is best forgotten. There does not appear to be enough variation in flower color to warrant formal recognition of any particular variants.

Phalaenopsis venosa has been widely used for the breeding of solid yellow flowers that do not fade with age. The brown barring of the sepals and petals usually diffuses to a solid color. The white area surrounding the base of the column is very dominant and readily seen in

P. venosa hybrids. The slightly unpleasant fragrance of the flowers is not passed along to its progeny.

Phalaenopsis violacea Witte

Ann. Hort. Bot. Leiden 4:129. 1860; *Polychilos violacea* (Witte) Shim, Malayan Nat. Journ. 36:26. 1982. Type: Indonesia. Sumatra, Palembang, leg. Teijsmann, drawing by *Witte* (holotype: L). Original watercolor of the holotype reproduced in Sweet (1980:105).

Stauritis violacea Rchb.f., Hamburg. Gartenz. 18:34. 1862; *Stauropsis violacea* Rchb.f., Xenia Orch. 2:7. 1862. Type: Indonesia. Sumatra, *Willink s.n.* (holotype: W).

Pendulous epiphytes. **Leaves** succulent, oblong-elliptic to obovate, tapered to the base, acute, rounded, pale to medium green, 20–25 × 7–12 cm. **Inflorescences** arching racemes, sequentially one- or two-flowered, shorter than the leaves but becoming subequal with age, the rachis fractiflex, the floral bracts ovate, acute, fleshy, bilaterally flattened, to 7 mm long. **Flowers** fleshy, fragrant, dark rose, the apices of the sepals and petals green, the inner margins of the lateral sepals and the midlobe of the lip darker, the lateral lobes of the lip and callus yellow. **Dorsal sepal** oblong-elliptic, acute-carinate, concave, 20–35 × 8–15 mm, the **lateral sepals** obliquely elliptic-ovate, acute-carinate, strongly divergent, 22–35 × 11–17 mm. **Petals** oblique, the upper half oblong, the lower half elliptic-obovate, acute, 20–30 × 7–17 mm. **Lip** three-lobed, 20–28 mm long, 16–23 mm wide across the expanded lateral lobes, the lateral lobes erect, oblong, truncate with a small tooth-like forward corner and a longer acuminate tooth-like rear corner, the midlobe elliptic-obovate, obtuse-rounded, with a dorsal keel ending in a raised subapical knob above and with a short, carinate keel beneath, the **callus** bi-

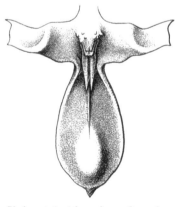

Phalaenopsis violacea drawn from the type of its synonym *Stauritis violacea*. Illustrator: H. R. Sweet.

seriate with an additional basal glandular field, the posterior callus a stack of +/− fused, short, blunt, apically notched calli, the anterior callus sulcate, bifid. **Column** lightly arching, dilated toward the apex (club-like), to 1.5 cm long. **Pedicel** and **ovary** to 3 cm long.

Distribution: Indonesia (Sumatra) and Malaysia (Malay Peninsula).

Etymology: From the Latin, *violaceus* ("violet"). **Illustrations**: Amer. Orchid Soc. Bull. 56:362. 1987; Amer. Orchid Soc. Bull. 58:380. 1989; Awards Quart. 15(1):18. 1984; Awards Quart. 16(1):33. 1985; Awards Quart. 16(2):68. 1985; Awards Quart. 21(4):196, 226. 1990; Awards Quart. 22(3):180. 1991; Awards Quart. 22(4):237. 1991; Die Orchidee 44(2):106. 1993; Fitch 1980a:860, 861; Gessner 1979:122, 123; Griesbach 1981b:220; Gruss 1990:115, 116; Gruss and Wolff 1995:130; Sweet 1969:41, 1980:105.

Phalaenopsis violacea has been treated in a broad sense by most authors. This concept included both solid rose-colored flowers from the Malay Peninsula and Sumatra (the "Malaysian" type) and greenish white flowers with purple pigment more or less restricted to the lateral sepals and the lip (the "Borneo" type) known from Borneo and also reported from the Malay Peninsula. The latter are now separated as a distinct species, *P. bellina*, on the basis of differences in morphology and floral fragrance analysis.

The flowers of *P. violacea* are usually a rather nondescript rose-purple with varying degrees of green at the tips of the sepals and petals. Recently, more brilliantly flowered clones have entered horticulture, reportedly from Sumatra. Several growers have tagged these with informal designations as a distinct new variety. This is actually a backward approach to the naming process. The type specimens of both the names listed here came from Sumatra. Thus, if one wanted to make a formal distinction, one would describe the more dull-colored Malay Peninsula entity as new, and the brilliantly flowered Sumatran entity would by definition become a tautonym bearing the epithet of *violacea* (as, when I published *P. fimbriata* subsp. *sumatrana*, that action automatically created the tautonym *P. fimbriata* subsp. *fimbriata* for the original Javan population).

I do not elect to formally differentiate these two supposed phases at this time. First, some of the "improved" *P. violacea* in cultivation are actually artificial hybrids of *P. violacea* with *P. bellina*. Second, the sampling data, mostly horticultural plants of unknown precise origin, is insufficient to make any definitive statements about the distribution of these phases in nature. For example, are they geographically isolated (subspecies) or do both phases occur throughout the range of the species (varieties)? It is quite likely that these differences represent a cline, or a more or less continuous gradation from one end of the species range to the other end. Finally, given the extremely wide range of variation in this species (Fitch 1980a), naming all the variants would be impractical. This is a case where descriptive clonal names and publication of color photographs in something like the *Awards Quarterly* would better serve the needs of horticulture.

A distinct population of *Phalaenopsis* occurs in the Mentawai Island group off the west coast of Sumatra. The flowers are larger and more full in shape than most *P. violacea*, and better forms have quite brilliant coloration with highly contrasting green tips to the sepals and petals. Only one color photograph of this entity has been published (as the clone 'Green Tips', see *American Orchid Society Bulletin* 49:261. 1980.). In the size and shape of the flowers they approach those of *P. bellina*. At first glance the flowers appear to resemble a hybrid swarm between *P. bellina* and *P. violacea*. Unlike either of those species, however, the Mentawai plants have much longer inflorescences, to ca. 50 cm, that lack a somewhat flattened, fleshy rachis. These plants require additional study before deciding on their status and making any name changes.

Two sporadically occurring color morphs, artificially propagated in quantity and much used in breeding programs, do require formal names.

Phalaenopsis violacea f. *alba*
(Teijsm. & Binn.) E. A. Christ., stat. nov.

> Basionym: *Phalaenopsis violacea* var. *alba* Teijsm. & Binn., Natuurk. Tijdschr. Nederl. Indië 24:320. 1862; *Phalaenopsis violacea* subvar. *alba* (Teijsm. & Binn.) Veitch, Man. Orchid. Pl., pt. 7:42. 1891. Type: Indonesia. Sumatra, Palembang, *Teijsmann s.n.* (? not preserved).

Distribution: Indonesia (Sumatra). **Etymology**: From the Latin, *albus* ("white"), a reference to the pure white sepals and petals. **Illustrations**:

Awards Quart. 19(2):71. 1988; Awards Quart. 20(3):151, 152. 1989; Awards Quart. 20(4):186. 1989; Awards Quart. 21(4):188. 1990; Awards Quart. 22(4):220. 1991; Awards Quart. 25(1):33. 1994; Die Orchidee 39(1):27. 1988; Fitch 1980a:860, 1983:709; Gruss 1990:115; Gruss and Wolff 1995:130; Sweet 1980:105.

This form differs from the typical purple-colored form by having white sepals and petals with or without green tips and a white lip with the lateral lobes bright yellow.

Phalaenopsis violacea f. *coerulea* E. A. Christ., f. nov.

A forma typica floribus caeruleis differt.

Type: Photograph labeled *P. violacea* 'Blue One' in Amer. Orchid Soc. Bull. 49:261. 1980.

Etymology: From the Latin, *caeruleus* ("blue"). **Illustrations**: Amer. Orchid Soc. Bull. 49:861. 1980; Amer. Orchid Soc. Bull. 69:330. 2000. Awards Quart. 19(3):160. 1988; Awards Quart. 26(3):129. 1995; Die Orchidee 46(4):56. 1995; Fitch 1980a:861; Gruss and Wolff 1995:130.

Although this lavender-bluish phase has been widely cultivated and artificially propagated, it has never been formally described. The intensity of color is highly variable, from pale washed-out colors to rather intense shades. A widely available color photograph that represents an average flower color of this form is selected as the holotype. Darker forms, approaching indigo, are being selected for propagation in horticulture.

Section *Zebrinae* Pfitz.

In Engler and Prantl., Pflanzenfam. 2(6):212. 1889; *Phalaenopsis* section *Zebrinorchis* Kuntze, Lex. Gen. Phan. 430. 1904. Type: *Phalaenopsis zebrina* Witte (= *Phalaenopsis sumatrana* Korth. & Rchb.f.).

This section comprises species with a cucullate (hooded) clinandrium (anther bed). This distinctive feature separates them from the often similarly colored species of section *Amboinenses*. The species of this section are uniform in morphology with the exception of highly variable color in *P. sumatrana.*

Key to the species of section *Zebrinae*

1. Midlobe of lip essentially glabrous; floral markings often intricate; flowers usually produced singly in succession. . . . . . *P. inscriptiosinensis*
1. Midlobe of lip with a prominent boss of trichomes at the apex.
   2. Outer halves of the sepals and petals and/or the entire surface solid dark purple. . . . . *P. speciosa*
   2. Outer halves of the sepals and petals not solid dark purple, variously pigmented from pure white to wine red, with or without barring.
      3. Sepals and petals white with at most a few scattered transverse bars of pigment at the base; inflorescences usually with several branches. . . . . *P. tetraspis*
      3. Sepals and petals variously pigmented, when white (some populations of *P. zebrina*) usually with numerous bars of pigment; inflorescences simple or branched.
         4. Posterior callus continuous with the anterior callus which extends to the midlobe; sepals and petals with longitudinal rows of barring toward their apices; flowers fragrant of candy.
         . . . . *P. corningiana*
         4. Posterior callus independent of and not continuous with the anterior callus; sepals and petals with transverse rows of barring; flowers with a slightly unpleasant fragrance. . . . . . . *P. sumatrana*

Phalaenopsis corningiana Rchb.f.

Gard. Chron., n.s., 11:620. 1879; *Polychilos corningiana* (Rchb.f.) Shim, Malayan Nat. Journ. 36:24. 1982. Type: "Borneo." Without precise locality, *Hort. Veitch s.n.* (holotype: W). Watercolor of the holotype reproduced in Gruss and Röllke (1993f:230) and in Sweet (1968:1096, 1980:80).

Phalaenopsis sumatrana var. *sanguinea* Rchb.f., Gard. Chron., n.s., 15:782. 1881; *Phalaenopis sumatrana* subvar. *sanguinea* (Rchb.f.) Veitch, Man. Orchid. Pl., pt. 7:40. 1891. Type: "Borneo." With-

out precise locality, *Hort. Veitch s.n.* (holotype: W). Watercolor of
the holotype reproduced in Sweet (1968:1096).

Epiphytes. **Leaves** elliptic-obovate, tapered to the conduplicate base,
rounded, acute, to 32 × 11 cm. **Inflorescences** arching to subpendent
racemes or panicles, to 30 cm long, the floral bracts triangular, acute,
concave, to 5 mm long. **Flowers** fragrant, the sepals and petals cream

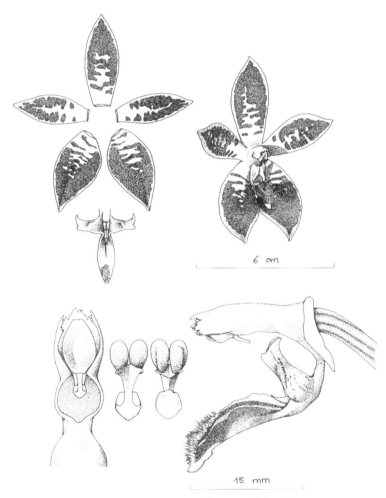

Phalaenopsis corningiana. Illustrator: F. Pupulin.

to greenish cream overlaid with brown barring, the bars transverse toward the base of the segments and typically longitudinally aligned toward the apex, extreme individuals bear nearly solid red flowers, the lip white with broad longitudinal purple stripes all but obscuring the ground color, the column white. **Dorsal sepal** oblong-elliptic, obtuse or minutely notched, convex, to 40 × 13 mm, the **lateral sepals** obliquely oblong-obovate, obtuse, shallowly convex, to 30 × 15 mm. **Petals** oblong-oblanceolate, bluntly subacute, to 35 × 12 mm. **Lip** three-lobed, to 20 mm long, to 17 mm wide across the expanded lateral lobes, the lateral lobes erect, oblong-elliptic, truncate with the elongate corners, the posterior corner falcate, the midlobe oblong, obtuse, with a central raised keel, with a boss of dense trichomes at the apex, the **callus** apparently uniseriate, sulcate, bifid, at the base continuous with a structure analogous to a posterior keel, forming a sunken pit. **Column** arching, with a coarsely erose-dentate hood over the anther bed. **Pedicel** and **ovary** to 4 cm long.

Distribution: Borneo (Sarawak and elsewhere on the island). **Etymology**: Named for Erasmus Corning, an early orchid grower in the United States. **Illustrations**: Awards Quart. 15(4):173. 1984; Awards Quart. 20(3):144. 1989; Christenson 1995:21; Die Orchidee 40(6):25. 1989 (cf.); Fowlie 1982:141, 1985b:209; Gruss and Wolff 1993:6, 1995:

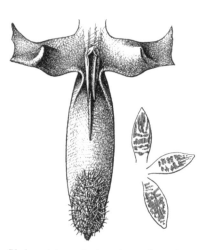

110; Orchid Digest 40:105. 1976; Orchid Digest 50:159. 161. 1986; Orchid Digest 52:73. 1988; Sweet 1968:1099, 1980:80, 90. **Note**: The plant figured in *Orchids of Borneo* (vol. 1, pl. 16d, as *P. sumatrana*) is typical *P. corningiana*.

Confusion has ever surrounded the identity of this species and the various darker color morphs of *P. sumatrana*, compounded by repeated misidentifications of *P. sumatrana* as *P. corningiana* in horticulture. In addition, *P. corningiana* is rare in cultivation, and most growers are therefore unacquainted with it. Though these two species are closely related sister species, once you

Phalaenopsis corningiana drawn from the type. Illustrator: H. R. Sweet.

have seen true *P. corningiana*, there is no mistaking it for *P. sumatrana*.

Maynard Michel (pers. comm.) relates that true *P. corningiana* came into cultivation in the 1970s in California, where a large seedling population was raised. But most growers found *P. corningiana* difficult to grow, and the species soon became rare again in cultivation. Plants currently in cultivation, however, do not appear to be any more difficult to grow than *P. sumatrana* and other species in this section.

In addition to the differences in callus morphology, *P. corningiana* has been distinguished from *P. sumatrana* by the pattern of markings on the sepals and petals. In *P. corningiana* the markings are arranged in longitudinal stripes toward the apex of the sepals and petals. In contrast, the markings in *P. sumatrana* are always transverse (from side to side), all the way to the apex of the sepals and petals. That difference does work most of the time, but it is a moot point in heavily pigmented clones of either *P. corningiana* or *P. sumatrana*, where the pattern of the markings is obscured.

The best character with which to separate these sister species is the floral fragrance. *Phalaenopsis corningiana* has wonderfully scented flowers reminiscent of old-fashioned ribbon candy. *Phalaenopsis sumatrana*, on the other hand, has a mildy acrid fragrance without any of the spicy tones of candy. Maynard Michel suggested the strong difference in fragrance between the species, and I was able to confirm these differences with side-by-side flowering plants in the collection of Jerry and Yoko Fischer in Minneapolis. Differences in floral fragrances implies separate pollinators and a degree of biological isolation in nature.

I follow Sweet in placing *P. sumatrana* var. *sanguinea* in synonymy, although his drawing of the type shows a callus more similar to true *P. sumatrana* than *P. corningiana*. In this regard, special note should be taken of the solid red clone recently illustrated in the *Orchids of Borneo* (vol. 1, pl. 16e, as *P. sumatrana*), which matches the phase of *P. corningiana* described as *P. sumatrana* var. san-

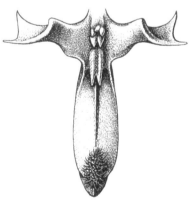

Phalaenopsis corningiana drawn from the type of its synonym *P. sumatrana* var. *sanguinea*. Illustrator: H. R. Sweet.

169

guinea. No transfer of this varietal name is taken here pending the results of studies in Borneo on the geographic distribution of these color morphs in nature.

Sweet (1980) recorded the inflorescences of *P. corningiana* as "much shorter than the subtending leaves." This was a bias from the very limited horticultural material available at the time. Weak or first-bloom seedlings typically bear short, few-flowered racemes. More robust plants typically have panicles somewhat longer than the leaves, similar to those found in *P. sumatrana.*

Phalaenopsis inscriptiosinensis Fowlie

Orchid Digest 47:11. 1983. Type: Indonesia. Central Sumatra, without precise locality, leg. Liem Khe Wie 81-S-1, *Hort. Los Angeles Arboretum s.n.* (holotype: LA).

Phalaenopsis sinensis Hort. Die Orchidee 34(1):39. 1983, nom. nud.

Epiphytes with short stems. **Leaves** three to five, elliptic-oblong, 8–16 × 4–8 cm. **Inflorescences** unbranched racemes, decurved, two- to five-flowered, the flowers opening sequentially with one or two open at a time, the peduncle terete, 7–11 cm long, the peduncular bracts sparse, distant, tubular, ovate, obtuse, clasping, the floral bracts triangular, concave, 6–8 mm long. **Flowers** to 3.5 cm wide, white or pale yellow +/– greenish suffusion toward the apices, the sepals and petals with intricate transverse bands of cinnamon brown, the sidelobes of the lip with bright yellow-orange anterior teeth, the midlobe of the lip white with dark red longitudinal stripes along the lower two-thirds, the column white, the sepals and petals convex with revolute margins. **Dorsal sepal** oblong-elliptic, obtuse, 17–19 × 7–9 mm, the **lateral sepals** subsimilar, divergent, apiculate, 16–18 × 9–11 mm. **Petals** oblong-oblanceolate, obtuse, to 13 × 6 mm. **Lip** three-lobed, the lateral lobes truncate, the lateral corners continued as small teeth, to 4 mm long, the midlobe oblong, subacute, 8 × 4 mm, with a central carinate keel, almost glabrous (Fowlie records "finely and barely ciliate, so much so as to appear bare"), the **callus** biseriate, the calli subsimilar and subequal, each bluntly bifid. **Column** hooded. **Pedicel** and **ovary** 1.8–2 cm long.

Distribution: Apparently endemic to Indonesia (Sumatra). **Illustrations**: Awards Quart. 26(1):29. 1995; Die Orchidee 42(3): Orchideenkartei Seite 649. 1991; Fowlie 1983:12, 1985a:51; Gruss and Wolff 1995: 111; Orchid Digest 49:51. 1985 (as *P. paucivittata*); Orchid Digest 49: 155. 1985.

The type of the name *P. sumatrana* was misinterpreted by Reichenbach, who applied the name to a different species. His misinterpretation has been consistently followed in both botany and horticulture. The type of the name *P. sumatrana* actually represents a species consistently known in horticulture and botany as *P. inscriptiosinensis*. To save both of these names in the sense of their established usage, I have proposed in the journal *Taxon* to conserve the name *Phalaenopsis sumatrana* (Orchidaceae) with a new type. This proposal, reproduced here, is under consideration as this book goes to press:

Phalaenopsis sumatrana Korth. & Rchb.f., Hamburg. Gartenz. 16:115. March 1860 [*Orchid.*], nom. cons. prop.

Type: Illustration in Ann. Hort. Bot. Leiden 4:145. 1860, typ. cons. prop.

Phalaenopsis sumatrana Korth. & Rchb.f. (l.c.) was based on Korthals' unpublished drawing 443. To paraphrase the discussion by Sweet (Genus *Phalaenopsis* 88. 1980), Reichenbach saw the original of Korthals' drawing at Leiden in 1856 but was not allowed to make a copy for his personal herbarium. After examining and duplicating a copy of this drawing in Lindley's personal herbarium, Korthals and Reichenbach published *P. sumatrana* with a short, minimally informative diagnosis.

Later in 1860 (after July), *P. zebrina* Witte was published with a full-page color illustration (Ann. Hort. Bot. Leiden, l.c.). Reichenbach later expanded his description of *P. sumatrana*, reducing *P. zebrina* to synonymy under the former (Gard. Chron. 506. 1865). Critical to an understanding of the taxonomy of this species and resulting nomenclatural issues are Reichenbach's comments that Korthals' drawing was a "not fully intelligible sketch" and his negative comments ("mishaps") concerning Witte's published drawing. Reichenbach stated that Witte's drawing was "indifferent" and "sufficiently

171

incorrect to secure its not being understood." In addition, using a flower sent him by Miquel in 1863 (*Icon Herb. Reichenbach 22343*, W) for comparison, he noted that Witte's drawing erred in not showing the lip with a terminal tuft of trichomes.

In hindsight, Korthals' drawing 443 is not problematic as opined by Reichenbach. This drawing represents a species otherwise unknown to Reichenbach or to Sweet and distinct from *P. zebrina*, a species only rediscovered by horticultural collectors in the 1980s. The first modern mention of this species was as *P.* "Djung Kwok" in a commercial advertisement (Amer. Orchid Soc. Bull. 51:1125. 1982). This taxon was later formally described as *P. inscriptiosinensis* Fowlie (Orchid Digest 47:11. 1983). *Phalaenopsis inscriptiosinensis*, clearly illustrated in Korthals no. 443, is characterized by inflorescences subequal to or shorter than the leaves and held beneath them, which bear solitary flowers in succession with completely glabrous lips.

In contrast, *P. zebrina* bears inflorescences subequal to or slightly longer than the leaves and held above them, which bear several flowers simultaneously with the flowers having a terminal tuft of trichomes on the lip. Reichenbach was correct in criticizing Witte's illustration for lacking the trichomes on the lip although this was recorded in the parallel description of *P. zebrina* by Teijsmann and Binnendijk (Natuur. Tijdschr. Nederl. Ind. 24:319. 1862). This was an error by the artist. What Reichenbach failed to realize was that Korthals' drawing also showed no trichomes on the lip. This was not an error and is a diagnostic character of *P. inscriptiosinensis*.

The result of Reichenbach linking *P. sumatrana*, based on a largely inaccessible unpublished drawing, with the more accessible illustration of *P. zebrina* was to mislead all subsequent workers into a misinterpretation of *P. sumatrana* in horticulture (Bechtel et al. in Man. Cult. Orch. Species 367. 1981; Hawkes in Encyc. Cult. Orch. 368. 1965; Schlechter in Die Orchideen, ed., 2:54. 1927; Stewart in RHS Man. Orch. 280. 1995; B. S. Wms. in Orchid-Grow. Man., ed 7:673. 1894; Veitch in Man. Orch. Pl. 40. 1893) and botany (Chan et al. in Orch. Borneo 1:252–253. 1994; Holttum in Fl. Malaysia, vol. 1, ed.

3: 670. 1964; Seidenfaden and Wood in Orch. Penin. Malaysia and Singapore 671. 1992; Sweet in Genus *Phalaenopsis* 88. 1980; Wood and Cribb in. Checkl. Orch. Born. 356. 1994).

Reichenbach was the primary orchid taxonomist in the late 19th century and his singular dominance created many problems. The case of *P. sumatrana* parallels Reichenbach's similar error in misapplying the name *Epidendrum atropurpureum* Willd. to a showy horticultural species correctly known as *Encyclia cordigera* (Kunth) Dressler (Dressler in Taxon 13:247. 1964).

The species interpreted in literature as *P. sumatrana* is widespread from Myanmar to Borneo (Seidenfaden in Opera Bot. 95:237. 1988) and the Philippines (Palawan). It is a widely grown horticultural plant that has played an active role in hybridization efforts. *Phalaenopsis inscriptiosinensis*, in contrast, is apparently narrowly endemic to central Sumatra and has had minimal impact on horticulture and hybridization efforts (Gruss and Wolff in *Phalaenopsis* 111–112. 1995).

No purpose would be served by honoring the type of *P. sumatrana* with the requisite application of the name to an obscure, insignificant species universally known as *P. inscriptiosinensis*. Conserving the name *P. sumatrana*, with a conserved type in agreement with established usage, serves nomenclatural stability and the needs of horticulture. The genus *Phalaenopsis* is preëminent in orchid horticulture and floriculture. Although the species known as *P. sumatrana* represents a small fraction of that commerce, no purpose is served by changing the name of that species.

Reichenbach recalled the early history of *P. inscriptiosinensis* (as *P. sumatrana*) in the *Gardeners' Chronicle* of 1865, which is repeated here:

The original discoverer of this plant was Korthals, who met with it in Sumatra before 1839,[*] Korthals, who would have been so happy

---

[*] Pieter Willem Korthals (1807–1892) is thought to have made his Sumatra collections in 1833.

to have worked on his plants. We saw a sketch of his in 1856 at Leyden, but were not allowed either to take a copy of it or to describe it. A few months later we found a copy of it, of the same sketch at Turnham Green with Dr. Lindley, and were most liberally allowed to make free use of it. We did so and a very short description was published by us from the not fully intelligible sketch.

The degree of variation in flower color in this species is unknown. Most of the specimens in cultivation are derived from limited original stock that has been artificially propagated in cultivation. I am accepting the plant illustrated by Fowlie as *P. paucivittata* (Fowlie 1985a:51) as an extremely darkly patterned *P. inscriptiosinensis*. It is certainly closer than most of the material in cultivation to Korthals' early drawing in having markings to near apices of the sepals and petals.

Fowlie described the leaves of *P. inscriptiosinensis* as "undulate," but both published photographs by him show leaves that are neither especially undulate nor with undulate margins.

Phalaenopsis speciosa Rchb.f.

Gard. Chron., n.s., 15:562. 1881; *Polychilos speciosa* (Rchb.f.) Shim, Malayan Nat. Journ. 36:26. 1982. Type: India. Nicobar Islands, *Berkeley s.n.* (holotype: W). Watercolor of the holotype reproduced in Sweet (1968:1097, 1980:77).

Phalaenopsis speciosa var. *maculata* Gower, The Garden 37:582. 1890, ex char. Type: *Hort. Smee s.n.* (not preserved).

Epiphytes. **Leaves** four or five, elliptic-obovate, tapered to the base, acute to obtuse, convex, to 20 × 8 cm. **Inflorescences** arching to subpendent, racemes or panicles, to 30 cm long. **Flowers** showy, fleshy, glossy, strongly fragrant, with +/− convex sepals and petals, variable in color, the sepals and petals purple with +/− white at the base, the lip purple, the column usually white. **Sepals** subsimilar, oblong-elliptic to elliptic-obovate, acute or obtuse, to 28 × 12 mm. **Petals** subsimilar to the sepals but usually somewhat shorter, to 28 × 10 mm. **Lip** three-lobed, to 18 mm long, to 16 mm wide across the expanded lateral lobes, the lateral lobes oblong-triangular, erect, the apices irregularly denticulate, falcate, the midlobe oblong-oblanceolate, obtuse-rounded, with a raised dorsal keel, the apex produced in an orbicular pad covered by dense trichomes, the **callus** biseriate, the posterior callus bifid, the anterior callus sulcate, bifid. **Column** straight, to 8 mm long, with a minutely erose-denticulate hood over the anther bed. **Pedicel** and **ovary** to 3 cm long.

Distribution: Endemic to India (Andaman and Nicobar Islands). **Etymology**: From the Latin, *speciosus* ("showy"). **Illustrations**: Gard. Chron., n.s., 18:745. 1882; Lindenia 6: t. 258. 1891; Sweet 1968:1098, 1980:83.

Phalaenopsis speciosa is problematic because apparently it was not in cultivation in the 20th century (see discussion at *P. speciosa* var. *imperatrix*). In addition, the flower color is highly variable; the first three clones brought into cultivation were each described as distinct entities. Added to this void is the closely related sister species, *P. tetraspis*, which is both sympatric (has an overlapping distribution) and also shows some variability in flower color. We know of *P. speciosa* only through a series of historic, and mostly cultivated, specimens preserved in herbaria and a few published drawings. The species can produce inflorescences longer than the leaves, although most historic illustrations show unbranched inflorescences subequal to the leaves in a manner similar to first-bloom seedlings of *P. sumatrana*. This may have been an artifact of cultivation and the "rushed" illustration of the first-bloom inflorescences after the plants re-established in Europe. Presumably *P. speciosa* initially produces racemes that subsequently reflower with lateral branches (panicles).

The original (type) plant of *P. speciosa* had flowers that were essentially purple with the bases of the sepals white with transverse purple barring, although other plants in contemporary cultivation at the time show white bases of both the sepals and petals without any barring. The reverse of the flower was white with clearly de-

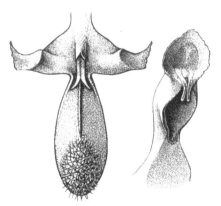

Phalaenopsis speciosa drawn from the type. Illustrator: H. R. Sweet.

175

fined purple spots, although here too other plants in contemporary cultivation did not show any spotting on the reverse. The column was white except in var. *christiana*.

Although *P. speciosa* var. *maculata* is included here in the synonymy of *P. speciosa* following Sweet, there is no particularly good reason—based on the brief original description ("sepals and petals pure white, beautifully spotted with lilac-mauve") and lack of preserved material—to consider this *P. speciosa* rather than *P. tetraspis*. *Phalaenopsis tetraspis* frequently produces a few transverse purple bars on the sepals and petals against a white ground color.

Two varieties have been published.

Phalaenopsis speciosa var. *christiana* Rchb.f.

Gard. Chron., n.s., 18:745. 1882; *Phalaenopsis speciosa* subvar. *christiana* (Rchb.f.) Veitch, Man. Orchid. Pl., pt. 7:39. 1891.
Type: India. Nicobar Islands, *Berkeley s.n.* (holotype: W).

Illustrations: No illustration is known.

This variety may represent a somewhat peloric clone or perhaps an unstable hybrid between *P. speciosa* and *P. tetraspis*. It was described as having purple sepals and column with contrasting white petals, although both the collector and Reichenbach commented that occasionally the petals would also be purple, rendering the flower similar to var. *imperatrix*. No other species of *Phalaenopsis* exhibits such an unstable pigment condition (although certain hybrid combinations produce flowers with petals a different color from the sepals).

Phalaenopsis speciosa var. *imperatrix* Rchb.f.

Gard. Chron., n.s., 18:745. 1882; *Phalaenopsis speciosa* subvar. *imperatrix* (Rchb.f.) Veitch, Man. Orchid. Pl., pt. 7:38. 1891.
Type: India. Nicobar Islands, *Berkeley s.n.* (holotype: W).

Phalaenopsis imperati Gower, The Garden 37:447. 1890, nom. nud.

Phalaenopsis speciosa var. *purpurata* Rchb.f. ex J. D. Hook., Fl. Brit. Ind. 6:30. 1890, nom. nud.

Etymology: Named, at Berkeley's suggestion, to honor the empress of India. **Illustrations**: Orchid Album 6: t. 158. 1885 (reproduced in Sweet 1980:77).

This variety, clearly the finest color morph for horticulture, differs from the type by having solid deep purple flowers without any barring at the base of the sepals. The reverse of the flowers do show some barring but not the spotting found in the type variety.

The solid purple flower of this variety has caused ongoing confusion with the similarly colored *P. pulchra* from the Philippines. Indeed, one widely grown clone of *P. pulchra*, mislabeled and sold as *P. speciosa* 'Orchidglade', SM/SFOS, continues to cause problems in horticulture. See the discussion under *P. pulchra* for the many differences between these two species.

A plant cultivated in Germany was illustrated as *P. speciosa* with a question mark (Gruss and Röllke 1990b:219). That flower is from a complex hybrid bred from some parent similar to *P.* George Vasquez and has nothing to do with the true *P. speciosa*. The anther bed lacks the hood characteristic of the species and this section.

I discount the report of an inflorescence in *P. speciosa* to "six feet in length" (*Orchid Review* 1:210. 1893) and presume this measurement was based on a misidentified plant of *P. pulchra*, which often produces very long inflorescences.

Phalaenopsis sumatrana Korth. & Rchb.f.

Hamburg. Gartenz. 16:115. March 1860; *Polychilos sumatrana* (Korth. & Rchb.f.) Shim, Malayan Nat. Journ. 36:26. 1982. Type: (proposed; pending approval). Type illustration in Ann. Hort. Bot. Leiden 4:145. 1860.

Phalaenopsis acutifolia Linden, Lindenia 2:11. 1886, nom. nud.

Phalaenopsis zebrina Witte, Ann. Hort. Bot. Leiden 4:145. 1860 (after July); Teijsm. & Binn., Natuurk. Tijdschr. Nederl. Indië 24:319. 1862, descr. ampl. Type: Indonesia. Sumatra, Prov. Palembang, *Gersen s.n.* (holotype: BO). Type illustration reproduced in Sweet (1968:1093, 1980:100).

177

Phalaenopsis sumatrana var. *paucivittata* Rchb.f., Gard. Chron., n.s., 17:628. 1882; *Phalaenopsis sumatrana* subvar. *paucivittata* (Rchb.f.) Veitch, Man. Orchid. Pl., pt. 7:40. 1891; *Phalaenopsis paucivittata* (Rchb.f.) Fowlie, Orchid Digest 49:51. 1985. Type: Origin unknown, *Hort. Veitch s.n.* (holotype: W). Original watercolor of the holotype reproduced in Sweet (1968:1096).

Phalaenopsis corningiana var. *flava* Hort. ex Fowlie, Orchid Digest 46:140. 1982, nom. nud., ex icon.

Pendent epiphytes. **Leaves** elliptic-obovate, tapered to the conduplicate base, rounded, acute, to 32 × 11 cm. **Inflorescences** arching to subpendent racemes or panicles, to 30 cm long, the floral bracts triangular, acute, concave, to 6 mm long. **Flowers** fleshy-rigid, mildly fragrant, extremely variable in color from white to green to wine red, with few to many transverse brown bars or with barring absent, the base of the sepals and petals without markings, the lip white with purple suffusion, the column white. **Dorsal sepal** oblong-elliptic, cuneate, acute-carinate, usually convex, to 24 × 15 mm, the **lateral sepals** obliquely elliptic, to 28 × 15 mm. **Petals** oblong-oblanceolate, acute, to 35 × 12 mm. **Lip** three-lobed, to 25 mm long, to 15 mm across the expanded lateral lobes, the lateral lobes erect, oblong, oblique-falcate, two-toothed, the midlobe oblong, obtuse, with a raised central dorsal keel,

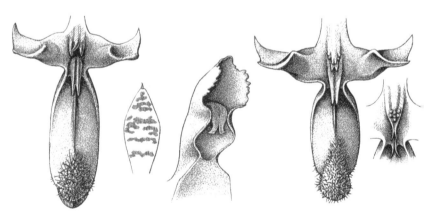

Phalaenopsis sumatrana drawn from the type of *P. zebrina* Witte.
Illustrator: H. R. Sweet.

the apex a raised boss of dense trichomes, the **callus** biseriate, the posterior callus four lobulate at the apex, at the base glandular, the anterior callus longer, sulcate, bifid. **Column** slightly arching, dilated toward the apex, to 1.5 cm long, the anther bed (clinandrium) hooded, with erose-dentate margins. **Pedicel** and **ovary** to 2.5 cm long.

Distribution: Widespread from Myanmar, Thailand, Vietnam, to Indonesia (Java, Sumatra), Malaysia (Perak, Johore), East Malaysia (Sabah), and the Philippines (Palawan). **Etymology**: Named for its place of origin on the island of Sumatra. **Illustrations**: Awards Quart. 18(2): 72. 1987; Awards Quart. 20(1):22. 1989; Awards Quart. 21(3):131, 156. 1990; Chan et al. 1994:252, 359; Die Orchidee 33(1):15, 19. 1982; Die Orchidee 33(6): back cover. 1982; Die Orchidee 44(2): Orchideenkartei Seite 721. 1993; Die Orchidee 45(6):47. 1994; Fowlie 1982:140, 141; Gordon 1989a:231; Griesbach 1981b:220; Gruss and Röllke 1993f: 230; Gruss and Wolff 1993:7 (as *P. corningiana* var. *flava*), 1995:114, 115; Martin 1985:417; Orchid Digest 40:105. 1976; Schettler 1989:154 (cf.); Sweet 1968:1099, 1980:87, 100; Vaughn 1969:752.

The original type of the name *P. sumatrana*, a drawing by Korthals, actually represents *P. inscriptiosinensis* and not the species consistently known as *P. sumatrana*. A proposal is pending to conserve a new type for the name *P. sumatrana* in keeping with its long-established usage. The text of the proposal can be found under *P. inscriptiosinensis*.

Fowlie (1982, 1985b) attempted to divide *P. sumatrana* (as accepted here) into several species. His divisions were largely unexplained and mostly based on minor color variations. He attempted to separate something called *P. zebrina* with a white ground color from similar plants with a yellowish ground color, calling the latter a pallid form of *P. corningiana*. His separation is contrary to the type of *P. zebrina*, which has a yellowish, not a white, ground color. On the basis of the published photographs, both Fowlie's *P. corningiana* var. *flava* and his *P. zebrina* are referrable to *P. sumatrana*. For example, Fowlie's *P. corningiana* from Tenom, Sabah, is perfectly good *P. sumatrana* (Fowlie 1985b:209).

Phalaenopsis sumatrana is very consistent in its morphology throughout its range with the exception of flower color, which is highly variable. The ground color may be white, pale straw yellow, pale green, or completely obscured by wine-red suffusion. The markings on the sepals and petals range from sparse to very dense and almost obscuring the

179

ground color. There does not appear to be any pattern to the distribution of these variants in nature (Comber pers. comm.).

The name *P. zebrina* has been misapplied in horticulture to plants bearing flowers with a stark white ground color. This is an error as the type illustration of *P. zebrina* clearly shows a yellowish ground color. The only described color morph of *P. sumatrana* with a stark white ground color is *P. sumatrana* var. *paucivittata*, a variety described as having white flowers with a few (three or four) transverse brown-purple bars (the epithet *paucivittata* literally means "few-striped"). Fowlie (1985a) elevated this variety to species rank and applied the name to a collection he made in Sumatra. The photograph of a richly marked flower that he supplied is clearly not in agreement with Reichenbach's concept and is correctly identified as *P. inscriptiosinensis*. The origin of Reichenbach's plant is still unknown. Recent collections of *P. sumatrana* from the Philippines appear to most closely resemble var. *paucivittata*, as does the clone *P. sumatrana* 'H. H.' (*Die Orchidee* 43(6):47. 1991).

Phalaenopsis tetraspis Rchb.f.

Xenia Orch. 2:146. 1968; *Phalaenopsis speciosa* var. *tetraspis* (Rchb.f.) Sweet, Amer. Orchid Soc. Bull. 37:1092. 1968. Type: [presumably India. Andaman Islands], *Lobb s.n.* (holotype. W).

Phalaenopsis barrii King ex J. D. Hook., Ann. Roy. Bot. Gard. Calcutta 5:38. 1895, nom. nud.

Phalaenopsis sumatrana var. *alba* G. Wilson, Orchid World 5:146. 1915. Type: *Hort. Schmid s.n.* (not preserved).

Epiphytes. **Leaves** four or five (to nine in robust plants), elliptic-obovate, tapered to the base, acute to obtuse, convex, to 20 × 8 cm. **Inflorescences** arching to subpendent, racemes or panicles, to 30 cm long. **Flowers** showy, fleshy, glossy, strongly fragrant, with +/− concave sepals and petals, variable in color, the sepals and petals white with a few transverse purple bars at the base, the lip white with faint purple suffusion, the lateral lobes of the lip bright yellow, the column usually white. **Sepals** subsimilar, oblong-elliptic to elliptic-obovate, acute or obtuse, to 28 × 12 mm. **Petals** subsimilar to the sepals but usually somewhat shorter, to 28 × 10 mm. **Lip** three-lobed, to 18 mm long, to 16 mm wide across the expanded lateral lobes, the lateral lobes ovate-triangular at the base, oblong toward the apices, erect, the apices irregularly denticulate, with a posterior falcate hook, the midlobe oblong, obtuse-subacute, with a raised dorsal keel, the apex produced in an elongate oblanceolate pad covered by dense trichomes, the **callus** triseriate, the posterior callus minutely four-lobulate, the median callus bifid, the anterior callus sulcate, bifid. **Column** straight, to 8 mm long, with a minutely erose-denticulate hood over the anther bed. **Pedicel** and **ovary** to 3 cm long.

Distribution: India (Andaman and Nicobar Islands) and Indonesia (Sumatra). **Etymology**: Obscure. Most likely the name is from the Greek, *tetra* ("four") and *aspes* ("rounded shield"), although what Reichenbach was alluding to is unknown. **Illustrations**: Awards Quart. 26(2):84. 1995; Gruss and Wolff 1995:118; Sweet 1971b:46, 1980:83, 85.

Sweet reduced the white-flowered *P. tetraspis* to a variety of *P. speciosa*, noting the lack of distinguishing morphological characters to separate the two entities. Sweet had little material of either species to examine and did not have access to the large population of *P. tetraspis* that has recently entered cultivation. The two species are clearly closely related sister species, but I think they are distinct for the following reasons.

First, there are differences, albeit subtle, in floral morphology as shown by Sweet's drawings of the respective types. In *P. tetraspis* the retrorse hooks terminating the lateral lip lobes are more pronounced, the midlobe is oblong rather than obovate, and the distribution of trichomes on the midlobe is different. The trichomes in *P. tetraspis* form an oblanceolate patch from the middle of the midlobe while *P. speciosa* bears a semicircular field of trichomes restricted to the apical third of the midlobe.

Second, the discovery of *P. tetraspis* in Sumatra (Fowlie 1992) casts doubt that the white *P. tetraspis* and the dark purple

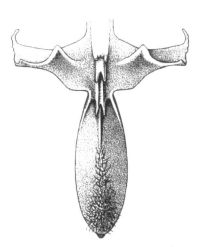

Phalaenopsis tetraspis drawn from the type. Illustrator: H. R. Sweet.

P. speciosa are merely varieties of one species. If they are both part of one entity, why is the purple phase apparently absent from Sumatra?

Third, plants of *P. tetraspis* now in cultivation produce either pure white sepals and petals or segments with a few, basal, irregularly dispersed transverse purple bars. This is not the usual pattern of pigmentation seen in alba forms of *Phalaenopsis*. Granted, however, that plants now in cultivation probably come from Sumatra and not the Andaman and Nicobar islands. Also I have seen no evidence whatsoever of pigment on the back surfaces of the sepals and petals in *P. tetraspis* in the manner that *P. speciosa* is marked.

Finally, the historic illustration of *P. tetraspis* published in the *Botanical Magazine* is misleading because it shows a two-flowered inflorescence. Plants of *P. tetraspis* recently introduced in cultivation typically bear panicles with many densely, few-flowered branches. Joe Palermo (pers. comm.) says that this character is enhanced when the plants are grown under lower than average light levels. Under low light levels even first-bloom seedlings produce panicles. I do not doubt the identification of this illustration because the tapered oblanceolate cluster of trichomes on the lip midlobe, characteristic of *P. tetraspis*, is clearly evident in the black-and-white lip dissections surrounding the color plate.

Until such a time that fresh material of both *P. speciosa* and *P. tetraspis* can be obtained from the Andaman and Nicobar islands, I see no reason to unite these two concepts.

Phalaenopsis sumatrana var. *alba* was minimally described as having pure white sepals and petals and a lip with wine-red longitudinal stripes on the midlobe. Without preserved material or other form of documentation Sweet assumed this was a color variant of *P. sumatrana*. The origin of this plant is unknown, but the grower remarked that unlike his plants of typical *P. sumatrana*, which did not grow well under his conditions (lowland, on the coast of Java), this *alba* variety thrived. The coloration of the lip and the vigor of the plant under sweltering conditions convince me that this variety actually represents *P. tetraspis*.

CHAPTER 9

Subgenus *Phalaenopsis*

Subgenus *Phalaenopsis*

This subgenus, which includes the type of the genus, is characterized by having a single callus and, with the exception of the three species of section *Deliciosae*, smooth lateral lobes of the lip without the characteristic tooth-like ridge found in other subgenera. With the exception of spots found at the base of the sepals and on the sepals and petals of some species (*P. stuartiana*, for example) all species in this subgenus bear essentially unmarked white or pink flowers. They lack the transverse barring patterns and yellow ground colors found in subgenus *Polychilos*. To the best of my knowledge, all species of this subgenus exhibit a post-pollination response of a withered, dry perianth. There is no evidence of the persistent, fleshy, chlorophyllous perianth seen in other sections.

Recent molecular work using the matK gene (Jarrell unpubl.) supports this grouping and indicates this subgenus is derived relative to subgenera *Polychilos* and *Aphyllae*.

Section *Phalaenopsis*

> *Phalaenopsis* section *Euphalaenopsis* Benth., Gen. Pl. 3:573. 1883. Type: *Epidendrum amabile* L. (= *Phalaenopsis amabilis* (L.) Bl.).
>
> *Synadena* Raf., Fl. Tellur. 4:9. 1838. Type: *Synadena amabilis* (L.) Raf. (= *Phalaenopsis amabilis* (L.) Bl.).

Species of this section bear flowers with broad petals, the petals much broader than the sepals. In addition, they bear prominent, erect, somewhat glossy calli. With one or two exceptions (such as *P. schilleriana*) the flowers of this section are not fragrant.

The pollination biology is known for *P. amabilis* (Chan et al. 1994: 234). The flowers are visited by large carpenter bees of the genus *Xylocopa*. Chan et al. report that pollination is highly successful and typically results in more than 50 percent fruit set.

Key to the species of section *Phalaenopsis*

1. Flowers white.
  2. Leaves marbled.
    3. Lateral lobes of the lip bright yellow, unspotted; midlobe of the lip not spotted. . . . . *P. philippinensis*
    3. Lateral lobes and midlobe of the lip densely spotted. . . *P. stuartiana*
  2. Leaves not marbled.
    4. Midlobe of the lip rose. . . . . *P. ×intermedia*
    4. Midlobe of the lip white.
      5. Callus shield-shaped with the upper edge terminating in one pair of divergent teeth. . . . . *P. amabilis*
      5. Callus not shield-shaped, the upper edge terminating in two pairs of subparallel teeth. . . . . *P. aphrodite*
1. Flowers pink.
      6. Leaves green or overlain with silver, generally not in a strong marbled pattern, the undersurface usually green; the callus bilobed with a deep central sinus; the apex of the lip extended in long, narrow tails longer than the midlobe; summer flowering. . . . . *P. sanderiana*
      6. Leaves strongly marbled deep green and silver, the undersurface usually purple; the callus shield-shaped with only a shallow notch at the apex; the apex of the lip bilobed with gently recurved falcate lobes less than half the length of the midlobe; spring flowering. . . . . *P. schilleriana*

Phalaenopsis amabilis (L.) Bl.

Bijdr. 7:294. 1825; *Epidendrum amabile* L., Sp. Pl., ed. 1:953. 1753; *Cymbidium amabile* (L.) Roxb., Hort. Beng. 63. 1814, nom. nud.,

Fl. Ind., ed. 3, 2:457. 1832; *Synadena amabilis* (L.) Raf., Fl. Tellur. 4:9. 1838. Type: Indonesia. Java, without precise locality, *Osbeck s.n.* (holotype: LINN). Photograph of the holotype reproduced in Sweet (1969:684, 1980:23).

Phalaenopsis grandiflora Lindl., Gard. Chron. 1848:39. 1848; *Phalaenopsis amabilis* var. *grandiflora* (Lindl.) Batem., Second Cent. Orch. Pl., t. 114. 1867. Type: Indonesia. Java, leg. ignot., *Hort. Veitch s.n.* (holotype: K).

Phalaenopsis grandiflora var. *gracillima* Burb., The Garden 22:118. 1882. Type: The Philippines. Palawan Island, *Burbidge s.n.* (holotype: BM).

Phalaenopsis gloriosa Rchb.f., Gard. Chron., ser. 3, 3:554. 1888; *Phalaenopsis aphrodite* var. *gloriosa* (Rchb.f.) Veitch, Man. Orch. Pl., pt. 7:25. 1891; *Phalaenopsis amabilis* var. *aphrodite* subvar. *gloriosa* (Rchb.f.) Ames, Orchid. 2:227. 1908. Type: Origin unknown, *Hort. Low s.n.* (holotype: W).

Phalaenopsis amabilis var. *fournieri* Cogn., Chron. Orchid. 166. 1898, ex char. Type: Origin unknown, *Hort. Regnier s.n.* (holotype: ? not preserved).

Phalaenopsis amabilis var. *rimestadiana* Linden, Lindenia 16:35, t. 736. 1901; *Phalaenopsis rimestadiana* (Linden) Rolfe, Orchid Rev. 13:260. 1905. Type: Origin unknown, *Hort. Linden s.n.* (holotype: ? not preserved); lectotype, effectively designated by Sweet: t. 736, loc. cit.

Phalaenopsis amabilis var. *rimestadiana alba* Hort., Orchis 1:27, t. 4. 1906. Type: Not preserved or if preserved, destroyed at B; lectotype, here designated: t. 4, loc. cit.

Phalaenopsis amabilis var. *ramosa* van Deventer, Orchideën 1:94, figs. 1 and 2. 1935. Type: Indonesia. Without precise locality, *Hort. van Deventer s.n.*, not preserved; lectotype, here designated: figs. 1 and 2, loc. cit.

Phalaenopsis ×elisabethae Hort., Rev. Hort., n.s., 20:534. 1927, ex char.

Robust epiphytes. **Leaves** variable, oblong-oblanceolate to elliptic-obovate, tapered to the folded base, obtuse, minutely and obliquely bilobed at the apex, arching to pendent, to 50 × 10 cm. **Inflorescences** scapose racemes or few-branched panicles, often producing secondary branches from quiescent nodes on the peduncle, arching to pendent, the peduncle terete, with distant appressed tubular sheaths, the floral bracts inconspicuous, triangular, concave, scarious, to 5 mm long. **Flowers** showy, membranous, white, the lip and callus variously marked with

8 cm

8 mm

Phalaenopsis amabilis. Illustrator: F. Pupulin.

yellow and red, alternately arranged in two ranks. **Dorsal sepal** erect, elliptic-ovate, obtuse-rounded, concave or convex, to 4 × 2.5 cm, the **lateral sepals** obliquely ovate-lanceolate to ovate-elliptic, acute, concave, to 4 × 2.5 cm. **Petals** subrotund from a cuneate-clawed base, broadly rounded, to 4.5 × 5 cm. **Lip** three-lobed, to 2.3 cm long, to 4.2 cm wide across the expanded lateral lobes, the lateral lobes obliquely elliptic, broadly clawed, obtuse-rounded, erect-incurved forming a cylinder, the midlobe in the form of a cross, the basal lobules triangular, variable in development over the range of the species, the apex bluntly obtuse flanked by long, flexuous tendril-like appendages (cirrhi), the **callus** uniseriate, peltate, shield-shaped, the posterior edge smoothly notched between one pair of blunt teeth, the anterior edge obtuse-rounded. **Column** straight, stout. **Pedicel** and **ovary** to 5 cm long.

Distribution: Widespread from Sumatra and Java to the southern Philippines, and east to New Guinea and Queensland, Australia. Plants from the eastern portion of the range are accepted as distinct subspecies. Chan et al. (1994) record *P. amabilis* in Borneo from sea level to 1500 m in elevation. **Etymology**: From the Greek, *amabilis* ("lovely"). **Illustrations**: Awards Quart. 15(4):177. 1984; Awards Quart. 18(1):47. 1987; Awards Quart. 19(4):196. 1988; Awards Quart. 24(3):211. 1993; Awards Quart. 25(3):174. 1994; Awards Quart. 25(4):225, 228, 229, 233. 1994; Chan et al. 1994:232; Nash 1995:263; Orchid Digest 46:7. 1982; Sweet 1968:871; Sweet 1969:682, 684, 686; Sweet 1980:20, 21, 22, 23, 41.

This is the largest-flowered species in the genus. With its broad petals and full form, in keeping with historic British flower-judging standards of an idealized round flower, *P. amabilis* has until very recently formed the primary basis for hybridization in the genus. Certainly the large, round flowers borne on an arching raceme define the general public's perception of a phalaenopsis as well as industry standards for pot-plant production of phalaenopsis. A showy orchid by virtue of

Phalaenopsis amabilis, the type flower in the Linnaean Herbarium. Photographer: L. A. Garay.

its large, numerous, pure white flowers, *P. amabilis* has been designated the national flower of Indonesia.

Lindley was confused over the identification of the true *P. amabilis* and consistently misapplied that name to plants of *P. aphrodite*. As a result of this confusion, Lindley needed a name for his "other" species and he redescribed true *P. amabilis* as *P. grandiflora*. Ironically the names *P. grandiflora* and it derivative *P. amabilis* var. *grandiflora* have been equally misapplied as informal designations for Philippine plants of *P. amabilis* in cultivation even though the type specimens of both are from Indonesia (Java).

One ongoing confusion with *P. amabilis* is the application of the name to white-flowered plants originating from southern Taiwan. Those Taiwanese plants are correctly a subspecies of *P. aphrodite*, which see. No true *P. amabilis* has been recorded from Taiwan or its neighboring islands.

In nature, the effective pollination of *P. amabilis* is usually quite high for an orchid. When the flowers are not effectively pollinated (i.e., do not result in fruit set), the inflorescences typically branch and reflower, a characteristic highly appreciated in horticulture. As a result, inflorescences in the wild sometimes reach great lengths of more than 1.5 meters. *Phalaenopsis amabilis* is an effective colonizing species, and it is not uncommon to find large numbers of seedlings in nature on a given host tree. This is one reason that collection for local horticulture in places like Sabah, in the absence of habitat destruction, does not appear to seriously deplete native populations.

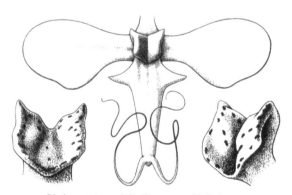

Phalaenopsis amabilis. Illustrator: H. R. Sweet.

188

Phalaenopsis amabilis is variable for many of its characters as one would expect in a species with a broad range rich with the genetic isolating mechanisms formed by the disjunctions of island biology. Most of the variation is minor and does not warrant formal recognition. This variation includes the total and relative amounts of red and yellow pigment on the lip, the presence and density of red spots on the lateral lobes of the lip, and the overall flower shape. This is not to say that this variation does not affect the aesthetics of this species and its hybrids. For example, some orchid breeders prefer the flowers wider than tall and the lateral sepals divergent; others, such as Amado Vasquez, prefer variants where the flowers are taller than wide and the lateral sepals are subparallel.

Minor variation aside, three variants require discussion. One is a color morph; the other two have apparent definable morphologic differences and appear to have distinct geographic ranges, and hence they are treated here as subspecies.

Phalaenopsis amabilis subsp. *moluccana*
(Schltr.) E. A. Christ., stat. nov.

Basionym: *Phalaenopsis amabilis* var. *moluccana* Schltr., Repert. Spec. Nov. Regni Veg. 10:193. 1911. Type: Indonesia. Sulawesi, Gunong Klabat (Minahassa), *Schlechter 20581* (holotype: B, destroyed; lectotype, designated by Sweet (1969:686): AMES).

Phalaenopsis celebica van Vloten, Die Orchidee 1:125. 1932, ex char. Type: Indonesia. Sulawesi, without precise locality, *Hort. van Vloten s.n.* (not preserved).

Distribution: Indonesia in Sulawesi and the Molucca Islands and East Malaysia in eastern Sabah. **Etymology**: Named for its place of origin in the Molucca Islands. **Illustrations**: Mayr 1986:179; Orchid Digest 46:29. 1982; Sweet 1969:687, 1980:25; Tharp et al. 1987:90, 91.

In the western portion of its range including the type locality in Java, *P. amabilis* produces a lip where the midlobe is cruciform (in the shape of a cross), the base with prominent triangular teeth (the arms of the cross). Toward the middle of its range in Sulawesi, the teeth at the base are far less prominent; these plants are recognized as subsp. *molucanna*.

189

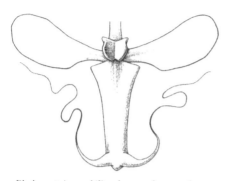

Phalaenopsis amabilis subsp. *moluccana* drawn from the type. Illustrator: H. R. Sweet.

This subspecies, which differs by having no lateral teeth at the base of the midlobe of the lip, has been considered endemic to Indonesia in Sulawesi and the Molucca Islands; however, it has also been collected in eastern Sabah by Shim and illustrated in the *Orchid Digest* (loc. cit.). Collecting in eastern Kalimantan has been insufficient, meaning the extent of subsp. *molucanna* in Borneo is unknown.

A note in passing might be made about historic collections of *Phalaenopsis* on Ambon (De Wit 1977), in which a Robinson collection from Amahoesoe on Ambon is referred to *P. amabilis*. The status of that Robinson collection is unknown but was probably destroyed by fire in Manila at the close of World War II. It should also be noted that the *Angraecum album majus* of Rumphius (see De Wit 1977, pl. 3-2) is clearly *P. amabilis* despite De Wit's speculations concerning *P. deliciosa* and *Dendrobium crumenatum* Sw. The growth habit, the presence and angle of the lateral branches on the inflorescence, and proportion of the flowers to the plant size can only apply to *P. amabilis*.

Phalaenopsis amabilis subsp. *rosenstromii*

(Bail.) E. A. Christ., comb. et stat. nov.

Basionym: *Phalaenopsis rosenstromii* Bailey, Queensland Agric. J. 17:231. 1906; *Phalaenopsis amabilis* (L.) Bl. var. *rosenstromii* (Bailey) Nicholls, Austral. Orchid Rev. 14:104. 1949. Type: Australia. Queensland, Daintree River, *Rosenstrom s.n.* (holotype: K; isotype: BRI).

Phalaenopsis amabilis (L.) Bl. var. *papuana* Schltr., Repert. Spec. Nov. Regni Veg. Beih. 1:968. 1913. Type: Papua New Guinea. Kaiser Wilhelms Land, Malia, at foot of Bismarck Mts., *Schlechter 18409* (holotype: B, destroyed; lectotype, designated by Sweet (1980:25): AMES; isolectotypes: E, K, L, NSW).

Distribution: New Guinea and Australia. Found from sea level to ca. 600 m (in Australia) or 1500 m (Papua New Guinea) in elevation. **Etymology**: Named for collector G. Rosenstrom. **Illustrations**: Dockrill 1992:1037; Grundon et al. 1993:461; O'Byrne 1994:513, color plate following p. 292; Sweet 1980:25. **Note**: The color photograph in Dockrill (1992: pl. 157), labeled *P. rosenstromii*, is *P.* ×*intermedia*, not *P. amabilis*.

In the eastern portion of the species' range in New Guinea and Australia are the plants recognized as subsp. *rosenstromii*. This subspecies has been defined by the shorter, narrowly triangular midlobe of the lip, with inconspicuous teeth at the base. When Schlechter described this entity (as *P. amabilis* var. *papuana*) he did not mention the shape of the midlobe but focused on perceived differences of the callus and the viscidium of the pollinarium. I do not see any significant differences in these characters when Schlechter's drawings and isotypes are compared with other material of *P. amabilis* from throughout its range.

Clements (1989:105) lectotypified *P. amabilis* var. *papuana* with the isosyntype specimen *Schlechter 18409* at Kew. This is superfluous and overlooks Sweet's earlier explicit lectotypification with the duplicate specimen at the Orchid Herbarium of Oakes Ames at Harvard University.

Recently, Australian workers, largely following Clements' treatment, have considered *P. amabilis* subsp. *rosenstromii* a separate species, calling it *P. rosenstromii*. That action is based in part on an extremely narrow species concept, which does not allow for infraspecific categories such as subspecies, and in part on an apparent miscommunication between Clements and Yoneo Sagawa. First, as is obvious from this treatment, I reject an approach that *requires* entities be treated as species (rather than as forms, varieties, or subspecies) if morphological differences can be perceived.

Theoretical philosophies aside, the case of *P. amabilis* and its two subspecies provides a particularly tricky example when trying to shoe-

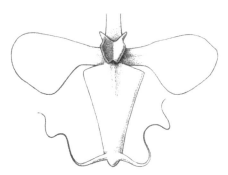

Phalaenopsis amabilis subsp. *rosenstromii* drawn from the type of its synonym, *P. amabilis* var. *papuana*. Illustrator: H. R. Sweet.

box variants into separate species. The variation among these subspecies is essentially clinal (variation that is continuous and directional
from one end of a species range to the antipodal end), with a general
narrowing and shortening of the midlobe of the lip from west to east.
The variation is discontinuous because of isolation resulting from the
well-established phytogeographic breaks between Borneo and Sulawesi
on the one hand and between Sulawesi and New Guinea on the other.

It also should be noted, however, that the perceived morphological
differences between these subspecies are based on the type specimens
together with a rather small sampling of plants, and they do not necessarily accurately represent the variability of these characters in the actual populations. Collections from Australia (Grundon et al. 1993) and
New Guinea (O'Byrne 1994) show pronounced lateral teeth at the
base of the midlobe of the lip in disagreement with the types of *P. rosenstromii* and *P. amabilis* var. *papuana*. This apparent variation signals caution and the need for additional research before elevating this subspecies to species rank, with the resulting havoc on hybrid registration.

Finally, Clements' strongest argument for elevating Australasian
plants of *P. amabilis* to species status as *P. rosenstromii* was the report that
they "have different chromosome numbers (Sagawa pers. comm.)."
Subsequently, Sagawa has told me that he suggested that Australasian
plants of *P. amabilis* might (!) have a different chromosome number
but that no actual chromosome counting has been done.

Phalaenopsis amabilis var. *aurea* (Hort.) Rolfe

Gard. Chron., n.s., 26:212. 1886; *Phalaenopsis grandiflora* var.
aurea Hort., Proc. Roy. Soc. 4:135. 1864. Neotype, designated by
Sweet (1969:686): Borneo, without precise locality, *Hort. Warner
s.n.* as illustrated in Sel. Orch. Pl., ser. 2, t. 7. 1869.

Phalaenopsis amabilis var. *fuscata* Rchb.f., Bot. Zeit. 20:214. 1862;
Phalaenopsis grandiflora var. *fuscata* (Rchb.f.) Burb., The Garden
22:118. 1882. Type: Borneo. Without precise locality, *Hort. Low
s.n.* (holotype: W).

Phalaenopsis grandiflora var. *ruckeri* Burb., The Garden 9:314.
1876, nom. nud.

Distribution: The geographic extent of this variety and the frequency of it within mixed populations in unknown; however, it is typical of plants originating in Sabah, East Malaysia (Borneo). **Etymology**: From the Latin, *aureus* ("golden yellow"), a reference to the deep lip color. **Illustrations**: Chan et al. 1994: pl. 15a.

This variety differs from other varieties and subspecies by having a yellow lip midlobe rather than a white midlobe with at most a brush of yellow at the base. It would appear to be the most desirable color variant for breeding purposes.

Phalaenopsis ×*amphitrite* Kraenzl.

Gard. Chron., ser. 3, 11:618. 1892. Type: The Philippines. No specimen is known.*

Phalaenopsis stuartiana var. *hrubyana* Rchb.f., Gard. Chron. 1:372. 1881. Type: The Philippines.

Phalaenopsis ×*wiganiae* Hort. (1899).

Phalaenopsis ×*schilleriano-stuartiana* Hort. (1900).

Distribution: Endemic to the Philippines. **Etymology**: Named to honor Amphitrite, wife of Neptune in Greek mythology. **Illustrations**: No illustrations are known.

This natural hybrid represents the combination of *P. sanderiana* and *P. stuartiana*. Although the ranges of the two species share a long border in the southern Philippines, the hybrid appears to be rare. This is no doubt because of the differences in the flowering seasons of the parents: *P. stuartiana* flowers in the spring, while *P. sanderiana* flowers later in the summer.

I have examined one plant grown by Diane Davis that appears to represent either *P.* ×*amphitrite* or part of a retrogressive swarm between *P.* ×*amphitrite* and *P. stuartiana*. The flowers superficially resemble *P. stuartiana* but have fuller petals that lack the narrow wedge-shaped

---

* The type material, if any was preserved, would have been deposited in Berlin or in Kraenzlin's personal herbarium. The Berlin herbarium was mostly destroyed during World War II; no *Phalaenopsis* specimens are known to have survived. The Kraenzlin herbarium at Hamburg is missing the Aeridinae.

bases typical of true *P. stuartiana*. Most noticeably, both the back of the sepals and the petals where they attach to the ovary are bright rose-purple, a character never seen in *P. stuartiana*.

I believe that *P. sanderiana* var. *marmorata* also may represent this hybrid.

Phalaenopsis aphrodite Rchb.f.

Hamburg. Gartenz. 18:35. 1862; *Phalaenopsis amabilis* var. *aphrodite* (Rchb.f.) Ames, Orchid. 2:226. 1908. Type: The Philippines. Luzon, Manila, *Cuming 2092* (W).

Phalaenopsis amabilis var. *longifolia* Don, Hort. Cantabrig., ed. 13:608. 1845. Type: The Philippines. Manila, *Hort. s.n.* (holotype: ? not preserved).

Phalaenopsis amabilis var. *rotundifolia* Don, Hort. Cantabrig., ed. 13:608. 1845. Type: The Philippines. Manila, *Hort. s.n.* (holotype: ? not preserved).

Phalaenopsis ambigua Rchb.f., Hamburg. Gartenz. 18:35. 1862; *Phalaenopsis amabilis* var. *ambigua* (Rchb.f.) Burb., The Garden 22:119. 1882. Type: The Philippines. Without precise locality, *Hort. s.n.* (holotype: W).

Phalaenopsis erubescens Burb., The Garden 9:314. 1876; *Phalaenopsis amabilis* var. *erubescens* (Burb.) Burb., The Garden 22:119. 1882; *Phalaenopsis amabilis* var. *aphrodite* subvar. *erubescens* (Burb.) Ames, Orchid. 2:227. 1908. Type: The Philippines. Without precise locality, *Hort. s.n.* (holotype: ? not preserved).

Phalaenopsis amabilis var. *dayana* Hort. ex Warn. & B. S. Wms., Orchid Album 1: t. 11. 1881; *Phalaenopsis aphrodite* var. *dayana* (Hort.) Veitch, Man. Orch. Pl., pt. 7:24. 1891; *Phalaenopsis amabilis* var. *aphrodite* subvar. *dayana* (Hort.) Ames, Orchid. 2:227. 1908. Type: The Philippines. Without precise locality, *Hort. Day s.n.* (holotype: W).

Epiphytes. **Leaves** elliptic to oblong-ovate, tapered to the base, acute or obtuse, green +/− red suffusion on the lower surfaces, to 25 × 6 cm.

Inflorescences arching to pendent racemes or few-branched panicles, the rachis somewhat fractiflex, the floral bracts minute, triangular, concave, scarious, to 5 mm long. **Flowers** showy, membranous, white, the lip and callus variably marked with yellow and red, the column white. **Dorsal sepal** elliptic to elliptic-ovate, obtuse-rounded, to 4×2 cm, the **lateral sepals** obliquely ovate, acute to subacute, to 4×2 cm. **Petals** broadly subrhomboid, clawed, obtuse-rounded, to 4×4 cm. **Lip** three-lobed, to 3 cm long, to 4 cm wide across the expanded lateral lobes, the lateral

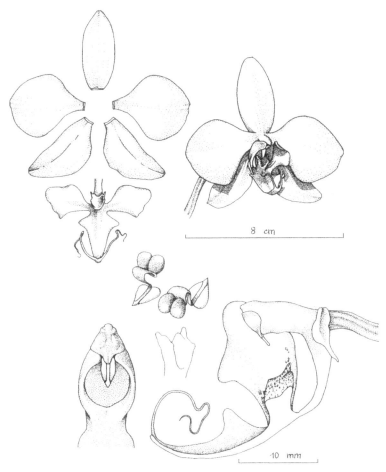

Phalaenopsis aphrodite. Illustrator: F. Pupulin

195

lobes obliquely ovate, clawed, broadly rounded-obtuse, incurved-erect forming a cylinder, the midlobe triangular-hastate, the apex bluntly obtuse flanked by a pair of tendril-like appendages (cirrhi), the **callus** uniseriate, the posterior edge notched forming four erect teeth, the anterior edge obtuse-rounded. **Column** stout, fleshy. **Pedicel** and **ovary** to 3.5 cm long.

Distribution: The northern Philippines and southeastern Taiwan, the latter a distinct subspecies. **Etymology**: Named for the Greek goddess of beauty and light, Aphrodite. **Illustrations**: Awards Quart. 20(1): 22. 1989; Awards Quart. 22(1):18. 1991; Awards Quart. 22(2):94. 95. 1991; Awards Quart. 26(4):190. 1995; Christenson 1999a:364; Die Orchidee 35(1):31. 1984; Fowlie 1991b:120; Gruss 1995:139; Gruss and Wolff 1995:44, 45; Sweet 1969:691, 693; Sweet 1980:20, 27, 29, 41; Tharp et al. 1987:91.

Phalaenopsis aphrodite is the other large, white-flowered species in the genus. The Philippine subspecies (subsp. *aphrodite*) was once widespread in cultivation but is rarely seen in modern collections. Recently, however, the Taiwan subspecies has been artificially propagated in vast quantities and is now commonly available, both from orchid growers and as mass-marketed pot-plants in supermarkets and other non-traditional sales outlets.

Phalaenopsis aphrodite has been confused with *P. amabilis*, whose flowers are very similar. In addition to having distinct ranges, with *P. amabilis* only recorded from the southern Philippines, their callus structures

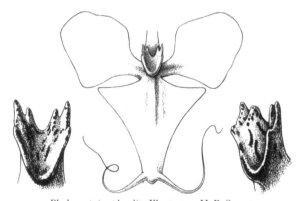

Phalaenopsis aphrodite. Illustrator: H. R. Sweet.

are distinct. *Phalaenopsis aphrodite* has the posterior edge of the callus divided into four teeth. This is unlike the callus of *P. amabilis*, which is divided into only two teeth. The species in section *Phalaenopsis* with a callus most similar to *P. aphrodite* is *P. sanderiana*. The callus of *P. sanderiana* is also four-toothed, but the teeth are highly unequal and the two inner teeth are significantly taller than the outer two. In *P. aphrodite* the teeth are subequal, with the outer teeth slightly taller than the inside two.

Sweet used leaf color to separate *P. amabilis* from *P. aphrodite*, suggesting that the undersurface of the leaves were green in *P. amabilis* and purple in *P. aphrodite*. I find this character variable in both species. For example, the plant described as *P. ambigua* represents a Philippine example of *P. aphrodite* that lacked the purple undersurface to the leaves, as do plants of subsp. *formosana*.

Phalaenopsis aphrodite subsp. *formosana*
E. A. Christ., subsp. nov.

Subspecies haec typo similis sed foliis porraceis, floribus parvioribus, et inflorescentiis ramosissimis differt.

Type: Taiwan. South Cape, *Henry 1705* (holotype: NY; isotype: K).

Phalaenopsis formosana Miwa, Pract. Hort. (Jissai Engei, Tokyo) 27:115. 1941, nom. illeg.

Phalaenopsis babuyana Miwa, Pract. Hort. (Jissai Engei, Tokyo) 27:117. 1941, nom. illeg.

Phalaenopsis formosum Hort., Sander's One-Table List of Orchid Hybrids 2:862. 1961, nom. nud.

Phalaenopsis amabilis var. *formosa* Shimadzu, Orchid Rev. 29:68. 1921, nom. nud.

Distribution: Endemic to Taiwan. Known only from a small region of the mainland and a few outlying islands (Babuyan, Lan-yeu, and Lu-tao), the mainland population has been reported as extinct (Cheng n.d.).
Etymology: Named for its place of origin in Taiwan, historically known as Formosa. **Illustrations**: Awards Quart. 18(1):18. 1987; Awards Quart.

22(1):50. 1991 (as *P. amabilis*); Awards Quart. 22(2):98. 1991 (as *P. amabilis*); Awards Quart. 24(1):38, 39. 1993; Awards Quart. 24(3):225, 236. 1993; Awards Quart. 25(2):75. 1994; Awards Quart. 25(3):159, 164. 1994; Cheng n.d.:68–70.

Phalaenopsis aphrodite subsp. *formosana* represents an isolated northern population of *P. aphrodite*, a species which is otherwise endemic to the Philippines. Plants of subsp. *formosana* bear apple-green leaves without any trace of anthocyanin pigments, somewhat smaller flowers, and much branched panicles that typically produce side branches from even the most basal nodes on the inflorescence. Although plants of this subspecies in cultivation have been confused with *P. amabilis*, both in the literature and for purposes of hybrid registration, wild-collected material clearly shows the four-toothed callus characteristic of *P. aphrodite* and unlike that of *P. amabilis*. The callus morphology of subsp. *formosana* is clearly shown in the photograph in Cheng (n.d.:70).

Miwa (1941) distinguished between the Taiwan populations found on the mainland versus those that occurred on the island of Babuyan. I do not think these differences are significant at the taxonomic level. Based on the flower size and gestalt, however, the mass-propagated plants of subsp. *formosana* in the trade appear to be of the Babuyan strain or infraspecific hybrids strongly influenced by the Babuyan strain.

Phalaenopsis ×*intermedia* Lindl.

In Paxton, Fl. Gard. 3:162. 1853. Type: The Philippines. Luzon, near Manila, leg. Lobb, *Hort. Veitch s.n.* (holotype: K).

Phalaenopsis lobbii Hort. ex Rchb.f., Bot. Zeit. 21:128. 1863, nom. nud.[*]

Phalaenopsis ×*aphroditi-equestris* Rchb.f., Bot. Zeit. 21:128. 1863, nom. nud.

Phalaenopsis delicata Rchb.f., Gard. Chron., n.s., 17:700. 1882. Type: The Philippines. Luzon, *Hort. Veitch 86* (holotype: W).

---

[*] Presumably this was a slip of the pen based on the type collection of *P.* ×*intermedia* by Lobb.

Phalaenopsis ×*brymeriana* Hort. ex Warn. & B. S. Wms., Orch. Album 9: t. 416. 1890, ex icon.

Phalaenopsis ×*intermedia* var. *vesta* Hort., Orchid Rev. 1:52. 1893; *Phalaenopsis* ×*vesta* (Hort.) Hort., Gard. Chron., ser. 3, 13:80. 1893. Type: The Philippines. *Hort. Veitch s.n.* (holotype: ? not preserved).

Phalaenopsis ×*intermedia* var. *diezii* Covera, Philippine Orchid Rev. 5:9. 1953, nom. illeg.; *Phalaenopsis* ×*diezii* (Covera) Quisumbing, Proc. 2nd World Orchid Conf. 31. 1958. Type: The Philippines. Leyte, *Hort. Diez s.n.* (holotype: ? not preserved).

Epiphytes. **Leaves** oblong-elliptic to elliptic, obtuse, dark green with purple suffusion on the lower surfaces, to 30 × 7.5 cm. **Inflorescences** initially erect, then arching to laxly pendent racemes or few-branched panicles, to 60 cm long, the branches and primary rachis many-flowered, the floral bracts minute, triangular, scarious, to 0.4 cm long. **Flowers** membranous, white, the lip reddish pink, the callus yellow. **Dorsal sepal** elliptic to elliptic-ovate, obtuse-rounded, to 4 × 1.5 cm, the **lateral sepals** obliquely ovate, sub-acute, to 4 × 1.5 cm. **Petals** subrhomboid-elliptic, cuneate-clawed, obtuse, broadly rounded, to 3.5 × 2.2 cm. **Lip** three-lobed, the lateral lobes obovate, obtuse, rounded with an irregular margin, erect-incurved forming a cylinder the midlobe ovate, the apex shallowly notched with variably developed lateral falcate, retrorse, tendril-like lobules (cirrhi), the **callus** uniseriate, peltate, subquadrate. **Column** straight, stout. **Pedicel** and **ovary** to 3 cm long.

Etymology: From the Latin, *intermedius* ("intermediate"). Its flowers are intermediate between those of its parents, leading Lindley to correctly surmise its hybrid origin. **Illustrations**:

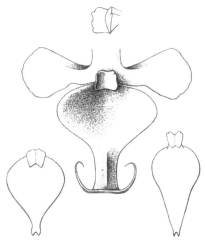

Phalaenopsis ×*intermedia* drawn from the types: the typical variety (center), var. *portei* (left), and the plant described as *P. delicata* (right). Illustrator: H. R. Sweet.

Awards Quart. 25(3):173. 1994 (peloric); Gruss and Wolff 1995:46, 48; Sweet 1969:898, 1980:39.

This is the natural hybrid between *P. aphrodite* and *P. equestris*. Unlike all other naturally occurring hybrids in the genus, *P. ×intermedia* has formed a genetically stabilized population that acts like a species and is self-reproducing in nature.

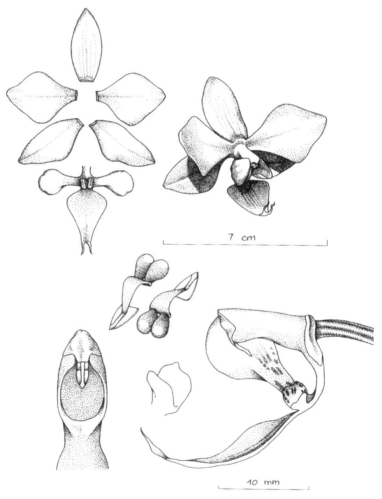

Phalaenopsis ×intermedia. Illustrator: F. Pupulin.

The varietal name *diezii* has been applied informally to peloric variants of this hybrid. That name has never been validly published, and I choose not to recognize what are clearly monstrous clones. Although these peloric variants are not particularly rare in nature, and especially on the island of Leyte (Manuel and Lee 1974), this is doubtless because *P. equestris* tends to produce peloric individuals and offspring rather than a self-perpetuating peloric population. Fertile flowers are very rare in these peloric variants, and their fertility is usually limited to part of a pollinarium on a nonfunctional, incomplete stipe and viscidium, where the rostellum is not developed as a delivery system.

Phalaenopsis × *intermedia* is a vigorous grower that typically produces keikis after flowering from the tips of the inflorescences, in the manner of its *P. equestris* parent.

Phalaenopsis × *intermedia* var. *portei* Rchb.f.

Bot. Zeit. 21:128. 1863; *Phalaenopsis* × *portei* (Rchb.f.) Denning, Gard. Chron., n.s., 5:370. 1876; *Phalaenopsis* × *intermedia* var. *porteana* Burb., The Garden 22:119. 1882; *Phalaenopsis* × *porteri* Hort., Index Kew. 2:486. 1895. Type: The Philippines. Luzon, *Hort. Warner s.n.* (holotype: W).

Etymology: Named for the collector of this variety, Marius Porte (d. 1866), who also collected the original plants of *P. schilleriana*. **Illustrations**: Amer. Orchid Soc. Bull. 56:588. 1987.

Phalaenopsis × *intermedia* normally bears flowers that have a lip of a rather nondescript brick red, uneven in color; *P.* × *intermedia* var. *portei* bears flowers with an intensely saturated, dark red lip.

Phalaenopsis × *leucorrhoda* Rchb.f.

Gard. Chron., n.s., 3:301. 1875. Type: The Philippines. *Hort. Low s.n.* (holotype: W).

Phalaenopsis × *casta* Rchb.f., Gard. Chron., n.s., 3:590. 1875; *Phalaenopsis* × *leucorrhoda* var. *casta* (Rchb.f.) Veitch, Man. Orch. Pl., pt. 7:46. 1891. Type: The Philippines. *Hort. Low s.n.* (holotype: W).

Phalaenopsis ×rothschildiana Rchb.f., Gard. Chron., ser. 3, 1:606. 1887. Type: The Philippines. *Hort. Veitch 389* (holotype: W).

Phalaenopsis ×leucorrhoda var. *grandiflora* Hort., Gard. Chron., n.s., 3:686. 1875, ex char.

Phalaenopsis ×leucorrhoda var. *alba* Hort., Florist and Pom. 42. 1883; Gard. Chron., n.s., 20:751. 1883, ex char.

Phalaenopsis ×cynthia Rolfe, Gard. Chron., ser. 3, 7:132. 1890; *Phalaenopsis ×leucorrhoda* var. *cynthia* (Rolfe) Veitch, Man. Orch. Pl., pt. 7:46. 1891, ex char.

Phalaenopsis ×youngii Hort., Gard. Chron., ser. 3, 15:211. 1894, ex char.

Phalaenopsis ×youngiana Hort., The Garden 47:122. 1895, ex char.

Phalaenopsis ×schilleriano-gloriosa Rolfe, Orchid Rev. 5:4. 1897, ex char.

Phalaenopsis ×casta var. *superbissima* Hort., Orchid Rev. 18:149. 1910, ex char.

Phalaenopsis ×rothschildiana var. *tatsuta* Iwakasi, Orchid Rev. 32:258. 1924, ex char.

Distribution: Endemic to the southern Philippines. **Etymology**: From the Greek, the comparative *leuco-* ("white") and *-rhodo* ("rosy red"), pre-sumably a reference to the two-toned petals of the type clone. **Illustrations**: Awards Quart. 17(4):215. 1986; Awards Quart. 21(3):155. 1990; Awards Quart. 23(2):110. 1992; Fowlie 1991b:119, 121; Gruss 1995:139.

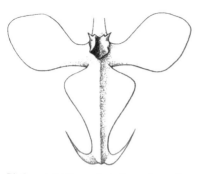

Phalaenopsis ×leucorrhoda drawn from the type. Illustrator: H. R. Sweet.

This is the sporadically occurring nat-ural hybrid between *P. aphrodite* and *P. schilleriana*. This combination has been remade in cultivation, and several select clones have been recognized with floral awards, although they have been little utilized in secondary hybridization. Unlike either parent species, the hybrid tends to produce non-flowering inflorescences under less than optimal conditions (i.e., consistently insufficient drops in night time temperatures). These long, sterile inflorescences often terminate in keikis, a feature seen to a limited extent in *P. schilleriana.*

When first introduced, *P. philippinensis,* from the northern Philippines, was consistently confused with *P. ×leucorrhoda.* The calli of the two entities are quite different: in *P. ×leucorrhoda* the posterior corners of the callus are sharply pointed teeth; in *P. philippinensis* the posterior corners of the callus are broadly rounded.

Phalaenopsis philippinensis Golamco ex Fowlie & Tang

Orchid Digest 51:92. 1987. Type: The Philippines. Luzon, near Madela, Nueva Vizcaya, *Hort. Usita s.n.* (holotype: LA; photograph: NY).

Pendent epiphytes. **Leaves** oblong-elliptic to oblong-oblanceolate, tapered to the base, obtuse-rounded, the upper surface dark green overlain with silvery gray marbling, the lower surface dark purple, to 36 × 13.5 cm. **Inflorescences** laxly arching-pendent panicles, to 120 cm long, the floral bracts minute, triangular, to 8 mm long. **Flowers** delicate, membranous, numerous (to 100+), white +/− pale pink suffusion, the lateral sepals with dark red spots at the base, the lip white with dark yellow lateral lobes, with dark red stripes at the base of the lateral lobes of the lip, the column white. **Dorsal sepal** elliptic to elliptic-ovate, obtuse-rounded, to 4.5 × 2.3 cm, the **lateral sepals** obliquely ovate, subacute, divergent, to 4.5 × 2.4 cm. **Petals** rhomboid, cuneate-clawed, obtuse, broadly rounded, to 4.5 × 4.5 cm. **Lip** three-lobed, to 2.5 cm long, to 4 cm wide across the expanded lateral lobes, the lateral lobes elliptic-obovate, obtuse-rounded, erect-incurved forming a cylinder, the midlobe oblong-ovate, the base hastate to subauriculate, the apex notched with the lanceolate lobules elongate and recurved, the **callus** uniseriate, peltate, channeled, the posterior edge extended in a pair of winglike teeth. **Column** stout, straight, to 0.8 cm long. **Pedicel** and **ovary** to 5 cm long.

Distribution: Endemic to the Philippines. **Etymology**: With the Latin suffix -*ensis*, indicating its place of origin in the Philippines. **Illustrations**: Awards Quart. 24(1):60. 1993; Die Orchidee 39(5):22. 1988 (as *P. ×leucorrhoda*); Die Orchidee 41(6):43. 1990; Die Orchidee 43(3): 144. 1992; Die Orchidee 46(4): Orchideenkartei Seite 809. 1995; Fessel 1989:219; Fowlie 1991b:121, 122; Gruss 1995:139; Gruss and Wolff 1995:47, 49; Orchid Digest 47:6. 1983 (as *P. ×leucorrhoda*).

This showy species has only recently been described. When first published (Golamco 1984) the name was invalid because no Latin diagnosis or description accompanied the English description and the binomial combination was not explicitly cited. These oversights were corrected by Fowlie and Tang. When *P. philippinensis* was first discovered and brought into cultivation, it was confused with the similar *P. ×leucorrhoda*. The richly marked leaves and the pure yellow lateral lobes of the lip have made it a very desirable species.

Like the closely related *P. schilleriana* and *P. stuartiana*, *P. philippinensis* tends to open all the flowers on an inflorescence quickly. Having all flowers open at once makes *P. philippinensis* a particularly excellent display plant. This quality of producing a massive display of flowers is dominant in its hybrids.

Phalaenopsis sanderiana Rchb.f.

Flora 65:466. 1882; *Phalaenopsis amabilis* var. *aphrodite* subvar. *sanderiana* (Rchb.f.) Ames, Orchid. 2:228. 1908; *Phalaenopsis aphrodite* var. *sanderiana* (Rchb.f.) Quisumbing, Philippine Journ. Sci. 74:182. 1941; *Phalaenopsis amabilis* var. *sanderiana* (Rchb.f.) Davis, Amer. Orchid Soc. Bull. 18:744. 1949, nom. illeg. Type: The Philippines. Mindanao, leg. Roebelen, *Hort. Sander s.n.* (holotype: W).

Pendent epiphytes. **Leaves** elliptic to oblong-elliptic, tapered to the conduplicate base, obtuse-rounded, green +/– purple suffusion and a silvery overlay, to 27 × 9 cm. **Inflorescences** arching-erect racemes or few-branched panicles, to 80 cm long, the floral bracts minute, triangular, concave, scarious, to 4 mm long. **Flowers** showy, membranous, white with variable degrees of pink suffusion, the callus and base of the lip marked with yellow and red. **Dorsal sepal** elliptic to elliptic-ovate, obtuse-rounded, to 3.5 × 2.3 cm, the **lateral sepals** obliquely ovate, obtuse, divergent, to 3.5 × 2.2 cm. **Petals** subrhomboid, cuneate, obtuse, broadly rounded, to 3.8 × 3.8 cm. **Lip** three-lobed, to 3 cm long, to 4 cm wide across the expanded lateral lobes, the lateral lobes spatulate, the blade oblique, obtuse-rounded, erect-incurved forming a cylinder, the midlobe hastate-cruciform, the basal tooth-like lobes triangular, acute, the apex notched, flanked by tendril-like flexuous appendages, the **callus** uniseriate, erect, peltate, the posterior edge deeply notched in the middle, each side with one larger, taller, inner, rounded tooth and one smaller, shorter, outer, acute tooth. **Column** stout, short. **Pedicel** and **ovary** to 3 cm long.

Distribution: Endemic to the Philippines. **Etymology**: Named to honor Frederick Sander, English orchid grower and importer. Latin scholars have flip-flopped over the appropriate spelling of this commemorative ending. Without delving into an extraneous, rather esoteric discipline, the "i" was initially added as -*iana* (this the opinion of Latin scholars when Sweet published his revision in 1969), then the "i" was dropped, as -*ana* (the prevailing opinion when Sweet reissued his revision in 1980), and finally opinion has reverted to the more euphonious original, including the "i" as -*iana* (the same scholarly shifts have affected *P. lueddemanniana, P. stuartiana,* and other like names). **Illustrations**: Amer. Orchid Soc. Bull. 56:588. 1987; Awards Quart. 15(1): 37. 1984; Christenson 1995:21; Die Orchidee 42(1): Orchideenkartei Seite 633. 1991; Martin 1985:419; Moses 1980:365; Orchid Digest 45: 49. 1981; Sweet 1969:889, 1980:31, 41.

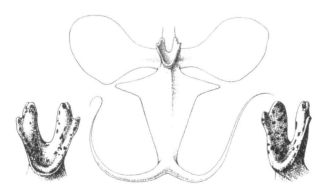

Phalaenopsis sanderiana drawn from the type. Illustrator: H. R. Sweet.

Phalaenopsis sanderiana has often been relegated to the status of poor cousin relative to other members of this section. It is not as large-flowered as *P. amabilis* and *P. aphrodite*, it bears flowers with pinkish flowers that are not as evenly or as darkly colored as *P. schilleriana*, and although the foliage is often patterned with a silvery overlay, it never has the rich marbling found in *P. schilleriana* and *P. stuartiana*. This is unfortunate because *P. sanderiana* deserves a special place in *Phalaenopsis* species collections and in modern pot-plant breeding programs. Unlike the other species in this section, which are strongly spring-flowered, *P. sanderiana* blooms in mid to late summer. This habit of flowering "off-season" has been underappreciated by both hobbyist growers and professional plant breeders. Hobbyists who grow *P. sanderiana* will have large, showy flowers during the otherwise depauperate summer season, and plant breeders should be able to obtain hybrid lineages that initiate inflorescences during the long days and consistently warm temperatures of summer. Unlike hybrid lines bred primarily or exclusively from *P. amabilis* and *P. aphrodite*, those bred from *P. sanderiana* do not show the sterile, gigantic-bracted, highly elongate inflorescences that typically blast buds during development in the summer heat.

Phalaenopsis sanderiana flowers are normally white with variable degrees of purple suffusion toward the edges of the sepals and petals. Although now rare in cultivation, strains of *P. sanderiana* have been line bred for solid, dark pink flowers. Most of the darker clones (F_4 to F_7 generations) were affected by inbreeding depression, a genetic weakness, and proved to be poor growers. In addition to the variability of pink coloring in the flowers, one dubious variety and one exceptional color form deserve formal status.

Phalaenopsis sanderiana var. *marmorata* Rchb.f.

Gard. Chron., n.s., 20:812. 1883; *Phalaenopsis sanderiana* subvar. *marmorata* (Rchb.f.) Veitch, Man. Orch. Pl., pt. 7:35. 1891; *Phalaenopsis amabilis* var. *aphrodite* subvar. *sanderiana* f. *marmorata* (Rchb.f.) Ames, Orchid. 2:228. 1908. Type: The Philippines. Without precise locality, leg. Barber, *Hort. Low s.n.* (holotype: W). Reichenbach's watercolor of the holotype reproduced in Sweet (1969:690).

Phalaenopsis sanderiana var. *punctata* O'Brien, Gard. Chron., ser.
3, 7:78. 1891; *Phalaenopsis sanderiana* subvar. *punctata* (O'Brien)
Veitch, Man. Orch. Pl., pt. 7:35. 1891; *Phalaenopsis amabilis* var.
aphrodite subvar. *sanderiana* f. *punctata* (O'Brien) Ames, Orchid.
2:229. 1908. Type: The Philippines. Without precise locality,
Hort. Low s.n. (holotype: W).

Etymology: From the Latin, *marmoratus* ("marbled"), a reference to
patterned midlobe of the lip. **Illustrations**: Sweet 1969:690.

Repeating Sweet's quote of Reichenbach, var. *marmorata* was described as having flowers with the "sepals and petals tinged outside yellowish white, with a certain green hue . . . The lateral sepals have numerous rows of purple spots at the base. The side laciniae show three broad
basilar purple bars, nearly parallel, and some purple spots. The mid
lacinia is neatly marbled with fine purple stains on the side, purple dots
in mid-line, and a very light purple wash between those three areas."
The use of the term lacinia (plural: laciniae) in these comments refers
to the lobes of the lip.

This entity may represent the sporadically occurring natural hybrid
between *P. sanderiana* and *P. stuartiana*, *P.* ×*amphitrite*. The former is
widespread in southern Mindanao, while the latter is widespread in
northern Mindanao, the two sharing an extensive overlapping marginal range. The midlobe of the lip in *P. sanderiana* is normally unmarked, and the marbled pattern recorded for this variety is in keeping
with possible influence from *P. stuartiana*. This name is retained at the
varietal level pending new modern collections that match the type(s).

Both var. *marmorata* and the synonymous var. *punctata* were described
from plants cultivated by Low. It is possible that Rolfe redescribed the
same plant(s) that had been described earlier by Reichenbach.

Phalaenopsis sanderiana f. *alba*
(Veitch) E. A. Christ., stat. nov.

Basionym: *Phalaenopsis sanderiana* subvar. *alba* Veitch, Man.
Orch. Pl., pt. 7:35. 1891; *Phalaenopsis sanderiana* var. *alba*
(Veitch) Stein, Orchideenbuch 511. 1892; *Phalaenopsis amabilis*
var. *aphrodite* subvar. *sanderiana* f. *alba* (Veitch) Ames, Orchid.

207

2:228. 1908. Type: The Philippines. Without precise locality, *Hort. Veitch s.n.* (holotype: not preserved). Neotype, designated by Sweet (1969:890), *Hort. Sander s.n.* (neotype: K).

Phalaenopsis alcicornis Rchb.f., Gard. Chron., ser. 3, 1:799. 1887. Type: [The Philippines]. *Hort. Sander s.n.* (holotype: K).

Phalaenopsis sanderiana var. *pulcherrima* Rolfe, Orchid Rev. 19:310. 1911. Type: The Philippines. *Hort. Sander s.n.* (K).

Etymology: From the Latin, *albus* ("white"), a reference to the flower color. **Illustrations**: Orchid Digest 45:49. 1981; Sweet 1980:41.

This form lacks any pink suffusion in the sepals and petals. Once common and artificially propagated in horticulture, this color morph appears to be extremely rare in modern collections.

Phalaenopsis schilleriana Rchb.f.

Hamburg. Gartenz. 16:115. 1860. Type: The Philippines. Luzon, leg. M. Porte, *Hort. Schiller s.n.* (holotype: W).

Phalaenopsis schilleriana var. *viridi-maculata* Ducharte, Journ. Soc. Imp. & Centr. d'Hort. 8:609, t. 17. 1862. Type: No specimen is known. Lectotype, designated by Sweet (1980:34): t. 17, loc. cit.

Phalaenopsis schilleriana var. *delicata* Dean, Floral Mag., n.s., 6: t. 257. 1877. Type: No specimen is known. Lectotype, designated by Sweet (1980:34): t. 257, loc. cit.

Phalaenopsis schilleriana var. *splendens* Warn., Sel. Orch. Pl., ser. 3: t. 5. 1878. Type: Not preserved. Neotype, designated by Sweet (1969:893): t. 5, loc. cit.

Phalaenopsis schilleriana var. *major* J. D. Hook. ex Rolfe, Gard. Chron., n.s., 26:212. 1886. Type: The Philippines. *Hort. Veitch s.n.* (holotype: K).

Phalaenopsis schilleriana var. *compacta nana* Hort., Gard. Chron., ser. 3, 7:356. 1890, nom. nud.

Phalaenopsis schilleriana var. *purpurea* O'Brien, Gard. Chron., ser.

3, 11:105. 1892. Type: The Philippines. Luzon, *Hort. Low s.n.* (holotype: K).

Phalaenopsis schilleriana var. *grandiflora* van Brero, Die Orchidee 4:23. 1935, nom. illeg.

Phalaenopsis schilleriana var. *odorata* van Brero, Die Orchidee 4:23. 1935, nom. illeg.

Epiphytes. **Leaves** oblong-elliptic to elliptic-obovate, tapered to the base, obtuse, dark green with the upper surface marbled with silvery gray and the lower surface purple suffused, to 45 × 11 cm. **Inflorescences** arching-pendent panicles, the floral bracts inconspicuous, ovate, concave, scarious, to 5 mm long. **Flowers** numerous (to 250+ per inflorescence), membranous, fragrant, pink, the callus and sidelobes of the lip marked with red and yellow, the midlobe of the lip +/− spotted at the base, the column darker pink. **Dorsal sepal** elliptic to elliptic-ovate, obtuse-rounded, to 3.5 × 1.6 cm, the **lateral sepals** obliquely elliptic-ovate, subacute, subparallel, subequal to the dorsal sepal. **Petals** rhomboid, cuneate-clawed, obtuse, broadly rounded, with lightly undulate margins, to 4 × 4 cm. **Lip** three-lobed, to 2.2 cm long, to 3.4 cm across the expanded lateral lobes, the lateral lobes obliquely elliptic, obtuse-rounded, erect, spreading, the midlobe elliptic-ovate, notched at the apex and flanked by retrorse falcate lobules in the form of an anchor, the **callus** uniseriate, peltate, channeled, both the posterior and

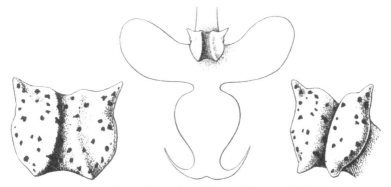

Phalaenopsis schilleriana drawn from the type. Illustrator: H. R. Sweet.

anterior edges notched, forming paired teeth to either side of the channel. **Column** stout, fleshy. **Pedicel** and **ovary** to 4 cm long.

   Distribution: Endemic to the Philippines. **Etymology**: Named for the original grower of this species, Consul Schiller of Hamburg, Germany. **Illustrations**: Awards Quart. 15(4):179. 1984; Awards Quart. 16(4):168. 1985; Awards Quart. 17(4):206. 1986; Awards Quart. 20(1): 2. 1989; Awards Quart. 21(2):106. 1990; Awards Quart. 21(3):167.

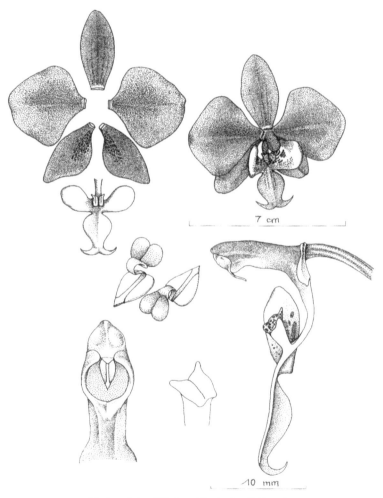

Phalaenopsis schilleriana. Illustrator: F. Pupulin.

1990; Awards Quart. 22(2):86. 1991; Awards Quart. 23(2):77. 1992; Awards Quart. 26(1):13. 1995; Awards Quart. 26(3):154. 1995; Awards Quart. 26(4):199. 1995; Batchelor 1982:1271; Die Orchidee 32(6):5. 1981; Die Orchidee 34(6): back cover. 1983; Die Orchidee 40(5):24. 1989; Die Orchidee 41(1): back cover. 1990; Fowlie 1991b:120; Gruss 1992a:135, 1995:139; Harper 1985:949; Kobayashi 1989:151; Moses 1980:363; Orchid Digest 45:49. 1981; Sweet 1969:892, 1980:34, 41.

Phalaenopsis schilleriana readily grows to specimen size and makes an excellent display plant. It has been said that the Miami Orchid Show was scheduled specifically to coincide with the flowering of *P. schilleriana* in South Florida. The bright pink flowers and richly marbled foliage recommend this species highly. In addition, *P. schilleriana* is one of the few species of this subgenus that has a noticeable, faint, pleasing fragrance, although not everybody is able to detect the fragrance.

Phalaenopsis schilleriana is still exported from the Philippines, reportedly from vegetative propagations. Regardless, select seed strains have been artificially propagated in cultivation for several generations, and all recent award-winning clones have arisen from this selected stock.

Several horticultural varieties have been recognized in the past. Varieties *purpurea* and *splendens*, however, merely represent superior clones with darker color and larger flowers. I see no reason to formally maintain them as distinct varieties of the species. Sweet also distinguished var. *splendens* on the basis of the leaf markings which consist of "parallel oblong meshes." Patterning of the leaves in *P. schilleriana* is extremely variable, both between populations and within the progeny of a single seed capsule. The particular pattern seen on the neotype illustration of var. *splendens* is not useful as a taxonomic character.

The following variant does deserve formal recognition, although I am not aware that it is in cultivation at this time.

Phalaenopsis schilleriana f. *immaculata*
(Rchb.f.) E. A. Christ., stat. nov.

Basionym: *Phalaenopsis schilleriana* var. *immaculata* Rchb.f., Gard. Chron., n.s., 3:429. 1875; *Phalaenopsis schilleriana* subvar. *immaculata* (Rchb.f.) Veitch, Man. Orch. Pl., pt. 7:37. 1891. Type: The Philippines, leg. Barber, *Hort. Low s.n.* (holotype: W).

Phalaenopsis schilleriana var. *advena* Rchb.f., Gard. Chron., n.s., 23:174. 1885. Type: The Philippines. *Hort. Low s.n.* (holotype: W).

Phalaenopsis curnowiana Hort., Gard. Chron., ser. 3, 9:268. 1891, nom. nud.

Etymology: From the Latin, *immaculatus* ("without spots"). This form lacks the characteristic spotting at the base of the lip and over the callus.

Phalaenopsis stuartiana Rchb.f.

Gard. Chron., n.s., 16:748. 1881; *Phalaenopsis schilleriana* var. *stuartiana* (Rchb.f.) Burb., The Garden 22:119. 1882. Type: The Philippines. Mindanao, leg. Boxall, *Hort. Low s.n.* (holotype: W).

Phalaenopsis schilleriana var. *vestalis* Rchb.f., Gard. Chron., n.s., 17:330. 1882; *Phalaenopsis schilleriana* subvar. *vestalis* (Rchb.f.) Veitch, Man. Orch. Pl., pt. 7:37. 1891. Type: [The Philippines]. *Hort. Low s.n.* (holotype: W).

Phalaenopsis stuartiana var. *bella* Rchb.f., Gard. Chron., ser. 3, 3:200. 1888. Type: The Philippines. Mindanao, *Hort. Low s.n.* (holotype: W).

Phalaenopsis schilleriana var. *alba* Roebelen, Gard. Chron., ser. 3, 7:459. 1890. Type: [The Philippines]. *Hort. Low s.n.* (holotype: W).

Epiphytes. **Leaves** oblong-elliptic to oblanceolate-obovate, tapered to the base, obtuse, dark green with the upper surface silvery gray marbled and the lower surface purple suffused, to 35 × 8 cm. **Inflorescences** arching-pendent panicles, to 60 cm long, the floral bracts ovate, concave, scarious, to 1 cm long. **Flowers** numerous, membranous, faintly fragrant, white, the inner halves of the lateral sepals greenish yellow with chestnut-brown spots, the lateral lobes of the lip with chestnut-brown spotting, the midlobe with similar larger spotting, the callus yellow, the column white. **Dorsal sepal** elliptic, tapered-constricted at the base, obtuse-rounded, to 3.5 × 1.5 cm, the **lateral sepals** obliquely elliptic-ovate, subacute, to 3.2 × 1.5 cm. **Petals** subrhomboid, cuneate-

clawed, obtuse, broadly rounded, occasionally shallowly notched at
the apex, to 3.3 × 2.6 cm. **Lip** three-lobed, to 2.5 cm long, to 3 cm
across the expanded lateral lobes, the lateral lobes obliquely oblong-
oblanceolate, obtuse-rounded, erect, spreading, the midlobe elliptic-
suborbicular, the apex shallowly notched and flanked by a pair of
retrorse, falcate lobules in the form of an anchor, the **callus** uniseriate,
peltate, channeled, the posterior edge notched with a long, triangular
tooth to each side, the anterior edge shallowly notched with a blunt

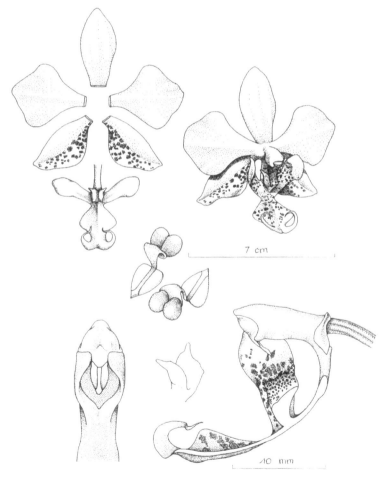

Phalaenopsis stuartiana. Illustrator: F. Pupulin.

213

tooth to each side. **Column** stout, straight. **Pedicel** and **ovary** to 4 cm long.

Distribution: Endemic to the island of Mindanao in the southern Philippines. **Etymology**: Named to honor Stuart Low of the British horticultural firm of Hugh Low & Co. **Illustrations**: Awards Quart. 17(1):30, 53. 1986; Awards Quart. 22(1):46. 1991; Awards Quart. 24(1):67. 1993; Awards Quart. 26(3):165. 1995; Batchelor 1982:1267; Collins 1983:795; Die Orchidee 30(2):43. 1979; Die Orchidee 34(6):213. 1983; Die Orchidee 41(1): back cover. 1990; Die Orchidee 42(4):32. 1991; Die Orchidee 44(2): Orchideenkartei Seite 719. 1993; Fessell 1989:218, 219; Fowlie 1987a:93; Freed 1981c:1458, 1984:1145; Orchid Digest 45:49. 1981; Orchid Digest 59:24. 1995; Sweet 1969:895, 1980:37, 41.

Phalaenopsis stuartiana, like its sister species *P. philippinensis* and *P. schilleriana*, makes a spectacular display plant, bearing hundreds of flowers in a mass above richly marbled foliage. Even though the flowers appear to be very delicate and thin-textured, they are long-lasting on the plant. With the propagation of f. *punctatissima* and the creation of tetraploid strains, *P. stuartiana* continues to be popular.

Long overlooked in breeding, *P. stuartiana* is regaining influence both from the production of floriferous triploid display plants bred with standard tetraploid white hybrids and in the production of multiflora pot-plants, especially through its contribution to *P.* Cassandra (*equestris × stuartiana*).

Reichenbach described var. *bella* on the basis of its "linear red marks on the side laciniae" and the lip with "very large, purple-chocolate

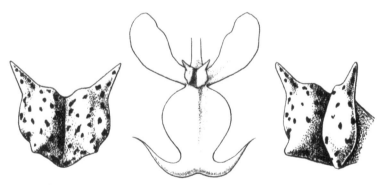

Phalaenopsis stuartiana drawn from the type. Illustrator: H. R. Sweet.

blotches on the mid lacinia of the lip." I consider this to be within the normal range of variation seen in the species and do not consider it worthy of formal designation.

Two color variants are worth recognizing, especially f. *punctatissima*, as it is the most significant variant for hybridization.

Phalaenopsis stuartiana f. *nobilis*
(Rchb.f.) E. A. Christ., stat. nov.

Basionym: *Phalaenopsis stuartiana* var. *nobilis* Rchb.f., Gard. Chron., n.s., 16:748. 1881. Type: The Philippines. Mindanao, *Hort. Low s.n.* (holotype: W).

The flowers of *P. stuartiana* are normally a creamy white (a brighter, starker white in tetraploid clones). They may be greenish, but this is usually caused by some form of physiological stress that inhibits the full expansion of the floral tissue. *Phalaenopsis stuartiana* f. *nobilis*, in contrast, produces pale, sulfur-yellow flowers. Cesar Zapata, Jr., of Wellington, New Zealand, comments (in litt.) that this rare form is in very limited cultivation in the Philippines, Taiwan, and private collections.

Phalaenopsis stuartiana f. *punctatissima*
(Rchb.f.) E. A. Christ., stat. nov.

Basionym: *Phalaenopsis stuartiana* var. *punctatissima* Rchb.f., Gard. Chron., n.s., 17:44. 1882. Type: The Philippines. Mindanao, *Hort. Low s.n.* (holotype: W).

Etymology: From the Latin superlative of *punctatus* ("dotted"). **Illustrations**: Gruss and Wolff 1995:57.

The dorsal sepal and petals of *P. stuartiana* are typically white without any significant spotting. Occasionally plants are seen with spotting on the dorsal sepal and petals similar to the spotting on the lateral sepals. This strain, exemplified by the clone 'Larkin Valley' developed by John Ewing, is considered to be the most desirable strain in cultivation.

The spotting of the dorsal sepal and petals appears to be regulated by the epidermis. This leads to a somewhat unstable system: environmental changes affect the physiology of the epidermis when the flowers are in bud. Typical specimens of *P. stuartiana* often show sectoring of spots against the otherwise white dorsal sepal and petals. Similarly, plants of f. *punctatissima* and hybrids derived from them also show the reverse sectoring, with portions of the dorsal sepal and petals appearing without spots. The presence of these sectors and their instability both from flower to flower and between clonal propagations has been falsely blamed on a virus.

Occasionally, while these spotted forms and their hybrids undergo tissue culture using whole-shoot propagation techniques, accidents occur that eliminate the original epidermis. The resulting propagations lack the original spotting on the dorsal sepal and petals upon flowering. This does not alter the breeding characteristics of these plants, however, since the cells producing gametes are unaffected by the replacement of the epidermis. A similar regulatory system appears to be in effect for peloric forms, and several laboratories have reported the loss of peloric characters when phalaenopsis are propagated by techniques that do not maintain the integrity of the epidermis (by using parenchyma from cut-leaf surfaces rather than whole-shoot proliferation).

Phalaenopsis ×*veitchiana* Rchb.f.

Gard. Chron. 1872:935. 1872. Type: The Philippines. Luzon, *Hort. Veitch 219* (holotype: W).

Phalaenopsis ×*intermedia* var. *brymeriana* Rchb.f., Gard. Chron., n.s., 5:366. 1876. Type: The Philippines. Without precise locality, *Brymer s.n.* (holotype: W).

Phalaenopsis ×*veitchiana* var. *brachyodon* Rchb.f., Gard. Chron., n.s., 21:270. 1884. Type: [The Philippines]. *Hort. Low s.n.* (holotype: W).

Phalaenopsis ×*gertrudeae* Quisumbing, Philippine Journ. Sci. 76:92. 1941. Type: The Philippines. Luzon, Prov. Tayabas, *Stewart s.n.* (holotype: AMES[*]).

---

[*] Prior to the destruction of the herbarium at Manila by fire during World War II, many orchid holotypes were removed from the Philippines and transferred to the Orchid Herbarium of Oakes Ames at Harvard University. In most cases, material at AMES of types cited for Manila (PNH) are the actual holotypes and not isotypes.

Phalaenopsis ×virataii Quisumbing, Philippine Orchid Rev. 6:4. 1956. Type: The Philippines. Luzon, Prov. Cavite, *Virata s.n.* (holotype: PNH).

Distribution: Endemic to the Philippines. **Etymology**: Named to honor British horticulturist Harry J. Veitch, who first flowered this hybrid in cultivation. **Illustrations**: Awards Quart. 23(1):44. 1992; Awards Quart. 23(2): 112. 1992.

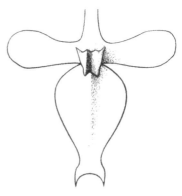

Phalaenopsis ×veitchiana drawn from the type. Illustrator: H. R. Sweet.

This is the recurring natural hybrid between *P. equestris* and *P. schilleriana*. This hybrid combination has been artificially recreated in cultivation on several occasions, and the resulting offspring fully agree with wild-collected material. Despite the charm of this hybrid and its high flower count, little secondary hybridization has taken place. Secondary hybrids of *P. ×veitchiana* would appear to offer great potential for spring-flowered display plants.

Section *Deliciosae* E. A. Christ.

Selbyana 9:167. 1986; *Kingidium* section *Deliciosae* (E. A. Christ.) Gruss & Röllke, Die Orchidee 44(3):121. 1993; *Kingidium* section *Kingidium*, sensu Gruss & Röllke, Die Orchidee 44(3):189. 1993. Type: *Phalaenopsis deliciosa* Rchb.f.

The three species of section *Deliciosae* are morphologically intermediate between other members of subgenus *Phalaenopsis*, on the one hand, and the remainder of the genus on the other. The flowers bear lateral lobes of the lip with tooth-like flaps, similar to those found in subgenus *Polychilos*, while having uniseriate calli as in other species of subgenus *Phalaenopsis*.

The close affinity of this section with section *Esmeralda* is suggested by molecular data, their breeding behavior, their both producing four pollinia, and the bifid structure of their callus (at least in *P. regnieriana*, reduced in the other two species of section *Esmeralda*).

Phalaenopsis deliciosa has been placed in the genus *Kingidium* by many authors, a genus relegated here to *Phalaenopsis* section *Aphyllae*. Species of section *Deliciosae* and section *Aphyllae* share the conditions of having small subsaccate lip bases and four pollinia, characters I do not consider necessarily significant at the generic level in the *Phalaenopsis* alliance (i.e., both characters have been found to be variable in otherwise well-defined genera in the subtribe Aeridinae, such as *Gastrochilus*). I do not think that *P. deliciosa* is closely related to section *Aphyllae*, a position supported by recent molecular data. Unlike species of section *Aphyllae*, *P. deliciosa* is not deciduous in nature, does not exhibit chlorophylly of the perianth after pollination, and is not restricted to the eastern Himalayas and southeast Asia.

Gruss and Röllke overlooked the typification of *Kingidium* by Hunt (1971a) with *P. taenialis*. This led them to needlessly publish a section *Kingidium* based on *P. deliciosa* and reduced section *Deliciosae* to synonymy.

The recently described and little-known *P. chibae* is included here with some reservations. It is the only species in the genus with a single transverse rather than a longitudinal callus (some members of subg. *Parishianae* have a transverse callus as part of a biseriate callus).

Key to the species of section *Deliciosae*

1. Callus transverse; sepals and petals with chestnut-brown markings.
 . . . . *P. chibae*
1. Callus longitudinal; sepals and petals unmarked.
 2. Inflorescences racemes or panicles, usually more than 10 cm long; lip purple. . . . . *P. deliciosa*
 2. Inflorescences short racemes, never panicles, usually less than 8 cm long; lip white. . . . . *P. mysorensis*

Phalaenopsis chibae Yukawa

Ann. Tsukuba Bot. Gard. 15:19. 1996; *Kingidium chibae* (Yukawa) Gruss & Röllke, Die Orchidee 48(6):261. 1997. Type: Vietnam. Vicinity of Dalat, 400–600 m, May 1994, *M. Chiba P-1795* (holotype: TNS).

Description after Yukawa: Presumably epiphytes. **Leaves** elliptic to obo-vate, obliquely emarginate, lightly suffused with purple, to 11 × 4.5 cm. **Inflorescences** erect racemes, dull purple, to 11 cm long, the floral bracts triangular, acute, to 3 mm long. **Flowers** to 13, to 1.2 cm wide, opening simultaneously, pale yellow with chestnut-brown irregular markings, the tips of the sepals and petals unmarked, the callus white

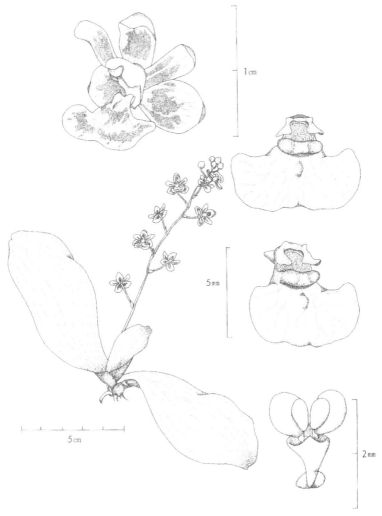

Phalaenopsis chibae from the original publication. Illustrator: F. Endo.

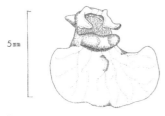

5 mm

Lip details of *Phalaenopsis chibae*.
Illustrator: F. Endo.

with purple markings. **Dorsal sepal** oblong, obtuse, concave, 4.5 × 3.5 mm, the **lateral sepals** obliquely elliptic-ovate, obtuse, 6 × 4.5 mm. **Petals** oblong, obtuse, concave toward the apex, 5.5 × 2.5 mm. **Lip** three-lobed, saccate, densely pubescent behind the callus, 6 × 8.5 mm, the lateral lobes much smaller than the midlobe, triangular, acute, 1 mm long, the midlobe transverse, broadly reniform, obtuse-rounded with a central shallow notched, 5 × 8.5 mm, the **callus** biseriate, the posterior callus a conspicuous transverse thick wall-like ridge across the entire base of the midlobe, the anterior callus a small raised pad. **Column** stout, with a prominent foot, to 4 mm long; the pollinia four in two highly unequal pairs. **Pedicel** and **ovary** terete, to 1.4 cm long.

Distribution: Endemic to Vietnam at 400–600 m in elevation. **Etymology**: Named for Masaaki Chiba of Japan, who discovered the species. **Illustrations**: Yukawa 1996:20, 21.

This recently discovered species is quite rare in cultivation, and I know the entity only from the original publication and observing one plant in bud in a private collection in Chicago. It is truly unique in the genus in having a single transverse callus. I agree with Yukawa that on the basis of its four pollinia and small spur it is best placed in this section—and I admit that the buds are superficially similar to those of *P. deliciosa*—but will emphasize the oddness of the callus. Future study may show that *P. chibae* deserves a separate section or subgenus.

Phalaenopsis deliciosa Rchb.f.

Bonplandia 2:93. 1854; *Kingidium deliciosum* (Rchb.f.) Sweet, Amer. Orchid Soc. Bull. 39:1095. 1970. Type: Java. Tjikoja, *Zollinger 1429* (W).

Aerides latifolia Thw., Enum. Pl. Zeyl. 429. 1861; *Doritis latifolia* (Thw.) Trim., Cat. 89. 1885. Type: Sri Lanka. *Thwaites C.P. 3495* (lectotype: K; isolectotypes: G, P).

Phalaenopsis bella Teijsm. & Binn., Natuurk. Tijdschr. Nederl. Indië 24:321. 1862; *Kingidium deliciosum* var. *bellum* (Teijsm. & Binn.) Gruss & Röllke, Die Orchidee 44(5):225. 1993. Type: Indonesia. Java, Rodjabasa, *Teijsmann s.n.* (syntype, non vide); Java, Salak, *Teijsmann s.n.* (syntype, non vide).

Phalaenopsis hebe Rchb.f., Hamb. Gartenz. 18:35. 1862; *Doritis hebe* (Rchb.f.) Schltr, Repert. Spec. Nov. Regni Veg. Beih. 1:968. 1913; *Kingiella hebe* (Rchb.f.) Rolfe, Orchid Rev. 25:197. 1917. Type: Indonesia. Sunda Islands, *DeVries s.n.*, non vide.

Phalaenopsis wightii Rchb.f., Bot. Zeitung (Berlin) 20:214. 1862; *Doritis wightii* (Rchb.f.) Benth. & J. D. Hook., Gen. Pl. 3:574. 1883; *Kingidium wightii* (Rchb.f.) Gruss & Röllke, Die Orchidee 46(1):23. 1995. Type: India. Malabar, *Wight s.n.* (holotype: K); *Icon. Herb. Reichenbach 22223* (W).

Phalaenopsis amethystina Rchb.f., Gard. Chron. 1865:602. 1865. Type: *Icon. Herb. Reichenbach 22230* (holotype: W). Photograph and watercolor of the holotype reproduced in Gruss and Röllke (1993g:273, 274).

Phalaenopsis alboviolacea Ridl., Trans. Linn. Soc. London, Bot., ser. 2, 3:373. 1893. Type: Malaysia. Pulau Tioman, *Nanson s.n.*, non vide.

Doritis philippinensis Ames, Orchid. 2:235. 1908; *Kingiella philippinensis* (Ames) Rolfe, Orchid Rev. 25:197. 1917. Type: The Philippines. Mt. Mariveles, *Hort. ex Merrill s.n.* (AMES).

Doritis steffensii Schltr., Repert. Spec. Nov. Regni Veg. 10:194. 1911. Type: Sulawesi. Menado, Minahassa, *Steffens s.n.* (B, destroyed).

Phalaenopsis hebe var. *amboinensis* J. J. Smith, Philippine Journ. Sci. 12:260. 1917. Type: Indonesia. Ambon.

Epiphytes rapidly forming clumps by basal shoots. **Leaves** obovate-oblong, obtuse to obliquely minutely bilobed at the apex, dark green, margins undulate on emerging leaves, to 15.5 × 3.5 cm. **Inflorescences** arching racemes or more commonly panicles, the peduncle to 12 cm long, the rachis slightly thicker than the peduncle, the floral bracts minute, triangular. **Flowers** produced continuously and sequentially over long periods, fleshy, the sepals and petals white or yellow (the latter in subsp. *hookeriana*) with variable amounts of rose suffusion and spotting at the base of the segments, the lip rose with darker venation, the column pastel pink, the anther white. **Dorsal sepal** oblong-elliptic, obtuse, to 0.9 × 0.4 cm, the **lateral sepals** obliquely elliptic, subfalcate with a revolute lower margin, to 0.6 × 0.4 cm. **Petals** obliquely oblong-elliptic, subacute, to 0.9 × 0.4 cm. **Lip** three-lobed, to 1.3 cm long, to 0.8 cm across the expanded lateral lobes, the lateral lobes erect, spreading, obliquely elliptic-obovate, obtuse, each with a central flaplike tooth, the midlobe obovate-suborbicular, cuneate, emarginate +/- with a terminal apicule, the lateral margins deflexed-subrevolute, to 0.6 × 0.6 cm, the **callus** uniseriate, bifid, the junction of the lip with the column foot subsaccate. **Column** straight, to 0.4 cm long. **Pedicel** and **ovary** to 0.8 cm.

Distribution: Widespread from Sri Lanka and India to the Philippines and Sulawesi. Chan et al. (1994) record this species in Borneo from sea level to 300 m in elevation; in Thailand it grows up to 600 m in elevation. Yellow-flowered plants from northeast India are recognized as a distinct subspecies. **Etymology**: From the Latin, *deliciosus* ("delicious," "delicate"). **Illustrations**: Awards Quart. 16(4):167. 1985; Chan et al. 1994:172, 347; Gruss and Röllke 1993c:184, 185, 186, 187; Gruss and Röllke 1993d: 226, 227, Gruss and Röllke 1993e: 229, 1993g: 273, 274; Gruss and Röllke 1994a:6 (lower right as *P. decumbens*), 1994b: 66 (as *P. hebe*); Gruss and Röllke 1995a:25, 1995c:116–117 (as *K. philippinense*); Sheehan and Sheehan 1984:1153.

Phalaenopsis deliciosa has been called *P. decumbens* (Griff.) Holtt. or a derivative of that name—*Aerides decumbens* Griff., *Biermannia decumbens* (Griff.) Tang & Wang, *Kingidium decumbens* (Griff.) P. F. Hunt, *Kingiella decumbens* (Griff.) Rolfe, *Polychilos decumbens* (Griff.) Shim—on the basis of a historic misidentification of the type specimen of *Aerides decumbens* Griff. (*Griffith 5236*, K). That specimen and all the names based on it are correctly *Phalaenopsis parishii* Rchb.f., which see.

Under the name *Kingiella philippinensis* for registration purposes, *P. deliciosa* has given rise to hybrids registered as ×*Phaliella*.

With a large distribution over most of tropical Asia, it is not surprising to find a long list of synonyms. In a series of papers, Gruss and Röllke (1993–95) have proposed to split a broadly defined *P. deliciosa* into several species. Based primarily on minor aspects of coloration, I do not find their arguments convincing and maintain a traditional, broad view of this species (Christenson 1986). One variant proposed by Gruss and Röllke is distinct and warrants subspecies status.

Phalaenopsis deliciosa subsp. *hookeriana*
(Gruss & Röllke) E. A. Christ., comb. et stat. nov.

> Basionym: *Kingidium hookerianum* Gruss & Röllke, Die Orchidee 46(1):23. 1995. Type: Myanmar. Moulmein, Tenasserim, *Parish 175* (holotype: K).

Distribution: Northeast India and probably adjacent China and Myanmar. **Etymology**: Named to honor Joseph Dalton Hooker, author of the monumental *Flora of British India*. **Illustrations**: Christenson 1995: 21; Die Orchidee 45(6): front cover. 1994; Gruss and Röllke 1994c:229, 230, 231, 232.

This yellow-colored phase has been imported from exporters in northeast India over time and appears to represent a well-defined subspecies, although the exact range is unknown. In addition to the flower color, these plants consistently have somewhat larger, fuller flowers. The name *Doritis wightii*, based on a white-flowered plant from southern India, has been consistently misapplied to these plants when exported.

Phalaenopsis mysorensis Saldanha

> Indian Forester 100:572. 1974; *Kingidium mysorensis* (Saldanha) Sathish, Cat. Indian Orch. 95. 1994. Type: India. Karnataka State, Hassan District, Vanagur, *Saldanha 15915* (JCB).

> *Kingidium niveum* Sathish, Cat. Indian Orch. 53. 1994, syn. nov. Type: India. Kerala State, Palghat District, Walghat, *Sathish Kumar 11264* (CALI).

Miniature epiphytes with very short stems. **Leaves** oblong-elliptic, conduplicate at the subpetiolate base, acute to minutely, obliquely two-lobed, 3–14 × 1.6–3.5 cm. **Inflorescences** short, few-flowered, erect racemes, 1–8 cm long, terete, the peduncle and rachis purplish violet, the one or two peduncle bracts scarious, sheathing, the floral bracts lanceolate, acute, to 1 × 1 mm. **Flowers** four to eight, white, the lateral lobes of the lip dark yellow. **Dorsal sepal** oblong-obovate, obtuse, 6–7 × 3–4 mm, the **lateral sepals** obliquely ovate, subacute, 5–6 × 4–5 mm, attached to the column foot forming a mentum. **Petals** obovate, obtuse, 5–6 × 3 mm. **Lip** articulated to the column foot, the lateral lobes erect, oblong, rounded with a toothed margin, the lamina with a thick, fleshy ridge, each 3 × 1.5 mm, the midlobe transversely triangular-reniform, with entire to obscurely toothed margins, with involute lateral margins, 3.7 × 7 mm, the disc with a slight depression bordered by two raised ridges, the **callus** uniseriate, of four teeth, the outer two short, the inner two long and antenna-like. **Column** 2 mm long, shallowly (obscurely) winged, the foot to 3 mm long. **Pollinia** four, in two unequal pairs, to 0.9 × 0.5 mm, the stipe ligulate, the viscidium triangular. **Pedicel** and **ovary** 6–7 mm long. **Capsule** oblong, to 2 cm long.

Distribution: Endemic to southern India (Mysore: Karnataka; Kerala). **Etymology**: With the Latin suffix *-ensis*, indicating its place of origin in Mysore, India. **Illustrations**: Gruss and Röllke 1997g:266; Saldanha and Nicolson 1976: fig. 128; Sathish, Cat. Indian Orch. 95. 1994: fig. 16; Sweet 1980:50.

I am reducing the recently described *Kingidium niveum* to the synonymy of *P. mysorensis*. Sathish distinguished *K. niveum* as related to *P. mysorensis* but differing by "having cupular floral bracts, shorter and slightly falcate leaves which are acute at apex, 5-veined petals, 2 pairs of unequal antennae and 3-fid rostellum." Before entering into a discussion on this subject, it should be stated that the original description and drawing of *P. mysorensis* were obviously based on a flower that had undergone post-pollination changes. The column apex in the type drawing is clearly swollen in a manner consistent with post-pollination physiology.

That said, I do not consider the differences used by Sathish significant at the species level. Both sets of floral bracts are described as 1 mm long. With a feature of that size, the distinction between "subulate" (*P. mysorensis*) and "acute" (*K. niveum*) is inconsequential and may be caused by differential drying of the type specimens. The cited differences in leaf size are not significant given the small sample size and the likely overlap of measurements. The leaves of *P. mysorensis* were described as *up to* 14 × 3.5 cm, those of *K. niveum*, as 3–9 × 1.6–2.6 cm. The character of having leaf apices minutely bifid is variably expressed, usually but not always linked to plant vigor. I do not consider this a species character in *Phalaenopsis* and related genera. Petal venation has not been given for *P. mysorensis* to my knowledge. The supposed differences in the lip callus (the antennae of Sathish) are simply inaccurate. The type illustration of *P. mysorensis* clearly shows a four-lobed structure as stated by Saldanha in Sweet as "a forked, filiform process flanked by two very short teeth." The lateral teeth of *K. niveum* are drawn as somewhat longer than those of *P. mysorensis*, but as stated elsewhere I have found these characters highly variable in the *P. cornu-cervi* complex and of little use taxonomically. The final character of the three-fid rostellum is partly the difference based on a fresh flower versus one that had been pollinated and partly the semantics of whether to count the small central lobule separating the two prominent rostellum divisions.

Sweet never saw material of this species. On the basis of the original description and drawing, he placed *P. mysorensis* in his section *Parishianae* with reservations, no doubt influenced by Saldanha's comparing his new species with *P. parishii*. When I collected a fruiting example of this species on a prop-root of an upland swamp *Pandanus*, I initially identified the collection as a depauperate *Phalaenopsis deliciosa* on the basis of its foliage. I agree fully with Sathish's placement of *P. mysorensis* in *Kingidium*, accepted here in part as subgenus *Phalaenopsis* section *Deliciosae*. Note should be made of Sathish's comments (*Cat. Indian Orch*. 95. 1994) that *P. mysorensis* has a distinct spur-like mentum and four pollinia, effectively emending Saldanha's original description.

This rare species is known only from a few collections. *Saldanha 18915* was collected at 900 m in elevation and Sathish gives a range of 750–1800 m. This suggests that *P. mysorensis* should be grown under intermediate to cool-intermediate temperatures rather than in a warm greenhouse.

Flowering has been recorded from December to March with fruiting specimens collected into June. Because of the rarity of this species in nature and the limited scientific literature, all known voucher specimens are cited here: India. Karnataka: Hassan District, Vanagur, *Saldanha 15915* (JCB; type of *Phalaenopsis mysorensis*); same data, *Saldanha 18915*

(JCB); same data, *Saldanha HFP-1581* (JCB); same data, *Saldanha HFP-1692* (JCB); Kerala: Coorg District, Mercara, Abbi Falls, *Christenson and Amy 947* (SEL); Palghat District, Walghat, *Sathish Kumar 11264* (CALI; type of *Kingidium niveum*); Pothumala, Nelliampathy, *Sasidharan 3086* (KFRI); Trichur District, Sholayar, *Sasidharana 5431* (KFRI).

Section *Esmeralda* Rchb.f.

Gard. Chron., n.s., 11:398. 1879. Lectotype, here designated: *Phalaenopsis esmeralda* Rchb.f. (= *Phalaenopsis pulcherrima* (Lindl.) J.J. Sm.).

Phalaenopsis section *Antenniferae* Pfitz. in Engler and Prantl., Pflanzenfam. 2(6):212. 1889; *Phalaenopsis* section *Antennorchis* Kuntze in Post and Kuntze, Lex. Gen. Phan. 430. 1904. Type: *Phalaenopsis antennifera* Rchb.f. (= *Phalaenopsis pulcherrima* (Lindl.) J.J. Sm.).

Doritis Lindl., Gen. and Sp. Orch. Pl. 178. 1833; *Phalaenopsis* section *Doritis* (Lindl.) J.J. Sm., Repert. Spec. Nov. Regni Veg. 32:366. 1933, nom. inval. Type: *Doritis pulcherrima* Lindl. (= *Phalaenopsis pulcherrima* (Lindl.) J.J. Sm.).

Doritis has alternatively been accepted as a genus separate from *Phalaenopsis* or as part of a broadly defined *Phalaenopsis*. The principal characters that have been used to separate *Doritis* are the long column foot, the long rostellum (and corresponding long stipe of the pollinarium), the presence of linear "appendages" toward the base of the lip, four pollinia, and the terrestrial habit.

While the column foot of species in this section is long, forming a saccate-like structure with the clawed base of the lip, it is completely homologous to other species of *Phalaenopsis* (*P. lobbii*, for example). The rostellum, although long in this group in absolute terms, occupies the same relative position over the stigmatic cavity found in other species (i.e., the stigmatic cavity of species in section *Esmeralda* is longer).

Earlier authors noted erect linear "appendages" toward the base of the lip in this group of species, an example of inaccurate descriptive morphology. The midlobes of species in this section are three-lobulate, with the resulting lateral lobules in *P. buyssoniana* and *P. pulcherrima* large and pronounced. This three-lobulate structure has been misinterpreted as a three-lobed lip homologous to other species of *Phalaenopsis*. The linear "appendages" noted by Holttum and others are actually homologous to the lateral lobes found in other species of *Phalaenopsis*. This has been proven time and again through character inheritance in intersectional hybrids.

The absolute separating character of four pollinia in *Doritis* versus two pollinia in *Phalaenopsis* has been proven false. In the circumscription of the genus used here, only two of the five subgenera bear two pollinia (subgenus *Polychilos* and part of subgenus *Phalaenopsis*). We are back to the old argument discussed previously that if one wants to accept *Doritis* on the absolute character of pollinia number, then *Phalaenopsis* must be split, according to the precepts of modern phylogenetic theory, into at least seven genera to have the end products represent holophyletic groups (monophyletic groups that include all derivatives). Such a solution needlessly emphasizes differences, is not required by scientific considerations, and is unacceptable in such an important genus as *Phalaenopsis*, where stability of names must be a pragmatic consideration.

Finally, preliminary molecular data using the matK gene (Jarrell unpubl.) reveals a phylogenetic pattern where *Doritis* falls in the middle of *Phalaenopsis*, between subgenera *Aphyllae* and *Polychilos* on the one hand and members of section *Phalaenopsis* on the other. Again, if *Doritis* is maintained as a separate genus, at the very least *Grafia* and *Polychilos* must also be maintained as distinct genera (otherwise *Phalaenopsis* would be paraphyletic). Such a classification would require about half the registered *Phalaenopsis* hybrids be renamed under a new hybrid combination between *Phalaenopsis* and *Polychilos*—similar to what would happen if *Vanda sanderiana* Rchb.f. were treated as *Euanthe sanderiana* (Rchb.f.) Schltr.: most hybrid *Vanda* plants would have to be renamed as ×*Vandanthe* plants (*Euanthe* × *Vanda*). This type of nomenclatural instability, not to say mayhem, is unacceptable.

The callus of section *Esmeralda* is uniseriate. In *P. regnieriana* the callus is bifid, similar to those found in sections *Deliciosae* and *Polychilos*; in the other two species the callus is simple, a character I take to be secondarily derived.

When all this is taken into account, I see no reason to separate *Doritis* from *Phalaenopsis*, outside of historic precedent. The "sinking" of *Doritis*, following the earlier positions of Holttum and J. J. Smith, does cause problems with the registration of hybrids, however. The hybrid genus ×*Doritaenopsis* (*Doritis* × *Phalaenopsis*) effectively disappears. But now that hybrid registration has been transferred to computers, this should not cause too much consternation away from the greenhouse potting bench. The duplication of names between hybrids registered as ×*Doritaenopsis* versus *Phalaenopsis* appears to be minimal.

One significant benefit of eliminating ×*Doritaenopsis* is that it would eliminate many modern "doritaenopsis" that never actually had any species of section *Esmeralda* in their ancestry. When the three species of section *Esmeralda* are used in combination with those of other subgenera, the characters of section *Esmeralda*, especially the erect inflorescences, flower shape, and flower color, are quite dominant. Since the 1960s and on through modern bloodlines, a number of "doritaenopsis" were produced that bore large round flowers, either white or white with red lip, on arching sprays unlike most ×*Doritaenopsis*. The chromosomes of species in section *Esmeralda* are longer than those of other members in the subgenus and can be differentiated in a karyotype (an analysis of an individual's chromosome complement). Recent work in Japan and Taiwan has shown that these aberrant "doritaenopsis" have no *Doritis*-length chromosomes and probably resulted from mislabeled flasks of standard *Phalaenopsis* hybrids (Christenson 1999b).

Lindley originally described *P. pulcherrima* as an epiphyte. That and similar reports over the years are in error. The three species of section *Esmeralda* are terrestrial (or lithophytic among humus and moss on rocks), and most characters that define this section are uniquely derived characters (autapomorphies) associated with the terrestrial habit. In particular, the stiffly erect inflorescences are an adaptation to a terrestrial habit. Also, unlike most *Phalaenopsis* species, which produce roots periodically throughout the growing season, plants of this section produce a principal flush of roots in a root collar all around the plant. This is presumably an adaptation to rooting in and rising above a fresh layer of leaf litter in nature.

Preliminary investigation of flavonoid co-pigments (Griesbach unpubl.) shows a complex pattern in *P. pulcherrima* that is similar to that

228

found in *P. equestris.* Curiously, anecdotal information from hybridizers also shows an affinity between these two species. They cross easily with each other and with their secondary hybrids.

Reichenbach placed both *P. antennifera* and *P. esmeralda* in his section *Esmeralda.* The name-giving species is selected as the lectotype.

Key to the species of section *Esmeralda*

1. Flowers large, the dorsal sepal to 2.2 cm long. . . . . *P. buyssoniana*
1. Flowers small, the dorsal sepal to 1.2 cm long.
  2. Lateral lobules of midlobe large, erect and subparallel, to 5.5 mm long; midlobe of lip not particularly tapered, 4 mm wide at base. . . . . *P. pulcherrima*
  2. Lateral lobules of midlobe small, involute, to 3 mm long; midlobe of lip tapered, 2–3 mm wide at base. . . . . *P. regnieriana*

Phalaenopsis buyssoniana Rchb.f.

Gard. Chron. 2:295. 1888. Type: Vietnam. Without precise locality, *Regnier s.n.* (holotype: W).

[*Doritis pulcherrima*] var. *buyssoniana* Seidenfaden & Smitinand, Orch. Thailand Prelim. List 821. 1965, nom. inval.

Robust terrestrials. **Leaves** oblong-elliptic to elliptic-obovate, concave, pale silvery green with fine purple spotting on the upper surface and purple suffusion and spotting on the lower surface, to 25 × 9.5 cm. **Inflorescences** stiffly erect, many-flowered racemes to 1 m long. **Flowers** rose-pink, the lip darker rose, the column dark rose, the anther white. **Dorsal sepal** elliptic to elliptic-obovate, obtuse-rounded, to 2.2 × 1.3 cm, the **lateral sepals** obliquely broadly triangular-ovate, acute, to 2.1 × 1.4 cm. **Petals** subrhomboid to obliquely broadly ovate, cuneate-clawed, obtuse-rounded, to 2.3 × 1.2 cm. **Lip** three-lobed, to 2.2 × 1.5 cm, the lateral lobes erect, linear-lanceolate, to either side of the callus, the midlobe three-lobulate, the lateral lobules erect, elliptic, obtuse-rounded, to 1.2 × 0.7 cm, the middle lobule ovate, obtuse, to 1.1 × 0.9 cm, the **callus** uniseriate, transverse, with the leading edge broadly rounded. **Column** straight, stout.

Distribution: Thailand and Indochina (see the discussion by Sagarik in Orchid Rev. 72:83. 1964). **Etymology**: Named in honor of French horticulturist Le Comte François Du Buysson. **Illustrations**: Awards Quart. 23(4):212. 1992; Batchelor 1982:1272; Freed 1969a:237.

Phalaenopsis buyssoniana traditionally has been placed in the synonymy of a broadly defined *P. pulcherrima*. With the advent of chromosome counting, *P. buyssoniana* was found to be a tetraploid with 76 chromosomes (2n = 4x = 76) and therefore different from *P. pulcherrima*, which is a diploid with 38 chromosomes (2n = 2x = 38). Thus, *P. buyssoniana* was simply considered a spontaneous tetraploid variant of *P. pulcherrima*. This assumption was supported by the similar floral morphology of the two entities, other than size differences attributed to ploidy levels (Holttum 1965).

Recently, however, diploid plants (protocorms) of *P. pulcherrima* have been treated with colchicine to effect doubling of the chromosome number. Upon flowering, such artificially created autotetraploids of *P. pulcherrima* resemble superimproved *P. pulcherrima* with somewhat larger flowers with fuller-formed segments and more intensely saturated floral pigments. They do not resemble *P. buyssoniana* in any manner, especially in flower color, flower size, and plant size and habit. Given this new evidence, there is no reason to accept *P. buyssoniana* as part of a broadly defined *P. pulcherrima*, despite similar floral morphology, and these plants are accorded species rank. This is logical as these two entities are biologically isolated in nature by virtue of their ploidy levels; natural hybridization events would normally result in the production of sterile triploids (2n = 3x = 57).

The flowers of *P. buyssoniana* are pale pink and show little variation in their coloration, although a white-flowered form with a yellow lip has been reported from Thailand.

Separating *P. buyssoniana* from *P. pulcherrima*, regardless of whether one accepts them in *Phalaenopsis* or retains them in *Doritis*, creates many problems for the interpretation of previous hybrids. Such an investigation is clearly outside the scope of this work; perhaps someone familiar with the breeding of "doritaenopsis" will publish a definitive article elucidating which species was actually used in early hybridization efforts, updating the information presented by Freed (1969a, 1969b).

Phalaenopsis pulcherrima (Lindl.) J. J. Sm.

Repert. Spec. Nov. Regni Veg. 32:366. 1933; *Doritis pulcherrima*
Lindl., Gen. and Sp. Orch. Pl. 178. 1833. Type: Vietnam. Da
Nang, *Finlayson 521* (holotype: K).

Phalaenopsis esmeralda Rchb.f., Gard. Chron. 1874:582. 1874.
Type: Cambodia. Yan Dong, *Godefroy s.n.* (holotype: W; isotypes:
K, W).

Phalaenopsis antennifera Rchb.f., Gard. Chron. 1879:398. 1879.
Type: Myanmar. Without precise locality, *Hort. Low s.n.* (holotype: W).

Phalaenopsis esmeralda var. *rubra* Hort. ex Stein, Orchideenbuch
506. 1892. Type: Not preserved.

Phalaenopsis mastersii King & Pantl., Journ. As. Soc. Bengal 66:591.
1897. Type: India. Assam, Nambur Falls, *Masters s.n.* (CAL?).

Terrestrials forming large clumps by basal offshoots. **Leaves** oblong to
elliptic, acute, concave, to 15 × 3 cm. **Inflorescences** stiffly erect racemes to 60 cm long, the peduncle to 30 cm long, the rachis many-
flowered, the floral bracts minute, scarious. **Flowers** brilliant saturated
cerise, the erect lateral lobules of the midlobe of the lip orange, the
disk of the midlobe white, the column white. **Dorsal sepal** elliptic to
elliptic-obovate, cuneate, obtuse-rounded, to 1.2 × 0.6 cm, the **lateral
sepals** obliquely broadly triangular-ovate, obtuse, attached to the long
column foot, to 1 × 0.9 cm. **Petals** subsimilar and subequal to the dorsal sepal. **Lip** three-lobed, to 1.2 cm long, the lateral lobes narrow,
antrorse, linear-lanceolate, lateral to the callus, the midlobe three-lobulate, the lobules subequal, the lateral lobules erect, broadly elliptic,
obtuse, broadly rounded, the middle lobule broadly triangular-ovate,
deflexed, obtuse to subacute, the **callus** uniseriate, small, transverse,
with a rounded leading edge. **Column** straight, stout, with a pair of
knee-like projections at the base. **Pedicel** and **ovary** to 1.6 cm long.

   Distribution: Widespread from northeast India and southern China
throughout Indochina to Malaysia (Malay Peninsula), Indonesia (Sumatra), and East Malaysia (Sabah). **Etymology**: From the Latin, *pulcher*
("beautiful"). **Illustrations**: Amer. Orchid Soc. Bull. 61(21): front cover,

113. 1992; Awards Quart. 23(3):183. 1992; Awards Quart. 24(2):136 (peloric), 145, 146. 1993; Awards Quart. 24(3):196. 1993; Awards Quart. 24(4):295. 1993; Awards Quart. 25(1):32. 1994; Awards Quart. 26(1):50 (peloric). 1995; Awards Quart. 26(2):72, 83. 1995; Die Orchidee 35(5):15. 1984; Die Orchidee 46(2):20. 1995 (peloric); Gruss 1992a:136; Gruss and Wolff 1995:163; Seidenfaden 1988a:32.

Seidenfaden and Smitinand (1965) and Seidenfaden (1988a) record an elevational range of 100–1200 m. It has been recorded to grow in sandy soil along the coast or on rocks near the sea.

Phalaenopsis pulcherrima readily produces basal offshoots, resulting in large clumps of stems in cultivation. Although the species is easy to grow, some people report difficulty getting the plants to flower: plants either do not flower at all or only produce a few inflorescences on a many-stemmed plant. All three species of section *Esmeralda* prefer higher light intensities than other species in the genus and poor flowering is usually the result of less than optimum light intensity.

Peloric clones of *P. pulcherrima* are not uncommon and have been given the informal varietal name *champornensis*. This name has never been validly published, and I resist giving a formal designation to a teratologic monstrosity.

Three sporadically occurring color morphs have been formally named and are sought after by horticulturists and orchid breeders.

Phalaenopsis pulcherrima f. *alba*
(Gruss & Roeth) E. A. Christ., comb. et stat. nov.

Basionym: *Doritis pulcherrima* f. *alba* Gruss & Roeth, Die Orchidee 50(6):671. 1999. Type: Thailand, leg. J. Roeth & O. Gruss, 1986, Hort. *F. Glanz 12.9.95* (holotype: HAL 063308).

Phalaenopsis esmeralda var. *candidula* Rolfe, Lindenia 6:49, t. 263. 1890; *Doritis pulcherrima* var. *candidula* (Rolfe) Guill., Fl. Gen. Indo-Chine 6:456. 1933. Lectotype, here designated: tabula 263 in Lindenia, loc. cit.

Etymology: From the Latin, *albus* ("white"). **Illustrations**: Awards Quart. 22(4):237. 1991 (as *Doritis pulcherrima* var. *alba*); Die Orchidee 42(3):9. 1991.

This form produces flowers with white sepals, petals, and lip, the lip highlighted with yellow markings on the sidelobes and callus.

Phalaenopsis pulcherrima f. *albiflora*
(Rchb.f.) E. A. Christ., comb. et stat. nov.

> Basionym: *Phalaenopsis esmeralda* var. *albiflora* Rchb.f., Otia Bot. Hamburg. 1:35. 1877; *Doritis pulcherrima* f. *albiflora* (Rchb. f.) Roeth & Gruss, Die Orchidee 50(6):671. 1999. Type: Kampuchea. Without precise locality, *Hort. Lueddemann s.n.* (holotype: W?).

Etymology: From the Latin, *albus* ("white") and *flos* ("flower").
This form produces flowers with white sepals and petals that contrast with a rose-colored lip.

Phalaenopsis pulcherrima f. *coerulea*
(Fowlie) E. A. Christ., comb. et stat. nov.

> *Doritis pulcherrima* var. *coerulea* Fowlie, Orchid Digest 33:241. 1969; *Doritis pulcherrima* f. *coerulea* (Fowlie) Gruss & Roeth, Die Orchidee 50(6):671. 1999. Type: Thailand. Without precise locality, *Freed s.n.* (holotype: LA; photograph: NY).

Etymology: From the Latin, *coeruleus* ("blue"). **Illustrations**: Awards Quart. 24(3):179. 1993.
This form produces bluish violet flowers unlike the standard cerise flowers of the typical form. The amount of cerise pigmentation is variable. Modern selections have favored less cerise pigment, resulting in bluish lavender (grayish) flowers.

Phalaenopsis regnieriana Rchb.f.

> Gard. Chron. 2:746. 1887; *Doritis regnieriana* (Rchb.f.) Holtt., Kew Bull. 19:212. 1965; *Phalaenopsis esmeralda* f. *regnieriana* J. J. Sm., Bull. Jard. Bot. Buitenz., ser. 3, 1:120. 1919 (nomen). Type: Thailand. Without precise locality, *Regnier s.n.* (holotype: W).

Terrestrials similar to *P. pulcherrima* in growth habit, leaf morphology, inflorescence structure, dimensions, and general characteristics of the flower, including column morphology. **Lip** three-lobed, to 1.4 cm long, to 0.5 cm wide across the expanded lobule of the midlobe, the lateral lobes linear-lanceolate, ca. 1.8 mm long, the midlobe three-lobulate, the lateral lobules small, suborbicular, rounded-obtuse, the middle lobule oblong-ovate, obtuse-rounded, the **callus** bifid.

Distribution: Recorded as endemic to Thailand. **Etymology**: Named to honor French horticulturist M. R. Regnier. **Illustrations**: Seidenfaden 1988a:33.

Phalaenopsis regnieriana spent most of its history in obscurity, placed by authors without scrutiny in the synonymy of *P. pulcherrima* as early as 1892 in Stein's *Orchideenbuch*. Holttum (1965) studied the holotype of

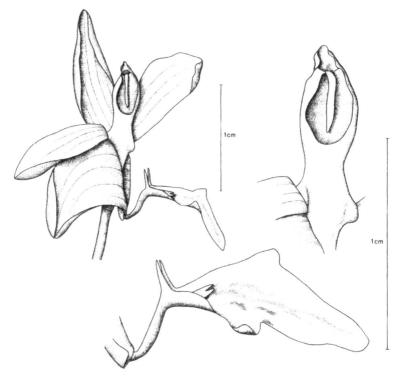

Phalaenopsis regnieriana drawn from the type. Illustrator: G. Seidenfaden.

P. regnieriana and established that this species deserved recognition. Seidenfaden (1988a) also examined the holotype and provided an illustration for the first time. At first glance a flower of *P. regnieriana* resembles a slightly deformed *P. pulcherrima*. The sepals, petals, and column are essentially identical. The lip is also similar but differs in *P. regnieriana* by having the lateral lobules of the midlobe as small, lightly incurved lobules, unlike the large, parallel, erect lobules found in *P. pulcherrima*. In addition, the callus of *P. regnieriana* is a well-developed bifid structure, unlike the rounded to very shallowly notched callus of *P. pulcherrima*.

Known only from the type collection, Seidenfaden questions the Thailand origin of this species, noting Regnier's horticultural connections with Indochina in addition to the total absence of modern Thai collections of this species. I will only add a comment about the existence of one unusual collection from Indochina (Annam, without precise locality, 2 Oct. 1921, *McClure 7494*), which I located in Zurich (Z). This collection bears very narrow, oblanceolate leaves less than 2 cm wide (resembling the very weak-growing, cultivated color variants that suffer from inbreeding depression) and may represent *P. regnieriana*. Unfortunately, the one sample of this collection, originally distributed by the Canton Christian College, has neither buds nor flowers remaining on the specimen.

Section *Stauroglottis* (Schauer) Benth.

J. Linn. Soc. 18:332. 1881; *Stauroglottis* Schauer, Nov. Act. Acad. Nat. Cur. 19, suppl. 1:432. 1843. Type: *Stauroglottis equestris* Schauer (= *Phalaenopsis equestris* (Schauer) Rchb.f.).

Plants of this section are very similar to and share several characteristics with those of section *Phalaenopsis*. They share a similar geographic range, small chromosome sizes, predominately white and pink flowers that lack transverse barring patterns, and sometimes marbled foliage. Unlike plants of section *Phalaenopsis*, plants of section *Stauroglottis* bear smaller flowers with mostly subsimilar sepals and petals and an undivided lip apex.

Key to the species of section *Stauroglottis*

1. Leaves green, variously suffused with purple, never marbled.
   . . . . *P. equestris*
1. Leaves richly marbled with dark green, silver, and purple.
   2. Petals with a central brown patch, with strongly revolute margins.
      . . . . *P. celebensis*
   2. Petals solid-colored or with longitudinal pink stripes, never with a central brown patch, flat (planar) without revolute margins.
      . . . . *P. lindenii*

Phalaenopsis celebensis Sweet

The Genus Phalaenopsis 66. 1980. Type: Sulawesi. Without precise locality, *Hort. Karthus and Dakkus s.n.* (BO).

Miniature epiphytes. **Leaves** oblong-obovate, obtuse, dark green marbled with silvery white, to 17 × 6 cm. **Inflorescences** densely manyflowered racemes, the peduncle erect, to 40 cm long, the rachis pendent, to 13 cm long, the floral bracts inconspicuous. **Flowers** white, the petals with a central brown suffusion, the base of the lip with brown stripes composed of spots, the base of the lateral lobes of the lip yellow suffused and brown spotted, the upper surface of the column rose. **Dorsal sepal** elliptic-suborbicular, obtuse, variously concave, convex, or both, to 1.3 × 1 cm, the **lateral sepals** obliquely elliptic-ovate, obtuse, divergent, with revolute basal margins, to 1.4 × 1 cm. **Petals** when flattened obliquely transverse, obtuse-rounded, minutely emarginate, in-

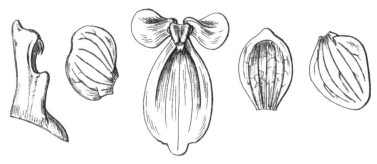

Phalaenopsis celebensis drawn from the type. Illustrator: H. R. Sweet.

curved with strongly revolute margins, to 0.9 × 1.2 cm. **Lip** three-lobed, the lateral lobes obovate, obtuse-rounded, to 0.5 × 0.3 mm, each with a posterior ridge, the midlobe elliptic-obovate, obtuse with a shallow constriction below the apex, to 1 × 0.6 cm, the **callus** solitary, triangular, acuminate. **Column** straight, with a pair of fleshy knees fused to the lateral margins of the base for half its length, to 0.8 cm long. **Pedicel** and **ovary** to 2.6 cm long.

Distribution: Endemic to Indonesia (Sulawesi). **Etymology**: With the Latin suffix -*ensis*, indicating its place of origin in Sulawesi (the Celebes). **Illustrations**: Awards Quart. 22(1):12. 1991; Awards Quart. 25(3):144.

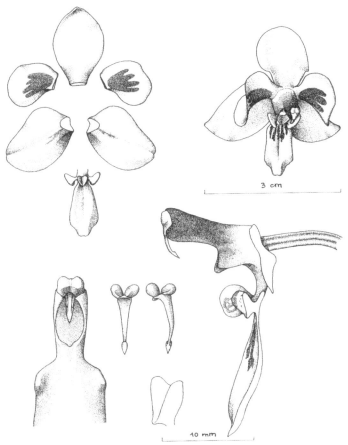

Phalaenopsis celebensis. Illustrator: F. Pupulin.

1994; Die Orchidee 33(6): back cover. 1982; Die Orchidee 36(1):15. 1985; Die Orchidee 36(5):3. 1985; Die Orchidee 44(6):39. 1993; Gruss and Wolff 1995:58, 60; Orchid Digest 55:73. 1991; Sweet 1980:64, 66.

This relatively recent introduction has been artificially propagated and is now widespread in cultivation. The species is highly regarded for its dwarf plant size, richly marked leaves (similar to *P. lindenii*), and numerous flowers.

The form of the petals of *P. celebensis* is unique in the genus. The petals are incurved with strongly revolute margins and bear a central brown

Phalaenopsis celebensis, a plant in flower. Illustrator: F. Pupulin.

stain. When crossed with other members of section *Stauroglottis, P. celebensis* has produced charming miniature multifloras; hybrid crosses to larger-flowered species and hybrids, however, have produced offspring with poor shape due to the dominance of the revolute petal margins.

Phalaenopsis celebensis is also unique in the genus for the form of the "knees" at the base of the column. In other species of *Phalaenopsis* these knees are free from the column. In *P. celebensis*, the knees are parallel to and fused to the column for half the column length. The architecture of the lip and incurved petals combined with the chamber created by the knees points to a specialized pollination biology for *P. celebensis*.

The type specimen, like subsequent material introduced to cultivation, was collected in Sulawesi without precise locality data. Nothing is known of its distribution in Sulawesi or its habitat and ecological preferences.

Phalaenopsis equestris (Schauer) Rchb.f.

Linnaea 22:864. 1850; *Stauroglottis equestris* Schauer, Nov. Act. Acad. Cur. 19, suppl. 1:432. 1843. Type: The Philippines. Luzon, Manila, *Meyens s.n.* (holotype: W).

Phalaenopsis rosea Lindl., Gard. Chron. 1848:671. 1848. Type: The Philippines. Luzon, Manila, *Lobb s.n.* (holotype: K; isotype: W).

Phalaenopsis stauroglottis Hort. ex Rollinson, Gen. Cat. 42. 1876, nom. nud.

Phalaenopsis equestris (Schauer) Rchb.f. var. *leucaspis* Rchb.f., Gard. Chron., n.s., 15:688. 1881; *Phalaenopsis rosea* Lindl. var. *leucaspis* (Rchb.f.) Rolfe, Gard. Chron., n.s., 26:276. 1886. Type: The Philippines. Without precise locality, *Hort. Barber s.n.* (W).

Phalaenopsis rosea var. *deliciosa* Burb., The Garden 22:119. 1882, ex char.

Phalaenopsis equestris (Schauer) Rchb.f. var. *leucotanthe* Rchb.f. ex Godefroy-Lebeuf, L'Orchidophile 3:490. 1883. Lectotype, designated by Sweet (Amer. Orchid Soc. Bull. 38:334. 1969): *Icon. Herb. Reichenbach 22208* (W).

Phalaenopsis rosea Lindl. var. *aurantiaca* Gower, The Garden 41: 216. 1892, ex char.

Phalaenopsis riteiwanensis Masamune, Trans. Nat. Hist. Soc. Formosa 24:213. 1934; *Stauroglottis riteiwanensis* Masamune, Trans. Nat. Hist. Soc. Formosa 24:213. 1934, in syn. Type: Taiwan. Syokotosyo (Riteiwan), *Segawa s.n.*, non vide.

Epiphytes. **Leaves** variable in size and shape, oblong-elliptic to oblong-ovate to elliptic, acute to subobtuse, green without any markings, gen-

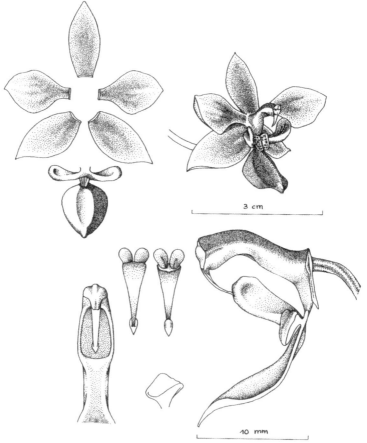

Phalaenopsis equestris. Illustrator: F. Pupulin.

240

erally to 20 × 6.5 cm but larger in some populations. **Inflorescences** densely many-flowered racemes or panicles, long-pedunculate, the peduncles erect, the rachis arching-subpendent, the apex frequently forming a plantlet following flowering, the floral bracts insignificant, to 2 mm long. **Flowers** variable in color and size, opening simultaneously, typically the sepals and petals white or pale pink with a central pink suffusion, the lip solid rose or red, the callus white or yellow +/– rose or red spotting, the column rose, the anther white. **Sepals** subsimilar, subequal, lightly reflexed, oblong-elliptic, acute, to 1.7 × 0.8 cm, the lateral sepals somewhat oblique, divergent. **Petals** elliptic-rhombic, clawed, obtuse to subacute, to 1.5 × 0.8 cm. **Lip** three-lobed, to 1.4 cm long, to 1.6 cm wide across the expanded lateral lobes, the lateral lobes oblong-oblanceolate, obtuse-rounded, erect-incurved, the midlobe ovate-trullate, acute with a laterally constricted blunt tip, the **callus** solitary, peltate, quadrangular with a truncate apex. **Column** lightly arching, to 0.9 cm long. **Pedicel** and **ovary** to 2 cm long.

Distribution: The Philippines and Taiwan. **Etymology**: From the Latin, *equester*, pertaining to riding and cavalry. The basis for this name is obscure. **Illustrations**: Awards Quart. 19(2):78, 102. 1988; Awards Quart. 20(4):184. 1989; Awards Quart. 21(4):196. 1990 (peloric); Awards Quart. 24(1):50. 1993 (peloric); Awards Quart. 24(2):142, 154. 1993; Awards Quart. 24(4):321. 1993; Awards Quart. 25(1):334. 1994 (peloric); Batchelor 1982:1273; Collins 1983:792; Die Orchidee 31(6): front cover. 1980; Die Orchidee 34(6): back cover. 1983; Die Orchidee 35(5):17. 1984; Die Orchidee 41(4):25. 1990 (peloric); Die Orchidee 42(5):273. 1991 (peloric); Die Orchidee 45(6):43. 1994; Die Orchidee 46(4):51. 1995; Die Orchidee 46(5):208. 1995; Gruss 1990:118; Gruss and Wolff 1995:61; Lückel 1980:223, 225; Sweet 1969:336, 1980:61, 62.

Phalaenopsis equestris is highly variable, both vegetatively and in flower color. Several independent genes control the expression of both anthocyanins and

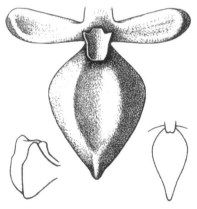

Phalaenopsis equestris drawn from the type. Illustrator: H. R. Sweet.

241

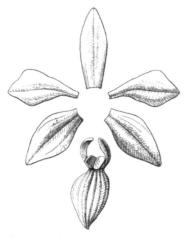

Phalaenopsis equestris drawn from Taiwanese material described as *P. riteiwanensis*. Illustrator: H. R. Sweet.

carotenoids in the lip of *P. equestris*, and several horticultural varieties have been published based on the permutations of whether or not these genes are expressed. Sweet recognized two of these: var. *leucaspis* Rchb.f., which lacks yellow pigments associated with the white callus; and var. *leucotanthe* Rchb.f. ex Godefroy-Lebeuf (= var. *aurantiaca* Gower), which has deep orange pigments associated with the callus. According to Cesar Zapata, Jr. (in litt.), these variants and others with different combinations of pigment appear to occur sporadically throughout all populations of *P. equestris* as part of the normal allele frequencies, and no evidence suggests any of these are linked to geographic isolation (i.e., candidates for recognition as subspecies). For this reason, and the requisite need to publish additional new varieties for consistency, I do not formally recognize these variants in this study.

Peloric forms of all color variants exist, and peloric-flowered hybrids are produced with some frequency from breeding with standard, non-peloric *P. equestris*. This is especially true of hybrid combinations that include *P. pulcherrima*. This tendency to produce peloric-flowered offspring also gave rise to the peloric form of *P.* ×*intermedia*, the informal var. *diezii*.

Phalaenopsis equestris is in the background of nearly all semi-alba (white with a contrastingly colored lip) and striped hybrids. Recently the species has gained favor in producing multiflora hybrids for the pot-plant trade.

Taiwanese plants, originally described as *P. riteiwanensis*, do not differ in any significant way from Philippine plants (see the drawing reproduced in Lückel 1980:223). In general, Taiwanese plants of *P. equestris* bear flowers with a more open form and rather nondescript coloration, making them less desirable in horticulture.

Three color variants, all important parents in modern breeding programs, are formally treated here.

Phalaenopsis equestris (Schauer) Rchb.f. var. *rosea*
Valmayor & Tiu

Philippine Orchid Rev. 3:18. 1983. Type: The Philippines. Without precise locality, *Valmayor & Tiu 108* (holotype: CAHP).

Etymology: From the Latin, *roseus* ("rose"), a reference to the evenly rose-colored flowers. **Illustrations**: Amer. Orchid Soc. Bull. 60(2): back cover. 1991; Amer. Orchid Soc. Bull. 64:127. 1995; Awards Quart. 19(1):5. 1988; Awards Quart. 23(1):27. 1992; Awards Quart. 23(4):230, 245. 1992; Awards Quart. 24(1):50. 1993; Awards Quart. 25(1):36, 48. 1994; Awards Quart. 25(3):141, 146, 154, 161 (peloric). 1994; Awards Quart. 25(4):220. 1994; Awards Quart. 26(1):44. 1995; Awards Quart. 26(4):206. 1995; Die Orchidee 41(4):25. 1990; Die Orchidee 41(5): 197. 1990; Die Orchidee 42(5):273. 1991; Gruss 1992a:134; Gruss and Wolff 1995:64 (peloric); Orchid Digest 59:24. 1995. **Notes**: All published photographs of this variety are, to the best of my knowledge, hybrids between wild-collected plants of this variety and standard *P. equestris*, which bears white to pale pink sepals and petals with a central suffusion of rose-pink. Even though the name was based on a wild-collected plant, the name should be applied to horticultural material of infraspecific hybrid origin. The plant figured in Gruss and Wolff (1995: pl. 61) as *P. equestris* 'Amethystina' appears to be an interspecific hybrid based on both lip and petal shape, and not this variety.

This variety of *P. equestris* has recently come into wide cultivation. Instead of bearing pale pink or white sepals and petals with a darker, central patch, the floral segments are uniformly dark rose-purple without any lighter borders. It is somewhat unfortunate that Valmayor and Tiu chose the epithet *rosea* for this variety, as that epithet could cause some confusion with the synonym of the typically colored form, *P. rosea* Lindl. There is no nomenclatural problem with the name, however, as names do not have priority outside their rank (i.e., there would be a problem only if someone had previously transferred Lindley's *P. rosea* to a variety of a species).

I am accepting the solid pink phase of *P. equestris* as a variety, as it was published, although some evidence suggests that the plants may come from a uniform, geographically isolated population. Cesar Zapata, Jr., offers the following comments (in litt.) on the concolor pink phase of

P. equestris: "This form exists in a very small area north of the Philippine Island of Luzon–Bangui, Ilocos Norte. We call this the 'Ilocos' type. It has the smallest leaves of all the forms of the species and has a slightly different lip structure, especially the callus."

My experience with wild-collected plants of this variety, obtained from Richella Orchids in the early 1970s, concurs with Zapata's observations. I would also add that the flowers are smaller than other variants of *P. equestris* and produce full, round flowers with overlapping floral segments. Zapata also notes that the typical phase "exists southwest of Luzon–Quezon province and this is where the Riverbend strain comes from. We call this the 'Tagalog' form. It has the largest leaves, up to and more than two feet long and flower spikes three to five feet long."

From that information one could draw the conclusion that these are distinct populations and that var. *rosea* should be elevated to a subspecies, in keeping with classification used here. I hesitate to do that at this time because of the extreme variability seen in wild-collected plants of *P. equestris*, including the huge-leaved plants mentioned by Zapata. The late Fred Fuchs imported some of the latter, and until they flowered with absolutely typical flowers for *P. equestris*, it was difficult to believe that they could be the same species. Zapata also notes, "An intermediate form exists from the northern tip of Luzon–Aparri and all along the northeastern side of the island until the Aurora province. We call this the 'Aparri' form. Other forms exist elsewhere."

A full study is needed on the patterns of variability in *P. equestris* before formally describing and naming variants for horticultural expediency (see Santiago et al. 1983). This is an ideal research project for a resident of the Philippines.

Phalaenopsis equestris (Schauer) Rchb.f. f. *alba*
(Hort.) E. A. Christ., stat. nov.

> *Phalaenopsis equestris* (Schauer) Rchb.f. var. *alba* Hort., Amer.
> Orchid Soc. Bull. 38:334. 1969. Lectotype, here designated: The
> Philippines. Without precise locality, *Hort. Shipley s.n.*, photograph in Amer. Orchid Soc. Bull. 36:144. 1967.

Etymology: From the Latin, *albus* ("white"), a reference to the white sepals and petals. **Illustrations**: Amer. Orchid Soc. Bull. 64(3): back cover. 1995; Awards Quart. 23(1):45. 1992; Awards Quart. 24(4):299. 1993 (peloric); Awards Quart. 25(1):27. 1994; Awards Quart. 25(2): 108. 1994; Awards Quart. 26(2):77, 78. 1995; Gruss and Wolff 1995:61; Harper 1991:110.

This is the pure white form of the species, with no pigment associated with the callus. Other white-flowered forms have a yellow callus.

Phalaenopsis equestris (Schauer) Rchb.f. f. *aurea* (Hort.) E. A. Christ., f. nov.

Differt a specie typica sepalis petalisque albo et labello aureo.

Type: Without precise locality, *Hort. Raven-Riemann s.n.* (holotype: photograph reproduced in the color plate section of this book).

Etymology: From the Latin, *aureus* ("golden yellow"), a reference to the pure golden yellow lip of this form. **Illustrations**: Christenson 1999a: 363; Die Orchidee 46(4):52. 1995.

This exceptional variant bears pure white flowers with a highly contrasting solid yellow lip. Recently brought into cultivation, *P. equestris* f. *aurea* has been seed propagated and widely distributed.

Phalaenopsis lindenii Loher

Loher, Journ. Orch. 6:103. 1895. Type: The Philippines. Luzon, *Loher 5384* (K).

Miniature epiphytes. **Leaves** dark green, marbled with silvery white, oblong-lanceolate to oblong-oblanceolate, acute, the apex minutely, obliquely bilobed, to 25 × 4 cm. **Inflorescences** densely many-flowered scapose racemes, occasionally branched, the peduncle suberect, the rachis arching-pendent, the floral bracts inconspicuous, to 2 mm long. **Flowers** opening simultaneously, the sepals and petals white +/– faint pink longitudinal stripes, the lip white, the basal half with five intense, bright pink longitudinal stripes, the apical half suffused with pink in a solid patch, the callus pale yellow with red spots, the column pink, the

245

anther white. **Dorsal sepal** oblong-elliptic, obtuse-rounded, to 1.6 × 7 cm, the **lateral sepals** obliquely oblong-ovate, acute, divergent, to 1.5 × 0.8 cm. **Petals** oblanceolate-subspatulate, cuneate, obtuse-rounded, to 1.4 × 0.8 cm. **Lip** three-lobed, to 1.4 cm long, to 1.8 cm wide across the expanded lateral lobes, the lateral lobes oblong-oblanceolate, obtuse-rounded, incurved, the midlobe broadly obovate-suborbicular, shallowly concave, the apex broadly rounded with an abrupt, blunt apicule, the **callus** solitary, peltate, elliptic with angular margins when viewed

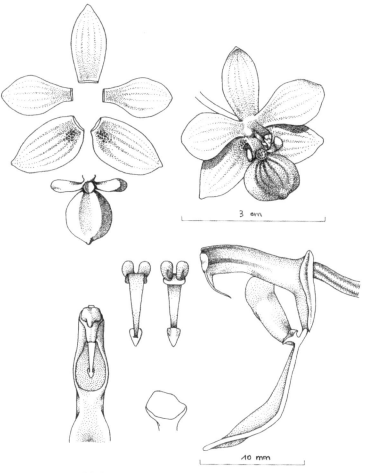

Phalaenopsis lindenii. Illustrator: F. Pupulin.

246

from above with a small notch on both the posterior and anterior margin. **Column** arching, dilated, to 1 cm long. **Pedicel** and **ovary** to 3.5 cm long.

Distribution: Endemic to the Philippines. **Etymology**: Named to honor Belgian horticulturist Jean Jules Linden (1817–1898). **Illustrations**: Awards Quart. 15(3):91. 1984; Awards Quart. 16(2):59. 1985; Awards Quart. 24(2):154. 1993; Awards Quart. 24(2):154. 1993; Die Orchidee 31(2):19. 1980; Die Orchidee 33(1):39. 1982; Die Orchidee 33(2): back cover. 1982; Die Orchidee 34(6): back cover. 1983; Die Orchidee 39(1): back cover. 1988; Die Orchidee 42(4):29. 1991; Die Orchidee 44(4): Orchideenkartei Seite 733. 1993; Gruss 1990:117; Gruss and Wolff 1995:62, 64; Harper 1990:62; Lückel 1980:225; Orchid Digest 45:49. 1981; Orchid Digest 46:6. 1982; Orchid Digest 47:6. 1983; Orchid Digest 55:72. 1991; Sweet 1969:336, 1980:64, 65.

Phalaenopsis lindenii is perhaps the most charming species in the genus, combining miniature plant size with richly marbled leaves and flowers with peppermint-candy striped lips. Most individuals of *P. lindenii* in nature have flowers with white sepals and petals with little, if any, visible stripes (usually just faint striping on the lateral sepals). Superior clones and most seedling populations now in cultivation have been selected for prominent striping on the sepals and petals.

Sweet (1980) refers peloric forms previously identified as *P. equestris* to *P. lindenii* based on their having marbled leaves. I have never seen a peloric clone of *P. lindenii*, although this feature is commonplace in *P. equestris*. I grew the clone mentioned by Sweet ('Fleur de Lys'), which I obtained from Fred Thornton in the early 1970s. It did not have marbled leaves and was clearly *P. equestris*, not *P. lindenii*. In addition, the clone 'Fleur de Lys' consistently produced keikis at the apex of the inflorescence in the manner of *P. equestris*, a feature only sporadically seen in *P. lindenii*.

Phalaenopsis lindenii is found in the northern mountains of the Philippines.

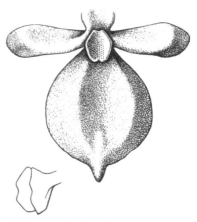

Phalaenopsis lindenii drawn from the type. Illustrator: H. R. Sweet.

All authors state that it occurs at "higher elevations," although I am unable to find any specific ranges cited in the literature. Certainly in cultivation, *P. lindenii* requires somewhat cooler conditions than most species. The relative rarity of *P. lindenii* in cultivation stems from growing the plants under temperatures that are too consistently warm. In subtropical and tropical areas, *P. lindenii* should be grown in front of cooling pads to keep the leaf temperatures from getting too hot. In temperate regions, *P. lindenii* should be grown under intermediate rather than warm conditions.

Phalaenopsis lindenii is notoriously difficult to use as a parent in hybrids, either as pollen donor or seed producer. This is unfortunate because the few hybrids that have been raised show great potential. When crossed with standard hybrids, *P. lindenii* produces multiflora, striped progeny. When crossed with other species of section *Stauroglottis*, *P. lindenii* has the potential to produce a new class of miniature, multiflora hybrids. The latter is exemplified by *P.* Little Skipper.

CHAPTER 10

Cultivation

With few exceptions, *Phalaenopsis* species have the same cultural requirements as the commonly grown complex hybrids. Two differences in their culture are a relatively slower overall growth rate and, in most cases, a seasonal aspect to their growth. Complex *Phalaenopsis* hybrids are typically grown under "soft" conditions of low light levels, high temperatures, and constant fertilizer to obtain maximum vegetative growth for the pot-plant market. In a diverse *Phalaenopsis* species collection, the plants generally do best when grown under "hard" or at least harder conditions of medium to bright light levels, intermediate temperatures, and seasonally modified fertilizer regimes. Some species show distinctly seasonal growth patterns, especially in their active root growth. Whereas most *Phalaenopsis* hybrids can be repotted any time of year and will respond with new root growth, some species, such as *P. parishii* and its relatives, should not be repotted during their dormant period or the root system will be adversely affected.

Growing orchids—and especially species—successfully depends on myriad interacting, regulatable factors, including light levels, temperatures, and humidity; more intangible factors, such as the grower's experience and knowledge of greenhouse microclimates, will also affect the outcome of the enterprise. Spend time observing your plants. Never stop learning from the experience of other growers; every grower has successes and failures with different species or their strains. Try to extract cultural guidelines from a grower who does well with a species that you systematically "grow to extinction." Often it is merely a matter of observing the plants in a different growing situation.

Everything stated in this chapter should be taken as a general guideline, given a relatively standard greenhouse operation. The worst thing a grower, and especially a novice grower, can do is to read what an "expert" says and then blindly convert to that system. Above all, try not to change anything without need. The old adage "if it ain't broke, don't fix it" is particularly apt in horticulture. For one excellent example: Beverly Harris, a friend in Connecticut, grew a specimen of the jewel-orchid *Ludisia discolor* so spectacular that it eventually covered a glass breakfast table. She joined the Connecticut Orchid Society and learned that her plant was actually an orchid—whereupon it quickly succumbed to all the new knowledge she had gained. Experimentation is an essential part of growing orchids, but always try a new system on a few nonessential plants before applying the system to an entire collection.

Potting containers

Phalaenopsis species can be grown in virtually any container that provides drainage and is nontoxic to plants. Commercial growers invariably use plastic pots for economic reasons: they cost less, weigh less, break less, and need to be watered less. Specialist growers of species, on the other hand, have a wider array of options and may choose a variety of containers tailored to the individual needs of the plants and their best method of display. The more commonly used containers are plastic pots, ceramic pots (glazed or unglazed), wooden baskets, and slabs.

The primary advantage of using plastic pots is their impermeability to water, which eliminates lateral water loss from the potting medium. This feature also tends to keep the growing medium uniformly moist, with no overly wet or dry areas. Additional advantages of using plastic pots are their very low cost and ready availability. Plastic pots are easily sterilized but are as often simply discarded because of their low unit cost.

Perhaps the greatest disadvantage of using plastic pots is their light weight, which, depending on the growing medium selected, often causes plants to be top-heavy. The likelihood that plants will fall over increases in species with substantial erect inflorescences. This can be offset to an extent by weighting the bottom of the pot with gravel or other heavy drainage material, or by placing the individual pots in a rack or tray designed to hold pots at equidistant lengths. A second disadvantage of using plastic pots is the inverse effect caused by their superb water retention. When a phalaenopsis loses its root system, through pathogens or physical damage during repotting, and is unable to draw sufficient water from the growing medium, the medium will stay overly damp and may lead to further root degradation.

Round or square, short or tall, plastic pots should be selected for their practicality under the specific growing conditions. They should also have the greatest amount of drainage possible; growers often add additional holes to plastic pots to increase drainage and prevent the media's stagnating ("going sour"). Plastic pots come in a variety of colors; the color used is not thought to have an effect on growth, with the exception of clear plastic pots, which may possibly benefit seasonally deciduous species from the Himalayas and southern China. Likely these species have significant photosynthetic activity in their roots and might benefit from a lighted root zone provided by clear growing containers.

Usually of high-fired terra cotta, unglazed ceramic pots are the traditional and beloved pots of horticulture. They offer several advantages for growing phalaenopsis. The weight of ceramic pots anchors plants. Their porous nature enables them to "breathe," allowing gas and water exchange between the growing medium and the ambient air. In addition to the beneficial distribution of gases, primarily oxygen and carbon dioxide, clay pots effectively evaporate water from the medium. While sometimes seen as a disadvantage, the evaporation of water through the pot surface benefits the plant by cooling the root zone during periods of excessive heat. In addition, the wicking action provided by this evaporation pulls water away from the center of the pot, preventing overly wet conditions to persist at the base of the plant.

With their advantages come a number of disadvantages, and that is why, perhaps, they are seen with greater rarity in horticulture and especially in commercial and hobbyist phalaenopsis production. The principal disadvantages of unglazed ceramic pots are these: their weight; their breakability; their high initial cost; their tendency to accumulate salts, especially calcium oxide; their tendency to promote the growth of algae; and the difficulty of sterilizing them for reuse. The accumulation of calcium deposits may be unsightly, especially in regions with naturally hard water. Even so, these deposits, in the face of good general culture, are rarely deleterious to *Phalaenopsis* species because of the frequency of repotting in standard culture. By the time these deposits have accumulated to the point of deleteriously affecting the plants, the plants are repotted into new or cleaned pots. Similarly, algal growth on the outside of the pots is an aesthetic call. Some people dislike the untidy nature of algal growth, while others regard it as a sign of healthy greenhouse culture. No evidence suggests that algal growth on the outside of ceramic pots is in any way deleterious to the growth of the orchid.

To summarize, standard clay pots offer many advantages in a collection with intensive management. They are used to best advantage where time allows for individual observation and hand-watering of each plant on a specific need basis.

For most growers, glazed ceramic pots are used almost exclusively as cachepots, a decorative accent that is used to hold—and hide—a more utilitarian pot. The reason for this is obvious: glazed ceramic pots are perhaps the most expensive type of container in which to grow a *Phalaenopsis* species. Horticulturally, glazed pots offer the same ability to hold a top-heavy plant in flower as do unglazed pots. Because of their non-porous surface, however, glazed pots prevent the growth of algae and the buildup of unsightly salts. Too, glazed pots are much easier and quicker to sterilize between uses. Perhaps the only downside to using glazed pots is their inability to "breathe" and provide gas exchange at the roots. I say "perhaps" because this is offset by their moisture-retaining ability, which is similar to that of plastic pots.

Many *Phalaenopsis* species with pendent inflorescences are shown to best effect in wooden baskets. In addition to being aesthetically pleasing, baskets provide excellent aeration of the roots. Because baskets are usually suspended in the greenhouse, plants in them usually receive better air circulation than their counterparts on the bench.

One drawback to potting in baskets: it is difficult to remove the plants for repotting without significantly damaging the roots. Of course overgrown plants in smaller baskets can simply be moved to a larger basket in their entirety—old basket and all—without the need to disturb the root system in any way. When removing certain species from baskets, especially *P. stuartiana* and closely related species, the old basket should be returned to the greenhouse and "grown" as one would a plant. In many cases the severed root segments, still firmly attached to the slats of the basket, will form adventitious buds and eventually rooted plantlets, which can be potted and grown on as clonal propagations.

Slab culture is an excellent method of growing *Phalaenopsis* species. Rough-textured cork bark is most widely available commercially, but any material recommended for orchids may be used. Everyone has their own method of mounting orchids. The standard technique is to use a small pad of moss at the base of the plant and fasten the moss and the orchid to the slab with nylon fishing line (nylon will not break down under normal greenhouse conditions). Others use putty-like compounds known as "liquid nails" to anchor the stem bases of miniature species or small seedlings. The primary drawback to mounting *Phalaenopsis* species is the need to water frequently, usually every day.

Potting mixtures

Regional cooking aside, few recipes match the diversity of ingredients seen in orchid potting mixtures. The optimal ingredients for one's plants will depend as much on the ambient conditions of light, humidity, air movement, and water quality, combined with one's own growing practices and experience, as on any specific formulation, whether "scientific" or "magical." Every component has both advantages and disadvantages—that cannot be stressed enough. And these qualities are greatly modified by other growing factors. Years ago, someone in the Greater New York Orchid Society stated that orchids could be grown in any medium. To prove his point, he later brought in two plants—one thriving in a pot filled with wine bottle corks, the other happily chugging along in a container of chopped woolen socks! How you grow is as important as what you grow in. The most commonly used media are osmunda, tree bark, tree fern fiber, sphagnum moss, rock wool, and charcoal.

Perhaps the earliest growing medium for epiphytic orchids, osmunda is now rarely used, expensive, and difficult to find of high quality. Even so, it is an outstanding growing medium because of its moisture retention and its high natural nutrient levels. Not uncommonly one enters a greenhouse of plants in various potting mixtures with a small corner devoted to the "super-select" favorites getting special treatment in osmunda.

Osmunda is the dried fibrous root mass of a temperate fern of the genus *Osmunda*. It comes in large, dense chunks, usually about the size of a large grapefruit or melon, which must then be cut into cubes, each one or two inches in diameter. The cubes, rinsed free of any soil or grit, are then used to firmly pot the orchid, usually with no other ingredient added save drainage crock. The "secret" to growing orchids well in osmunda involves the orientation of the fibers in each cube: the fibers must be aligned vertically to allow for free drainage of water. Cubes placed with the fibers oriented horizontally do not drain and will become undesirable pockets of stagnant water.

As an organic component in orchid mixes, chopped tree bark is most frequently encountered. The two most commonly used barks are redwood (*Sequoia sempervirens*) and Douglas fir (*Pseudotsuga menziesii*). Bark is inexpensive, readily available, easy to use, and a good combination of moisture retention and aeration.

The primary drawbacks to using bark are its demand for supplemental nitrogen and its often rapid decomposition. Bark utilizes nitrogen in its decomposition and can compete directly with the orchid for this nutrient. Phalaenopsis planted in a bark mixture, more so than other potting materials, require regularly applied supplemental nitrogen for optimal growth. The quality of commercially available bark also varies widely, depending on how quickly the bark is dried prior to bagging and shipping. Bark that remains moist prior to processing, especially in bulk in large piles at the timber mill, begins to decompose long before it arrives in the hands of the orchid grower. High-quality bark can last for three full years under greenhouse conditions, while low-quality bark barely lasts a year.

Bark is usually graded by size: fine bark of about one-quarter inch in diameter is called seedling bark; bark pieces of about an inch in diameter are referred to as medium-grade bark; larger nuggets of 1.5 inches or more are coarse grade. Coarse-grade nuggets are rarely used in phalaenopsis culture and are reserved for orchids with thicker, coarser root systems, such as vandas. Most barks, even though graded prior to shipping, also contain quantities of small dust-like pieces. Screening out this fine material before use is recommended.

Fresh bark is quite difficult to wet initially. Before being incorporated as a potting medium, fresh bark should be soaked in water until the pieces are moist and water no longer rolls off the flat surfaces. Either soak fresh bark overnight or add a few drops of surfactant to the water to break the surface tension. Wet only enough bark for your immediate purposes, since the bark will begin decomposition if stored wet for any length of time.

Two types of tree fern fiber have been used. One is black and rigid and obtained mostly from Central America; the other is brown and pliable. The latter is called Hawaiian tree fern or hapu. The black fiber was once commonly available and widely used in the orchid industry. Commercial sources for tree fern have become increasingly scarce, and the cost is largely prohibitive. Today one mostly finds fine-grade tree fern about one-quarter inch long as a minor component of seedling mixes.

Tree ferns metabolize silica and deposit silica in their vascular fibers. This chemistry makes tree fern fiber extremely long-lasting. A potting mixture with significant amounts of tree fern is almost immune to loss of aeration over time from decomposition. Although the chemical nature of the fibers is thought to change with time, the three-dimensional structure of the fibers remains intact.

Semiaquatic mosses of the genus *Sphagnum* are found throughout the world. (Partially decomposed and preserved sphagnum moss, known as peat, is increasingly used in phalaenopsis culture and is something else entirely.) What orchid growers know as sphagnum moss is long-fiber strands of intact dried moss that has undergone minimal decomposition. Nearly all commercial sources provide high-quality sphagnum moss from New Zealand. It is a relatively expensive potting material but has many excellent qualities that compensate for the higher initial outlay. Its most important qualities are its extremely high moisture retention and naturally fungistatic properties.

Sphagnum moss absorbs an incredible amount of water, and it would casually seem to be too wet a substance for growing epiphytic orchids like phalaenopsis. Sphagnum moss, however, naturally contains fungistatic compounds that kill or at least suppress most fungi. Thus, even though appearing at times to be waterlogged, the moss makes a fine growing medium for orchids provided other conditions, and especially light quality, are adequate.

Perhaps the greatest attribute of using sphagnum moss is that it all but eliminates daily moisture stress during warm months of the year. Regardless of the specific watering regimes and ambient greenhouse humidity, most orchids suffer significant moisture stress in the afternoon and early evening during warm summer months. This is particularly true of phalaenopsis, which lack storage organs such as pseudobulbs. During peak hours of heat, the plants are unable to absorb water through the roots as quickly as they transpire it through the leaves, resulting in a deficit that negatively impacts their metabolism. The nearly saturated root zone produced by using sphagnum moss minimizes this stress. This is particularly important in subtropical regions such as Florida, where afternoon heat loads are considerable and can be deleterious.

Sphagnum moss comes in dried bales and should be moistened prior to use. Some moss includes fungal spores, which may be transmitted to humans, causing localized dermititis. Anyone repotting phalaenopsis plants in quantity should use disposable plastic gloves as a precaution. Saturate the moss with water in a bucket or tub, and then squeeze it tightly to remove most of the water. There are two schools of thought when it comes to using sphagnum moss for potting orchids—the loose-packed school and the tightly packed school. In my experience, phalaenopsis do best when potted *very* loosely in sphagnum moss: pack the moss just enough to prevent the orchid from flopping around in the pot or falling over when watered.

Because sphagnum moss is resistant to decomposition, it appears to be largely unchanged over time; but experience suggests that it does undergo chemical changes, and the plants should be repotted regularly. Phalaenopsis left in the same sphagnum moss over many years invariably decline in health presumably from these implied chemical changes. Under very wet or shady conditions, the surface of the moss may get a somewhat slimy, dark coating of blue-green algae. This may be controlled with a gentle algicide/bacteriocide such as Physan.

Rock wool is a wool-like substance that results from extruding liquified rock in the manner of cotton candy. Rock wool comes in bags and resembles a dirty green version of the fiberglass commonly used in fish tank filters. Although widely used in general horticulture, it has found a small audience among orchid growers. The primary benefits of rock wool are its inert nature and great moisture-retaining capability. It is one of the few horticultural products that is of a consistent quality, impervious to the vagaries of weather and methods of processing. Because it is a mineral product and literally does not break down under greenhouse conditions, plants potted in rock wool never require repotting due to degradation of the potting medium. Because of its high moisture retention, rock wool, like sphagnum moss, eleviates daily moisture stress.

Rock wool has not become a popular phalaenopsis medium primarily due to its poor visual appeal at the retail sales end. In addition to looking like some sort of errant mattress stuffing, rock wool is particularly well suited to growing a top layer of slimy blue-green algae. Growers have reported success using rock wool as the primary medium with a top dressing of a more attractive medium. Most growers, however, find it easier and less expensive to use some other medium entirely.

Rock wool is normally offered in two classes, one highly water absorbent and the other largely water repellent. Different growers report personal success with one or the other extreme, or various combinations of the two classes. No definitive consensus concerning these relative formulations has emerged for phalaenopsis.

It would be tempting to use rock wool for its moisture-retaining qualities as a minor component of a medium. The wool-like quality of the substance, however, and its predilection to clump frustrate most commercial attempts to mechanically mix rock wool into diverse media.

The addition of charcoal offers two primary advantages to a growing medium. First, although derived from wood, it is largely immune to degradation during its normal time span in an orchid pot. Thus it offers many of the same qualities of aeration seen in the inert mineral-derived components often added to orchid media. Second, it has a high co-efficient for adsorbing toxins, both those introduced through the watering system and those produced as metabolic by-products by the orchid root system (this is why activated charcoal forms a standard component of drinking water filtration systems).

Charcoal for orchid use must be unadulterated hardwood charcoal. Commercially available briquets for home barbeques and other such compressed products have toxic additives and must never be used for horticulture. High-quality charcoal is available from horticultural supply houses and from manufacturers supplying grills at upscale restaurants. In the deep tropics, where daily rainfall may exceed an inch a day during the wet season, growers often use large chunks of charcoal (often with equal-sized pieces of broken brick) as the sole potting component. Such a high percentage of charcoal is not recommended for phalaenopsis under standard greenhouse conditions outside the deep tropics. The ability of charcoal to adsorb toxins is a two-edged sword—eventually a medium with a very high charcoal component will re-release toxins, especially under watering regimes that do not guarantee regular leaching of these toxins by dilution.

Many other ingredients may be added to a medium as minority components. These invariably serve one of two functions, either to increase the mixture's moisture-retaining capability or to increase its aeration. So-called German peat moss, a preserved peat moss that comes in chunks about one inch in diameter, has been an integral part of general orchid mixes for more than a century. Noted for its moisture-retaining ability while remaining intact, thus promoting aeration, German peat moss is a major component of the famous Off-Mix (named for premier grower George Off), the standard and perhaps best cattleya potting mixture. Peat moss also serves a strong function in its ability to absorb sporadic fertilizer applications and re-release them to the growing plant in a more or less steady state.

A second moisture-retaining component added to general mixes is redwood wool—the result of compressing redwood chips to produce small bundles of wool-like fibers. A particularly choice ingredient in general mixtures, redwood wool suffers the same problem as rock wool: a difficulty to uniformly combine in a mixture given standard commercial equipment.

Without a doubt the favored component for aeration is perlite, a highly porous, artificially heat-expanded rock. Various grades of perlite are available and the largest sizes, about three-eighths of an inch in diameter, are preferred for orchids albeit curiously difficult to obtain. Perlite is thought to be essentially neutral, although popular myth suggests that it is a source of damaging fluorides when it interacts with certain ammoniacal compounds, such as Physan.

Historically the best additive to achieve superior aeration in a medium was vermiculite. This is an artificially expanded mica schist. While a superb additive for soil mixtures used for "normal" plants like petunias and roses, vermiculite is rarely used for phalaenopsis on a day-to-day basis. While it appears to be a fine additive on the surface, in practice it is overly prone to compaction and therefore not useful for orchid culture.

The latest addition to orchid media is styrofoam. The so-called styrofoam peanuts are often used as a bottom layer in pots to provide drainage. Styrofoam peanuts offer a host of pros and cons over more traditional drainage material. On the plus side, styrofoam is lightweight (a superficial improvement over crock) and inherently free of pathogens; plants grown with a drainage layer of styrofoam usually exhibit excellent growth. The minus is that styrofoam is so lightweight that the resulting plants, if grown for pot-plant production, are overly top-heavy once the raceme matures and the flowers begin to open. While plants grown in clay pots usually are well anchored, those grown in plastic pots, especially with styrofoam peanuts for drainage, are invariably top-heavy, requiring a rack to merchandize the plants en masse or a cachepot to display individual plants. Anyone who has perused pot-plant phalaenopsis at local mass-market venues such as Home Depot can bear witness to the flipped-over plants, styrofoam peanuts clinging to their roots.

The other, and far more common, use of styrofoam is as an addition to potting media, as minute spheres, usually about one-tenth of an inch in diameter. Being functionally inert, these bits of styrofoam are a superb, sterile addition to mixes. The greatest complaint concerning them is the minor nuisance they cause in the greenhouse, where ventilator fans create a steady-state vortex of tiny styrofoam pellets. No amount of sweeping will eliminate these minute invaders!

The final class of minor additives are the various clay pellets. The most commonly available product is marketed as Turface. These partially fired products can be used to great advantage, especially as small granules, about one-eighth of an inch in diameter, in aggressively monitored seedling production. Larger pellets, of about half an inch in diameter, are more commonly available and may be incorporated with success in the media of most epiphytic genera, but they are most unsatisfactory when used with phalaenopsis. Under standard phalaenopsis conditions these pellets break down to too great a degree, forming an unhealthy sludge-like clay stratum that all but obliterates normal drainage.

Artificial soil or soilless mixes—composed mostly of pulverized preserved peat moss with the addition of perlite, styrofoam pellets, and other minor components—are increasingly being used for commercial phalaenopsis production. Although good-naturedly described by some growers as "mud," they are inexpensive, readily available through standard horticultural suppliers, have high water retention, and are flowable, making potting much faster, simpler, and cheaper. Perhaps the greatest quality of these mixes is their considerable nutrient storage and re-release capacity, due to the high amount of peat moss in the mix (usually greater than 50 percent by volume). This nutrient storage and re-release capacity provides a nearly constant flow of nutrients to the orchid. Peat-based mixes are also capable of lateral water movement by capillary action, thus avoiding the uneven watering of a container that can occur with more porous epiphyte mixtures.

The greatest difference between these peat-based mixes and the more porous epiphyte mixtures is that peat dries out at a very slow rate. Unlike most potting mixtures, which must be watered several times a week, peat-based mixes rarely need watering more frequently than every seven to ten days. It takes some experience to be able to judge when the pots need watering. Most first-time failures of phalaenopsis planted in these mixes are due to overwatering by growers familiar with more traditional epiphyte media, especially by incorrectly judging the moisture level in the pot based on the moisture content of the exposed surface layer.

Using peat-based mixes for certain phalaenopsis may require extra consideration of the watering regime. Because they are so slow to dry out, peat-based mixes may remain too wet during the cycle of root dormancy for some *Phalaenopsis* species. These include Himalayan and Chinese species that have a strong dormancy involving loss of leaves in nature as well as most species of subgenus *Polychilos*. Growers may wish to segregate species plants potted in soilless mixes from hybrid collections, which, as they are bred primarily from species of subgenus *Phalaenopsis*, show little cyclic root growth.

Potting

Phalaenopsis are among the most forgiving orchids when it comes to potting and repotting. With few exceptions they have rapidly growing roots that tolerate and sometimes thrive as a result of root disturbance.

Whether to pot phalaenopsis loosely or firmly is a matter of personal preference that, in my experience, has more to do with the nature of the medium used: pot loosely in sphagnum moss versus firmly in bark mixtures. The most important considerations are to pot phalaenopsis based on their root mass and to ensure that the plants do not wobble after repotting.

A common mistake when repotting a phalaenopsis is to select a pot based on the size of the leaves, or for an aesthetic visual balance with the overall plant size, whereas the sole consideration ought to be that the pot be only slightly larger than the root mass. This is especially true of plants with distressed root systems, where overpotting will most likely lead to rot and loss of the plant. By using a pot size in balance with the root mass you minimize the tendency to overwater. If the plant is vigorous and new roots quickly fill the pot, the plant can always be moved into a larger container, ahead of the normal repotting schedule. Underpotting is easily remedied, overpotting is more treacherous.

In general, phalaenopsis are repotted once a year, shortly after their peak bloom period. Species grown in media that resist degradation or under conditions that tend to slow degradation, such as basket culture, can be left for two or three years without incident. Unlike more temperamental orchids such as cattleyas and paphiopedilums, phalaenopsis can be repotted at any time of the year, including when they are in flower, but this is not usually recommended unless the plant is exceptionally vigorous: it is a double strain to the plant to carry flowers and undergo some root loss or disturbance. If a flowering plant requires repotting, the inflorescences should be removed during the potting procedure.

It is standard practice to remove dead leaves and roots when repotting a mature plant. Functional phalaenopsis roots are firm, dead roots are hollow. The easiest way to distinguish the two is to grab a root between two fingers and gently tug on it. A live root will not yield, while a dead root will strip off with ease, leaving behind a wiry central core. These wiry remnants can be cut off or left intact as they do serve to anchor the plant in the new medium. No evidence has been presented that leaving these cores in any way promotes disease.

The other task that needs attending to during repotting mature plants is to remove the old stem base. Although phalaenopsis have short stems, over time the stems grow to several inches, especially on large plants such as *P. amabilis* and its relatives. Growers either cut the old stem base with a sterilized tool or gently flex the stem and find the place where the stem will naturally break when snapped. The latter method occasionally misfires, yielding a very short stem with frighteningly few roots and a rather unhappy grower!

It is normal for phalaenopsis to produce some aerial roots in addition to those that are growing among the potting material. In repotting, these aerial roots are usually tucked into the new pot, more for aesthetics than for any particular horticultural reason. If a phalaenopsis has an abundance of aerial roots and few to no roots in the container it usually indicates one of two things: either the potting material has decomposed and lost its aeration or the watering regime is one of frequent, shallow waterings rather than deep waterings that thoroughly moisten the media in the pot.

Temperature, watering, humidity, and air movement

Although they sound like four separate aspects of culture, temperature, watering, humidity, and air movement are so deeply intertwined that modification of any one will affect all. While one can discuss ideal levels for each of these variables, any or all may need adjustment for a given growing area.

With the exception of deciduous species of subgenera *Aphyllae* and *Parishianae* and to a lesser extent *P. celebensis* and *P. lindenii*, species of *Phalaenopsis* require consistently warm conditions. A minimum night temperature of 62°F (17°C) is recommended. Many species can be grown or maintained under cooler night temperatures if they are "hardened" by growing under drier conditions with minimal nitrogenous fertilizer. Growth will not be optimal under cool conditions, and the plants are susceptible to a broader range of bacterial and fungal pathogens, but it can be done.

No maximum heat level for phalaenopsis has been determined, but in general day temperatures should be kept below 90°F (32°C) where possible. At higher temperatures care should be given to increase shading and raise humidity to offset heat stress. *Phalaenopsis celebensis* and *P. lindenii* are considered cooler growing than other species of subgenus *Phalaenopsis* but don't appear to actually need cool night temperatures. Instead they seem to decline if grown with high day temperatures that would not harm typical lowland phalaenopsis. These two species should be given special care, such as placement directly in front of a cool-pad system or evaporative cooler, during extended periods of high day temperatures.

The other temperature consideration is the need for a sharp difference (a swing of 10 to 15 degrees Fahrenheit, 5 to 8 degrees Celsius) in day versus night temperatures. This difference ensures proper respiration and regular development of the flower buds and allows the initiation of inflorescences. Under most circumstances this is the natural result of the growing area's being warmed by sunlight during the day. The exceptions occur during the dead of winter in northern climates, where few growers have the resources to artificially raise the day temperature to this degree, and during the doldrums of summer, where the opposite is true. This temperature difference is relative. In warm summer months or in tropical climates, the night temperatures may stay rather high for long periods of time. Even so, a substantial temperature differential usually occurs. A northern greenhouse might have 80°F (27°C) days and 65°F (18°C) nights, while a southern greenhouse might have 90°F (32°C) days and 75°F (24°C) nights. Both have a similar day/night differential.

The deciduous species of subgenera *Aphyllae* and *Parishianae* are the exceptions to these general rules and should be given cooler winter temperatures during their dormancy period. Although the minimum night temperatures have not been definitively established for these groups, most of their species will succeed with night temperatures between 52° and 55°F (11° and 13°C), and some will tolerate even colder temperatures provided other conditions of limited watering and lower humidity are met.

Although phalaenopsis are succulent plants with modifications to conserve water, they lack any true storage organs. Because of this (and again with the exception of the deciduous species), they should not be allowed to fully dry out for extended periods of time. But neither should they remain waterlogged for any period of time, since the roots require aeration. Like so many aspects of cultivation there is no one answer for how frequently to water. A particular plant's need for water is dependent on the ambient weather, relative humidity, pot type and size, potting material, air circulation, and a host of other variables that affect greenhouse microclimates. On one extreme, plants of phalaenopsis mounted on slabs should be watered daily; at the other, plants potted in a peat-based mix require watering only every seven to ten days.

In general the potting material should almost dry out between waterings. With experience the moisture content of a pot can be determined by the heft of the potted plant or by inserting a finger into the medium. Coolness indicates a high moisture content.

As with all orchids, phalaenopsis should be watered thoroughly and periodically rather than shallowly and frequently, for a number of reasons. Because of the limited ability of most potting materials to laterally transfer water by capillary action, only a thorough, heavy watering can ensure complete wetting of the medium. Some media components, like new bark, are resistant to moistening after they dry and require immersion in the pot to absorb any significant amount of water. Finally, heavy watering promotes leaching of possibly phytotoxic levels of some salts, which otherwise can accumulate in the potting medium.

In nature nearly every *Phalaenopsis* species grows under conditions of high humidity, often associated with swamps, rivers, and other bodies of water. In cultivation they also thrive best when kept at a high relative humidity. High humidity alleviates daily moisture stress during warm months of the year, buffers fluctuations in the ambient environment, and allows flowers to attain their maximum potential size. The only times when low relative humidity is desirable for phalaenopsis are during the winter, for those deciduous species from higher elevations with a pronounced dormancy, and when it is necessary to help combat widespread bacterial and fungal outbreaks such as botrytis, which thrive in highly humid environments.

All plants benefit from brisk air movement and phalaenopsis are no exception. Unless taken to a ridiculous extreme, the general rule is to have as much air movement as possible. Ample air movement can be seen by the gentle swaying or fluttering of at least some of the inflorescences in a greenhouse. Abundant air movement greatly diminishes the growth and spread of pathogenic bacteria and fungus and, by disrupting and "stirring" surface diffusion layers, encourages active plant growth by promoting gas and vapor exchange from the orchid leaves.

Fertilizer

Phalaenopsis are no different from other plants in their basic nutritional needs for nitrogen, phosphorus, and potassium, the three elements supplied in commercially available fertilizers. These elements can be delivered in an organic matrix, like fish emulsion or manure, or more commonly as inorganic salts. Both are used on phalaenopsis.

Phalaenopsis, like other epiphytic orchids, do require slightly different applications of fertilizer. Because most phalaenopsis have no or only limited dormancy, the plants grow best under conditions of continuous feed. Time-release fertilizers, which yield a low-dose continuous supply of nutrients and have become an industry standard for non-orchids, are rarely used on phalaenopsis because traditionally most epiphytic potting media based on tree bark did not have enough lateral water movement in the pot to make time-release fertilizers effective. This is changing, and time-release fertilizers can be used to advantage with peat-based soilless mixes.

Most growers fertilize phalaenopsis plants with a liquid solution of nutrient salts that includes a colorful marker dye. In general phalaenopsis and other orchids are fertilized "twice as often but half as much" as non-orchids. Thus if a package calls for ornamentals to receive one tablespoon per gallon of water per month, phalaenopsis should receive half a tablespoon per gallon of water twice a month. Ideally fertilizer strength should be adjusted so that a dilute fertilizer solution is given the plants with most waterings; break the pattern periodically by leaching the pots with plain water.

Fertilizer application too is tied to other aspects of cultivation, including water quality, water alkalinity, and choice of potting material. Most growers have personal favorites and fertilizing regimes. Recent applied physiological research by Dr. Y. T. Wang (see Bibliography) has proven or disproven many commonly held notions on fertilizing phalaenopsis, especially as related to maximum growth for the pot-plant market.

Pests and diseases

Phalaenopsis species are remarkably free from most pests and disease. Nearly all those that do attack the genus do so selectively, affecting only those individual plants that are under some form of stress—most often those that have suffered some root loss, which leads to partial desiccation of the leaves.

No specific chemicals are mentioned here. Laws regulating the use of compounds and formulations vary from place to place, and readers are therefore advised to contact their local Agricultural Extension Agent for specific advice. The most significant pests and diseases of phalaenopsis follow, together with specific preventive measures and the occasional cure.

Cockroaches can be problematic in some greenhouses and in areas where they are native, such as Florida. The most frequently seen symptom is the loss of all active aerial roots, although roaches also will chew completely through young inflorescences and even the margins of younger leaves. Some of the several chemicals used to control roaches are phytotoxic to orchids; if the possible side effects to orchids are unknown, limit the application of powders or sprays to areas beneath the benches and along walls, where the pesticides will not come into direct contact with the phalaenopsis.

Silvery slime trails leading away from tipless roots and leafless seedlings are sure signs of either snails or slugs. Both of these are ubiquitous in orchid collections, and both are controlled with formulations containing the chemical metaldehyde. The higher the concentration of metaldehyde, the more effective they are at curing an infestation. Both liquid formulations and granular or pelleted forms are available. The liquid formulations appear to offer greater efficacy against snails.

Granular or pelleted preparations are generally broadcast. A good method for spreading the material is to stand at one end of a growing space and throw a handful toward the far end and then do the same from the other end. This scattering effect generally avoids the possibility of the product gathering in any one phalaenopsis crown. Some of the pellet formulations will grow mold under greenhouse conditions, which can in turn cross-contaminate the orchid if the pellet is resting in the phalaenopsis crown. Pet owners should also be aware that some of the pelleted preparations resemble dry pet food, and they may want to be selective in the brand they purchase.

Slugs, more than any other pest, bring about a sort of blood fever among phalaenopsis growers. Most will attest that a slug can easily devour one or more community pots of seedlings in a night. In addition to metaldehyde, several organic solutions may be tried, such as placing shallow saucers of beer or buttermilk below the benches at night. Both of these liquids attract slugs, which subsequently enter the liquids and drown when their surface respiration is impaired. Great success may be had using a combination of metaldehyde and beer or buttermilk, but again: exercise great caution if household pets have access to the growing area.

It is always good practice to repot new plants upon their arrival, especially if you have purchased them from an unfamiliar vendor. The obvious reason is that this allows you to examine the quality of the root system and transfer the plant to the uniform potting medium used under your conditions. The less obvious reason is that snails and their eggs often lurk in the inoculated potting medium during the day. Snails reproduce rapidly, and potting media newly imported to your conditions can quickly produce an infestation.

Of the many kinds of scale that attack plants and most orchids, only soft brown scale is commonly found on phalaenopsis. These sucking insects are found on the lower leaf surface and especially along the lower leaf margins. Their thin shells, which resemble miniature brown army helmets, are easily popped when squeezed between your fingers, revealing a small whitish insect inside. Scale infestations usually begin in plants that have root damage and some leaf desiccation.

Soft brown scale is easily controlled by any number of commonly available pesticides. Even with the addition of a surfactant to the spraying solution, however, it usually takes several applications of insecticide to eliminate an infestation: the outer shell of the insect is difficult to penetrate, and the insects are further protected by their largely inaccessible location on the lower leaf surfaces.

Mealybugs are small sucking insects that generally have a shaggy, white, waxy coating over their bodies. Many of the species are brilliant red when crushed (mealybugs are the source of red lacquer used in East Asian lacquerware). In phalaenopsis they usually attack the back of flower buds and flowers or are found in the leaf axils at the base of the plant. The latter is particularly true of plants that have lost all or part of their root system and have somewhat desiccated, limp leaves.

Mealybugs are controlled by a broad array of commonly available insecticides. Their waxy coating often makes it difficult for sprays to penetrate the bodies, and it is generally recommended that a surfactant be added to the solution before application. Small infestations can be eliminated by hand using a cotton-tipped ear swab dipped in alcohol.

Aphids are small insects that feed by directly sucking plant juices. They usually attack only young flower buds of phalaenopsis, unless there are major problems with the growing conditions and the health of the plants. They rob the plant of nutrients, and they can disfigure the flowers. The greater threat from aphids is that they effectively transmit plant viruses, and thus no infestation should go untreated. Aphids are parthenogenic: offspring are produced directly from ovarian tissue without the need for sexual reproduction. Because they are quite literally "born pregnant," populations of aphids can grow exponentially and quickly become a problem.

Aphids are not difficult to control, and a broad range of commonly available insecticides will eradicate them, often with a single application. Small infestations can often be spot-eliminated by using a strong water jet from a hose or by spraying with dilute soapy water (be sure to thoroughly rinse the plant afterward). Many hobbyist growers keep their phalaenopsis plants in a mixed collection with other orchids and ornamental plants. The non-orchid plants are far more likely to serve as hosts for aphids, which spill over to the orchids only when the population reaches critical mass. Once again, good greenhouse hygiene can help avoid recurring aphid infestations: eliminate extraneous plants and especially weeds beneath the benches.

The scourge of phalaenopsis growers is bacterial rot, which can quickly liquify a plant. Bacterial rot either attacks the center of the plant (and is then known as crown rot) or it appears as semitranslucent watery patches on the leaves. The latter should be surgically removed; be sure to remove about one-quarter inch of seemingly unaffected tissue from around the rot. The cut surface should then be treated with a bacteriocide or sterilizing agent, and the leaves should be kept completely dry for several days. With crown rot little can be done except to remove the affected leaves (which usually pull out without any resistance) and to keep the center of the plant dry. Sometimes the crown will resprout and sometimes the plant will produce a sideshoot from one of the lower leaf nodes.

Despite an improved arsenal of chemicals, bacterial rot remains difficult to control directly. Prevention is vitally important here, especially good greenhouse hygiene and buoyant air circulation. Spraying with an algicide/bacteriocide like Physan helps prevent bacterial rot both directly and indirectly, because its surfactant qualities keep plant surfaces dry. By breaking up large water droplets on the leaves, allowing them to evaporate more quickly, such products reduce subsequent bacterial infection.

Dormant fungal spores of botrytis are quite literally everywhere. Under most conditions the fungus is not pathogenic and goes largely unnoticed in a collection. Close conditions (especially those caused by extreme high humidity during long overcast periods of weather) and an abundance of older flowers (such as occurs at the end of spring) are ripe conditions for an outbreak of botrytis. The first symptom of botrytis is the appearance of discolored spots on the older flowers. This is followed by a rapid spread of more spots on fresher flowers and a hoary mold that grows from the older spots as they enlarge.

Botrytis is not a particularly virulent fungus and is easily controlled by a variety of liquid, powdered, or gaseous fungicides. More than fungicides, however, botrytis can be largely controlled prior to an outbreak by good greenhouse hygiene and regulated growing practices. Dead leaves, old flowers, and other breeding grounds of botrytis should be religiously removed both from the plants and from the growing areas. If an older spray of flowers is unwanted, it should be cut from the plant and removed from the growing area. This saves the plant from expending further energy maintaining the flowers and removes a potential host for initial botrytis infection. Lowering the humidity and raising the amount of air movement will also forestall the onset of botrytis and other fungal pathogens.

If your growing area is particularly susceptible to botrytis, special attention should be given young seedlings, particularly newly deflasked seedlings in community pots. Only these young, extremely tender seedlings are likely to be directly threatened by botrytis.

Viral diseases of phalaenopsis are largely ignored for several reasons. First, most viruses that attack *Phalaenopsis* appear primarily to affect overall vigor without the type of floral crippling and growth anomalies seen in other orchid genera. Second, the rapid growth of the plants, especially of *Phalaenopsis* hybrids, makes it cost-effective to simply discard seemingly infected plants, unless they are particularly select studs. Third, even under the best growing conditions, most individual phalaenopsis plants have a rather limited life. A 10- or 15-year-old specimen of *Phalaenopsis* is truly old in contrast to some *Cattleya* or *Paphiopedilum* hybrids that have been in cultivation for more than a century. Finally, unlike many other genera of orchids, *Phalaenopsis* can be routinely repotted without the need for cutting tools. This combined with routine sterilization of cutting tools has decreased the overall spread of viruses in modern *Phalaenopsis* species collections.

Viruses in phalaenopsis are most commonly spread by raising seedlings from a virus-infected parent or by pollinating a flower with pollinia from an infected plant. Most viruses are efficiently transferred in orchid pollinia. The conventional wisdom, rarely followed even by conscientious breeders, is to propagate a superior clone before pollinating any of its flowers. In that way virus-free backup plants are available should the mother plant become infected.

Viruses are not transmitted through fully mature, "dry" seed, which is harvested after the capsular fruit of the orchid dries and splits open. But almost no modern grower propagates phalaenopsis from dry seed. Instead, phalaenopsis are uniformly raised through a form of embryo rescue known as "green pod" culture. An unripe, green phalaenopsis fruit that is old enough to have fully viable embryos is opened under sterile conditions, and the embryos (young seed) are removed and grown in the laboratory. The problem with this method is that along with the embryos, some placental tissue is removed from the fruit. If the mother plant is infected with a virus, then so is this placental tissue. In the laboratory the placental tissue remains alive, and as the virus-free embryos swell and begin to grow they are cross-contaminated with virus from the adjacent placental tissue.

Thus the frequently heard statement that "seedlings are always virus free" requires some consideration of the laboratory practices that generated the plants. In my experience, virus-infected seedlings frequently exhibit growth anomalies at an early age and often appear more symptomatic than their similarly infected parent plants.

CHAPTER 11

Conservation

Phalaenopsis hybrids—without a doubt the most widely grown orchids in today's market and the most commonly seen accents in upscale magazines—may finally bring orchids out of a snobbish connoisseur cul-de-sac and into a preëminent position in floriculture. Yet despite their popularity among orchid growers, florists, and mass-market venues, comparatively little effort is paid to the conservation of the species, which are the building blocks of exciting new hybridization trends in the genus.[*]

Status in the wild

Although little reliable and documented information is available in the literature, all parties agree that natural populations of phalaenopsis are under significant pressure. Habitats are being degraded by man through forest-cutting and the clearing of land for agriculture, and existing populations stripped for horticultural export. Even so, the lack of hard data from the secretive world of commercial plant collectors hobbles policy-making bodies from acting on those species that are truly threatened or endangered.

Some species are exceedingly rare in cultivation, and nothing is known of their status in the wild, either historically or currently. For example, *P. stobartiana* is known only from four clones, and *P. robinsonii* is known only from a single preserved plant.

---

[*] A portion of this chapter originally appeared in 1999 in the journal *Orchids* 68(4):362–367.

At this time, three species or certain of their populations are purported to be endangered or extinct in the wild. *Phalaenopsis aphrodite* is found throughout the northern Philippines with three isolated disjunct populations on outlying islands in Taiwan. This distinct subspecies, *P. aphrodite* subsp. *formosana*, has been confused with *P. amabilis*, has been registered in many hybrids as *P. amabilis*, and is widely available in the trade under that name. Ironically, although said to be extinct in the wild on the mainland (Cheng n.d.), this subspecies is without a doubt the most widely artificially propagated species in the genus and can often be found mass-marketed at astonishing low retail prices.

The second imperiled species, *P. gigantea*, is endemic to Borneo; the status of this vegetatively massive species is unknown. Concurrent with its reintroduction to horticulture in the 1960s, *P. gigantea* has been speculated to be on the brink of extinction in the wild; however, no hard data is available. Certainly the high economic value put on these plants combined with their slow growth rate in cultivation makes the continued harvesting from the wild an all-too-grim reality.

Jim Comber (pers. comm.) mentions the rarity of *P. javanica*, endemic to Java, and places the blame for its scarcity squarely on horticultural collecting: "In 1975 it was discovered by a party from Bogor Botanic Gardens further west on a mountain south of Cianjur, where it occurred in some abundance in the forest and on coffee bushes. Unfortunately, an Indonesian orchid species exporter learned about the discovery and persuaded the local population to collect it to extinction from this small mountain. Whether or not it still occurs elsewhere is not known."

Status in cultivation

With their rapid growth and ease of culture, *Phalaenopsis* species are particularly well adapted to *ex situ* propagation. The successful mass propagation of some species, spurred in part by limited availability of wild-collected plants due to CITES restrictions, is dramatic. Alas, the overall impact of artificially propagated stock is too often obscured by the tediously secretive business practices of many commercial phalaenopsis growers and their focus on flower qualities over greenhouse culture and propagation. Even casual visitation of nurseries reveals the profound yet unheralded effect that artificial propagation has on species populations in cultivation.

One important lesson learned in *Phalaenopsis*, however, is that award-quality species come from selfings and sib-crossings—and almost never from wild-collected imports. One has only to look at the parentage of recently awarded, improved species to reveal their lineage in directed, select breeding lines.

A second important lesson is that artificially raised seedlings of species are more vigorous than their wild counterparts, except under unusual circumstances. Sadly there exists a great myth to the opposite, that wild-collected plants are somehow "better" than their cultivated counterparts. Some of this can be attributed to the often slower growth rate of certain historic clones; in many cases these clones have accumulated a cryptic viral load in cultivation, or it may simply be that they were not vigorous clones in the first place. Select clones from the wild are initially chosen for their flower quality and rarely for their vigor. With each generation of artificially raised *Phalaenopsis* species, the largest protocorms are replated, the largest *in vitro* seedlings are transferred to their final flask, and the most vigorous seedlings survive in the community pots and are grown on to maturity. The rapid generation time of *Phalaenopsis* quickly allows the selection of exceptionally vigorous plants.

The vagaries of the commercial marketplace, however, remain notoriously fickle. Some species are given high priority based on commercial demand for the species or their hybrids. Thus we see abundant selections of *P. amboinensis, P. schilleriana, P. stuartiana, P. venosa,* and their fellows. Less "sexy" species of limited appeal to present tastes, such as *P. mannii* and *P. pallens,* in contrast, teeter on the edge of extinction in cultivation.

Problems with *ex situ* conservation

Perhaps the greatest problem facing growers who raise populations of artifically propagated species is the purity of their breeding stock. Martin Motes, a specialist grower of vandas and their allies in Homestead, Florida, has an apt expression for this situation: "Bad hybrids replace good species." For, as in *Phalaenopsis*, many hybrid vandas masquerade as pure species. Such hybrids, either naturally occurring or mislabeled greenhouse stock, are all too often selected and awarded because of their vigor and form, often an improvement over their species parents. Examples in *Phalaenopsis* abound.

One such naturally occurring hybrid is *P. fasciata* 'J & L', AM/AOS, clearly a hybrid between *P. hieroglyphica* and either *P. fasciata* or *P. reichenbachiana*. The clone 'J & L' in turn gave rise to such progeny as the clone 'Stone River' (Harper pers. comm.), a benchmark in modern judging of *P. fasciata* that is, in part, a hybrid with *P. hieroglyphica*. In cultivation and especially in the *Awards Quarterly*, one sees an increasing number of "select" *P. venosa* that are actually the man-made *P.* Ambonosa (*amboinensis* × *venosa*). Serious orchid breeders should always record their parent plants, either by taking photographs or (and this is preferred) by pickling flowers of their stud plants in alcohol. In this way it may be possible to retroactively undo some of the confusion resulting from questionable parents.

One stumbling block to long-term conservation of certain species is our inability to keep the individual plants alive for long periods of time. Like so many rare species grown only by specialist growers, certain species are imported en masse only to be grown, flowered, awarded, used in hybrids, and then—after only a few years—disappear from collections. The missing piece of the puzzle is accurate habitat information, which would allow growers to adjust their greenhouse conditions and identify appropriate microclimates for the long-term survival of individual plants.

Certain authors, such as Jack Fowlie, excelled at conveying useful habitat information to growers, but no serious study has been made of *Phalaenopsis* species *in situ*. My favorite example of this lacuna is the ecology of the difficult-to-grow *P. lindenii*. In 1947 this Philippine endemic was reported by Eduardo Quisumbing as coming from "higher altitudes." Now into the next century, our limited knowledge of their elevation remains the same. Interestingly, *P. celebensis*, a sister species to *P. lindenii*, is similarly difficult to maintain in cultivation.

The future

The long-term potential of conserving *Phalaenopsis* species is positive—and twofold: there must be both *in situ* conservation in the wild and *ex situ* conservation in cultivation.

Global tropical deforestation is a problem beyond the scope of any orchid group, whether the International Phalaenopsis Alliance or the American Orchid Society. While all members of the greater orchid community are rabid advocates of saving tropical forests, any impact we may have is, sadly, miniscule compared to the economic realities and unwavering population pressures on tropical forest resources. One way that we can make an impact, however, is to gather hard data on *Phalaenopsis* species in the wild. Phalaenopsis growers remain almost exclusively focused on plants in cultivation. For the long-term conservation of the plants in the wild, hard data must be generated on their real distribution, ecology, and pollination biology. As a taxonomist I can testify that such data is sorely lacking; even the elevational range of most species is unknown.

A permanent germplasm bank is a necessity for the long-term conservation of *Phalaenopsis* species in cultivation. Because phalaenopsis are not a "real" crop, there is little chance of a Federal/USDA germplasm bank as there is for maize, soybeans, wheat, and almost all other staple food crops. The patchwork system of commercial and hobbyist growers—while remarkably successful in its chaos—suffers the vagaries of market forces, grower's whims, power failures, Benlate, and other assorted horticultural glitches. Until a permanent integrated germplasm bank is established, lesser species in cultivation will always face the possibility of going out of cultivation "through the cracks," only to be missed when trends in taste invariably change.

CHAPTER 12

Hybrids

Phalaenopsis hybrids, once the rare prizes of wealthy collectors, have transformed orchid pot-plant production. Flamboyant cattleyas had once defined the public's concept of "orchid"; these were the flowers dear to wartime sweethearts and seen conspicuously adorning the décolletage of opera stars and Hollywood starlets. Later this image was supplanted by less costly and more durable cymbidiums, the first mass-marketed orchids. Pre-made cymbidium corsages in individual plastic boxes became a springtime staple in supermarkets, and it was tetraploid cymbidiums that first brought the price of orchid cut-flowers down to a populist level.

Memories of cattleyas and cymbidium now seem like images from an old newsreel or a sepia-toned dream. Few floriculture crops have swamped the marketplace as suddenly as phalaenopsis. Where once the purview of tony architectural magazines, hardly any glossy magazine today is without a photograph of a *Phalaenopsis* hybrid as decorative accent. The same applies to most televised interviews and other occasions where a touch of beauty and understated elegance is required. Add to this the increasing mass-marketing of *Phalaenopsis* hybrids through supermarkets and other outlets that directly reach the general public and have helped eliminate the misconception of orchids as temperamental conservatory plants, and you have the makings of an orchid revolution.

Ironically, much of the success of phalaenopsis as a pot-plant is due to the lackluster performance of the first designer phalaenopsis, a hybrid known as *P.* Toyland, registered by Griesbach in 1983 as a cross between *P.* Hummingbird and *P.* ×*leucorrhoda* (actually *P. philippinensis*, which was then considered a form of *P. ×leucorrhoda*). This hybrid, a remarkably vigorous and uniform grex, genetically designed to be a superior pot-plant, failed because the flowers were on the small side, of open shape, and pastel-colored, with shades of white and pale to medium pink. In short, they failed to ignite a retail revolution. Toyland, however, was marketed by the USDA—not to established orchid growers, but largely to commercial nurseries that had never attempted to grow a crop of orchids. The arrival of Toyland also coincided with the earliest uses of artificial soil mixture for orchids.

Foliage growers, miniature rose growers, and other horticultural firms that tried Toyland with mixed results also tried a few other phalaenopsis. The lessons they learned were many-fold. First, orchids—or at least phalaenopsis—were not the prima donnas that most people thought. Second, they could be grown in the same commercially available soilless media used elsewhere in the greenhouse on other, non-orchid crops. Third, orchids were a high-return product relative to other commercial pot-plants. Finally, phalaenopsis often could be raised suspended above the benches, utilizing growing space that was unavailable for the production of foliage and other terrestrial crops. So while Toyland is relegated to a footnote in orchid history, supplanted by large-flowered hybrids favored in the retail market, its introduction and method of marketing helped lay the foundation for today's widespread mass-production of phalaenopsis as a pot-plant.

Traditionally, seven classes of *Phalaenopsis* hybrids have been recognized: whites, whites with colored lip, pinks, stripes, yellows, novelties, and ×*Doritaenopsis*. The past two decades have seen a diversification of the novelty class into four additional classes, namely multifloras, spots, reds, and miniatures. Some overlap occurs in these latter four classes, but pure blood lines and uniform strains are slowly emerging.

Phalaenopsis hybrids come in every color imaginable except scarlet red, green, and true blue, although some greenish and lavender-gray hybrids have been produced on a limited basis. The introduction to cultivation of *P. braceana* and *P. stobartiana* promises to generate truly dark green-flowered hybrids. Several crosses that have flowered with *P. stobartiana* as a parent reveal the dominance of the dark green flower color.

The following discussion cites the names of the species actually used in making the hybrid, with the names used for registration purposes cross-referenced where possible. Thus, even though one parent of *P.* Micro-Nova is listed as *P. parishii* by the Orchid Registrar at the Royal Horticultural Society, the hybrid was actually made using *P. lobbii* (*P. parishii* was not in cultivation at the time the hybrid was made and registered). This review is historic in nature and intended to introduce the reader to the species that went into different blood lines and their particular influences as well as the jumping off points for current hybridization efforts. Modern phalaenopsis breeding is so extensive that a complete review is clearly outside the scope of this book. In the case of modern hybrids, so many species are mingled that specific influences from each species are all but obscured except to the professional phalaenopsis breeder.

Whites

Although a brief bout of experimental breeding in the mid-19th century involved diverse species, most hybridization efforts over the next century were devoted to perfecting white hybrids. The two species used in these hybrids, *P. amabilis* and *P. aphrodite*, are the largest-flowered species in the genus and most resemble Victorian ideals of round form and overlapping segments. At a time when smaller-flowered species were relegated to the unflattering category of "botanicals," it is easy to understand why spectacular sprays of large white flowers dominated popular taste.

Early white hybrids were registered using several species names. Some of these, such as *P. grandiflora* and *P. rimestadiana*, have been subsequently included in the synonymy of *P. amabilis*. When analyzed, it is clear that modern standard white *Phalaenopsis* hybrids are essentially line-bred selections of *P. amabilis* and *P. aphrodite*, with a very small infusion of genes from *P. stuartiana*, and *P. schilleriana*.

Although large flower size and round form were perfected at an early stage, early white hybrids produced diaphanous flowers that were short-lived and highly susceptible to air pollution. This all changed with the production of *P.* Doris, registered by Duke Farms in 1940 as a cross between *P.* ×*elisabethae* (now *P. amabilis*) and *P.* Katherine Siegwort. Many plants of Doris were tetraploids, having twice the normal number of chromosomes. These tetraploids exhibited flowers with

278

thick substance and long-lasting qualities. *Phalaenopsis rimestadiana,* the parent in the background of *P.* Doris, was actually a naturally occurring tetraploid form of *P. amabilis.* This was a watershed moment in hybridizing white phalaenopsis and also influenced other bloodlines, since standard white hybrids were routinely used as one parent in pink- or red-lip hybrids.

Since the time of Doris, hybridization of whites has largely been a process of selecting larger, better-shaped flowers. By the late 1960s whites had been nearly perfected with the production of *P.* Grace Palm (Doris × Winged Victory), registered by Ryerson in 1950; *P.* Dos Pueblos (Doris × Grace Palm), registered by Bean in 1956; *P.* Juanita (Chief Tucker × Grace Palm), registered by Shaffer in 1957; *P.* Cast Iron Monarch (Louise Georgiana × Doris), registered by Kieswetter in 1957; *P.* Elinor Shaffer (Juanita × Doris), registered by Shaffer in 1960; *P.* Gladys Read (Juanita × Grace Palm), registered by Santa Cruz in 1961; and *P.* Joseph Hampton (Monarch Glen × Doris), registered by Dos Pueblos in 1966.

Without a doubt, modern white hybrids exhibit the most uniform and highest quality flowers of any group. Unfortunately, concurrent with the selection of large, round flowers, the total flower count of an inflorescence and its tendency to produce side branches diminished. Recently, as part of the prominence of pot-plant phalaenopsis over display plants, orchid breeders have started to intentionally generate triploid hybrids by backcrossing tetraploid hybrids with diploid species, especially Taiwanese forms of *P. aphrodite.* The resulting hybrids, strongly influenced by the diploid species, have tremendous vigor and typically produce branched inflorescences with high flower counts. While not usually competitive for flower awards, the triploid hybrids have many commercially desirable qualities, including increased vigor, earlier flowering from seed, and consistently branched inflorescences. These triploid hybrids are mostly sterile and represent an endpoint in breeding generated specifically for the retail market.

In a similar vein, the recently described *P. philippinensis* (whose dominant trait of opening all its flowers at once is inherited by its hybrids) is being crossed with standard tetraploid white and pink hybrids. The complete burst of flowers—although considered a negative for pot-plants (it shortens the overall bloom period and shelf life)—makes for spectacular display plants.

Whites with colored lip

White-flowered phalaenopsis with a contrasting red lip, also known as semi-albas, trace their parentage back to *P. ×intermedia* and especially *P. ×intermedia* var. *portei*. *Phalaenopsis ×intermedia*, a natural hybrid between *P. aphrodite* and *P. equestris*, typically produces a pale red-rose lip. Variety *portei*, however, produces a solid, dark red-rose lip. This feature has been line-bred into hybrids that today produce sepals and petals equal to the very best white hybrids and dark red-rose lips. Although these hybrids are called red-lip hybrids, the lip color is actually a red-rose. Truly red lips (scarlet) come only from hybridization with species of subgenus *Polychilos* (see the discussion under yellow hybrids). Another line of semi-albas (*P.* Show Girl is one example) has *P. lueddemanniana* as a forebear.

Early red-lip hybrids, such as *P.* Ruby Lips (Roselle × Doris), registered by McCoy in 1955, produced only a small percentage of progeny with darkly colored lips. With the advent of hybrids such as *P.* Mildred Karleen (Judy Karleen × Sharon Karleen), registered by Hager in 1960; *P.* Cher Ann (Ann Hatter × Karleen's Wendy), registered by Hughes in 1969; and *P.* Mad Lips (Ann Hatter × Mad Hatter), registered by McClellan in 1969, red-lip hybrids achieved most of the flower qualities of standard white or pink hybrids. Now hybrids such as *P.* Fifi (Minouche × Redfan), registered by Vacherot and LeCoufle in 1974, produce uniform crops of stark white flowers with boldly contrasting dark lips and flower size equal to that found in standard white hybrids.

Pinks

In early hybridization efforts, the two showy pink-flowered Philippine species, *P. sanderiana* and *P. schilleriana*, were interbred with white hybrids to produce pink hybrids with larger, rounder flowers. Despite the superior shape and wide petals of *P. sanderiana*, this species did not induce strong pink color into its progeny, and *P. schilleriana* quickly became the parent of choice for producing pink hybrids. While understandable, this is somewhat unfortunate as *P. sanderiana* has the unique feature of being a late summer bloomer, unlike all other larger-flowered Philippine species, which flower in the early spring.

Early pink hybrids were pale in color and often had unevenly distributed pigment, the latter considered a very serious flaw by both breeders and judges. Pink hybrids neared the qualities seen in white hybrids with the production of crosses such as *P.* Zada (Doris × San Songer), registered by Fields Orchids in 1958; *P.* Barbara Beard (Virginia × Zada), registered by Beard in 1962; and *P.* Ann Marie Beard (Palm Beach Rouge × Rosada), registered by Beard in 1966. These hybrids had larger flower size, full shape, and even pigment distribution.

In Germany Hark created a strain of quality pink hybrids that dominate modern pink breeding. Starting with *P.* Lipperose (Ruby Wells × Zada) registered in 1968 and *P.* Lippezauber (Doris Wells × Zada) registered in 1969, Hark produced an assortment of large-flowered, evenly pigmented, dark pink hybrids including the pivotal *P.* Zauberrose (Lipperose × Lippezauber), registered in 1972; *P.* Abendrot (Lippezauber × Lippstadt), registered in 1974; and *P.* Lippeglut (Lippstadt × Zauberrose) also registered in 1974. A parallel line breeding in France also produced high-quality modern pinks, mostly arising from *P.* Danse (Romance × Abondance), registered by Vacherot and LeCoufle in 1976. Today's pink hybrids are fully comparable to standard white hybrids.

Recent efforts have attempted to produce darker pink hybrids, by introducing purple-flowered species or by layering the pink pigments (anthocyanins) over yellow pigments (carotenoids). Unfortunately, the use of purple-flowered species, while significantly intensifying the color, produced hybrids with commercially unacceptable qualities. One early hybrid, *P.* Zadian (Zada × *pulchra*), registered by Jones and Scully in 1967, caused a sensation when introduced because of its deep plum-colored flowers; however, Zadian produced significant numbers of progeny that had open shape, irregularly distributed pigments, or other drawbacks. Most of these early hybrids are remembered for their exceptional awarded clones and not for the range of seedlings or any subsequent progeny.

The overlaying of pink pigments over a yellow base produced far superior results. Not only did these hybrids produce darker pink and purple shades, but the resulting flowers often glowed with intense raspberry or mulberry shades. As the diversity of good yellow hybrids increased in the 1970s, so did the combinations of yellow and pink, resulting is a subclass called art-shades. Hybrids such as *P.* Painted Desert

(Mrs. J. H. Veitch × Juanita), registered by Shaffer in 1966, and *P.* Cinnamon Candy (Zada × Painted Desert), registered by Ewing in 1973, exemplify this type of breeding. When a seedling is good, these art-shades produce interesting desert shades and watermelon tones. Unfortunately, art-shade hybrids typically produce a broad range of colors including many less-than-desirable flesh tones and muddy brownish pink flowers. Most select art-shade hybrids could be termed happy accidents rather than an actual subclass of hybrids.

Stripes

A secondary influence of *P. equestris* through its natural hybrid *P.* ×*intermedia* is the production of striped hybrids. The early hybrids with magenta veins against a stark white background were often called candy-stripe hybrids because their stripes were reminiscent of those on a peppermint candy-cane. Initially the stripes were either pale-colored or expressed only on the central portions of the sepals and petals. Today's hybrids show clearly defined dark veins throughout the sepals and petals.

Other species can produce striped hybrids. *Phalaenopsis lindenii,* a Philippine species with a naturally striped flower, produces charming striped hybrids such as *P.* Peppermint (*lindenii* × Pink Profusion), registered by Freed in 1964, and *P.* Baguio (*lindenii* × *schilleriana*), registered by Moir in 1966. Some breeders believe that many of the early striped hybrids (*P.* Ruby Lips, for example) actually used *P. lindenii* as a parent and not *P. equestris*. During this period in breeding, species identification was not very precise. No keys were available, and many species were incorrectly identified.

Phalaenopsis fuscata, P. javanica, and a few other species of subgenus *Polychilos* produce striped flowers, but these hybrids tend to fall between the standard hybrid definitions. The "stripes" are actually composed of fine spots, which alternative pattern has not been pursued by mainstream phalaenopsis breeders.

Only striped hybrids that had a white ground color were initially produced. This changed when innovative hybrids such as *Dtps.* (×*Doritaenopsis*) George Moler (Barbara Moler × Jason Beard), registered by Beard in 1976, and *P.* Firewater (Goldiana × Hugo Freed), registered by Ewing in 1977, were created in an attempt to produce magenta stripes on a yellow background. The blending of yellow with stripes actually produced very few striped yellow progeny; only a few clones clearly expressed darker veins against a yellow background. In some hybrids, like George Moler, the range of variation was extreme, from pure yellow flowers to dark rose-pink flowers. In the case of Firewater, one combination of parents produced yellowish backgrounds with dark veins and a ground color suffused with rose. A subsequent remake, using different parental clones, produced creamy white backgrounds with dark veins. One thing stands out in this line of breeding, however. Hybrids between traditional striped hybrids, obtained from *P. equestris*, and yellow hybrids, obtained from *P. fasciata*, produce remarkably vigorous progeny. Indeed, it is hard to imagine a more vigorous hybrid than Firewater or similar combination. Similarly, standard striped hybrids have been bred with pink hybrids to produce pink flowers with darker pink-purple veins.

Yellows

The search for yellow hybrids is a story with two threads: on the one hand there is the search for dark-yellow flowers; on the other, the elusive search for clear yellow flowers, devoid of any spotting or other markings. The goal has always been to have an unmarked yellow hybrid that mimics the large, round flowers of a modern white hybrid. Although strides have been made, the goal of a large, round, clear yellow flower has not been fully attained.

The first yellow hybrids were made by crossing large white hybrids with *P. mannii*, in the main because this species was imported in large numbers as wild-collected plants from northeast India. Although common in cultivation, *P. mannii* has many faults as a parent, including an open shape lent by its very narrow petals, yellow color that rapidly fades with age, and brown-barred segments. Early yellow hybrids, such as *P.* Golden Louis (Doris × *mannii*), registered by Vaughn in 1957, *P.* Golden Chief (Chieftain × *mannii*), registered by Vaughn in 1958, and *P.* Golden Martha (Joanna Magale × *mannii*) registered by Alberts and Merkel in 1962, were indeed yellow. The many poor qualities seen in *P. mannii* were quite evident, however, especially the rapid color fading that in a matter of days resulted in a white flower marred by extremely pale brown patches. The primary strength of this breeding was in the very high flower count brought from *P. mannii*. While the flowers were hardly award-quality by today's standards, the hybrids made spectacular display plants, with mature plants regularly displaying more than 100 open flowers at a time on large branched sprays. This is important to remember as today's yellow hybrids, dominated by *P. amboinensis*, *P. fasciata*, and *P. venosa*, often suffer from relatively low flower count.

Yellow breeding might have ended there if parallel breeding hadn't occurred using *P. fasciata* as the yellow parent. Unlike *P. mannii*, *P. fasciata* (incorrectly identified as *P. lueddemanniana* var. *ochracea*) has intense yellow color that doesn't fade, with fewer brown spots. On the negative side, *P. fasciata* bears fewer flowers per inflorescence and usually has sepals and petals with strongly revolute margins. These early hybrids, such as *P.* Inspiration (Juanita × *fasciata*), registered by Santa Cruz in 1961, and *P.* Golden Sands (Fenton Davis Avant × *fasciata*), registered by Fields Orchids in 1964, represented a quantum leap forward relative to hybrids with *P. mannii*. In good clones they produced larger, rounder flowers of an unfading, bright yellow. A by-product of breeding with *P. fasciata* was the production of flowers with truly red (scarlet) lips, unlike the rose-red lips derived primarily from *P. equestris*. Many hybrid seedlings retained the revolute margins of *P. fasciata* and produced open flowers with nearly tubular segments ("soda straws"). Still, the intensity of the color spurred hybridization for yellow phalaenopsis, which activity continues to this day.

About this time hybridizers experimented with many other yellow-flowered species. *Phalaenopsis cochlearis*, used to make hybrids such as *P.* Zephyr (Daryl Beard × *cochlearis*), registered by Beard in 1971, produced beautiful clear yellow flowers, but the color was so pale that breeding with the species was all but forgotten. Its sister species, *P. fuscata*, was also used to make hybrids like *P.* Janet Kuhn (Dos Pueblos × *fuscata*), registered by Beard in 1956. The strongly revolute margins of the sepals and petals in *P. fuscata* were dominant in those early hybrids, partly because of the relatively poor quality of the available white hybrids at the time, yielding a high percentage of poorly shaped and commercially undesirable progeny. Both *P. cochlearis* and *P. fuscata* produce large numbers of flowers on branched inflorescences; *P. fuscata* frequently produces hybrids with stripes composed of small reddish brown spots.

Next on the scene was the introduction of yellow-flowered strains of *P. amboinensis*. Unlike *P. fasciata* and *P. mannii*, *P. amboinensis* bears flowers with flat segments and relatively wide petals. In breeding, the brown barring of the sepals and petals is largely recessive, and hybrids of *P. amboinensis* are mostly clear yellow with, at most, fine brown spots toward the center of the flower. Early attempts, such as *P.* Paula Hausermann (Kenneth Stromsland × *amboinensis*), registered by Hausermann in 1977, quickly showed the great potential of this species in breeding yellow hybrids that produced flat flowers of exceptional substance and lasting quality. Very quickly, *P. amboinensis* was incorporated in almost all yellow breeding.

Phalaenopsis breeders next combined yellow-flowered species into primary hybrids and other "breeder" crosses. This multiplied the number of genes and alleles for yellow pigmentation, allowing for richer yellow colors that exhibited less overall fading. One early hybrid was *P.* Mambo (*amboinensis* × *mannii*), registered by Thornton in 1965. The yellow pigments from *P. amboinensis* successfully intensified the yellow color and allowed its hybrids to hold yellow color even after the *P. mannii* component faded. A second early hybrid was *P.* Spica (*fasciata* × *lueddemanniana*), registered by Osgood in 1969. *Phalaenopsis* Spica led to a number of successful yellow bloodlines through the hybrids *P.* Barbara Moler (Donnie Brandt × Spica), registered by Beard in 1971; *P.* Daryl Lockhart (Suemid × Spica), registered by Lockhart in 1975; and *P.* Golden Buddha (Cher Ann × Spica), registered by Lista in 1977. Golden Buddha has been particularly influential in subsequent breeding, in part because selfed and sib-crossed strains of Golden Buddha allowed breeders to select more homozygous clones, which in turn generated a higher percentage of quality hybrids lacking the undesirable qualities of *P. fasciata*, such as poor shape. A third hybrid along this line was *P.* Golden Pride (*amboinensis* × *fasciata*), registered by Dobkin in 1975.

The final building block of yellow hybrids was the introduction of *P. venosa* to cultivation. *Phalaenopsis venosa* has all the advantages of *P. amboinensis* plus the petals are wider and the flowers are darker yellow. This darker shade of yellow is dominant in its hybrids, and unlike all other yellow-flowered species of *Phalaenopsis*, the yellow color of *P. venosa* actually darkens after the flowers open. These qualities have made *P. venosa* the premier species for breeding modern yellow hybrids. Its progeny are immediately identifiable: the flowers of *P. venosa* have a characteristic white center that is dominant in breeding.

Modern yellow hybrids may combine any number of species in their heritage but are dominated by *P. amboinensis*, *P. fasciata*, and *P. venosa*. In the past, these species have led to hybrids with branched inflorescences, relatively few-flowered terminal sprays, and waxy, long-lasting, star-shaped, medium-sized flowers that are either clear yellow or with minimal spotting. As this class of hybrids is bred with other groups of *Phalaenopsis*, yellow hybrids improve with increased flower count, increased flower size, and a more classic, round flower shape.

Novelties

At one point any hybrid that was not a standard, large-flowered cross was called a novelty. With the coalescence of multifloras and reds as distinct classes, novelty *Phalaenopsis* hybrids are primarily interspecific hybrids of subgenus *Polychilos* or crosses with similarly sized species and hybrids. These plants are produced primarily for the hobbyist and orchid breeder markets. They lack the large flower size and elegant erect-arching inflorescences of standard hybrids.

Hybrids such as *P.* Princess Kaiulani (*amboinensis* × *bellina*), registered by Kirsch in 1961, *P.* Sunfire (*lindenii* × *lueddemanniana*) registered by Miller in 1964, and *P.* Tigress (*fasciata* × *mariae*), registered by Dewey in 1970, represent the variable class known as novelties.

Multifloras

Phalaenopsis equestris, although an ancestor of nearly all red-lip and striped hybrids through *P.* ×*intermedia*, was rarely used directly as a parent until recently, when it was crossed with tetraploid white or pink hybrids. The results were plants that produced large, branched inflorescences with large numbers of flowers more or less intermediate between the parents. Although spectacular display plants, this class of hybrids had the drawback of producing individual flowers that, by judging standards, were inferior since they were smaller and tended to have a more open shape than their tetraploid standard counterparts. These hybrids were very popular in the late 1800s.

When public taste and resulting market trends changed to appreciate smaller flower size with its concomitant smaller plant size, multiflora hybrids bred from *P. equestris* were rediscovered and gained enormous popularity. The resulting dense, much-branched, short, erect inflorescences render the orchids azalea-mimics. The commercial advantages include greatly reduced shipping costs, and the hobbyist advantages, manageable plant size and large "bang for the buck." The building blocks of this type of breeding are *P.* Cassandra (*equestris* × *stuartiana*), registered by Veitch in 1896; *P.* Swiss Miss (Mildred Karleen × *equestris*), registered by Hager in 1974; *P.* Be Glad (Cassandra × Swiss Miss), registered by Hager in 1978; and *P.* Carmela's Pixie (Terilyn Fujitake × Cassandra), registered by Carmela Orchids in 1990. Terry Root of the Orchid Zone coined the trademarked term Sweetheart for these hybrids. Not all multiflora hybrids are compact when mature; many become quite large after several years' growth.

Spots

When discussing spotted phalaenopsis, one is actually discussing two completely different classes of hybrids. First one must discuss the French spots, bred exclusively from *P. stuartiana*. These French spotted hybrids are so called because they were bred and perfected by the French firm of Vacherot and LeCoufle. Such hybrids as *P.* Alida (Artigny × Minouche), registered by Vacherot and LeCoufle in 1976, *P.* Snow Leopard (Alida × Francine), registered by Southwood in 1982, and *P.* Mary Krull (Alida × Red-Hot Chili), registered by Krull-Smith in 1985, bear the boldly spotted sepals and petals seen in similarly marked clones of *P. stuartiana* such as 'Larkin Valley', AM/AOS. Through repeated hybridization and selection of spotted clones over time, these hybrids are nearly equal in quality to modern standard white and pink hybrids.

Because these hybrids rely on heavily spotted clones of *P. stuartiana* for their patterning, their flowers are susceptible to the same environmentally induced sectoring or color-break seen in the species. Thus it is normal in this group of hybrids for the occasional wedge-shaped portions of the sepals and petals to have markings that differ in some way from the rest of the flower (lighter, darker, smaller, or larger spots). The presence of color-break in this line of breeding rarely indicates the presence of virus as it would in, say, a cattleya.

A different kind of spotting can be obtained using *P. lueddemanniana*. In early hybrids such as *P.* Cabrillo Star (Ramona × *lueddemanniana*), registered by Santa Cruz in 1961, and *P.* Texas Star (Evening Star × *lueddemanniana*), registered by Lawrence in 1958, the spotting varied from extremely pale to quite bold. Most of the early hybrids in this class were bred from crossing standard tetraploid white hybrids with diploid forms of *P. lueddemanniana*. Because of this, the color of the spots was suppressed to an extent by the higher proportion of white genes to spotted genes in the progeny. Even when the spotting wasn't as dark as hoped for by the breeder, this group of hybrids produced flowers of extremely heavy substance, rivaling parallel modern *P. amboinensis* hybrids bred specifically for substance such as *P.* Artienne (Clyde × *amboinensis*), registered by Hager in 1972.

Bloodlines that originated with the select clone *P. lueddemanniana* 'Woodlawn' have been interwoven, especially by orchid breeders in Taiwan, to produce a range of boldly spotted hybrids with markings as dark or darker than the *P. lueddemanniana* parent. Most of these hybrids are derived from *P.* Paifang's Queen (Mount Kaala × *lueddemanniana*), registered by Paifang Orchids Garden in 1977. Only one exceptional clone of *P.* Paifang's Queen was used in further breeding, the clone 'Brother' owned by Brothers Nursery. Hybrids with this clone and its offspring (usually with names that start with "brother") led to modern select strains through hybrids, such as *P.* Brother Fancy (Brother Grape × Brother Peacock), registered by Brothers Nursery in 1992, and *P.* Brother Purple (Golden Peoker × Brother Glamour), registered by Brothers Nursery in 1995. All these hybrids share the extremely heavy substance of *P. lueddemanniana*; on the negative side, these hybrids often exhibit the low flower count and somewhat crowded flowers seen in that species, although this fault is diminishing with each hybrid generation. It is worth noting that the 'Woodlawn' clone is unusual for *P. lueddemanniana* and may be a natural hybrid; the intensity of the spots seen in its offspring suggests the influence of *P. pulchra*.

Spotting patterns in hybrids bred from *P. lueddemanniana* are some-what unstable. This is especially true when clones are mass-produced for the pot-plant market, and somaclonal mutations are known. Unlike most mutations, many of the somaclonal mutations seen in these hy-brids are not deleterious, and many are actually improvements over the mother plant. The variability in these cases is due to regulation of the pigment genes in the cells that eventually produce the spots. If the genes responsible for the purple pigments are activated early in the development of the buds, the resulting cell lineages are sizeable, and the spots will be large; if the genes are activated late in the develop-ment of the buds, the spots will be small. Many of the selected soma-clonal mutations activate the pigment genes early in development, yielding sepals and petals that are nearly solid purple or with a very few, very large spots.

Reds

Much effort has been expended recently on producing red *Phalaenop-sis* hybrids. Red sepals and petals do not naturally occur in the genus, and red hybrids are the result of selectively overlaying purple pigment over yellow. To our eyes, this overlay appears red. It is doubtful we will ever see a "red" phalaenopsis comparable to *Sophronitis coccinea*, but hybrids that are solid deep reddish purple can be obtained.

Most red hybrids result from a combination of various yellow hybrids bred primarily from *P. amboinensis* and *P. fasciata* combined (for the purple) with *P. bellina*, *P. mariae*, *P. pulchra*, and a few other species. For example, *P.* Luedde-violacea (*bellina* × *pulchra*), a dark purple form backcrossed to *P. bellina* to produce *P.* George Vasquez, has been crossed with various yellow hybrids to produce red-purple flowers. Other significant building blocks of red breeding are *P.* Coral Isles (Princess Kaiulani × *lueddemanniana*), registered by Thornton in 1967, and *P.* Malibu Imp (*amboinensis* × Luedde-violacea), registered by Freed in 1977.

Hybridizers of a truly red phalaenopsis are at the threshold of suc-cess. At this time, however, red hybrids have many of the drawbacks of their parents, especially small flower size, very low flower count, and poor flower production given the size of the plant. Superior red hybrids such as *P*. Mahalo (Penang × Malibu Heir), registered by Fukuyama, bear intensely red-colored flowers but lack the display qualities required for sales to the general public as a pot-plant.

Miniatures

A small class of hybrids are what could be called truly miniature *Phalaenopsis* hybrids. These are plants that are fully mature in a 4-inch pot and tend to produce short, few-flowered inflorescences in scale with the miniature plant size. Miniature hybrids are typically bred from *P. lobbii, P. maculata, P. parishii*, and related species. Hybrids with these species are few and far between, however, as they tend to be reluctant to hybridize. Filling a specialist niche for connoisseurs and windowsill and artificial-light growers with limited space, miniature hybrids have a certain charm absent in large standard hybrids.

Perhaps the most successful miniature hybrid is *P*. Micro-Nova (*maculata* × *lobbii*), registered by Wallbrunn in 1980 (*P. lobbii* is treated as a synonym of *P. parishii* for purposes of hybrid registration). This hybrid is actually fully mature in a 3-inch pot, becoming a veritable specimen plant in a 4-inch pot. The recent introduction to cultivation of several Chinese species of subgenus *Aphyllae*, such as *P. wilsonii*, and the reintroduction of *P. lowii* offer a broad palette of genetic material for breeding truly miniature hybrids.

Crosses involving subgenera *Aphyllae* and *Parishianae*, without the introduction of genes from large-flowered species, promise to create semideciduous hybrids that are quite cold-tolerant in addition to their miniature status. Although not usually fully deciduous in cultivation, species of these subgenera tolerate cold winter conditions as long as they are kept on the dry side.

×*Doritaenopsis*

×*Doritaenopsis* is formed by crossing *Doritis* with *Phalaenopsis*. In this book, *Doritis* is included in a broadly defined *Phalaenopsis*, so even though there is technically no longer any such hybrid genus, the hybrid combination is retained for purposes of hybrid registration and in this discussion.

Phalaenopsis buyssoniana would appear to be the best possible parent in section *Esmeralda* because of its large flower size. Experience, however, has shown it to be a less desirable parent than *P. pulcherrima*. All hybrids with *P. pulcherrima* produce stiffly erect inflorescences with numerous magenta-cerise flowers. Occasionally white-flowered clones are produced. A great uniformity typifies ×*Doritaenopsis* hybrids, and they are easily recognized as a group. Good examples of the important blood lines in ×*Doritaenopsis* are *Dtps.* Red Coral (*P.* Doris × *P. pulcherrima*), registered by Claralen in 1959; *Dtps.* Memoria Clarence Schubert (*P. pulcherrima* × *P.* Zada), registered by Fields Orchids in 1965; and *Dtps.* Fire Cracker (*Dtps.* Red Coral × *P. pulcherrima*), registered by Beard in 1966.

Many plants registered and in cultivation as ×*Doritaenopsis* produce large, round flowers on arching sprays. These typically produce white flowers or white flowers with a red lip and are nearly identical to standard *Phalaenopsis* hybrids. Recent karyological research in Japan and Taiwan has shown these plants resulted from historic mislabeling of flasks. These plants, such as *Dtps.* Pueblo Jewel (*P.* Dos Pueblos × *Dtps.* Pink Jewel), registered by Beard in 1968, *Dtps.* Lady Jewel (*Dtps.* Pueblo Jewel × *P.* Mildred Karleen), registered by McClellan in 1971, and *Dtps.* Jason Beard (*Dtps.* Pueblo Jewel × *P.* Mad Hatter), registered by Beard in 1972, do not have any *P. buyssoniana* or *P. pulcherrima* in their genetic make-up (Christenson 1999b).

The Future

Phalaenopsis, of all orchid genera, holds the most exciting possibilities for future research. Despite the greater floral and vegetative intricacy of many other genera, *Phalaenopsis* reigns supreme as the most important economic orchid crop for the foreseeable future. This status, combined with their adaptability to *in vitro* culture and manipulation, assures preferential funding and study of the genus. A discussion of possible avenues of research within *Phalaenopsis* is worth considering.

Several straightforward taxonomic problems are unresolved at this time. The least known entity in the genus, the Mentawai Island population of *P. violacea*, needs to be rigorously compared with *P. bellina* and typical *P. violacea* using modern laboratory techniques. Similar techniques should be applied to *P. cornu-cervi* throughout its range, to ascertain a pattern, if any, to the extreme variations seen in this species' lip morphology.

Despite their popularity, we know virtually nothing about the natural habitats of *Phalaenopsis* species. Perhaps more than with other genera, wild-collected plants of *Phalaenopsis* are bought by growers from agents, not personally gathered in the wild; in many cases even the agents, who tend to rely on local collectors to actually gather the plants, have never seen the natural habitats. Detailed habitat information is needed for nearly every species of *Phalaenopsis* and is critically needed for *P. lindenii, P. maculata,* and other species that remain problematic in cultivation.

Within the genus are several clearly distinct groups of species, based on shared floral characters, that appear to exhibit different pollination strategies: some flowers have no scent, others are strongly fragrant; some have mobile lips, other have rigidly positioned lips; some are diaphanous and short-lived, others are extremely long-lasting. There is virtually no information available on the pollination biology of any species of *Phalaenopsis*. This total lack of knowledge precludes an integrated management system that includes the orchid's pollinators and therefore impedes long-term conservation efforts. In particular the species pair of *P. fuscata* and *P. kunstleri* offers an excellent opportunity to study two astonishingly similar species that differ solely by their column and callus structures.

The time is coming when species will become extinct or exceedingly difficult to reintroduce to cultivation. What might be called the greater phalaenopsis community, therefore, needs to plan for a permanent gene bank of *Phalaenopsis* species. Such a bank can take many forms (and redundancy is to be encouraged in this situation), including a centralized living collection, a decentralized satellite network of living collections, seed storage and distribution, protocorm production and distribution (a method spearheaded by the Australian Orchid Foundation), seedling distribution programs, or one of several still unperfected techniques, such as cryopreservation.

Finally, more formalized figures on commercial phalaenopsis trade are needed. Efforts are being made, especially by the American Orchid Society, in this direction, but insufficient data has been generated to date. Because of the vast quantities of *Phalaenopsis* hybrids produced for the pot-plant trade, the significant numbers of artificially raised species seedlings, and their regular shipments across national borders, *Phalaenopsis* could serve as a shining example of successful commerce combining with responsible and remarkably successful *ex situ* conservation. *Phalaenopsis*, unlike any other orchid genus, has the potential to alter CITES and influence other conservation legislation at both the national and international levels.

Bibliography

This bibliography is intended to be a complete listing of *Phalaenopsis*-specific literature (including hybridization) and research articles in which *Phalaenopsis* was used as a primary research organism. The citations include all aspects of horticulture, hybridizing, physiology, propagation, and taxonomy. English translations are used for some foreign-language titles. The author is interested in learning about any references not included here.

Abdullah, M., J. L. K. Eng, M. C. On, N. Soediono, L. P. Nyman, and J. Arditti. 1983. Dissection of a *Phalaenopsis* flower: important organs revealed. *Orchid Rev.* 91:288–289.

Agusni, S., and P. Rumawas. 1978. Treatment of bacterial soft rot [*Erwinia carotovora*] of the moth orchid (*Phalaenopsis amabilis* (L.) Bl.). *Bogor Inst.* 2(1):19–25.

Ahmed, M., M. K. Pasha, and M. A. Aziz Khan. 1989. *Phalaenopsis cornu-cervi* (Breda) Par. and Reichb.f. (Orchidaceae), a new record for Bangladesh. *Bangladesh J. Bot.* 18:105–108.

Alvarez-Gardeazabal, G. 1979. Practical observations on the cultivation of *Phalaenopsis* in the Cauca River Valley. *Orquideologia* 13(3):277–281.

Anonymous. 1988. Cultivation of *Phalaenopsis*. Aalsmeer Proefstation voor de Bloemisterij (The Netherlands). 75 pp.

Aoyama, M. 1993. Polyploidy in *Phalaenopsis* hybrids. *Bull. Hiroshima Prefect. Agric. Res. Center* no. 57:55–62.

Aoyama, M., K. Kojima, and M. Kobayashi. 1994. Morphology of microspore in *Phalaenopsis* hybrids. *Kinki Chugoku Agric. Res.* 88:49–53.

Arditti, J., E. A. Ball, and D. M. Reisinger. 1977. Culture of flower-stalk buds: a method for vegetative propagation of *Phalaenopsis*. *Amer. Orchid Soc. Bull.* 46:236–240.

Arditti, J., J. A. Johnson, and R. G. Perera. 1982. Culture media which do not require sterilization: *Phalaenopsis* flower stalk node. *Orchid Rev.* 89:49–52.

Arends, J. C. 1970. Cytological observation on genome homology in eight interspecific hybrids of *Phalaenopsis*. *Genetica* 41:88–100.

Bachner, M. 1976. *Phalaenopsis* Joseph Hampton—progenitor supreme. *Amer. Orchid Soc. Bull.* 45:521–525.

Baker, K. M., M. C. Mathes, and B. J. Wallace. 1987. Germination of *Ponthieva* and *Cattleya* seeds and development of *Phalaenopsis* protocorms. *Lindleyana* 2:77–83.

Baker, M. L., and C. O. Baker. 1989. Climate guide to orchid species culture: *Phalaenopsis mannii* Rchb.f. *Orchid Digest* 53:71–72.

———. 1990. Climate guide to orchid species culture: *Phalaenopsis violacea* Witte. *Orchid Digest* 54:132–134.

———. 1991. *Orchid Species Culture: Pescatorea, Phaius, Phalaenopsis, Pholidota, Phragmipedium, Pleione.* Timber Press, Portland, Ore.

Bassin, H. 1986. *Phalaenopsis* Deventeriana 'Treva'. *Amer. Orchid Soc. Bull.* 55:347–350.

Batchelor, S. R. 1982. Beginner's series: *Phalaenopsis*, pt. 1. *Amer. Orchid Soc. Bull.* 51:1267–1275.

———. 1983. Beginner's series: *Phalaenopsis*, pts. 2–5. *Amer. Orchid Soc. Bull.* 52:4–13, 124–128, 243–250, 364–374.

Baxter, P. 1995. *Phalaenopsis* Spring Silk. *Orchid Digest* 59:36–37.

Berkeley, E. S. 1971. Notes on orchids in the jungle, *Phalaenopsis speciosa. Orchid Digest* 35:49.

Bhattacharjee, S. K. 1979. Photoperiodism effects on growth and flowering in some species of orchids. *Sci. Cult. Calcutta* 45(7):293–295.

Birk, L. 1973. The Orchid Digest guide on the culture of orchids: *Phalaenopsis. Orchid Digest* 37:215–217.

Bouriquet, R., H. Broly, and B. Legrand. 1982. Clonal propagation of *Phalaenopsis* (Orchidaceae) by *in vitro* culture. In E. D. Earle, ed., *Variability in Plants Regenerated from Tissue Culture*. Praeger, New York. Pp. 35–46.

Boyle, F. 1979. The story of *Phalaenopsis sanderiana. Orchid Rev.* 87:136–138.

Brandange, S., B. Luning, C. Moberg, and E. Sjostrand. 1971. Studies of Orchidaceae alkaloids, pt. 24: a pyrrolizidine alkaloid from *Phalaenopsis cornu-cervi* Reichb.f. *Acta Biochem. Pol.* 25(1):349–350.

———. 1972. Studies on Orchidaceae alkaloids, pt. 30: investigation of fourteen *Phalaenopsis* species. *Acta Chem. Scand.* 26(6):2558–2560.

Brown, R. C., and B. E. Lemmon. 1991a. Pollen development in orchids, pt. 1: cytoskeleton and the control of division plane in irregular patterns of cytokinesis. *Protoplasma* 163(1):9–18.

————. 1991b. Pollen development in orchids, pt. 2: the cytokinetic apparatus in simultaneous cytokinesis. *Protoplasma* 165(1–3):155–166.

————. 1991c. Pollen development in orchids, pt. 5: a generative cell domain involved in spatial control of the hemispherical cell plate. *J. Cell Sci.* 100(3):559–565.

————. 1992. Pollen development in orchids, pt. 4: cytoskeleton and ultrastructure of the unequal pollen mitosis in *Phalaenopsis*. *Protoplasma* 167(3–4):183–192.

Bruns, A. 1992. Irrigation of orchids. *Gaertnerboerse & Gartenwelt* 92(4): 159–161.

Butler, J. 1976a. Simple culture of *Phalaenopsis* in a Brisbane suburb. *Australian Orchid Rev.* 41(2):69.

————. 1976b. Application of light, heat, water and fertiliser to *Phalaenopsis* in relation to photosynthesis. *Australian Orchid Rev.* 41(2):69.

Cabalquinto, L. 1978. A new *Phalaenopsis* species? from the Philippine Islands. *Amer. Orchid Soc. Bull.* 47:1100.

Cammard, J. 1982. *Phalaenopsis* (L.) Blume, pts. 1 and 2. *L'Orchidophile* 13:179–185; 14:341–345.

————. 1983a. *Phalaenopsis* (L.) Blume, pts. 3–5. *L'Orchidophile* 14:382–386, 434–439, 492–495.

————. 1983b. Les *Phalaenopsis*. *L'Orchidophile* 14:299–304.

Capesius, I., and W. Nagl. 1978. Molecular and cytological characterization of nuclear DNA and chromatin for angiosperm systematics: DNA diversification in the evaluation of four orchids. *Plant Syst. Evol.* 129(3):143–166.

Chan, C. L., A. Lamb, P. S. Shim, and J. J. Wood. 1994. *Orchids of Borneo*, vol. 1. The Sabah Society, Kota Kinabalu.

Chen, C. S., and S. P. Y. Hsieh. 1978. *Phytophthora palmivora* and *Phytophthora parasitica* black rot of *Phalaenopsis* in Taiwan. *Plant Prot. Bull. Taipei* 20(2):161–170.

Chen, S. C., and Z. H. Tsi. 1985. *Iconographia Cormophytorum Sinicorum*, vol. 5. Institute of Botany, Beijing.

Chen, S. C., Z. H. Tsi, and Y. B. Luo. 1998. *Native Orchids of China in Color*. Science Press, Beijing.

Chen, W. H., Y. M. Fu, R. M. Hsieh, W. T. Tsai, M. S. Chyou, C. C. Wu, and Y. S. Lin. 1995. Application of DNA amplification fingerprinting in the breeding of *Phalaenopsis* Orchid. In M. Terzi et al., eds., *Current Issues in Plant Molecular and Cellular Biology*. Pp. 341–346.

Chen, W. H., R. M. Hsieh, W. T. Tsai, Y. M. Fu, M. S. Chyou, C. C. Wu, and Y. S. Lin. 1995. *Phalaenopsis* at the TSC. *Amer. Orchid Soc. Bull.* 64:492–495.

Chen, W. H., R. M. Hsieh, W. T. Tsai, and C. C. Wu. 1990. Application of biotechnology in the improvement of *Phalaenopsis*. *Taiwan Sugar Taipei* 37(5):20–24.

Chen, W. H., W. T. Tsai, C. C. Wu, and R. M. Hsieh. 1991. Electrofusion and cell division of *Phalaenopsis* protoplasts. *Taiwan Sugar Taipei* 38(2):14–18.

Chen, W. S., H. Y. Liu, Z. H. Liu, L. Yang, and W. H. Chen. 1994. Gibberellin and temperature influence carbohydrate content and flowering in *Phalaenopsis*. *Physiol. Plant.* (Denmark) 90(2):391–395.

Chen, Y., and C. Piluek. 1995. Effects of thidiazuron and N6-bensylaminopurine on shoot regeneration of *Phalaenopsis*. *Plant Growth Regul.* 16:99–101.

Cheng, C. n.d. [1990s]. *Formosan Orchids*, vol. 2: *Epiphytes*. Privately published by the author, Taichung, Taiwan.

Christenson, E. A. 1986. Nomenclatural changes in the Orchidaceae subtribe Sarcanthinae. *Selbyana* 9:167–170.

———. 1995. An overview of the genus *Phalaenopsis*. *Orchid Digest* 59:19–22.

———. 1998. Orchid portrait: a misunderstood *Phalaenopsis*. *Orchids* 67(5): 490–492.

———. 1999a. Conserving *Phalaenopsis*. *Orchids* 68(4):362–367.

———. 1999b. When is a *Doitaenopsis* not a *Doritaenopsis? The Phalaenopsis Newsl.* 9(3): 8–9.

Christenson, E. A., and M. W. Whitten. 1995. *Phalaenopsis bellina* (Rchb.f.) Christenson, a segregate from *P. violacea* Witte (Orchidaceae: Aeridinae). *Brittonia* 47:57–60.

Clements, M. A. 1989. Catalogue of Australian Orchidaceae. *Austral. Orch. Res.* 1:1–160.

Coll, C. A. 1985. Breeding and growing *Phalaenopsis* in South Africa. *Proc. 11th World Orchid Conf.*, Miami. Pp. 142–144.

Collins, R. 1983. Some thoughts on contemporary *Phalaenopsis* hybridizing. *Amer. Orchid Soc. Bull.* 52:792–800.

Collins, R., and R. Peterson. 1975. Basic orchid culture, 7. Potting *Phalaenopsis*. *Amer. Orchid Soc. Bull.* 44:624–626.

Comber, J. B. 1976. The rediscovery of *Phalaenopsis viridis* on a limestone ridge in Indonesia. *Orchid Digest* 40:84–89.

———. 1990. *Orchids of Java*. Royal Botanic Gardens, Kew.

Cory, E. N., and H. A. Highland. 1959. Dipping *Phalaenopsis* for the control of mealybugs. *Amer. Orchid Soc. Bull.* 28:344–345.

Curry, R. D. 1975. Mesophyll collapse in *Phalaenopsis*. *Amer. Orchid Soc. Bull.* 44:497–498.

Daerr, M. 1967. Vegetative Vermehrung bei *Phalaenopsis*. *Die Orchidee* 18(6): 322–324.

Dam, D. P., and S. N. Dam. 1984(1986). *Phalaenopsis cornu-cervi* (Breda) Bl. and Reichb.f., an orchid record for the tropical rain forest of Assam (India). *Bull. Bot. Surv. India* 26(3, 4):195–196.

Davis, D., and P. Finkelstein. 1990. *Phalaenopsis* Lipperose and its influence on modern pink hybridizing. *Amer. Orchid Soc. Bull.* 59:352–360.

De Wit, H. C. D. 1977. Orchids in Rumphius' *Herbarium Amboinense*. In J. Arditti, ed., *Orchid Biology: Reviews and Perspectives*, vol. 1. Cornell University Press, Ithaca, N.Y.

Dockrill, A. W. 1992. *Australian Indigenous Orchids*. Surrey Beatty & Sons, Chipping Norton, New South Wales.

Doi, M., H. Oda, N. Ogasawara, and T. Asahira. 1992. Effects of CO_2 enrichment on the growth and development of *in vitro* cultured plantlets. *J. Jap. Soc. Hort. Sci.* 60(4):963–970.

Doi, O., T. Kokubu, and Y. Miyaji. 1971. A method of asexual propagation making use of the peduncle of Kocho orchid (*Phalaenopsis*). *Kagoshima Univ. Fac. Agric. Bull.* 21:83–86.

Dourado, F. M. 1978. *Phalaenopsis violacea* of Malaya. *Amer. Orchid Soc. Bull.* 47:699–700; see also *Orchid Digest* Jul.–Aug. 1974.

Duncan, R. E., and J. T. Curtis. 1942. Intermittent growth of fruits of *Phalaenopsis*. A correlation of the growth phases of an orchid fruit with internal development. *Bull. Torr. Bot. Cl.* 69(3):167–183.

Endo, M., and I. Ikusima. 1989. Diurnal rhythm and characteristics of photosynthesis and respiration in the leaf and root of a *Phalaenopsis* plant. *Plant and Cell Physiol.* (Japan) 30(1):43–47.

———. 1992. Changes in concentrations of sugars and organic acids in the long-lasting flower clusters of *Phalaenopsis*. *Plant and Cell Physiol.* (Japan) 33(1):7–12.

Ernst, R. 1967. Effect of select organic nutrient additives on growth *in vitro* of *Phalaenopsis* seedlings. *Amer. Orchid Soc. Bull.* 36:694–704.

———. 1975. Studies in asymbiotic culture of orchids. *Amer. Orchid Soc. Bull.* 44:12–18.

———. 1994. Effects of thidiazuron on *in vitro* propagation of *Phalaenopsis* and *Doritaenopsis* (Orchidaceae). *Plant Cell* 39(4):273–275.

Ernst, R., J. Arditti, and P. L. Healey. 1971. Biological effects of surfactants, pt. 1: influence on the growth of orchid seedlings. *New Phytol.* 70(3): 457–475.

Ewing, J., Jr. 1985. New trends in *Phalaenopsis* breeding. *Proc. 11th World Orchid Conf.*, Miami. Pp. 162–165.

Fast, G. 1979. Klonvermehrung von *Phragmipedium* Sedenii und *Phalaenopsis* hybr. aus Blütenknospen. *Die Orchidee* 30(6):241–244.

Fessel, H. H. 1989. Kindelbildung bei *Phalaenopsis*. *Die Orchidee* 40(6): 218–220.

Fessel, H. H., and E. Lückel. 1994. Eine neue *Phalaenopsis* aus der Sektion *Amboinenses*: *Phalaenopsis floresensis*. *Die Orchidee* 45(3):101–104.

Fighetti, C. F. 1993. The pleasures of *Phalaenopsis*. *Amer. Orchid Soc. Bull.* 62:276–277.

Fighetti, C. F., D. W. Frank, J. Martin, H. P. Norton, and M. Rose. 1993. Yellow *Phalaenopsis*. *Amer. Orchid Soc. Bull.* 62:134–141.

Finnell, R. B. 1992. Aging: seeds of destruction. *Nat. Hist.* no. 2:54–57.

Firpo, E. J. 1998. How do you bloom your *Phalaenopsis equestris*? *Orchids Austral.* 10(4):8–11.

Fischer, P. 1992. Comparison of potted *Phalaenopsis* in hydroculture and peat substrates. *Zierpflanzenbau* 32(13):547–548.

Fitch, C. M. 1977. *Phalaenopsis*—flask to flowering. *Amer. Orchid Soc. Bull.* 46:214–215, 315–317.

———. 1979. Malaysian *Phalaenopsis* specialist. *Amer. Orchid Soc. Bull.* 48:129–135.

———. 1980a. Commercial orchid firms: color variations of *Phalaenopsis violacea*. *Amer. Orchid Soc. Bull.* 49:860–861.

———. 1980b. A few, different *Phalaenopsis* hybrids. *Amer. Orchid Soc. Bull.* 49:996–999.

———. 1983. Malaysian orchid conservationist. *Amer. Orchid Soc. Bull.* 52:705–711.

———. 1996. *Phalaenopsis lowii* in Thailand. *Orchids* 65(8):806–809.

Flamee, M., and G. Boesman. 1977. Clonal multiplication of *Phalaenopsis* hybrids, by means of sections of the flower stalk. *Meded. Rijksuniv. Fac. Landbouwwet* 42(3–4):1865–1868.

———. 1981. Preliminary investigations on the use of benzyladenin (BA) for the multiplication *in vivo* *Paphiopedilum*- and *Phalaenopsis*-hybrids. *Meded. Rijksuniv. Fac. Landbouwwet* 46(1):241–245.

Fowlie, J. A. 1979. Two additional lost species of *Phalaenopsis* refound in Indonesia, *Phalaenopsis psilantha* Schltr. and *Phalaenopsis modesta* J. J. Smith. *Orchid Digest* 43:212–213.

———. 1981. Speciation amongst the Orchidaceae as a function of climate change and topophysiography. *Orchid Digest* 45:44–49.

———. 1982. Malaya revisited, pt. 21: *Phalaenopsis corningiana* on saplings and streamside trees near waterfalls. *Orchid Digest* 46:138–142.

————. 1983. A new *Phalaenopsis* species of the section *Zebrinae* from central Sumatra, *Phalaenopsis inscriptiosinensis* Fowl., sp. nov. *Orchid Digest* 47:11–12.

————. 1985a. Malaya revisited, pt. 27: *Paphiopedilum curtisii* in the Barisan Mountains of Sumatra. *Orchid Digest* 49:48–52.

————. 1985b. Malaya revisited, pt. 31: *Paphiopedilum victoria-mariae* (Sander ex Masters) Rolfe refound in Sumatra at high elevation on Andesite Lava Cliffs. *Orchid Digest* 49:204–210.

————. 1987a. A peculiar means of vegetative reproduction by *Phalaenopsis stuartiana*. *Orchid Digest* 51:93–94.

————. 1987b. Growing orchids in live moss, pt. 2: a visit with Ernie Campuzano of Butterfly Orchids. *Orchid Digest* 51:100–101.

————. 1991a. Malaya revisited, pt. 36: the Wallace Line and orchids. *Orchid Digest* 55:71–74.

————. 1991b. Some further observations on *Phalaenopsis philippinense* and *Phalaenopsis leucorrhoda*. *Orchid Digest* 55:118–122.

————. 1992. The re-emergence of *Phalaenopsis tetraspis* from collections from extreme NW Sumatra. *Orchid Digest* 56:4–9.

————. 1993. A new species of *Phalaenopsis* from Flores Island, Indonesia: *Phalaenopsis floresensis* Fowl., sp. nov. *Orchid Digest* 57:35–36.

Frank, D. W. 1988. Control of bacterial soft rot caused by *Pseudomonas cattleya* in the culture of *Phalaenopsis*. *Orchid Digest* 52:66–67.

Franke, H. 1981. Vegetative Vermehrung von *Phalaenopsis* durch Kultivierung von Blütenstammnodien in Wasser und Levatit HD 5 (Bayer). *Die Orchidee* 32(6): (235–239).

Freed, H. 1969a. The a-*dor*-able *Doritaenopsis*. *Orchid Digest* 33:236–239.

————. 1969b. A newly discovered blue *Doritis*. *Orchid Digest* 33:240–241.

————. 1975a. Those spectacular eye-catchers—peppermint-striped *Phalaenopsis*. *Amer. Orchid Soc. Bull.* 44:103–108.

————. 1975b. The exquisite semi-alba *Phalaenopsis*. *Orchid Digest* 39:24–25.

————. 1976a. Those golden gems—the yellow *Phalaenopsis*. *Orchid Digest* 40:204–211.

————. 1976b. *Phalaenopsis* are easy to grow. *Amer. Orchid Soc. Bull.* 45:405–408.

————. 1978a. Breeding with the Borneo-type *Phalaenopsis violacea*. *Amer. Orchid Soc. Bull.* 47:689–697.

————. 1978b. The twelve most important white *Phalaenopsis* stud plants. *Amer. Orchid Soc. Bull.* 47:1104–1111.

————. 1978c. The superb white *Phalaenopsis* exhibition quality plants. *Orchid Digest* 42:16–18.

————. 1980a. *Phalaenopsis amboinensis. Amer. Orchid Soc. Bull.* 49:468–476.

————. 1980b. An update on breeding with the Borneo-type *Phalaenopsis violacea. Amer. Orchid Soc. Bull.* 49:843–849.

————. 1980c. The fabulous *Phalaenopsis fasciata. Amer. Orchid Soc. Bull.* 49:1099–1106.

————. 1981a. The unpredictable *Phalaenopsis fuscata* hybrids. *Amer. Orchid Soc. Bull.* 50:937–941.

————. 1981b. The versatile *Phalaenopsis lueddemanniana. Amer. Orchid Soc. Bull.* 50:1077–1082, 1325–1332.

————. 1981c. Novelty *Phalaenopsis* species and their hybrids, *Phalaenopsis stuartiana. Amer. Orchid Soc. Bull.* 50:1458–1463.

————. 1984. Novas of the *Phalaenopsis* world. *Amer. Orchid Soc. Bull.* 53:927–935, 1029–1034, 1145–1150.

Frier, M. C. 1991. Golden pink—a sunrise color for *Phalaenopsis. Amer. Orchid Soc. Bull.* 60:210–216.

Fu, F. M. L. 1978. Studies on the tissue culture of orchids, pt. 1: clonal propagation of *Phalaenopsis* by lateral buds from flower stems. *Orchid Rev.* 87:308–310.

————. 1990. Micro-propagation of *Phalaenopsis. Trop. Crop Res.* (China) no. 2:24–27.

Fu, Y. M., W. H. Chen, R. M. Hsieh, W. T. Tsai, C. C. Wu, M. S. Chyou, and Y. S. Lin. 1994. Studies on DNA amplification fingerprinting techniques of *Phalaenopsis* orchid. *Rep. Taiwan Sugar Res. Inst.* 146:9–22.

Garay, L. A., F. Haner, and E. S. Siegerist. 1995. Inquilina orchidacea: Orchidaceae plaerumque Levyanae. *Lindleyana* 10:174–182.

Gavin, A., and R. J. Griesbach. 1991. *Phalaenopsis parishii*—color variations and hybrids. *Amer. Orchid Soc. Bull.* 60:121–124.

Gessner, U. 1979. Neunzig Jahre *Phalaenopsis violacea*-Zucht von 1887–1976. *Die Orchidee* 30(3):120–127.

Gil, J. Y. 1987. The propagation of *Phalaenopsis*, pt. 2. *Malayan Orchid Rev.* 21:45–46.

Ginsberg, H. S. 1999a. Novelty *Phalaenopsis* breeding in Taiwan, pt. 1. *Orchid Digest* 63:4–10.

————. 1999b. Novelty *Phalaenopsis* breeding in Taiwan, pt. 2. *Orchid Digest* 63:83–88.

Golamco, A. 1984. A new species in the guise of *Phalaenopsis* ×*leucorrhoda. Philippine Orchid Rev.* 6:17–25.

Gomi, K., Y. Ogino, and T. Tanaka. 1980. Fertilization and potting media for *Phalaenopsis* hybrid. *Bull. Fac. Agric. Miyazaki Univ.* 27(2):267–276.

Goo, E. 1998. Red alert. *Orchids* 67(5):478–483.

Gordon, B. 1985. Culture of the *Phalaenopsis* orchid. Laid-Back Publ., Rialto, Calif.

———. 1987. Good drainage. *Orchid Digest* 51:100–101.

———. 1988a. *Phalaenopsis* culture = pest control. *Orchid Digest* 52:107–115.

———. 1988b. *Phalaenopsis* culture: a beginner's guide. *Amer. Orchid Soc. Bull.* 57:14–20, 152–157, 261–265, 368–373.

———. 1989a. The breedin' o' the green (*Phalaenopsis*, that is). *Amer. Orchid Soc. Bull.* 58:226–237.

———. 1989b. *Phalaenopsis* flower induction (or, how to make them bloom). *Amer. Orchid Soc. Bull.* 58:908–910.

———. 1990. Botrytis on *Phalaenopsis* blooms . . . and how to prevent it. *Orchid Digest* 54:15–16.

———. 1994. Springtime culture of *Phalaenopsis* seedlings. *Orchid Digest* 58:81.

Griesbach, R. J. 1981a. Colchicine-induced polyploidy in *Phalaenopsis* orchids. *Plant Cell Tissue Organ Cult.* 1(2):103–107.

———. 1981b. Genetics and taxonomy. *Orchid Digest* 45:219–224.

———. 1983a. *Phalaenopsis mariae*, as a parent. *Orchid Digest* 47:204–206.

———. 1983b. The use of indolacetylamino acids in the *in vitro* propagation of *Phalaenopsis* orchids. *Sci. Hortic.* (The Netherlands) 19(3, 4):363–366.

———. 1984. The *in vivo* propagation of *Phalaenopsis* orchids. *Amer. Orchid Soc. Bull.* 53:1303–1305.

———. 1985a. *Doritaenopsis* Grebe, the making of an AQ/AOS. *Amer. Orchid Soc. Bull.* 54:595–596.

———. 1985b. Polyploidy in orchid improvement. *Amer. Orchid Soc. Bull.* 54:1445–1451.

———. 1985c. Polyploidy in *Phalaenopsis* orchid improvement. *J. Hered.* 76(1):74–75.

———. 1990. Flavonoid copigments and anthocyanin of *Phalaenopsis schilleriana. Lindleyana* 5:231–234.

———. 1995. A *Phalaenopsis* in every pot. *Orchid Digest* 59:42–43.

———. 1998. *Phalaenopsis violacea. Orchids* 67(5):484–489.

Griesbach, R. J., and T. M. Klein. 1993. *In situ* genetic complementation of a flower color mutant in *Doritis pulcherrima* (Orchidaceae). *Lindleyana* 8:223–226.

Grimes, J. 1987. An easy method to induce *Phalaenopsis* "stem props." *Amer. Orchid Soc. Bull.* 56:369–371.

Grundon, N., M. Swann, and W. T. Upton. 1993. Australasian orchids illustrated, no. 9: *Phalaenopsis amabilis* Blume var. *papuana* Schltr. *Orchadian* 10(12):459–461.

Gruss, O. 1990. Primärhybriden—Reizvolle Ergänzung der Natur, Teil 2: Primärhybriden der *Phalaenopsis violacea* Witte. *Die Orchidee* 41(4):115–119.

———. 1992a. Primärhybriden—Reizvolle Erganzung der Natur, Teil 6: Primärhybriden der kleinwüchsigen Arten der Gattung *Phalaenopsis—Phalaenopsis lobbii—Phalaenopsis parishii—Phalaenopsis wilsonii. Die Orchidee* 43(3):132–139.

———. 1992b. Primärhybriden—Reizvolle Ergänzung dur Natur, Teil 7: Primärhybriden der *Phalaenopsis maculata. Die Orchidee* 43(5):206–210.

———. 1995. *Phalaenopsis philippinensis* Golamco ex Fowlie & Tang, C. Z. 1987. *Die Orchidee* 46(4):138–143.

Gruss, O., and L. Röllke. 1990a. Die lange verschollene *Phalaenopsis parishii* wieder aufgetaucht *P. parishii—P. parishii* var. *lobbii—P. lobbii. Die Orchidee* 41(5):158–161.

———. 1990b. *Phalaenopsis*-Arten von den Andamanen und Nicobaren-Inseln: *Phalaenopsis speciosa* und *Phalaenopsis tetraspis. Die Orchidee* 41(6): 219–221.

———. 1991a. Eine weitere *Phalaenopsis* von den Philippinen—*P. bastianii* Gruss & Röllke. *Die Orchidee* 42(2):76–79.

———. 1991b. *Phalaenopsis wilsonii* Rolfe—*Phalaenopsis stobartiana* Rchb.f. Lange verschollene *Phalaenopsis*-Arten der sektion *Aphyllae* Sweet wieder in Kultur. *Die Orchidee* 42(5):238–243.

———. 1992a. *Phalaenopsis parishii* var. *lobbii* forma *flava*—eine "neue" Form dieser reizvollen Art. *Die Orchidee* 43(1):42–43.

———. 1992b. Seit 100 Jahren verschollen, *Phalaenopsis lowii* Rchb.f. *Die Orchidee* 43(4):153–156.

———. 1992c. Kleinode der Gattung *Phalaenopsis* in ihrer Vielfalt, Teil 1: *Phalaenopsis fimbriata* J. J. Smith 1921. *Die Orchidee* 43(2):87–89.

———. 1992d. Kleinode der Gattung *Phalaenopsis* in ihrer Vielfalt, Teil 2: *Phalaenopsis modesta* J. J. Smith 1906. *Die Orchidee* 43(5):203–205.

———. 1993a. Gattung *Kingidium. Die Orchidee* 44(1):33–36.

———. 1993b. Gattung *Kingidium*, Teil 2. *Die Orchidee* 44(3):119–122.

———. 1993c. *Kingidium deliciosum* (Rchb.f.) Sweet, Teil 3. *Die Orchidee* 44(4):183–189.

———. 1993d. *Kingidium deliciosum* var. *bellum* (Teisjm. & Binn.) Gruss & Röllke comb. nov., Teil 4. *Die Orchidee* 44(5):225–227.

———. 1993e. Die Synonyma von *Kingidium deliciosum—Phal. alboviolacea* Ridley, Teil 5. *Die Orchidee* 44(5):228–229.

———. 1993f. Bilder aus dem Reichenbach-Herbarium im Naturkundlichen Museum in Wien, Teil 1: Die Gattung *Phalaenopsis. Die Orchidee* 44(5):230–233.

————. 1993g. Die Synonyma von *Kingidium deliciosum—Phal. amethystina* Rchb.f., Teil 6. *Die Orchidee* 44(6):273–274.

————. 1994a. Die Synonyma von *Kingidium deliciosum—Kingidium decumbens* (Griff.) Hunt, Teil 7. *Die Orchidee* 45(1):5–7.

————. 1994b. Die Synonyma von *Kingidium deliciosum—Kingiella hebe* (Rchb.f.) Rolfe, Teil 8. *Die Orchidee* 45(2):65–67.

————. 1994c. *Kingidium hookerianum* Gruss & Röllke, Teil 9. *Die Orchidee* 45(6):229–233.

————. 1995a. *Kingidium wightii* (Rchb.f.) Gruss & Röllke comb. nov., Teil 10. *Die Orchidee* 46(1):23–28.

————. 1995b. Synonym von *Kingidium wightii—Doritis latifolia* (Thwaites) Trimen. *Die Orchidee* 46(1):29–30.

————. 1995c. *Kingidium philippinense* (Ames) Gruss & Röllke comb. nov., Teil 11. *Die Orchidee* 46(3):115–118.

————. 1995d. Synonym von *Kingidium philippinense*. *Die Orchidee* 46(3): 118–119.

————. 1995e. *Kingidium×stobartianum* (Rchb.f.) Seidenfaden (pro. spec.). *Die Orchidee* 46(6):233–236.

————. 1995f. Synonym von *Kingidium×stobartianum*. *Die Orchidee* 46(6): 236–237.

————. 1996. *Kingidium wilsonii* (Rolfe) Gruss & Röllke comb. nov. *Die Orchidee* 47(3):149–155.

————. 1997a. *Kingidium taeniale* (Lindley) Hunt. *Die Orchidee* 48(2):49–53.

————. 1997b. Die Synonyma von *Kingidium taeniale*. *Die Orchidee* 48(2): 53–55.

————. 1997c. *Kingidium naviculare* (Tang & Wang) Tsi ex Hashimoto nomen nudum. *Die Orchidee* 48(2):56–57.

————. 1997d. *Kingidium minus* Seidenfaden. *Die Orchidee* 48(6):259–268.

————. 1997e. *Kingidium chibae* (T. Yukawa) Gruss & Röllke comb. nov. *Die Orchidee* 48(6):261–263.

————. 1997f. Nachtrag—Die Synonyma von *Kingidium wilsonii*. *Die Orchidee* 48(6):264.

————. 1997g. Zweifelhafte Art *Phalaenopsis mysorensis* Saldanha. *Die Orchidee* 48(6):265–267.

————. 1997h. Nachtrag—Die Synonyma von *Kingidium wilsonii*. *Die Orchidee* 48(6):265–267.

————. 1997i. Zu den Sektionen der Gattung *Kingidium*. *Die Orchidee* 48(6): 267–268.

Gruss, O., and M. Wolff. 1993. Die Hybriden der *Phalaenopsis corningiana* Rchb.f. *Die Orchidee* 44(1):5–11.

———. 1994. Geschichte der weißen Hybriden der Gattung *Phalaenopsis. Die Orchidee* 45(3):126–133.

———. 1995. *Phalaenopsis.* Verlag Eugen Ulmer, Stuttgart.

Guillaumin, A. 1923a. Les *Phalaenopsis* cultivés et leurs hybrides. *Revue Horticole,* n.s., 18:294, 316–318.

———. 1923b. Nouveaux hybrides de *Phalaenopsis. Revue Horticole,* n.s., 18:499–501.

———. 1929a. Les "*Phalaenopsis*" hybrides issus du "*P. amabilis*" Bl. *Arch. Mus. Nat. Hist. Natur.,* ser. 6, 4:33–36.

———. 1929b. Nouveaux *Phalaenopsis* cultivés. *Revue Horticole,* n.s., 21:484–485.

———. 1930. Les "*Phalaenopsis*" hybrides autres que ceux issus du "*P. amabilis*" Bl. *Arch. Mus. Nat. Hist. Natur.,* ser. 6, 6:75–79

Guo, D., K. Liu, and M. Chai. 1991. Study on rapid clonal propagation of *Dendrobium, Cattleya* and *Phalaenopsis in vitro. Acta Agric. Zhejiangensis* 3(1): 34–38.

Haas von Schmude, N. F. 1977. Orchid Keiki Fix, eine neue Methode zur Erzeugung von Kindeln an Blütenstielen von *Phalaenopsis. Die Orchidee* 28(4): (109–111).

———. 1983. Klonale Massen Vermehrung von *Phalaenopsis. Die Orchidee* 34(6):242–248.

———. 1984. Tissue culturing *Phalaenopsis* using leaves and leaf segments. *Proc. 11th World Orch. Conf.,* Miami. P. 311.

Hagar, G. T. 1979. *Phalaenopsis amboinensis,* the "rediscovered" species. *Amer. Orchid Soc. Bull.* 48:1224–1228.

Hager, H. 1985. Breeding *Phalaenopsis* for new color and form—a new horizon. *Proc. 11th World Orch. Conf.,* Miami. Pp. 192–194.

Harper, T. 1985. *Phalaenopsis* culture for beginners. *Amer. Orchid Soc. Bull.* 54:947–954.

———. 1990. *Phalaenopsis lindenii*—its first 95 years. *Orchid Digest* 54:62–67, 69.

———. 1991. Multiflora *Phalaenopsis:* the contributions of *Phal. equestris* in breeding multifloras. *Amer. Orchid Soc. Bull.* 60:106–114.

———. 1993. Multiflora *Phalaenopsis. Amer. Orchid Soc. Bull.* 62:126–133.

Healey, P. L., R. Ernst, and J. Arditti. 1971. Biological effects of surfactants, pt. 2: influence on the ultrastructure of orchid seedlings. *New Phytol.* 70(3):477–482.

Herman, D. 1993. Mister *Phalaenopsis. Amer. Orchid Soc. Bull.* 62:118–125.

Hermann, S. 1987. *Phalaenopsis* micropropagation started with explants like flower nodes, internode sections and heel nodes. *Symposium Plant Microprop. Hort. Industr.,* Arlon, Belgium. Pp. 278–281.

Hermann, S., and Y. Sell. 1988. Several parameters for characterization of the floral axes of *Phalaenopsis* (Orchidaceae) in view of studying the morphogenic potentials. *Beitr. Biol. Pflanz.* (Berlin) 63(3):351–374.

Hetherington, E. 1981. *Phalaenopsis* hybridizing—today and tomorrow orchids. *Orchid Digest* 45:95–97.

———. 1993. The history makers: Consul Schiller's pink *Phalaenopsis*. *Orchid Digest* 57:143–144.

———. 1995. Keith Shaffer and Shaffer's Orchids. *Orchid Digest* 59:12–13.

Hinnen, M. G. J., R. L. M. Pierik, and F. B. F. Bronsema. 1989. The influence of macronutrients and some other factors on growth of *Phalaenopsis* hybrid seedlings *in vitro*. *Sci. Hortic.* (The Netherlands) 41(1):105–116.

Hiryati, Abdullah, and Saleh Kadzimin. 1993. Etiology of bacterial soft rot of orchids. *Pertanika J. Trop. Agric. Sci.* (Malaysia) 16(1):1–4.

Hoffman, K. 1989. Development of orchid production on member farms of orchid subgroup of the product group for ornamentals. *Gartenbau* 36(4): 118–119.

Holman, R. T., and P. C. Nichols. 1972. Characterization of the lipids of some orchids. *Phytochemistry* 11(1):333–337.

Hölters, J. 1983. Möglichkeiten der vegetativen Vermehrung von *Phalaenopsis*, 1–4. *Die Orchidee* 34(2):78–82; 34(3):119–122; 34(5):208–210; 34(6): 231–235.

Holttum, R. E. 1965. Cultivated species of the orchid genus *Doritis* Lindl. *Kew Bull.* 19:207–212.

———. 1966. The genus *Kingiella*. *Orchid Rev.* 74:128.

Homma, Y., and T. Asahira. 1985. New means of *Phalaenopsis* propagation with internodal sections of flower stalk. *J. Jap. Soc. Hort. Sci.* 54(3):379–387.

Hsiang, R. C. 1987. *Phalaenopsis Superior Parentage.* Orch. Soc. Rep. China.

Hsieh, R. M., W. H. Chen, W. T. Tsai, M. S. Chyou, and C. C. Wu. 1992. Electrophoretic pattern of isozymes in *Phalaenopsis* spp.: the impact of biological research on agricultural productivity. *Proc. SABRAO Int. Symp.* Pp. 319–329.

Hunt, P. F. 1971a. The correct name for *Phalaenopsis parishii*. *Amer. Orchid Soc. Bull.* 40:1093–1094.

———. 1971b. Registration of *Phalaenopsis* hybrids. *Orchid Rev.* 79:23–25.

Ichihashi, Y. 1992. Micropropagation of *Phalaenopsis* through the culture of lateral buds from young flower stalks. *Lindleyana* 7:208–215.

Intuwong, P., J. T. Kunisaki, and Y. Segawa. 1972. Vegetative propagation of *Phalaenopsis* by flower stalk cuttings. *Hawaii Orchid J.* 1(4):13–18.

Intuwong, P., and Y. Segawa. 1974a. Clonal propagation of *Phalaenopsis* by shoot tip culture. *Amer. Orchid Soc. Bull.* 43:893–895.

———. 1974b. Plantlet (keiki) formation in *Phalaenopsis*. *Hawaii Orchid J.*
3(3):17–20.

Ito, I., A. Momiyama, T. Namiki, and S. Takashima. 1972. Controlling the
flowering period of *Phalaenopsis*, pt. 1: on the flower bud differentiation
and development in *Phalaenopsis*. *Kyoto Prefect. Univ. Fac. Agric. Sci. Rep.*
24:9–12.

Jin, K. S., J. J. Kim, H. Ryu, and H. Y. Kim. 1994. Identification of bacterial
isolates obtained from diseased orchid and aloe plants caused by *Erwinia
chrysanthemi. J. Agric. Sci.* (Korea) 36(1):301–306.

Johnson, J. A., R. Perera, and J. Arditti. 1982. Clonal propagation of *Phalaenopsis* from flower-stalk nodes in anticontaminant-containing media. *Australian Orchid Rev.* 47(1):21–25.

Kaiser, B. 1987. More phosphorus and potassium instead of cool treatment.
Gaertnerboerse & Gartenwelt 87(25):896.

Karnehl, J. F. 1991. *Phalaenopsis parishii—Phalaenopsis lobbii? Schlechteriana*
2(4):138–142.

———. 1992a. *Phalaenopsis lindenii* Loher—questions, nothing but questions. *Schlechteriana* 3(1):16–19.

———. 1992b. *Kingidium deliciosum* (Rchb.f.) Sweet. *Schlechteriana* 3(1):
28–31.

Keithly, J. H., D. P. Jones, and H. Yokoyama. 1991. Survival and growth of
transplanted orchid seedlings enhanced by DCPTA. *HortScience*
26:1284–1286.

Keithly, J. H., and H. Yokoyama. 1990. Regulation of plant productivity, pt. 1:
improved seedling vigor and floral performance of *Phalaenopsis* by 2- (3,4-
dichlorophenoxy) triethylene [DCPTA]. *Plant Growth Regul.* 9:19–26.

Kimura, Y. 1991. Improvements of mass clonal *Phalaenopsis* propagation.
Gunma J. Agric. Res., ser. D, Hort. 6:33–40.

Kobayashi, G. 1989. *Phalaenopsis* Hilo Lip 'Lightfoot'. *Orchid Digest* 53:
148–151.

Kobayashi, G., and S. Yonai. 1990. Studies on the vegetative propagation of
Phalaenopsis by tissue culture. *Bull. Tochigi Prefect. Agric. Exp. St.* no.
37:57–70.

Kobayashi, M., M. Komatuda, and S. Yonai. 1991. Studies on the vegetative
propagation of *Phalaenopsis* through root-tip culture. *Abstr. Jap. Soc. Hort.
Sci.* 59(2):664–665.

Koch, L. 1973. Studies on the vegetative increase of *Phalaenopsis in vitro*.
Ph.D. diss., Hannover. P. 169.

———. 1974. Ergleiche Vermehrung von *Phalaenopsis in vitro. Gartenwelt*
74:482–484.

Koopowitz, H., and N. Hasegawa. 1985a. Golden Buddha—golden parent. *Amer. Orchid Soc. Bull.* 54:1308–1313.

———. 1985b. Trends in breeding modern *Phalaenopsis*: art shades. *Orchid Digest* 49:196–197.

Krizek, D. T., and R. H. Lawson. 1974. Accelerated growth of *Cattleya* and *Phalaenopsis* under controlled-environment conditions. *Amer. Orchid Soc. Bull.* 43:503–510.

Kubota, S., and K. Yoneda. 1990. Fertilizer retentivity of sphagnum medium for *Phalaenopsis* culture and relation between fertilizer concentration and times of irrigation. *Bull. Coll. Agric. Vet. Med. Nihon Univ.* (Japan) no. 47:75–80.

Kuhn, J., and L. Kuhn. 1965. *Phalaenopsis violacea. Amer. Orchid Soc. Bull.* 34:204–208.

Lagrelle, B. 1998. Les ennemis des *Phalaenopsis. Orchid. Cult. & Protect.* 33(1):21–25.

Lam, T. W., R. Ernst, J. Arditti, and S. Ichihashi. 1991. The effects of complex additives and 6-(g,g-dimethylallylamino)-purine on the proliferation of *Phalaenopsis* protocorms. *Lindleyana* 6:24–26.

Lamb, T., and J. A. Fowlie. 1980. Malaya revisited, pt. 18: the climate of Sabah, North Borneo, with cultural hints on the cultivation of certain *Paphiopedilum* and *Phalaenopsis* species which occur there. *Orchid Digest* 44:187–189.

LeCoufle, M. 1979. *Phalaenopsis equestris* Rchb.f. (*Phalaenopsis equestre*) *Phalaenopsis rosea* Ldl. (*Phalaenopsis* aux fleurs roses) synonymes. *L' Orchidophile* 10:1392.

———. 1985. French breeding lines of *Phalaenopsis. Proc. 11th World Orch. Conf.*, Miami. P. 230.

———. 1993. *Phalaenopsis leucorrhoda* et *Phalaenopsis philippinensis. L'Orchidophile* 108:151–157.

LeCoufle, M., and M. Vacherot. 1989. *Phalaenopsis* plant named Velmer. *Plant Pat. U.S. Pat. Trademark Off.* no. 6510:2.

Lee, J. S., M. S. Roh, R. J. Griesbach, and K. C. Gross. 1988. Growth responses of *Phalaenopsis* Toyland seedlings affected by different light intensity and temperature. *J. Korean Soc. Hortic. Sci. Suweon* 29(1):58–63.

Lee, N., and G. M. Lin. 1984. Effect of temperature on growth and flowering of *Phalaenopsis* white hybrid. *J. Chinese Soc. Hort. Soc.* 30:223–231.

Leigh, D. 1982a. *Phalaenopsis*: an introduction to the genus. *Orchid Rev.* 90:26–29.

———. 1982b. *Phalaenopsis*: the species and their hybrids. *Orchid Rev.* 90:48–51, 81–83, 135–137, 155–157, 185–187, 253–254, 335–337, 345–348, 395–398.

————. 1983. *Phalaenopsis celebensis. Orchid Rev.* 91:195.

Lesemann, D., and J. Begtrup. 1971. Electron microscopic demonstration of a bacilliform virus in *Phalaenopsis. Phytopath. Z.* 71(3):257–269.

Lim, D. 1983. *Phalaenopsis amboinensis. Malayan Orchid Rev.* 16:20–23.

Limartha, I. 1975. Influence of media and seed storage time on orchid germination. *Hawaii Orchid J.* 4(2):6–8.

Lin, C.-C. 1985. Clonal propagation of *Phalaenopsis* and *Doritaenopsis* by internodes of flower stalk *in vitro. J. Chinese Soc. Hort. Sci.* 31:84–93.

————. 1986. *In-vitro* culture of flower stalk internodes of *Phalaenopsis* and *Doritaenopsis. Lindleyana* 1:158–163.

————. 1987. Histological observations on *in-vitro* formation of protocorm-like bodies from flower stalk internodes of *Phalaenopsis. Lindleyana* 2:58–65.

Lin, J. S. 1980. Studies on the clonal propagation of *Phalaenopsis amabilis* by leaf tissue culture. *J. Agric. Res. China Taichung* 29(3):195–201.

Lin, R. S. 1981. Studies on the clonal propagation of *Phalaenopsis* by root culture. *J. Agric. Res. China Taichung Hsien* 30(2):141–145.

Lin, W. H., and G. Chon. 1987. *Phalaenopsis Kingdom from Formosa.* Asia Agri-Business Corp., Taipei.

Litwin, L. M. 1992. Into the light: selecting the best environment can lead to quality floral displays in *Phalaenopsis. Amer. Orchid Soc. Bull.* 61:38–43.

Liu, F. 1988. A new species of *Phalaenopsis* from Yunnan. *Acta Bot. Yunnan.* 10:119–120.

Lückel, E. 1980. *Phalaenopsis rosea* Lindley gleich *Phalaenopsis equestris* (Schauer) Rchb.f. *Die Orchidee* 31(6):221–226.

Magie, R. O. 1969. Control of *Botrytis cinerea* diseases on chrysanthemum, carnation, rose, snapdragon, petunia and phalaenopsis flowers. *Fla. State Hort. Soc. Proc.* 82:373–378.

Manuel, P. K., and T. C. Lee. 1974. *Phalaenopsis intermedia,* "the star of Leyte." *Amer. Orchid Soc. Bull.* 43:977–980.

Martin, J. G. 1985. In search of red *Phalaenopsis. Amer. Orchid Soc. Bull.* 54:411–420.

Martin, J., H. P. Norton, M. Rose, C. F. Fighetti, and D. W. Frank. 1993. Red *Phalaenopsis* hybrids. *Amer. Orchid Soc. Bull.* 62:250–257.

Mau, R. F. L. 1983. Development of the orchid weevil, *Orchidophilus aterrimus* (Waterhouse). *Proc. Hawaii Entomol. Soc.* 24(2, 3):293–297.

Mayer, L. 1993. How to grow *Phalaenopsis. Australian Orchid Rev.* 58(1):33–36.

Mayhew, D. E., A. L. Cook, and R. D. Raabe. 1992. Special report: a new virus is reported for *Phalaenopsis. Amer. Orchid Soc. Bull.* 61:574–577.

May Lay, F. F. 1978. Studies on the tissue culture of orchids, pt. 1: clonal propagation of *Phalaenopsis* by lateral buds from flower stems. *Orchid Rev.* 86:308–310.

Mayr, H. 1986. Am Standort von *Phalaenopsis gigantea, Phalaenopsis amabilis* und *Phalaenopsis cornu-cervi. Die Orchidee* 37(4):177–180.

McConnell, D. B., and T. J. Sheehan. 1978. Anatomical aspects of chilling injury to leaves of *Phalaenopsis* Bl. *HortScience* 13:705–706.

McCorkle, J. K., L. E. Reilly, and T. O'Dell. 1969. Pseudomonas infection of *Phalaenopsis. Amer. Orchid Soc. Bull.* 38:1073–1078.

McDowell, D. 1992. At home with *Phalaenopsis. Amer. Orchid Soc. Bull.* 61:150–153.

McFarlane, K. 1977. Hormone node culture of *Phalaenopsis. Australian Orchid Rev.* 42(1):30–31.

Miller, J. 1974a. Notes on the distribution of *Phalaenopsis* in the Philippines— with a useful climate summary, pt. 1: *Phalaenopsis lueddemanniana* and the miniature species most often confused with it. *Orchid Digest* 38:139–141.

———. 1974b. Notes on the distribution of *Phalaenopsis* in the Philippines— with a useful climate summary, pt. 2: the large, white-flowered species: *Phalaenopsis aphrodite* and *Phalaenopsis amabilis. Orchid Digest* 38:191–193.

———. 1974c. Notes on the distribution of *Phalaenopsis* in the Philippines— with a useful climate summary, pt. 3: the large, colored species: *Phalaenopsis schilleriana, Phalaenopsis stuartiana,* and *Phalaenopsis sanderiana. Orchid Digest* 38:219–221.

———. 1975. Notes on the distribution of *Phalaenopsis* in the Philippines— with a useful climate summary. *Orchid Digest* 39:24–25.

Minne, S. L. 1969. *Phalaenopsis* Harriettiae revisited. *Amer. Orchid Soc. Bull.* 38:882–884.

Mitchell, B., and L. Mitchell. 1993. *Phalaenopsis* as houseplants. *Orchid Digest* 57:136–140.

Miwa, A. 1941. *Phalaenopsis* of Formosa. *Pract. Hort.* 27:113–120.

Mohd, N. I., and S. J. Mohd. 1992. Micropropagation of orchids using scape nodes as the explant material. *Acta Hortic. Wageningen* 1(292):169–172.

Momose, H., and K. Yoneda. 1988. Protocorm-like body (PLB) formation by flower stalk node bud culture by means of cutting off the top of inflorescence of *Phalaenopsis. Bull. Coll. Agric. Vet. Med. Nihon Univ.* (Japan) no. 45:197–202.

Moses, J. R. 1980. *Phalaenopsis*—the search for pink. *Amer. Orchid Soc. Bull.* 49:363–370.

———. 1981. Improving on white *Phalaenopsis. Amer. Orchid Soc. Bull.* 50:796–804.

———. 1994. Development of semi-alba *Phalaenopsis*. *Amer. Orchid Soc. Bull.* 63:1000–1008.

Nadeau, J. A., A. Q. Bui, X. Zhang, and S. D. O'Neill. 1993. Interorgan regulation of post-pollination events in orchid flowers. *Curr. Plant Sci. Biotechnol. Agric.* 16:304–309.

Nadeau, J. A., X. S. Zhang, H. Nair, and S. D. O'Neill. 1993. Temporal and spatial regulation of 1-aminocyclopropane-1-carboxylate oxidase in the pollination-induced senescence of orchid flowers. *Plant Physiol.* 103(1): 31–39.

Nash, N. 1995. Flavor of the month: white *Phalaenopsis*. *Amer. Orchid Soc. Bull.* 64:262–265.

Nash, N., with J. Watson. 1997. *Phalaenopsis*. *Orchids* 66(10):1018–1027.

Neal, J. 1975. More light on *Phalaenopsis*, pt. 2. *Australian Orchid Rev.* 40(2):85.

Nicholas, P. 1969. *Phalaenopsis* in Tasmania. *Australian Orchid Rev.* 34(1): 29–30.

Niemann, D. A. 1974. Introgressive hybridization in *Phalaenopsis equestris* (Schauer) Rchb.f. *Amer. Orchid Soc. Bull.* 43:866–870.

Nishimura, G. 1981. Comparative morphology of *Cattleya aurantiaca* and *Phalaenopsis lueddemanniana* (Orchidaceae) seedlings. *Bot. Gaz. Chicago* 142(3):360–365.

Nishimura, G., K. Kosugi, and J. Furukawa. 1972. Flower bud formation in orchids, pt. 2: on the floral initiation and development in *Phalaenopsis*. *J. Jap. Soc. Hort. Sci.* 41(3):297–300.

Noble, M. 1991. You can grow *Phalaenopsis*. Jacksonville, Fla.

Northen, R. T. 1981. Book review: *The Genus Phalaenopsis*. *Orchid Digest* 45:122.

Norton, H. P., C. Raven-Riemann, and C. Fighetti. 1995. New horizons for novelties. *Amer. Orchid Soc. Bull.* 64:470–477.

Nuraini, I., and M. J. Shaib. 1990. Micropropagation of orchids using scape nodes as the explant material. *Rec. Adv. Hort. Sci. Trop.*, Serdang, Selangor, Malaysia. Pp. 169–172.

O'Byrne, P. 1994. *Lowland Orchids of Papua New Guinea*. Singapore Botanic Gardens, Singapore.

O'Neill, S. D., J. A. Nadeau, X. S. Zhang, A. Q. Bui, and A. H. Halevy. 1993. Interorgan regulation of ethylene biosynthetic genes by pollination. *Plant Cell* 5(4):419–432.

Os, P. van, and Y. Hermes. 1984. Cooling-induced bloom advance in *Phalaenopsis* [Aalsmeer Research Station]. *Vakbl. Bloemisterij.* 39(24):29.

Ota, K. , K. Morioka, and Y. Yamamoto. 1991. Effects of leaf age, inflorescence, temperature, light intensity, and moisture conditions on CAM photosynthesis in *Phalaenopsis. J. Jap. Soc. Hort. Sci.* 60(1):125–132.

Paek, K. Y., J. T. Jo, and Y. K. Hong. 1993. Selection of somaclonal variants from tissue culture in horticultural plants. *J. Agric. Sci.* (Korea) 35:151–162.

Pelz, H. W. 1979. Gedanken zur *Phalaenopsis*-Systematik. *Orchideen* (DDR) 14(1, 2):7–14, 37–44.

Peterson, R. 1976. Different *Phalaenopsis. Amer. Orchid Soc. Bull.* 45:118–120.

Pieper, W., and K. Zimmer. 1976. Clonal propagation of *Phalaenopsis in vitro. Acta Hortic.* 64:21–23.

Ploch, M. 1983. A short history of some of the lesser known *Phalaenopsis. Florida Orchidist* 26(3):99–102.

Poole, H. A., and J. G. Seeley. 1977. Effects of artificial light sources, intensity, watering frequency and fertilization practices on growth of *Cattleya, Cymbidium* and *Phalaenopsis* orchids. *Amer. Orchid Soc. Bull.* 46:923–928.

————. 1978. Nitrogen, potassium, and magnesium nutrition of three orchid genera. *J. Amer. Soc. Hort. Sci.* 103(4):485–488.

Porat, R. 1994. Comparison of emasculation and pollination of *Phalaenopsis* flowers and their effects on flower longevity, ethylene production, and sensitivity to ethylene. *Lindleyana* 9:85–92.

Porat, R., A. Borochov, and A. H. Halevy. 1994. Pollination-induced senescence in *Phalaenopsis* petals: relationship of ethylene sensitivity to activity of GTP-binding proteins and protein phosphorylation. *Physiol. Plant.* 90:679–684.

Porat, R., A. Borochov, A. H. Halevy, and S. D. O'Neill. 1994. Pollination-induced senescence of *Phalaenopsis* petals: the wilting process, ethylene production and sensitivity to ethylene. *Plant Growth Regul.* 15:129–136.

Porat, R., M. Serek, A. H. Halevy, and A. Borochov. 1995. An increase in ethylene sensitivity following pollination is the initial event triggering an increase in ethylene production and enhanced senescence of *Phalaenopsis* orchid flowers. *Physiol. Plant.* 93:778–784.

Pradhan, G. M. 1977. The natural conditions of *Phalaenopsis mannii* and *Phalaenopsis parishii* (with notes on their jungle mimics). *Orchid Digest* 41:94–97.

————. 1981. *Phalaenopsis* species of northern India. *Amer. Orchid Soc. Bull.* 50:30–34.

————. 1982. Dreierlei Arten *Phalaenopsis* aus dem Norden Indiens. *Die Orchidee* 33(6):233–236.

Reichenbach, H. G. 1860. Eine neue Phalaenopsis (mit Revision der damals bekannten Arten). *Hamburger Garten- & Blumenzeitung* 16:114–117.

Reinecke, T., and H. Kindl. 1994. Inducible enzymes of the 9, 10-dihydro-phenanthrene pathway: sterile orchid plants responding to fungal infection. *Mol. Plant. Microb. Interact.* 7(4):449–454.

Reisinger, D. M., E. A. Ball, and J. Arditti. 1976. Clonal propagation of *Phalaenopsis* by means of flower-stalk node cultures. *Orchid Rev.* 84:45–52. 1977.

———. 1977. Culture of flower-stalk buds: a method for vegetative propagation of *Phalaenopsis. Amer. Orchid Soc. Bull.* 46:236–240.

Richter, M., J. Matschke, and A. Sommer. 1999. Einfluss der Düngungskonzentration auf die Qualität und Haltbarkeit von *Phalaenopsis*-Hybriden. *J. Orchideenfr.* 6(2):72–80.

Richter, W. 1979. *Phalaenopsis*-Pflege. *Die Orchidee* 30(2):70–71.

Rittershausen, W. 1981. Yesterday's orchids—today: *Phalaenopsis schilleriana. Orchid Rev.* 89:248–249.

Roberts, J. M. 1998. Building a *Phalaenopsis* light garden. *Orchids* 67(9): 930–937.

Roebelen, C. 1992. *Phalaenopsis* in the Philippines. *Orchid Digest* 56:22–26.

Roedjito, S. W. 1975. Some notes on the moonlight orchid (*Phalaenopsis amabilis* Bl.). *Bul. Kebun Raya* 2(3):85–91.

Rolfe, R. A. 1886. A revision of the genus *Phalaenopsis. Gard. Chron.*, n.s., 26:168–170, 212–213, 276–277, 372.

———. 1905. Notes on the genus *Phalaenopsis. Orchid Rev.* 13:225–232.

Röllke, L. 1981. Berlin, ein Kongress mit Tradition und der Gattung *Phalaenopsis* als zentrales Vortragsthema. *Die Orchidee* 32(1):1–5.

Rose, M., H. P. Norton, J. Martin, C. F. Fighetti, and D. W. Frank. 1993. Artshade *Phalaenopsis. Amer. Orchid Soc. Bull.* 62:372–379.

Rossignol, L., and M. Vo-Thi-Bach. 1988. Further development of an *in vitro* method for the propagation of some *Phalaenopsis* genotypes. *Proc. 8th Eur. Cong. Orchids,* Paris. Pp. 103–122.

Rotor, G. B. 1949. A method of vegetative propagation of *Phalaenopsis* species and hybrids. *Amer. Orchid Soc. Bull.* 18:738–739.

———. 1980. *Phalaenopsis violacea* var. *alba* 'Crestwood' AM/AOS. *Amer. Orchid Soc. Bull.* 49:855.

Sagawa, Y. 1961. Vegetative propagation of *Phalaenopsis* by stem cuttings. *Amer. Orchid Soc. Bull.* 30:808–809.

———. 1962. Cytological studies of the genus *Phalaenopsis. Amer. Orchid Soc. Bull.* 31:459–465.

Sahavacharin, O. 1981. Induction of plantlets on inflorescence of *Phalaenopsis* by application of N-6-benzyl adenine. *Kasetsart J. Nat. Sci. Bangkok* 15(2):54–64.

Saldanha, L. J., and D. H. Nicolson. 1976. *Flora of Hassan District, Karnataka, India.* Amerind Publishing Co., New Delhi.

Sakanashi, Y., H. Imanishi, and G. Ashida. 1980. Effect of temperature on growth and flowering of *Phalaenopsis amabilis. Bull. Univ. Osaka Pref.*, ser. B, 32:1–9.

Salazar, L. M. [1989]. Papaya pulp as an organic nutrient supplement to a basal medium for the germination of selected species of orchids. *Fruit Bowl* (The Philippines) 5(1):57–60.

Saldanha, J. C. 1974. Three new orchids from southern India. *Indian For.* 100(9):566–572.

Santiago, F. S., T. L. Rosario, and C. V. Mujer. 1983. Peroxidase activity and protein banding pattern in the orchid *Phalaenopsis equestris* [Chemotaxonomic differences]. *Kalikasan Philipp. J. Biol.* 12(1, 2):51–60.

Sato, M. 1991. The *Phalaenopsis* business by Sapporo Breweries Ltd. *Proc. Nagoya Intern. Orchid Show, '91.* Pp. 107–111.

Schettler, R. 1983. Erfahrungen mit der *Phalaenopsis*-Kultur. *Die Orchidee* 34(5):199–200.

———. 1989. Die Benennung von Arten und Varietäten. *Die Orchidee* 40(4):154.

Schmidt, K., and D. Lauterbach. 1987. Pot culture of *Phalaenopsis:* regulated flowering by cool culture. *Deutsch. Gartenbau* 41(22):1324–1327.

Schmidt, T. 1985. Gedanken zum Naturschutz und meine *Phalaenopsis fuscata. Die Orchidee* 36(5):216–217.

Scully, R. M. 1966. Stem propagation of *Phalaenopsis. Amer. Orchid Soc. Bull.* 35:40–42.

———. 1971. February is *Phalaenopsis* time in Florida. *Amer. Orchid Soc. Bull.* 40:103–108.

Seidenfaden, G. 1988a. *Doritis. Opera Bot.* 95:31–34.

———. 1988b. *Kingidium. Opera Bot.* 95:182–189.

———. 1988c. *Phalaenopsis. Opera Bot.* 95:236–241.

———. 1992a. *Doritis. Opera Bot.* 114:411.

———. 1992b. *Kingidium. Opera Bot.* 114:411.

———. 1992c. *Phalaenopsis. Opera Bot.* 114:424–426.

Seidenfaden, G., and T. Smitinand. 1965. *The Orchids of Thailand: A Preliminary List.* The Siam Society, Bangkok.

Seidenfaden, G., and J. J. Wood. 1992. *Phalaenopsis.* In *The Orchids of Peninsular Malaysia and Singapore*, Olsen & Olsen, Fredensborg. Pp. 667–671.

Senghas, K. 1990. *Kingidium. Die Orchideen*, ed. 3(1):1400.

Sheehan, T., and M. Sheehan. 1970. Orchid genera illustrated, pt. 16: genus *Phalaenopsis* Blume. *Amer. Orchid Soc. Bull.* 39:606–607.

———. 1984. Orchid genera illustrated, pt. 102: *Kingidium. Amer. Orchid Soc. Bull.* 53:1152–1153.

Shim, P. S. 1981a. New records of Sabah orchids, pt. 10: a new natural hybrid *Phalaenopsis* from Sabah. *Bull. Sabah Orchid Soc.* 2(4):1–2.

———. 1981b. *Phalaenopsis fuscata* Rchb.f. *Bull. Sabah Orchid Soc.* 2(6):3–5.

———. 1981c. New records of Sabah orchids, pt. 13: *Phalaenopsis modesta. Bull. Sabah Orchid Soc.* 2(6):8–10.

———. 1982. A new generic classification in the *Phalaenopsis* complex (Orchidaceae). *Malayan Nat. J.* 36:1–28; reprinted in 1984, *Malayan Orchid Rev.* 18:48–61.

Shim, P. S., and J. A. Fowlie. 1983. A new species of *Phalaenopsis* from Sulawesi (Celebes) formerly confused with *Phalaenopsis psilantha* Schltr., *Phalaenopsis venosa* Shim & Fowl., sp. nov. *Orchid Digest* 47:124–128.

Shindo, K., and H. Kamemoto. 1963. Karyotype analysis of some species of *Phalaenopsis. Cytologia* 28:390–398.

Shoji, T. 1980. Cytological studies on Orchidaceae, pt. 4: chromosome numbers and karyotypes in the *Phalaenopsis* alliance 1. *Senshokutai Kromosomo* (Japan) 2 (17):481–486.

Siegerist, E. S. 1989. *Kingidium deliciosum. Amer. Orchid Soc. Bull.* 58:674–675.

Smeltz, K. C. 1995. An alternative method of *Phalaenopsis* stem propagation. *Amer. Orchid Soc. Bull.* 64:496–500.

Smirnova, E. S. 1985. Similarities and differences in the biomorphology of species of the genus *Phalaenopsis* Bl. *Bull. Gl. Bot. Sada Moskva* ("Nauka") 9137:65–72.

Smith, F. 1987. Spotted *Phalaenopsis. Amer. Orchid Soc. Bull.* 56:228–231.

Smythe, R. 1993. *Phalaenopsis*, the botanicals. *Australian Orchid Rev.* 58(1):9–13.

———. 1994. *Phalaenopsis psilantha. Australian Orchid Rev.* 59(5):41–43.

Srivastava, S. K. 1985. A critical note on *Phalaenopsis parishii* Reichb.f. (Orchidaceae) from W. Siang, Arunachal Pradesh. *J. Econ. Tax. Bot.* 7(1):141–143.

Strauss, M. S., and J. Arditti. 1984. Postpollination phenomena in orchid flowers, pt. 12: effects of pollination, emasculation, and auxin treatment on flowers of *Cattleya* Porcia 'Cannizaro' and the rostellum of *Phalaenopsis. Bot. Gaz. Chicago* 145(1):43–49.

Summerhayes, V. S. 1966. The gender of the generic name *Aerides* Loureiro. *Orchid Rev.* 74:81–82.

Sweet, H. R. 1968. Revision of the genus *Phalaenopsis*, pts. 1 and 2. *Amer. Orchid Soc. Bull.* 37:867–877, 1089–1104.

————. 1969. Revision of the genus *Phalaenopsis*, pts. 3–8. *Amer. Orchid Soc. Bull.* 38:33–43, 225–239, 321–336, 505–519, 681–694, 888–901.

————. 1970a. *Phalaenopsis* section *Parishianae*. *Amer. Orchid Soc. Bull.* 39:1094–1097.

————. 1970b. The genus *Phalaenopsis*, pt. 1: the lavender species. *Orchid Digest* 34:235–236.

————. 1970c. Observations on the genus *Phalaenopsis*, pt. 2: the yellow-flowered Philippine species. *Orchid Digest* 34:301–302.

————. 1971a. *Phalaenopsis*, the moth orchids. *Horticulture* 49(11):25, 44–45.

————. 1971b. Observations on the genus *Phalaenopsis*, pt. 3: the miniature white-flowered species. *Orchid Digest* 35:45–46.

————. 1972a. Observations on the genus *Phalaenopsis*, pt. 7: *Phalaenopsis violacea* Witte. *Orchid Digest* 36:11–12; reprinted in 1981, *Bull. Sabah Orchid Soc.* 2(5):11–12.

————. 1972b. Observations on the genus *Phalaenopsis*, pt. 8: *Phalaenopsis gigantea*. *Orchid Digest* 36:67–68; reprinted in 1981, *Bull. Sabah Orchid Soc.* 2(6):8–10.

————. 1973a. Observations on the genus *Phalaenopsis*, pt. 12: *Phalaenopsis fuscata* and its related species. *Orchid Digest* 37:107–108.

————. 1973b. Observations on the genus *Phalaenopsis*, pt. 13: *Phalaenopsis parishii* var. *lobbii* Rchb.f. *Orchid Digest* 37:167–168.

————. 1975. *Phalaenopsis*—a study of the importance of documentation. *Proc. 8th World Orch. Conf.*, Frankfurt. Pp. 217–220.

————. 1980. *The Genus Phalaenopsis*. Orchid Digest Corp., Pomona, Calif.

Tabei, H. 1978. Bacterial brown spot of *Phalaenopsis* orchids in the Philippines. *Jap. Agric. Res. Q. Ibaraki* 12(4):241–242.

Takasaki, S. 1989. Recent *Phalaenopsis* breeding in the Hawaiian Islands. *Amer. Orchid Soc. Bull.* 58:8–15.

Talia, M. A. C., and B. De Lucia. 1994. Influence of oasis substratum on *Phalaenopsis* soilless culture. *Acta Hort. Wageningen* no. 361:464–469.

Tanaka, M. 1978. Nutrient medium propagation of orchids, *Phalaenopsis* species. *Agric. Hortic. Tokyo* 53(9):1158–1164.

————. 1987. Studies on the clonal propagation of *Phalaenopsis* through *in vitro* culture. *Mem. Fac. Agric. Kagawa Univ.* 49:1–85.

————. 1992. Micropropagation of *Phalaenopsis* spp. *Biotechnol. Agricult. For.* Berlin 20:246–268.

Tanaka, M., A. Hasegawa, and M. Goi. 1975. Studies on the clonal propagation of monopodial orchids by tissue culture, pt. 1: formation of protocorm-like bodies from leaf tissue in *Phalaenopsis* and *Vanda*. *J. Jap. Soc. Hortic. Sci.* 44(1):47–58.

Tanaka, M., M. Ikeda, S. Fukai, and M. Goi. 1992. Effect of different films used for film culture vessels on plantlet development of *Phalaenopsis* and *Cymbidium. Acta Hortic. Wageningen* 1(319):225–230.

Tanaka, M., M. Kumura, and M. Goi. 1983. Surface sterilization for *in vitro* culture of *Phalaenopsis* flower-stalk cuttings using antimicrobials. *Acta Hortic.* no. 131:321–328.

––––––. 1988. Optimal conditions for shoot production from *Phalaenopsis* flower-stalk cuttings cultured *in vitro. Sci. Hortic.* (The Netherlands) 35(1):117–126.

Tanaka, M., and Y. Sakanishi. 1977. Clonal propagation of *Phalaenopsis* by leaf tissue culture. *Amer. Orchid Soc. Bull.* 46:733–737.

––––––. 1985. Regenerative capacity of *in vitro* leaf segments excised from mature *Phalaenopsis* plants. *Bull. Univ. Osaka Prefect.*, ser. B, 37:1–4.

Tanaka, M., Y. Senda, and A. Hasegawa. 1976. Plantlet formation by root-tip culture in *Phalaenopsis. Amer. Orchid Soc. Bull.* 45:1022–1024.

Tanaka, T., T. Matsuno, M. Masuda, and K. Gomi. 1988. Effects of concentration of nutrient solution and potting media on growth and chemical composition of a *Phalaenopsis* hybrid. *J. Jap. Soc. Hort. Sci.* 57(1):78–84.

Teo, C. K. H. 1990. *Phalaenopsis*—what is there for Malaysia and ASEAN. *Int. Conf. and Exhib. Orchids and Orn. Plants*, Kuala Lumpur, 22–28 Aug. 1990. Pp. 48–51.

Teuscher, H. 1970. *Phalaenopsis, Doritis* and *Kingidium. Amer. Orchid Soc. Bull.* 37:216–228.

Tharp, A. G., J. A. Fowlie, and C. Z. Tang. 1987. A recently described *Phalaenopsis* species from the Philippines: *Phalaenopsis philippinensis* Golamco ex Fowl. & Tang. *Orchid Digest* 51:87–92.

Thornton, F. L. 1975. *Asconopsis*, the making of a new genus. *Amer. Orchid Soc. Bull.* 44:40–43.

Timmerman, D. 1983. Culture of *Phalaenopsis. Vakbl. Bloemisterij.* 38(7): 34–35, 37.

Tokuhara, K., and M. Mii. 1993. Micropropagation of *Phalaenopsis* and *Doritaenopsis* by culturing shoot tips of flower stalk buds. *Plant Cell Reports* 13:7–11.

Trippi, V. S., and M. T. T. Van. 1971. Changes in the pattern of some isoenzymes of the corolla after pollination in *Phalaenopsis amabilis* Blume. *Plant Physiol.* 48(4):506–508.

Tse, A. T. Y., R. J. Smith, and W. P. Hackett. 1971. Adventitious shoot formation on *Phalaenopsis* nodes. *Amer. Orchid Soc. Bull.* 40:807–810.

Uesato, K. 1978. Studies on the formation and development of protocorm in growth cycle of orchids *Cattleya, Dendrobium, Phalaenopsis, Vanda. Sci. Bull. Coll. Agric. Univ. Ryukyus* no. 25:1–76.

Vacherot, M. 1991. Genus *Phalaenopsis*: 100 years of hybridization. *Proc. 8th Eur. Cong. Orchids*, Paris. Pp. 145–150.

Valmayor, H. L. 1985. Breeding of *Phalaenopsis* for cut flower trade in the Philippines. *Philippine Council Agric. Resources Res. Develop.*, Los Banos. P. 32.

Van Delden, R. J. 1979. The new hybrid genus *Doriellaopsis*. *Orchid Digest* 43:99–101.

van Holle-de Raeve, A. 1990a. *Phalaenopsis violacea*. *Schlechteriana* 1(1):3–7.

———. 1990b. *Phalaenopsis lueddemanniana*. *Schlechteriana* 1(2):67–70.

———. 1990c. *Phalaenopsis cornu-cervi*. *Schlechteriana* 1(3):111–116.

———. 1990d. *Phalaenopsis schilleriana*. *Schlechteriana* 1(4):163–167.

———. 1991. *Phalaenopsis gigantea*. *Schlechteriana* 2(1):3–8.

Vasquez, G., and M. C. Frier. 1991. International tastes in *Phalaenopsis* hybrids. *Amer. Orchid Soc. Bull.* 60:10–14.

Vaughn, L. C. 1969. Adventures in hybridizing *Phalaenopsis*. *Amer. Orchid Soc. Bull.* 35:745–758.

Vaughn, L. C., and V. Vaughn. 1971. On the judging of *Phalaenopsis*. *Amer. Orchid Soc. Bull.* 40:811–820.

———. 1973. An account of moth orchids: the ascendancy of white *Phalaenopsis*. *Amer. Orchid Soc. Bull.* 42:231–237.

Velisek, V. 1974. *Phalaenopsis* and its hybridization. *Ziva* 22(1):6–7.

Vergano, P. J., and A. J. Pertuit, Jr. 1993. Effects of modified atmosphere packaging on the longevity of *Phalaenopsis* florets. *HortTech.* 3(4):423–427.

Wallace, B. 1990. Natural ecology, cultivation and conservation of *Phalaenopsis rosenstromii*. *Australian Orchid Rev.* 55(4):9–11.

Wallbrunn, H. M. 1966. The *Stauroglottis* (or confusing) group of *Phalaenopsis*. *Amer. Orchid Soc. Bull.* 35:12–19.

———. 1971. A second look at the "Revision of the genus *Phalaenopsis*." *Amer. Orchid Soc. Bull.* 40:223–231.

———. 1989. When is a hybrid not a hybrid? *Orchid Rev.* 97:92–94.

Walter, R. 1977. Exotic orchids: *Phalaenopsis* species. *Rev. Hortic. Suisse* 50(6): 192–193.

Wang, B. Z., and S. M. Juang. 1971. The polyembryony in *Phalaenopsis*. *Taiwan Orchid Soc. Bull.* 10:165–166.

Wang, H. 1989. Rapid clonal propagation of *Phalaenopsis* by tissue culture. *Acta Hortic. Sinica* 16(1):73–77.

Wang, Y. T. 1995a. *Phalaenopsis* orchid light requirement during the induction of spiking. *HortScience* 30:59–61.

———. 1995b. Gibberellic acid on *Phalaenopsis*. *Amer. Orchid Soc. Bull.* 64:744–745.

———. 1997. *Phalaenopsis* light requirements and scheduling of flowering. *Orchids* 66(9):934–939.

Wang, Y. T., and L. L. Gregg. 1994. Medium and fertilizer affect the performance of *Phalaenopsis* orchids during two flowering cycles. *HortScience* 29:269–271.

Wang, Y. T., and T. Y. Hsu. 1994. Flowering and growth of *Phalaenopsis* orchids following growth retardant applications. *HortScience* 29:285–288.

Whang, L. K. 1985. Growing *Phalaenopsis* in the tropics. *Bull. Orchid Soc. S.E. Asia* 3(3):47.

Widiastoety, D. 1990. Application of gibberellic acid (GA3) on orchid *Phalaenopsis cornu-cervi* Bl. and Rchb.f. *Bul. Penelitian Hort.* (Indonesia) 19(1):19–24.

Wie, L. K. 1977. The rediscovery of *Phalaenopsis viridis*. *Orchid Digest* 41:177.

———. 1979. In search of the lost species *Phalaenopsis javanica*. *Orchid Digest* 43:57.

Williams, T. 1984. Yellow *Phalaenopsis*—86 years of hybridizing. *Amer. Orchid Soc. Bull.* 53:238–250.

Woltering, E. J., and F. Harren. 1989a. Early changes in ethylene production during senescence of carnation and *Phalaenopsis* flowers measured by laser photoacoustic detection. *Adv. Agric. Biotechnol.* 26:263–270.

———. 1989b. Role of rostellum desiccation in emasculation-induced phenomena in orchid flowers. *J. Exp. Bot. Oxford* 40(217):907–912.

Woltering, E. J., F. Harren, and D. D. Bicanic. 1989. Laser photoacoustics: a novel method for ethylene determination in plant physiological studies. *Acta Hortic. Wageningen* no. 261:201–208.

Wood, M. W. 1976. An orchid lighting experiment at Bardfield. *Amer. Orchid Soc. Bull.* 45:337–338.

Woodward, G. P. 1971. *Phalaenopsis* species can be fun. *Amer. Orchid Soc. Bull.* 40:772–778.

Wolter, M., C. Seuffert, and R. Schill. 1988. The ontogeny of pollinia and elastoviscin in the anthers of *Doritis pulcherrima* (Orchidaceae). *Nordic J. Bot.* 8:77–88.

Yang, Z. H., Q. Zhang, Z. H. Feng, K. Y. Lang, and H. Li. 1995. *Orchids.* China Esperanto Press, Beijing.

Yasugi, S. 1983. Ovule and embryo development in *Doritis pulcherrima* (Orchidaceae). *Amer. J. Bot.* 70:555–560.

Yeung, E. C., and S. K. Law. 1987. The formation of hyaline caudicle in two vandoid orchids. *Can. J. Bot.* 65(7):1459–1464.

Yoneda, K. 1985. Effects of plant age and time of transfer to highland during summer on *Phalaenopsis* flowering. *J. Jap. Soc. Hort. Sci.* 54(1):101–108.

————. 1986. A study on the culture of the inflorescence tip of the *Phalae-nopsis. Bull. Coll. Agric. Vet. Med. Nihon Univ.* (Japan) no. 43:124–127.

Yoneda, K., and H. Momose. 1988. PLB and plantlet formation by root-tip culture in *Phalaenopsis. Bull. Coll. Agric. Vet. Med. Nihon Univ.* (Japan) no. 45:191–196.

————. 1990. Effects on flowering of *Phalaenopsis* caused by spraying growth regulators when transferred to highland. *Bull. Coll. Agric. Vet. Med. Nihon Univ.* (Japan) no. 47:71–74.

Yoneda, K., H. Momose, and S. Kubota. 1991a. Effects of daylength and temperature on flowering in juvenile and adult *Phalaenopsis* plants. *J. Jap. Soc. Hort. Sci.* 60(3):651–657.

————. 1991b. Effects of light conditions on flowering of *Phalaenopsis* plants before transference to highland. *Bull. Coll. Agric. Vet. Med. Nihon Univ.* (Japan) no. 48:1–5.

————. 1993a. Comparison of flowering behavior between mature and pre-mature plants of *Phalaenopsis* under different temperature conditions. *Jap. J. Trop. Agric.* 36(3):207–210.

————. 1993b. Effects of organic solvents on the preservation and subse-quent seed formation in the pollinia of *Phalaenopsis. Jap. J. Trop. Agric.* 37(4):259–263.

Yoneda, K., T. Sakamoto, and H. Sasaki. 1983. Clonal propagation of *Phalae-nopsis* by means of flower-stalk bud culture and shoot-tip culture. *Bull. Coll. Agric. Vet. Med. Nihon Univ.* (Japan) no. 40:1–13.

Young, R. 1978. The discovery of *Phalaenopsis gigantea* in Sabah. *Sandakan Orchid Soc. Ann. Orchid Show.* Pp. 52–53.

Zachariah, C. F. 1991. Successfully growing *Phalaenopsis* in New Zealand sphagnum. *Amer. Orchid Soc. Bull.* 60:885–887.

Zakrejs, J. 1974. *Phalaenopsis* and its hybridization. *Zahradnicke Listy* 67(8):243.

Zhang, X. S., and S. D. O'Neill. 1993. Ovary and gametophyte development are coordinately regulated by auxin and ethylene following pollination. *Plant Cell* 5(4):403–418.

Zhou, G. 1992. Identification of plant parasitic nematodes on Taiwan orchids. *Acta Phytopath. Sinica* 22(3):235–239.

Zimmer, K., and W. Pieper. 1977. Zur vegetativen Vermehrung von *Phalae-nopsis in vitro. Die Orchidee* 28(3):118–122.

————. 1978. Clonal propagation of *Phalaenopsis* by excised buds. *Orchid Rev.* 87:223–227.

————. 1979. *Phalaenopsis*, zur vegetativen Vermehrung. *Gärtnerbörse u. Gartenwelt* 79:258–260.

Index to Plant Names

Accepted names are given in bold type. The page numbers of formal species treatments are given in bold type.

denticulata Rchb.f., 148, 150
devriesiana Rchb.f., 81
×*diezii* (Covera) Quisumb., 199
doweryensis Garay & E. A. Christ.,
103, **115**, 117
×*elisabethae* Hort., 185, 278
equestris (Schauer) Rchb.f., 25, 30,
35, 154, 200, 201, 217, 229, 235,
236, **239**, 241, 242, 243, 244, 247,
280, 282, 284, 286, 287
equestris var. *alba* Hort., 244
equestris var. *leucaspis* Rchb.f., 239,
242
equestris var. *leucotanthe* Rchb.f. ex
Godefroy-Lebeuf, 239, 242
equestris var. *rosea* Valmayor & Tiu,
243
equestris f. *alba* (Hort.) E. A. Christ.,
244
equestris f. *aurea* (Hort.) E. A.
Christ., **245**
erubescens Burb., 194
esmeralda Rchb.f., 226, 229, 231
esmeralda var. *albiflora* Rchb.f., 233
esmeralda var. *candidula* Rolfe, 232
esmeralda var. *rubra* Hort. ex Stein,
231
esmeralda f. *regnieriana* J. J. Sm., 233
fasciata Rchb.f., 103, **117**, 119, 120,
133, 134, 135, 155, 274, 283, 284,
285, 286, 289
fimbriata J. J. Sm., 102, **120**, 121,
122, 147
fimbriata subsp. *sumatrana* (J. J.
Sm.) E. A. Christ., **121**, 122, 163
fimbriata var. *sumatrana* J. J. Sm., 121
fimbriata var. *tortilis* Gruss & Röllke,
121, 122
fimbriata f. *alba* Gruss & Röllke, **122**
floresensis Fowlie, 76, 102, **122**, 123,
125
foerstermanii Rchb.f., 148
forbesii Ridl., 98

formosana Miwa, 197
formosum Hort., 197
fuscata Rchb.f., 22, 92, 93, **94**, 96,
98, 282, 284, 293
fuscata var. *kunstleri* Hort., 97
×*gersenii* (Teijsm. & Binn.) Rolfe,
124, 125
×*gertrudeae* Quisumb., 216
gibbosa Sweet, 64, **67**, 68
gigantea J. J. Sm., 21, 22, 102, 107,
117, **125**, 126, 127, 272
gigantea var. *aurea* E. A. Christ., **127**
gigantea var. *decolorata* Braem, 128
gigantea f. *decolorata* (Braem) E. A.
Christ., **128**
gloriosa Rchb.f., 185
grandiflora Lindl., 185, 188, 278
grandiflora var. *aurea* Hort., 192
grandiflora var. *fuscata* (Rchb.f.)
Burb., 192
grandiflora var. *gracillima* Burb., 185
grandiflora var. *ruckeri* Burb., 192
hainanensis Tang & Wang, 48, **50**,
51, 52, 54, 57, 62
hebe Rchb.f., 221, 222
hebe var. *amboinensis* J. J. Sm., 221
hieroglyphica (Rchb.f.) Sweet 104,
128, 130, 133, 274
hombronii Finet, 104
honghenensis F. Y. Liu, 48, **53**, 54, 57,
58, 62
imperati Gower, 176
inscriptiosinensis Fowlie, 166, **170**,
171, 172, 173, 174, 179, 180
×*intermedia* Lindl., 17, 184, 191,
198, 200, 242, 280, 282, 286
×*intermedia* var. *brymeriana* Rchb.f.,
216
×*intermedia* var. *diezii* Covera, 199,
201, 242
×*intermedia* var. *porteana* Burb., 201
×*intermedia* var. *portei* Rchb.f., **201**,
280